GLEIM® | Aviation

THIRD EDITION

REMOTE PILOT
FAA Knowledge Test Prep

Unmanned Aircraft - General

by
Irvin N. Gleim, Ph.D., CFII
and
Garrett W. Gleim, CFII

Gleim Publications, Inc.

PO Box 12848
Gainesville, Florida 32604

(352) 375-0772
(800) 874-5346

www.GleimAviation.com
aviationteam@gleim.com

Our answers have been carefully researched and reviewed. Inevitably, there will be differences with competitors' books and even the FAA. For updates to the first printing of the third edition of

Remote Pilot FAA Knowledge Test Prep

Go To: www.GleimAviation.com/updates

Or: Email update@gleim.com with **RPKT 3-1** in the subject line. You will receive our current update as a reply.

Updates are available until the next edition is published.

ISSN 2643-8836
ISBN 978-1-61854-545-9

This edition is copyright © 2022 by Gleim Publications, Inc. Portions of this manuscript are taken from previous editions copyright © 2017-2018 by Gleim Publications, Inc.

First Printing: June 2022

ALL RIGHTS RESERVED. No part of this material may be reproduced in any form whatsoever without express written permission from Gleim Publications, Inc. Reward is offered for information exposing violators. Contact copyright@gleim.com.

Let Us Know!

Feedback and suggestions for improvement will be received immediately through www.GleimAviation.com/questions.

Returns of books purchased from bookstores and other resellers should be made to the respective bookstore or reseller. For more information regarding the Gleim Return Policy, please contact our offices at (800) 874-5346 or visit www.GleimAviation.com/returnpolicy.

Gleim offers free technical support to all users of the current versions. Fill out the technical support request form online (www.GleimAviation.com/contact), email support@gleim.com, or call (800) 874-5346.

ABOUT THE AUTHORS

Irvin N. Gleim, who began publishing pilot training books over 40 years ago and received both the Excellence in Pilot Training Award and the Wright Brothers Master Pilot Award, earned his private pilot certificate in 1965 from the Institute of Aviation at the University of Illinois, where he subsequently received his Ph.D. He then became a commercial pilot and flight instructor (instrument) with multi-engine and seaplane ratings and was a member of the Aircraft Owners and Pilots Association, American Bonanza Society, Civil Air Patrol, Experimental Aircraft Association, National Association of Flight Instructors, and Seaplane Pilots Association. He authored flight maneuvers and practical test prep books for the sport, private, instrument, commercial, and flight instructor certificates/ratings and developed study guides for the remote, sport, private/recreational, instrument, commercial, flight/ground instructor, fundamentals of instructing, airline transport pilot, and flight engineer FAA knowledge tests. Three additional Gleim pilot training books are *Pilot Handbook*, *Aviation Weather and Weather Services*, and *FAR/AIM*.

The late Dr. Gleim also wrote articles for professional accounting and business law journals and authored widely used review manuals for the CIA (Certified Internal Auditor) exam, the CMA (Certified Management Accountant) exam, the CPA (Certified Public Accountant) Exam, and the EA (IRS Enrolled Agent) exam. He was Professor Emeritus at the Fisher School of Accounting, University of Florida, and a CFM, CIA, CMA, and CPA.

Garrett W. Gleim leads production of Gleim pilot training and resources. He earned his private pilot certificate in 1997 in a Piper Super Cub. He is a commercial pilot (single- and multi-engine), ground instructor (advanced and instrument), and flight instructor (instrument and multi-engine) and a member of the Aircraft Owners and Pilots Association, the National Association of Flight Instructors, and the Society of Aviation and Flight Educators. He is the author of study guides for the remote, sport, private/recreational, instrument, commercial, flight/ground instructor, fundamentals of instructing, and airline transport pilot FAA knowledge tests. He received a Bachelor of Science in Economics from The Wharton School, University of Pennsylvania. Mr. Gleim is also a CPA, CIA, and CGMA.

REVIEWERS AND CONTRIBUTORS

Ryan Jeff, CFI, AGI, IGI, Remote Pilot, graduated summa cum laude from Embry-Riddle Aeronautical University with a degree in Aeronautics and a minor in Applied Meteorology. He is our Part 141 Chief Ground Instructor and Flight Simulation Specialist. He researched changes, wrote and edited additions, and incorporated revisions into the text.

The CFIs who have worked with us throughout the years to develop and improve our pilot training materials.

The many FAA employees who helped, in person or remotely, primarily in Gainesville; Orlando; Oklahoma City; and Washington, DC.

The many pilots and learners who have provided comments and suggestions about *Remote Pilot FAA Knowledge Test Prep*.

A PERSONAL THANKS

This manual would not have been possible without the extraordinary effort and dedication of Jedidiah Arnold, Jacob Bennett, Julie Cutlip, Ethan Good, Fernanda Martinez, Bree Rodriguez, Veronica Rodriguez, Bobbie Stanley, Joanne Strong, Elmer Tucker, and Ryan Van Tress, who typed the entire manuscript and all revisions and drafted and laid out the diagrams, illustrations, and cover for this book.

The authors also appreciate the production and editorial assistance of Brianna Barnett, Michaela Giampaolo, Doug Green, Jessica Hatker, Sonora Hospital-Medina, Bryce Owen, David Sox, and Alyssa Thomas.

The authors also appreciate the video production expertise of Gary Brook, Philip Brubaker, and Matthew Church, who helped produce and edit all Gleim Aviation videos.

Finally, we appreciate the encouragement, support, and tolerance of our families throughout this project.

TABLE OF CONTENTS

	Page
Preface	vi
Introduction: The FAA Remote Pilot Knowledge Test	1
Study Unit 1. Regulations	11
Study Unit 2. Airspace Classification and Operating Requirements	73
Study Unit 3. Aviation Weather Services	113
Study Unit 4. Weather Effects on Performance	141
Study Unit 5. Loading and Performance	171
Study Unit 6. Radio Communications Procedures	189
Study Unit 7. Airport Operations	207
Study Unit 8. Aeronautical Decision Making and Physiology	247
Study Unit 9. Emergency Procedures, Maintenance, and Inspections	271
Appendix A: Remote Pilot Practice Test	281
Appendix B: Interpolation	287
Cross-References to the FAA ACS Codes	289
Abbreviations and Acronyms	291
Index of Legends and Figures	292
Index	293

NOTE: The FAA does not release the complete database of test questions to the public. Instead, sample questions are released on the Airman Testing page of the FAA website on a quarterly basis. These questions are similar to the actual test questions, but they are not exact matches.

Gleim utilizes customer feedback and FAA publications to create additional sample questions that closely represent the topical coverage of each FAA knowledge test. In order to do well on the knowledge test, you must study the Gleim outlines in this book, answer all the questions under exam conditions (i.e., without looking at the answers first), and develop an understanding of the topics addressed. You should not simply memorize questions and answers. This will not prepare you for your FAA knowledge test, and it will not help you develop the knowledge you need to safely operate an sUAS.

If you see topics covered on your FAA knowledge test that are not contained in this book, please contact us at www.GleimAviation.com/questions to report your experience and help us fine-tune our test preparation materials.

Thank you!

PREFACE

The primary purpose of this book is to provide you with the easiest, fastest, and least expensive means of passing the FAA knowledge test for the remote pilot certificate. We have

1. Reproduced all previously released knowledge test questions published by the FAA. We have also included many additional similar test questions.
2. Organized these topics into 9 study units.
3. Explained the answer immediately to the right of each question.
4. Provided an easy-to-study outline at the beginning of each study unit.

You can thoroughly prepare for the FAA pilot knowledge test by

1. Studying the outlines at the beginning of each study unit.
2. Answering the questions on the left side of each page while covering up the answer explanations on the right side of each page.
3. Reading the answer explanation for each question that you answer incorrectly or have difficulty answering.
4. Reinforcing this Gleim process with our **FAA Test Prep Online**, which emulates the FAA test.

This book will introduce our entire series of pilot training texts, which use the same presentation method: outlines, illustrations, questions, and answer explanations. In addition, **Pilot Handbook** is a textbook of aeronautical knowledge presented in easy-to-use outline format, with many charts, diagrams, and figures included. While this book contains only the material needed to pass the FAA pilot knowledge test, **Pilot Handbook** contains the textbook knowledge required to be a safe and proficient pilot.

We are confident this book and the **FAA Test Prep Online** will facilitate speedy completion of your knowledge test. We wish you the very best as you complete your remote pilot certification and in related flying as the remote pilot in command.

Enjoy Flying Safely!

Irvin N. Gleim
Garrett W. Gleim

INTRODUCTION: THE FAA REMOTE PILOT KNOWLEDGE TEST

What Is a Remote Pilot Certificate?	1
Eligibility Requirements for Remote Pilot Certification	2
FAA Pilot Knowledge Test and Testing Supplement	2
Knowledge Tests: Cheating or Unauthorized Conduct Policy	3
Knowledge Test Question Bank	3
How to Prepare for the Remote Pilot Knowledge Test	4
Gleim FAA Test Prep Online	5
Knowledge Test Question-Answering Technique	6
Educated Guessing	7
Simulated FAA Practice Test	7
When to Take the Remote Pilot Knowledge Test	7
Knowledge Testing Centers and Procedures	7
Your FAA Knowledge Test Report	8
Retaking the Remote Pilot Knowledge Test	9

WHAT IS A REMOTE PILOT CERTIFICATE?

A remote pilot certificate is much like a driver's license. A remote pilot certificate will allow you to operate a small unmanned aircraft system (sUAS) in accordance with the Small Unmanned Aircraft Regulations in 14 CFR Part 107. These regulations cover a broad spectrum of commercial uses for drones weighing less than 55 pounds.

ELIGIBILITY REQUIREMENTS FOR REMOTE PILOT CERTIFICATION

1. You must be able to read, speak, write, and understand the English language.
2. You must be at least 16 years of age and in a physical and mental condition allowing safe flight operation.
3. You must pass an initial aeronautical knowledge test with a score of 70% or better at an FAA-approved knowledge testing center.
4. If you already have a Part 61 pilot certificate, other than a student pilot certificate, you must have completed a flight review in the previous 24 months, and you must take an sUAS online training course provided by the FAA.
5. If you have a non-student pilot Part 61 certificate, you will immediately receive a temporary remote pilot certificate when you apply for a permanent certificate. Other applicants will obtain a temporary remote pilot certificate upon successful completion of a security background check.
6. The knowledge test or online FAA course covers the following sUAS topics:
    a. Regulations
    b. Airspace
    c. Aviation weather
    d. Unmanned aircraft loading
    e. Emergency procedures
    f. Crew Resource Management
    g. Radio communication procedures
    h. Human factors
    i. Aeronautical Decision Making
    j. Airport operations
    k. Maintenance
    l. Operations at night

FAA PILOT KNOWLEDGE TEST AND TESTING SUPPLEMENT

1. This book will help you prepare for and pass the Unmanned Aircraft General – Small (UAG) FAA knowledge test, consisting of 60 questions. The time limit is 2 hours.
2. The legends and figures in this book are taken from the FAA *Airman Knowledge Testing Supplement*.

 As you practice answering questions, keep in mind that, on test day, you may need to refer to the legends in Appendix 1 of the testing supplement.

3. In an effort to develop better questions, the FAA frequently **pretests** questions on knowledge tests by adding "pretest" questions.
    a. When you notice a question **not** covered by Gleim, it might be a pretest question.
    b. Please contact us at www.GleimAviation.com/questions or 800-874-5346 with your recollection of any possible pretest questions so we may improve our efforts to prepare future remote pilots.

KNOWLEDGE TESTS: CHEATING OR UNAUTHORIZED CONDUCT POLICY

The Administrator has authorized testing centers to terminate a test any time a test proctor suspects that a cheating incident has occurred.

The FAA will investigate, and if the agency determines that cheating or unauthorized conduct has occurred, any airman certificate or rating you hold may be revoked. You will also be prohibited from applying for or taking any test for a certificate or rating under 14 CFR 107.69 for a period of 1 year.

KNOWLEDGE TEST QUESTION BANK

In an effort to keep applicants from simply memorizing test questions, the FAA does not currently disclose all the questions you might see on your FAA knowledge test.

The questions and answers provided in this book include questions developed from current FAA reference materials that closely approximate the types of questions you should see on your knowledge test. We are confident that by studying our knowledge transfer outlines, answering our questions under exam conditions, and not relying on rote memorization, you will be able to successfully pass your FAA knowledge test and begin learning to become a safe and competent pilot.

Using this book and other Gleim test preparation material to merely memorize the questions and answers is unwise and unproductive, and it will not ensure your success on your FAA knowledge test.

HOW TO PREPARE FOR THE REMOTE PILOT KNOWLEDGE TEST

1. Begin by carefully reading the rest of this introduction. You need to have a complete understanding of the examination process prior to initiating your study. This knowledge will make your studying more efficient.

2. After you have analyzed this introduction, set up a study schedule, including a target date for taking your knowledge test.

    a. Do not let the study process drag on and become discouraging; i.e., the quicker, the better.

    b. Determine where and when you are going to take your knowledge test.

3. Work through Study Units 1 through 9.

    Study Unit 1: Regulations
    Study Unit 2: Airspace Classification and Operating Requirements
    Study Unit 3: Aviation Weather Services
    Study Unit 4: Weather Effects on Performance
    Study Unit 5: Loading and Performance
    Study Unit 6: Radio Communications Procedures
    Study Unit 7: Airport Operations
    Study Unit 8: Aeronautical Decision Making and Physiology
    Study Unit 9: Emergency Procedures, Maintenance, and Inspections

    a. For each question, we present

        1) The correct answer.

        2) The appropriate source document for the answer explanation. These publications can be obtained from the FAA (www.faa.gov) and aviation bookstores.

14 CFR	Federal Aviation Regulations	FAA-H-8083-1B	*Weight and Balance Handbook*
AC	Advisory Circular	FAA-H-8083-25B	*Pilot's Handbook of Aeronautical Knowledge*
ACUG	Aeronautical Chart Users' Guide	Sectional Chart	
AIM	Aeronautical Information Manual	sUASSG	*Small Unmanned Aircraft Systems Study Guide*
Chart Supplement			

   a) A complete list of abbreviations and acronyms used in this book is on page 291.

        3) A comprehensive answer explanation, including

            a) A discussion of the correct answer or concept and

            b) An explanation of why the other two answer choices are incorrect.

4. Begin by studying the outlines slowly and carefully. They are designed to help you pass the FAA knowledge test.

5. Answer the questions under exam conditions. Cover the answer explanations on the right side of each page with a piece of paper while you answer the questions.

 Remember, it is very important to the learning (and understanding) process that you honestly commit yourself to an answer. If you are wrong, your memory will be reinforced by having discovered your error. Therefore, it is crucial to cover up the answer and make an honest attempt to answer the question before reading the answer.

    a. Study the answer explanation for each question in detail.

    b. Use our **FAA Test Prep Online** to ensure that you do not refer to answers before committing to one **and** to simulate actual testing center exam conditions.

6. Keep track of your progress. As you complete a subunit, grade yourself with an A, B, C, or ? (use a ? if you need help on the subject).

   a. The A, B, C, or ? is self-evaluation of your comprehension of the material in that subunit and your ability to answer the questions.

   A means a good understanding.
   B means a fair understanding.
   C means a shaky understanding.
   ? means to ask others about the material and/or questions.

   b. This procedure will provide you with the ability to quickly see how much studying you have done (and how much remains) and how well you have done.

   c. This procedure will also facilitate review. You can spend more time on the subunits that were more difficult for you.

   d. **FAA Test Prep Online** provides you with your historical performance data.

GLEIM FAA TEST PREP ONLINE

Gleim **FAA Test Prep Online** is an all-in-one program designed to help anyone with a computer, Internet access, and an interest in flying pass the FAA knowledge tests. Order today at www.GleimAviation.com or (800) 874-5346, or demo Study Unit 1 for **free** at www.GleimAviation.com/free-demos.

Recommended Study Program

1. Start with Study Unit 1 and proceed through study units in chronological order. Follow the three-step process below.

   a. First, carefully study the Gleim Outline.

   b. Second, create a Study Session of all questions in the study unit. Answer and study all questions in the Study Session.

   c. Third, create a Test Session of all questions in the study unit. Answer all questions in the Test Session.

2. After each Study Session and Test Session, create a new Study Session from questions answered incorrectly. This is of critical importance to allow you to learn from your mistakes.

Practice Test

Take an exam in the actual testing environment of the PSI testing centers. **FAA Test Prep Online** simulates the testing formats of these testing centers, making it easy for you to study questions under actual exam conditions. After studying with **FAA Test Prep Online**, you will know exactly what to expect when you go in to take your pilot knowledge test.

On-Screen Charts and Figures

One of the most convenient features of **FAA Test Prep Online** is the easily accessible on-screen charts and figures. Several of the questions refer to drawings, maps, charts, and other pictures that provide information to help answer the question. In **FAA Test Prep Online**, you can pull up any of these figures with the click of a button. You can increase or decrease the size of the images, and you may also use our drawing feature to calculate the true course between two given points (required only on the private pilot knowledge test).

KNOWLEDGE TEST QUESTION-ANSWERING TECHNIQUE

Because the remote pilot knowledge test has a set number of questions and a set time limit, you can plan your test-taking session to ensure that you leave yourself enough time to answer each question with relative certainty. The following steps will help you move through the knowledge test efficiently and produce better test results.

1. **Budget your time.** We make this point with emphasis.
    a. If you utilize the entire time limit for the test, you will have about 2 minutes per question. Use any extra time you have to review questions that you are not sure about and similar questions in your exam that may help you answer other questions.
    b. Time yourself when completing study sessions in this book to track your progress and adherence to the time limit and your own personal time allocation budget.
2. **Answer the questions in consecutive order.**
    a. Do **not** agonize over any one item. Stay within your time budget.
    b. Mark any questions you are unsure of and return to them later as time allows.
        1) Once you initiate test grading, you can no longer review/change any answers.
    c. Never leave a multiple-choice question unanswered. Make your best educated guess in the time allowed. Remember, your score is based on the number of correct responses.
3. **For each multiple-choice question,**
    a. **Try to ignore the answer choices.** Do not allow the answer choices to affect your reading of the question.
        1) Two of them are incorrect. These choices are called **distractors** for good reason and are written to appear correct at first glance until further analysis.
        2) In computational items, the distractors are carefully calculated such that they are the result of making common mistakes. Be careful, and double-check your computations if time permits.
    b. **Read the question carefully** to determine the precise requirement.
        1) Focusing on what is required enables you to ignore extraneous information, to focus on the relevant facts, and to proceed directly to determining the correct answer.
            a) Be especially careful to note when the requirement is an **exception**; e.g., "Which of the following is **not** an operation allowed under Part 107?"
    c. **Determine the correct answer** before looking at the answer choices.
    d. **Read the answer choices carefully.**
        1) Even if the first answer appears to be the correct choice, do **not** skip the remaining answer choices. Questions often require the "best" answer of the choices provided. Thus, each choice requires your consideration.
        2) Treat each answer choice as a true/false question as you analyze it.
    e. **Click on the best answer.**
        1) For many multiple-choice questions, at least one answer choice can be eliminated with minimal effort, thereby increasing your educated guess to a 50-50 proposition.
4. After you have been through all the questions in the test, consult the question status list to determine which questions are unanswered and which are marked for review.
    a. Go back to the marked questions and finalize your answer choices.
    b. Verify that all questions have been answered.

EDUCATED GUESSING

 The FAA knowledge test sometimes includes questions that are poorly worded or confusing. Expect the unexpected and move forward. Do not let confusing questions affect your concentration or take up too much time; make your best guess and move on.

1. If you do not know the answer, make an educated guess as follows:
    a. Rule out answers that you think are incorrect.
    b. Select the best answer or guess between equally appealing answers. Your first guess is usually the most intuitive. If you cannot make an educated guess, re-read the stem and each answer choice and pick the most intuitive answer.

SIMULATED FAA PRACTICE TEST

Appendix A, "Remote Pilot Practice Test," beginning on page 281, allows you to practice taking the FAA knowledge test without the answers next to the questions. The test contains a selection of questions from our remote pilot knowledge test bank. Topical coverage in the practice test is similar to that of the FAA knowledge test.

WHEN TO TAKE THE REMOTE PILOT KNOWLEDGE TEST

1. You must be at least 14 years of age to take the Unmanned Aircraft General – Small (UAG) knowledge test.
2. Take the FAA knowledge test within 30 days of beginning your study.

KNOWLEDGE TESTING CENTERS AND PROCEDURES

PSI has testing centers throughout the country. More information can be found at www.GleimAviation.com/testingcenters.

You may take the following items to the testing center:

1. A navigational plotter
2. A pocket calculator you are familiar with and have used before (no instructional material for the calculator is allowed)
3. Proper identification (as discussed below)

NOTE: Paper, pencils, and a testing supplement are supplied at the examination site.

Identification will be required to provide positive proof of your identity and documentary evidence of your age. The identification must include your photograph, signature, date of birth, and actual residential address if different from the mailing address. This information may be presented in more than one form of identification.

Next, you will sign in on the testing center's daily log. Your signature on the logsheet certifies that, if this is a retest, you meet the applicable requirements (see "Retaking the Remote Pilot Knowledge Test" on page 9) and that you have not passed this test in the past 2 years.

A person from the testing center will assist you in logging onto the system, and you will be asked to confirm your personal data (e.g., name, Social Security number, etc.). Then you will be given an online introduction to the computer testing system, and you will take a sample test. If you have used our **FAA Test Prep Online**, you will be conversant with the computer testing methodology and environment.

YOUR FAA KNOWLEDGE TEST REPORT

1. You will receive your FAA Knowledge Test Report upon completion of the test. An example test report is reproduced below.
   a. The expiration date is the date by which you must take your FAA practical test.
   b. The report lists the ACS codes of the questions you missed so you can review the topics you missed.
2. Reach out to us at Gleim with your test report at FAAKTR@gleim.com.
3. Keep your FAA Knowledge Test Report in a safe place because you must submit it to the FAA when you apply for the remote pilot certificate.

U.S. DEPARTMENT OF TRANSPORTATION
Federal Aviation Administration
Airman Knowledge Test Report

NAME:

FAA TRACKING NUMBER (FTN):   **EXAM ID:**

EXAM: Unmanned Aircraft General – Small (UAG)

EXAM DATE: 06/23/2022   **EXAM SITE:**

SCORE: 96%   **GRADE:** Pass   **TAKE:** 1

The Airman Certification Standards (ACS) codes listed below represent incorrectly answered questions. These ACS codes and their associated Areas of Operation/Tasks/Elements may be found in the appropriate ACS document at http://www.faa.gov/training_testing/testing/acs.

A single code may represent more than one incorrect response.

UA.I.F.K1   UA.I.E.K3d

EXPIRATION DATE: 06/30/2024

DO NOT LOSE THIS REPORT

AUTHORIZED INSTRUCTOR'S STATEMENT: (if applicable)

On _____ (date) I gave the above named applicant _____ hours of additional instruction, covering each subject area shown to be deficient, and consider the applicant competent to pass the knowledge test.

Name _____

Cert. No. _____ (print clearly)

Type of instructor certificate _____

Signature _____

FRAUDULENT ALTERATION OF THIS FORM BY ANY PERSON IS A BASIS FOR SUSPENSION OR REVOCATION OF ANY CERTIFICATES OR RATINGS HELD BY THAT PERSON.
ISSUED BY: PSI Services LLC
FEDERAL AVIATION ADMINISTRATION

THIS INFORMATION IS PROTECTED BY THE PRIVACY ACT. FOR OFFICIAL USE ONLY.

RETAKING THE REMOTE PILOT KNOWLEDGE TEST

1. If you fail (score less than 70%) the knowledge test (which is virtually impossible if you follow the Gleim system), you may retake it after 14 days.
2. Upon retaking the test, you will find that the procedure is the same except that you must also submit your FAA Knowledge Test Report indicating the previous failure to the computer testing center.
3. Reasons for failure include
    a. Failure to study the material tested and mere memorization of correct answers. (Relevant study material is contained in the outlines of Study Units 1 through 9 of this book.)
    b. Failure to practice working through the questions under test conditions.
    c. Poor examination technique, such as misreading questions and not understanding the requirements.

STUDY UNIT ONE
REGULATIONS

(47 pages of outline)

1.1	General	(34 questions)	11, 58
1.2	Operating Rules	(22 questions)	16, 64
1.3	Remote Pilot Certification with an sUAS Rating	(3 questions)	30, 69
1.4	Waivers	(2 questions)	34, 69
1.5	Operations over People	(6 questions)	36, 70
1.6	Remote Identification (RID)	(6 questions)	51, 71

1.1 GENERAL

1. **14 CFR Part 107, Small Unmanned Aircraft Systems**, contains the operational rules for routine commercial use of small unmanned aircraft systems (sUAS or "drones").

    a. Part 107 includes operational limitations, requirements for certifications and responsibilities of the remote pilot in command (rPIC), and aircraft requirements.

      1) Part 107 allows sUAS operations for many different non-hobby and nonrecreational purposes without requiring airworthiness certification, exemption, or a Certificate of Waiver (CoW) or Authorization (CoA).

    b. This section provides guidance regarding the applicability of Part 107 to civil sUAS operations conducted within the National Airspace System (NAS). However, Part 107 does not apply to the following:

      1) Limited recreational operations of UAS that occur in accordance with 49 CFR 44809;
      2) Operations conducted outside the United States;
      3) Amateur rockets;
      4) Moored balloons;
      5) Unmanned free balloons;
      6) Kites;
      7) Public aircraft operations;
      8) Military operations; and
      9) Air carrier operations.

2. **Definitions Used in 14 CFR Part 107**

    a. **Applicant** is a person who submits a declaration of compliance (DOC) to the FAA for review and acceptance. An applicant may be anyone who designs, produces, or modifies a small unmanned aircraft.

    b. **Control station (CS)** is an interface used by the remote pilot or the person manipulating the controls to control the flight path of the small unmanned aircraft.

    c. **Corrective lenses** are spectacles or contact lenses.

    d. **Declaration of compliance (DOC)** is a record submitted to the FAA that certifies the small unmanned aircraft conforms to the Category 2 or Category 3 requirements under Part 107, Subpart D.

    e. **Means of compliance (MOC)** is the method an applicant uses to show its small UAS would not exceed the applicable injury severity limit upon impact with a human being, does not contain any exposed rotating parts that would cause lacerations, and does not have any safety defects.

    f. **Person manipulating the controls** is a person other than the rPIC who is controlling the flight of a small unmanned aircraft under the supervision of the rPIC.

    g. **Remote pilot in command (rPIC)** is a person who holds a remote pilot certificate with a small UAS rating and has the final authority and responsibility for the operation and safety of a small unmanned aircraft operation conducted under Part 107.

    h. **Small unmanned aircraft (sUA)** is an unmanned aircraft weighing less than 55 pounds, including everything that is onboard or otherwise attached to the aircraft, and can be flown without the possibility of direct human intervention from within or on the aircraft.

    i. **Small unmanned aircraft system (sUAS)** is a small unmanned aircraft and its associated elements (including communication links and the components that control the sUA) that are required for the safe and efficient operation of the sUA in the NAS.

    j. **Unmanned aircraft (UA)** is an aircraft operated without the possibility of direct human intervention from within or on the aircraft.

    k. **Visual observer (VO)** is a person the rPIC designates as a flightcrew member who assists the small unmanned aircraft rPIC and the person manipulating the controls to see and avoid other air traffic or objects aloft or on the ground.

    l. **Voluntary consensus standards bodies** are domestic or international organizations that plan, develop, establish, or coordinate voluntary standards using agreed-upon procedures. These bodies may include nonprofit organizations, industry associations, accredited standards developers, professional and technical societies, committees, task forces, or working groups.

3. **Falsification, reproduction, or alteration of a certificate, rating, authorization, record, or report** carries penalties that may include civil sanctions and the suspension or revocation of a certificate or waiver.

    a. The FAA relies on information provided by owners and remote pilots of sUAS when it authorizes operations or when it has to make a compliance determination.

        1) Accordingly, the FAA may take appropriate action against an sUAS owner, operator, rPIC, applicant for a Declaration of Compliance, or anyone else who fraudulently or knowingly provides false records or reports, or otherwise reproduces or alters any records, reports, or other information for fraudulent purposes.

SU 1: Regulations

4. **Accident Reporting**
    a. The rPIC is required to report an accident to the FAA within 10 days if it meets any of the following thresholds:
        1) At least serious injury to any person or any loss of consciousness
            a) A serious injury is an injury that qualifies as Level 3 or higher on the Abbreviated Injury Scale (AIS) of the Association for the Advancement of Automotive Medicine (AAAM).
                i) The AIS is an anatomical scoring system that provides a means of ranking the severity of an injury and is widely used by emergency medical personnel.
                ii) The FAA currently uses serious injury (AIS Level 3) as an injury threshold in other FAA regulations.
                iii) AIS 3 EXAMPLE: A person requires hospitalization but the injury is fully reversible [including head trauma, broken bone(s), laceration(s) to the skin that requires suturing, etc.].
        2) Damage to any property, other than the sUA, if the cost is greater than $500 to repair or replace the property (whichever is lower)
            a) EXAMPLE: An sUA damages a property whose fair market value is $200, and it would cost $600 to repair the damage. Because the fair market value is below $500, this accident is not required to be reported.
                i) Similarly, if the aircraft causes $200 worth of damage to property whose fair market value is $600, that accident is also not required to be reported because the repair cost is below $500.
    b. The accident report must be submitted to the appropriate FAA Regional Operations Center (ROC) electronically or by telephone within 10 calendar days of the operation that created the injury or damage.
        1) Electronic reporting can be completed at https://faadronezone.faa.gov. Alternatively, contact the appropriate FAA Regional Operations Center.

FAA Regional Operations Centers

Location Where Accident Occurred	Telephone
DC, DE, MD, NJ, NY, PA, WV, and VA	404-305-5150
AL, CT, FL, GA, KY, MA, ME, MS, NC, NH, PR, RI, SC, TN, VI, and VT	404-305-5156
AK, AS, AZ, CA, CO, GU, HI, ID, MP, MT, NV, OR, UT, WA, and WY	425-227-1999
AR, IA, IL, IN, KS, LA, MI, MN, MO, ND, NE, NM, OH, OK, SD, TX, and WI	817-222-5006

        2) Reports may also be made to the responsible Flight Standards office (www.faa.gov/about/office_org/field_offices/fsdo).

c. The report should include the following information:
   1) Small UAS rPIC's name and contact information
   2) Small UAS rPIC's FAA airman certificate number
   3) Small UAS registration number issued to the aircraft (FAA registration number)
   4) Location of the accident
   5) Date of the accident
   6) Local time of the accident
   7) Whether any serious injury or fatality occurred
   8) Property damaged and extent of damage, if any or known
   9) Description of what happened
d. National Transportation Safety Board (NTSB) Reporting
   1) In addition to the report submitted to the ROC, and in accordance with the criteria established by the NTSB, certain sUAS accidents must also be reported to the NTSB. NTSB's regulations, codified at 49 CFR Part 830, require immediate notification when an aircraft accident occurs. For more information, visit www.ntsb.gov.

5. **Inspection, testing, and demonstration of compliance.** For safety of flight, 14 CFR 107.15 requires the rPIC to perform checks of the UA prior to each flight to determine if the sUAS is in a condition for safe operation.

   a. **Preflight inspection and testing** must ensure that all control links between the CS and the UA are working properly.
      1) For example, before each flight, the rPIC must determine that the UA flight control surfaces necessary for the safety of flight are moving correctly through the manipulation of the UA CS.
      2) If the rPIC observes that one or more of the control surfaces are not responding correctly to CS inputs, then the rPIC may not conduct flight operations until correct movement of all flight control surface(s) is established.
      3) Ensure there is sufficient power to continue controlled flight operations to a normal landing. One of the ways this could be done is by following the manufacturer's operating manual power consumption tables.
      4) Ensure the UA anti-collision lights function properly prior to any flight that will occur during civil twilight or at night. The rPIC must also consider, during the preflight check, whether the anti-collision light(s) could reduce the amount of power available to the UA.
         a) The rPIC may need to reduce the planned duration of the UA operation to ensure that sufficient power exists to maintain the illuminated anti-collision lights and that sufficient power exists for the UA to proceed to a normal landing.
      5) Ensure that any object attached or carried by the UA is secure and does not adversely affect the flight characteristics or controllability of the aircraft.
   b. **Demonstration of compliance.** Ensure that all necessary documentation is available for inspection, including the rPIC's pilot certificate, identification, aircraft registration, and Certificate of Waiver (CoW), if applicable.

SU 1: Regulations

6. **Multiple-category sUAS.** 14 CFR 107.150 states that a small unmanned aircraft system may be eligible for one or more categories of operation over human beings, as long as an rPIC cannot inadvertently switch between modes or configurations.

7. **Record retention** is especially important in matters of compliance.

    a. A person who submits a declaration of compliance must retain and make available to the Administrator, upon request, the information in item 1) below for the period of time described in item 2) below:

    1) All supporting information used to demonstrate the UA meets the requirements of 14 CFR 107.120(a) for operations in Category 2 and 14 CFR 107.130(a) for operations in Category 3.

    2) The following time periods apply:

        a) If the person who submits a declaration of compliance produces a small unmanned aircraft, that person must retain the information described above for 2 years after the cessation of production of the small unmanned aircraft system for which the person declared compliance.

        b) If the person who submits a declaration of compliance designs or modifies a small unmanned aircraft, that person must retain the information described above for 2 years after the person submitted the declaration of compliance.

    b. A person who submits a means of compliance under this subpart must retain and make available to the Administrator, upon request, and for as long as the means of compliance remains accepted, the detailed description of the means of compliance and a justification showing how it meets the requirements of 14 CFR 107.120(a) for operations in Category 2 and 14 CFR 107.130(a) for operations in Category 3.

8. A **previously manufactured sUAS** may not be operated unless the pilot verifies that the label meets the requirements of 14 CFR 107.120(b)(1) and 107.130(b)(1), as applicable. If the UA was manufactured before the effective date of this rule, or the UA was otherwise not labeled, the remote pilot is responsible for determining whether the UA is listed on an FAA-accepted DOC. If the UA is eligible to operate over people, the remote pilot is responsible for labeling the aircraft in accordance with 14 CFR 107.135.

1.2 OPERATING RULES

1. **Registration requirements for sUAS** state that each UA must be registered, as provided for in 14 CFR Part 47 or Part 48, prior to operating under Part 107.

    a. The Federal Aviation Administration requires all owners of model aircraft, UA or drones, or other RC aircraft weighing between 0.55 and 55 pounds to register online before taking to the skies.

    1) Part 48 is the regulation that establishes the streamlined online registration option for sUAS that will be operated only within the territorial limits of the U.S.

    2) The online registration system requires drone owners 13 years and older to submit their name, email, and home address to receive a Certificate of Aircraft Registration/Proof of Ownership.

        a) This includes a unique registration number that must be affixed to the UA so that it is legibly displayed on an external surface.

    3) The UA registration cannot be transferred between types and is valid for 3 years.

    b. Guidance regarding UAS registration and marking may be found at www.faa.gov/licenses_certificates/aircraft_certification/aircraft_registry/UA.

    1) Alternatively, sUAS operators can elect to register under Part 47 in the same manner as manned aircraft.

    c. Registration of Foreign-Owned and Operated sUAS

    1) If sUAS operations involve the use of foreign civil aircraft, the operator needs to obtain a Foreign Aircraft Permit pursuant to 14 CFR 375.41 before conducting any commercial air operations under this authority.

    2) Foreign civil aircraft is defined as

        a) An aircraft of foreign registry that is not part of the armed forces of a foreign nation or

        b) A U.S.-registered aircraft owned, controlled, or operated by persons who are not citizens or permanent residents of the United States.

    3) Application instructions are specified in 14 CFR 375.43.

    4) Foreign-owned and operated sUAS must be registered, as provided for under Part 47 or Part 48, including submission of an Affidavit of Ownership for Unmanned Aircraft, if necessary. Additional information can be obtained at www.faa.gov/licenses_certificates/aircraft_certification/aircraft_registry/UA.

    d. The owner must use the traditional aircraft registration process under 14 CFR Part 47, (paper N-number), if any of the following apply:

    1) The UA is 55 pounds or greater;
    2) The owner wants to qualify a small unmanned aircraft for operation outside the U.S.;
    3) The owner holds title to an aircraft in trust;
    4) The owner uses a voting trust to meet U.S. citizenship requirements; or
    5) Public recording is desired for a UA loan, lease, or ownership documents.

SU 1: Regulations

    e. After September 16, 2023, most small unmanned aircraft that are registered or required to be registered must comply with remote identification requirements.

        1) The serial number of a standard remote identification unmanned aircraft, or of the remote identification broadcast module, if one is installed on the unmanned aircraft, must be listed on the Certificate of Aircraft Registration.

           a) The serial number may only be listed on one Certificate of Aircraft Registration at a time.

           b) The remote identification broadcast module may be moved from one UA operated under Part 107 to another as long as both UA are on the same registration number and the module's serial number is listed on the registration.

2. The requirement for the sUAS to be in a **condition for safe operation** is covered under 14 CFR 107.15.

    a. Prior to each flight, the rPIC must check the sUAS to determine whether it is in a condition for safe operation.

        1) A flight may not continue when the operator knows or has reason to know that the sUAS is no longer in a condition for safe operation.

           a) It is important to review the manufacturer's guidance about maintenance, replacement, or disposal of components.

    b. The rPIC must complete a preflight familiarization, inspection, and other actions, such as crewmember briefings, prior to beginning flight operations.

3. It is important for the rPIC to understand **medical conditions** that can interfere with safe operation of an sUAS.

    a. Being able to safely operate the sUAS relies on, among other things, the physical and mental capabilities of the rPIC, person manipulating the controls, VO, and any other direct participant in the sUAS operation.

        1) 14 CFR 107.17 states that no person may manipulate the flight controls of an sUAS or act as rPIC, VO, or direct participant in the operation of the UA if they know any medical condition would interfere with the safe operation of the sUAS.

    b. Physical or mental incapacitations could render an rPIC, person manipulating the controls, or VO incapable of performing their sUAS operational duties. These may include

        1) The temporary or permanent loss of the dexterity necessary to operate the CS to safely control the UA

        2) The inability to maintain the required "see and avoid" vigilance due to blurred vision

        3) The inability to maintain proper situational awareness of the UA operations due to illness and/or medication(s), such as after taking medications with cautions not to drive or operate heavy machinery

        4) A debilitating physical condition, such as a migraine headache or moderate or severe body ache(s) or pain(s) that would render the rPIC, person manipulating the controls, or VO unable to perform sUAS operational duties

        5) A hearing or speaking impairment that would inhibit the rPIC, person manipulating the controls, and VO from effectively communicating with each other

           a) In such a situation, the rPIC must ensure that an alternative means of effective communication is implemented. For example, a person who is hearing impaired may be able to effectively use sign language to communicate.

4. The rPIC has the **responsibility and authority** to identify, delegate, and manage tasks for each UA operation.

    a. Tasks vary greatly depending on the complexity of the small UAS operation.

        1) Supporting crewmembers can help accomplish those tasks and ensure the safety of flight. For example, visual observers and other ground crew can provide valuable information about traffic, airspace, weather, equipment, and aircraft loading and performance.

    b. According to 14 CFR 107.19, the rPIC

        1) Must be designated before or during the flight of the UA
        2) Is directly responsible for and is the final authority as to the operation of the sUAS
        3) Must ensure that the UA will pose no undue hazard to other people, other aircraft, or other property in the event of a loss of control of the UA for any reason
        4) Must ensure that the sUAS operation complies with all applicable regulations
        5) Must have the ability to direct the UA to ensure compliance with the applicable provisions of 14 CFR Part 107

5. **Regulatory deviation and reporting requirements for in-flight emergencies** permit the rPIC to deviate from any rule of Part 107 to the extent necessary to respond to an emergency.

    a. An in-flight emergency is an unexpected and unforeseen serious occurrence or situation that requires urgent, prompt action.

    b. 14 CFR 107.21 requires, upon FAA request, an rPIC who exercises this emergency power to deviate from the rules of Part 107 to send a written report to the FAA explaining the deviation.

    c. Emergency action should be taken in such a way as to minimize injury or damage to property.

6. **Hazardous operations.** 14 CFR 107.23 prohibits rPICs from engaging in **careless or reckless** operation of an sUAS.

    a. Because sUAS have additional operating considerations that are not present in manned aircraft operations, additional activity may be careless or reckless if conducted using an sUAS.

        1) For example, failure to consider weather conditions near structures, trees, or rolling terrain when operating in a densely populated area could be determined as careless or reckless operation.

        2) Flying an sUAS while driving a moving vehicle is considered to be careless or reckless because the person's attention would be hazardously divided.

            a) Therefore, the rPIC or person manipulating the controls cannot operate an sUAS and drive a moving vehicle in a safe manner and remain in compliance with Part 107.

    b. 14 CFR 107.23(b) states that no items may be **dropped** from a UA in a manner that creates an undue hazard to persons or property.

SU 1: Regulations

7. **Operating from a moving aircraft or moving land- or water-borne vehicle** is regulated under 14 CFR 107.25, which permits operation of an sUAS from a moving land- or water-borne vehicle over a sparsely populated area.
    a. However, operation from a moving aircraft is prohibited.
        1) Additionally, UA transporting another person's property for compensation or hire may not be operated from any moving vehicle.
    b. Waiving the sparsely-populated area provision. Although the regulation states that operations from a moving vehicle may only be conducted over a sparsely populated area, this provision may be waived.
        1) The operation is subject to the same restrictions that apply to all other Part 107 operations. For instance, the rPIC operating from a moving vehicle is still required to maintain visual line of sight (VLOS), and operations are still prohibited over persons not directly involved in the operation of the sUAS unless under safe cover.
        2) The rPIC is also responsible for ensuring that no person is subject to undue risk as a result of loss of control (LOC) of the UA for any reason. If a VO is not located in the same vehicle as the rPIC, the VO and rPIC must still maintain effective communication.

8. **Alcohol or drugs and the provisions on prohibition of use.** 14 CFR 107.17 does not allow operation of an sUAS if the rPIC, person manipulating the controls, or VO is unable to safely carry out his or her responsibilities. It is the rPIC's responsibility to ensure all crewmembers are not participating in the operation while impaired.
    a. While drug and alcohol use are known to impair judgment, certain over-the-counter medications and medical conditions could also affect the ability to safely operate the UA. For example, certain antihistamines and decongestants may cause drowsiness.
        1) 14 CFR 107.27 and 14 CFR 91.17 prohibit a person from serving as an rPIC, person manipulating the controls, VO, or other crewmember if (s)he
            a) Consumed any alcoholic beverage within the preceding 8 hours,
            b) Is under the influence of alcohol,
            c) Has a blood alcohol concentration of .04% or greater, and/or
            d) Is using a drug that affects his or her mental or physical capabilities.
    b. Certain medical conditions, such as epilepsy, may also create a risk to operations. It is the responsibility of the rPIC to determine that his or her medical condition is under control and (s)he can safely conduct a UAS operation.

9. **Daylight operations.** Remote pilot operations must be conducted during daylight unless the UA is equipped and authorized for operations during civil twilight or at night.

10. **Visual line of sight (VLOS) aircraft operations.** 14 CFR 107.31 requires the rPIC and person manipulating the controls to be able to see the UA at all times during flight. Therefore, the UA must be operated closely enough to the CS to ensure visibility requirements are met during UA operations.
    a. This requirement also applies to the VO, if used during the aircraft operation. However, the person maintaining VLOS may have brief moments in which (s)he is not looking directly at or cannot see the UA but still retains the capability to see the UA or quickly maneuver it back to VLOS.
        1) It may be necessary for the rPIC to look at the controller to determine remaining battery life or for operational awareness.

2) Should the rPIC or person manipulating the controls lose VLOS of the UA, (s)he must regain VLOS as soon as practicable.

   a) Even though the rPIC may briefly lose sight of the small unmanned aircraft, the rPIC always has the see-and-avoid responsibilities set out in 14 CFR 107.31 and 14 CFR 107.37.

   b) The circumstances that may prevent an rPIC from fulfilling those responsibilities will vary, depending on factors such as the type of sUAS, the operational environment, and the distance between the rPIC and the small unmanned aircraft. Therefore, no specific time interval exists in which interruption of VLOS is permissible, as it would have the effect of potentially allowing a hazardous interruption of the operation.

   c) If the rPIC cannot regain VLOS, the rPIC or person manipulating the controls should follow predetermined procedures for loss of VLOS. The capabilities of the sUAS will govern the rPIC's determination as to the appropriate course of action.

      i) For example, the rPIC may need to land the UA immediately, enter hover mode, or employ a return-to-home sequence.

   d) The VLOS requirement does not prohibit actions such as scanning the airspace or briefly looking down at the small unmanned aircraft CS.

b. VLOS must be accomplished and maintained by unaided vision, except vision that is corrected by the use of eyeglasses (spectacles) or contact lenses.

   1) Vision aids, such as binoculars, may be used only momentarily to enhance situational awareness. For example, the rPIC, person manipulating the controls, or VO may use vision aids to avoid inadvertently flying over persons or conflicting with other aircraft.

   2) Similarly, first-person-view devices may be used during operations but do not satisfy the VLOS requirement.

   3) As with other operations in Part 107, sUAS operations involving the transport of property must be conducted within VLOS of the remote pilot.

      a) While the VLOS limitation can be waived for some operations under the rule, it cannot be for transportation of property.

      b) Additionally, Part 107 does not allow the operation of an sUAS from a moving vehicle or aircraft if the UA is being used to transport property for compensation or hire. This limitation cannot be waived.

      c) The maximum total weight of the UA (including any property being transported) is limited to under 55 pounds.

         i) Additionally, other provisions of Part 107 require the remote pilot to know the UA's location; to determine the UA's attitude, altitude, and direction; to yield the right-of-way to other aircraft; and to maintain the ability to see and avoid other aircraft.

SU 1: Regulations

11. The requirements when a **visual observer** (VO) is used are listed under 14 CFR 107.33.

    a. A VO is a person acting as a flightcrew member who assists the UA rPIC and the person manipulating the controls to see and avoid other air traffic or objects aloft or on the ground.

    b. The rPIC may choose to use a VO to supplement situational awareness and VLOS.

     1) Although the rPIC and person manipulating the controls must maintain the capability to see the UA, using one or more VOs allows the rPIC and person manipulating the controls to conduct other mission-critical duties (such as checking displays) while still ensuring situational awareness of the UA.

     2) The VO must be able to effectively communicate

        a) The UA location, attitude, altitude, and direction of flight;
        b) The position of other aircraft or hazards in the airspace; and
        c) The determination that the UA does not endanger the life or property of another.

     3) To ensure that the VO can carry out his or her duties, the rPIC must ensure the VO is positioned in a location where they remain able to see the UA sufficiently to maintain VLOS. The rPIC can do this by specifying the location of the VO. The FAA also requires that the rPIC and VO coordinate to

        a) Scan the airspace where the UA is operating for any potential collision hazard and
        b) Maintain awareness of the position of the UA through direct visual observation.

           i) This is accomplished by the VO communicating to the rPIC and person manipulating the controls the flight status of the UA and any hazards that may enter the area of operation, so that they can take appropriate action. The VO's visual observation of the UA and surrounding airspace will enable the VO to inform the rPIC of the status.

     4) To make this communication possible, the rPIC, person manipulating the controls, and VO must work out a method of effective communication that does not create a distraction and allows them to understand each other.

     5) The communication method must be determined prior to operation.

        a) This effective communication requirement would permit the use of communication-assisting devices, such as a hand-held radio, to facilitate communication from a distance.

     6) Prior to a small UAS operation at **night**, the rPIC should ensure the ability to keep the UA within the intended area of operation and within VLOS for the duration of the operation.

        a) In almost all cases involving operations at night, the rPIC may need to restrict the operational area of the UA.
        b) Reduced lighting and contrast at night may make it difficult for remote pilots to fulfill the requirements of 14 CFR 107.31(a), which requires remote pilots to maintain the ability to visually discern the location, attitude, altitude, and direction of the flight of the aircraft.
        c) A remote pilot cannot rely solely on the UA anti-collision lighting, ground control station (GCS) telemetry data displays, or a combination of the two for compliance with 14 CFR 107.31.

12. **Prohibition of operating multiple sUAS.** 14 CFR 107.35 restricts a person from manipulating the flight controls or acting as an rPIC or VO in the operation of more than one unmanned aircraft at the same time.

13. **Prohibition of carrying hazardous material.** 14 CFR 107.36 states that the carriage of any hazardous material on a small unmanned aircraft may only occur if the operator holds an exemption that permits such carriage. 14 CFR Part 11 applies to petitions for exemption.

    a. Part 107 permits transportation of property by sUAS for compensation or hire. These operations must be conducted within a confined area and in compliance with the operating restrictions of Part 107.

       1) When conducting the transportation of property, the transport must occur wholly within the bounds of a state.

14. **Staying safely away from other aircraft and right-of-way rules** are required under 14 CFR 107.37. Each UA must yield the right of way to all aircraft, airborne vehicles, and launch and reentry vehicles. Yielding the right of way means that the UA must give way to the aircraft or vehicle and may not pass over, under, or ahead of it unless well clear.

    a. Potential hazard considerations of the rPIC are to see and avoid other aircraft while remaining clear. Each rPIC has a responsibility to operate the UA so it remains clear of and yields to all other aircraft.

       1) To satisfy this responsibility, the rPIC must know the location and flight path of the UA at all times.

          a) The rPIC must be aware of other aircraft, persons, and property in the vicinity of the operating area, and maneuver the UA to avoid a collision as well as prevent other aircraft from having to take action to avoid the UA.

       2) No person may operate a UA so close to another aircraft that it creates a collision hazard.

15. **Prior authorization** is required for operation in certain airspace. 14 CFR 107.41 states that operations in Class B, C, or D airspace, or within the lateral boundaries of the surface area of Class E airspace designated for an airport, are not allowed unless that person has prior authorization from ATC.

    a. Though many sUAS operations will occur in uncontrolled airspace, there are some that may need to operate in controlled airspace.

       1) The current authorization process can be found by logging into the FAADroneZone at https://faadronezone.faa.gov.

    b. The rPIC must understand airspace classifications and requirements. Failure to do so could be contrary to Part 107 regulations and may adversely affect safety of operations.

    c. Although sUAS may not be subject to Part 91, the equipage and communications requirements outlined in Part 91 were designed to provide safety and efficiency in controlled airspace.

       1) Accordingly, while sUAS operating under Part 107 may not be subject to Part 91, as a practical matter, ATC authorization or clearance may depend on operational parameters similar to those found in Part 91.

    d. The FAA has the authority to approve or deny aircraft operations based on traffic density, controller workload, communication issues, or any other type of operations that could potentially impact the safe and expeditious flow of air traffic in that airspace.

16. When **operating in the vicinity of airports**, the rPIC must avoid operating anywhere that the presence of the sUAS may interfere with operations at the airport, such as approach corridors, taxiways, runways, or helipads. Furthermore, the rPIC must yield right-of-way to all other aircraft, including aircraft operating on the surface of the airport.
    a. Unless the flight is conducted within controlled airspace, no notification or authorization is necessary to operate at or near an airport.
        1) When operating in the vicinity of an airport, the rPIC must be aware of all traffic patterns and approach corridors to runways and landing areas.
    b. 14 CFR 107.43 states that rPICs are prohibited from operating their UA in a manner that interferes with operations and traffic patterns at airports, heliports, and seaplane bases.
        1) A UA must always yield right-of-way to a manned aircraft, but a manned aircraft may alter its flight path, delay landing, or delay takeoff to avoid an sUAS that may present a potential conflict or otherwise affect the safe outcome of the flight.
            a) For example, a UA hovering 200 feet above a runway may cause a manned aircraft holding short of the runway to delay takeoff or a manned aircraft on the downwind leg of the pattern to delay landing. While the UA in this scenario would not present an immediate traffic conflict to the aircraft on the downwind leg of the traffic pattern or to the aircraft intending to take off, nor would it violate the right-of-way provision of 14 CFR 107.37(a), the UA would have interfered with the operations of the traffic pattern at an airport.
    c. To avoid interfering with operations in a traffic pattern, the rPIC should avoid operating in a traffic pattern or published approach corridors used by manned aircraft.
        1) When operational necessity requires the rPIC to operate at an airport in uncontrolled airspace, the rPIC should operate the UA in such a way that the manned aircraft pilot does not need to alter the flight path in the traffic pattern or on a published instrument approach in order to avoid a potential collision.
17. **Operating in prohibited or restricted areas** is covered under 14 CFR 107.45, which states that no person may operate an sUAS in prohibited or restricted areas unless that person has permission from the using or controlling agency, as appropriate.
18. **Flight restrictions** in the proximity of certain areas designated by Notices to Air Missions (NOTAMs) are covered under 14 CFR 107.47.
    a. A person acting as an rPIC must comply with the provisions of 14 CFR 99.7, Special security instructions, and the following sections of 14 CFR Part 91, Subpart B, Flight Rules:
        1) 14 CFR 91.137, Temporary flight restrictions in the vicinity of disaster/hazard areas
        2) 14 CFR 91.138, Temporary flight restrictions in national disaster areas in the State of Hawaii
        3) 14 CFR 91.139, Emergency air traffic rules
        4) 14 CFR 91.141, Flight restrictions in the proximity of the Presidential and other parties
        5) 14 CFR 91.143, Flight limitation in the proximity of space flight operations
        6) 14 CFR 91.144, Temporary restriction on flight operations during abnormally high barometric pressure conditions
        7) 14 CFR 91.145, Management of aircraft operations in the vicinity of aerial demonstrations and major sporting events

b. Certain temporary flight restrictions (http://tfr.faa.gov/tfr2/list.html) may be imposed by way of a NOTAM (https://notams.aim.faa.gov/notamSearch/nsapp.html#/). Therefore, it is necessary for the rPIC to check for NOTAMs before each flight to determine if there are any applicable airspace restrictions.

   1) According to 14 CFR 91.137, the Administrator will issue a NOTAM designating an area within which temporary flight restrictions apply and specifying the hazard or condition requiring their imposition, whenever necessary in order to

      a) Protect persons and property on the surface or in the air from a hazard associated with an incident on the surface,

      b) Provide a safe environment for the operation of disaster relief aircraft, or

      c) Prevent an unsafe congestion of sightseeing and other aircraft above an incident or event which may generate a high degree of public interest.

   2) The NOTAM will specify the hazard or condition that requires the imposition of temporary flight restrictions.

   3) When a NOTAM has been issued for a temporary flight restriction, no person may operate within the designated area unless that UA is participating in the hazard relief activities and is being operated under the direction of the official in charge of on scene emergency response activities.

   4) According to 14 CFR 91.145, the FAA will issue a NOTAM designating an area of airspace in which a temporary flight restriction applies when it determines one is necessary to protect persons or property on the surface or in the air, to maintain air safety and efficiency, or to prevent the unsafe congestion of aircraft in the vicinity of an aerial demonstration or major sporting event.

19. **Preflight familiarization, inspection, and actions for aircraft operations** are covered under 14 CFR 107.49, which requires the rPIC to complete preflight familiarization, inspection, and other actions, such as crewmember briefings, prior to beginning flight operations.

   a. The FAA has produced many publications providing in-depth information on topics such as aviation weather, aircraft loading and performance, emergency procedures, ADM, and airspace, which should all be considered prior to operations.

   b. Prior to flight, the rPIC must

      1) Conduct an assessment of the operating environment, including at least the following:

         a) Local weather conditions

         b) Local airspace and any flight restrictions

         c) The location of persons and moving vehicles not directly participating in the operation and property on the surface

         d) If conducting operations over people or moving vehicles, ensuring the small unmanned aircraft is eligible for the category or categories of operations

         e) Considering the potential for persons and moving vehicles not directly participating in operations entering the operational area for the duration of the operation

         f) Considering whether the operation will be conducted over an open-air assembly of persons

         g) Other ground hazards

         NOTE: Remote pilots are prohibited from operating as a Category 1, 2, or 4 operation in sustained flight over open-air assemblies unless the operation meets the requirements of 14 CFR 89.110 or 14 CFR 89.115(a).

2) Ensure that all persons directly participating in the sUAS operation are briefed on
   a) Operating conditions
   b) Emergency procedures
   c) Contingency procedures, including those for persons or moving vehicles not directly participating in the operation that enter the operational area
   d) Roles and responsibilities of each person involved in the operation
   e) Potential hazards
3) Ensure that all control links between the CS and the UA are working properly.
   a) Before each flight, the rPIC must determine that the UA flight control surfaces necessary for the safety of flight are moving correctly through the manipulation of the UA CS.
   b) If the rPIC observes that one or more of the control surfaces are not responding correctly to CS inputs, the rPIC may not conduct flight operations until correct movement of all flight control surface(s) is established.
4) Ensure sufficient power exists to continue controlled flight operations to a normal landing.
   a) This can be done by following the sUAS manufacturer's operating manual power consumption tables.
   b) Another method would be to include a system on the sUAS that detects power levels and alerts the remote pilot when remaining aircraft power is diminishing to a level that is inadequate for continued flight operation.
5) Ensure the UA anti-collision lights function properly prior to any flight that will occur during civil twilight or at night.
   a) The rPIC must also consider, during the preflight check, whether the anti-collision lights could reduce the amount of power available to the UA.
   b) The rPIC may need to reduce the planned duration of the small unmanned aircraft operation to ensure sufficient power exists to maintain the illuminated anti-collision lights and to ensure sufficient power exists for the UA to proceed to a normal landing.
6) Ensure that any object attached to or carried by the UA is secure and does not adversely affect the flight characteristics or controllability of the aircraft.
7) Ensure that all necessary documentation is available for inspection, including the rPIC's pilot certificate, identification, aircraft registration, and Certificate of Waiver (CoW), if applicable.

c. These preflight familiarizations, inspections, and actions can be accomplished as part of an overall safety risk assessment.
   1) The FAA encourages the rPIC to conduct the overall safety risk assessment as a method of compliance with the restriction on operating over any person who is not directly involved in the operation, unless the UA is eligible for an operation over people in accordance with Part 107, Subpart D. The safety risk assessment also assists with ensuring the UA will remain clear of other aircraft.

20. **Operating limitations for sUAS** must be in accordance with the following:
    a. **Maximum groundspeed**
       1) According to 14 CFR 107.51(a), the sUAS cannot be flown faster than a groundspeed of 87 kt. (100 mph).
       2) There are many different types of sUAS and different ways to determine groundspeed. Therefore, this guidance will only touch on some of the possible ways for the rPIC to ensure that the UA does not exceed a groundspeed of 87 kt. during flight operations. Examples of methods to ensure compliance with this limitation are
          a) Installing a Global Positioning System (GPS) device on the UA that reports groundspeed information to the remote pilot, wherein the remote pilot takes into account the wind direction and speed and calculates the UA airspeed for a given direction of flight.
          b) Timing the groundspeed of the UA when it is flown between two or more fixed points, taking into account wind speed and direction between each point, then noting the power settings of the UA to operate at or less than 87 kt. groundspeed.
          c) Using the UA manufacturer design limitations (e.g., installed groundspeed limiters).
    b. **Altitude limitations**
       1) According to 14 CFR 107.51(b), the sUAS cannot be flown higher than 400 feet AGL, unless flown within a 400-foot radius of a structure and does not fly higher than 400 feet above the structure's immediate uppermost limit.
          a) On the knowledge test, you may be required to interpret the altitude of a structure, such as a tower, on a sectional chart. Identify the height of the structure in feet AGL and add 400 feet to determine the maximum altitude that the UA may be flown.
       2) In order to comply with the maximum altitude requirements of Part 107, as with determining groundspeed, there are multiple ways to determine UA altitude above the ground or structure. Some possible ways for a remote pilot to determine altitude are as follows:
          a) Installing a calibrated altitude reporting device on the UA that reports the UA altitude above mean sea level (MSL) to the remote pilot, wherein the remote pilot subtracts the MSL elevation of the CS from the UA reported MSL altitude to determine the UA AGL altitude above the terrain or structure.
          b) Installing a GPS device on the UA that also has the capability of reporting MSL altitude to the remote pilot.
          c) With the UA on the ground, having the remote pilot and VO pace off 400 feet from the UA to get a visual perspective of the UA at that distance, wherein the remote pilot and VO maintain that visual perspective or closer while the UA is in flight.
          d) Using the known height of local rising terrain and/or structures as a reference.

SU 1: Regulations

   c. **Minimum visibility**
      1) Minimum visibility, as observed from the location of the CS, may not be less than 3 SM.
   d. **Cloud clearance requirements**
      1) The sUAS must have a minimum distance from clouds of no less than 500 feet below a cloud and no less than 2,000 feet horizontally from the cloud.

   NOTE: These operating limitations are intended, among other things, to support the remote pilot's ability to identify hazardous conditions relating to encroaching aircraft or persons on the ground, and to take the appropriate actions to maintain safety.

21. The requirements for a **remote pilot certificate** with an sUAS rating are covered under 14 CFR 107.7.
    a. A person exercising the authority of PIC in compliance with Part 107 is considered a "remote PIC." As such, prior to acting as rPIC, (s)he must obtain a remote pilot certificate with an sUAS rating.
    b. An rPIC, owner, or person manipulating the flight controls of an sUAS must
       1) Have in their physical possession and readily accessible the remote pilot certificate with an sUAS rating and identification when exercising the privileges of that remote pilot certificate.
       2) Present their remote pilot certificate with an sUAS rating and identification that contains the information listed in 14 CFR 107.67(b)(1)-(3) for inspection, upon a request from
          a) The Administrator;
          b) An authorized representative of the National Transportation Safety Board;
          c) Any federal, state, or local law enforcement officer; or
          d) An authorized representative of the Transportation Security Administration.
       3) Make available, upon request, to the Administrator any document, record, or report required to be kept under Part 107.

22. **Automated operations** are generally considered any operations in which the remote pilot inputs a flight plan into the CS, which sends the flight plan to the autopilot on board the small unmanned aircraft.

    a. During automated flight, flight control inputs are made by components on board the aircraft, not from a CS. If the rPIC loses the control link to the small unmanned aircraft, the aircraft would continue to fly the programmed mission and/or return home to land.

    b. During automated flight, the rPIC must have the ability to change routing/altitude or command the aircraft to land immediately. The ability to direct the small unmanned aircraft may be through manual manipulation of the flight controls or through commands using automation.

        1) The rPIC must retain the ability to direct the small unmanned aircraft to ensure compliance with the requirements of 14 CFR Part 107. The rPIC may transmit a command for the automated aircraft to climb, descend, land now, proceed to a new waypoint, enter an orbit pattern, or return to home. Any of these methods may be used to avoid a hazard or give right-of-way.

        2) The use of automation does not allow a person to operate more than one small unmanned aircraft simultaneously.

23. For **civil twilight operations**, the UA must be equipped with anti-collision lighting visible for at least 3 SM. However, the rPIC may reduce the visible distance of the lighting to less than 3 SM during flight if it is in the interest of safety to do so.

    a. Night is defined in 14 CFR 1.1 as the time between the end of evening civil twilight and the beginning of morning civil twilight, as published in The Air Almanac, converted to local time.

        1) In the continental United States, evening civil twilight is the period of sunset until 30 min. after sunset and morning civil twilight is the period of 30 min. prior to sunrise until sunrise.

24. A certificated remote pilot receives **night operations** privileges and may operate at night only after completing either a knowledge test or recurrent training that contains questions on night physiology and night visual illusions.

    a. Small UAS operations at night may occur only under the two risk mitigation measures listed in 14 CFR 107.29, as follows:

        1) The rPIC must have completed either an initial knowledge test or recurrent training that has been updated to include night operations.

        2) The UA must have lighted anti-collision lighting that is visible for at least 3 SM.

            a) The remote pilot may rely upon manufacturer statements indicating the anti-collision lighting is visible for 3 SM. However, the remote pilot ultimately remains responsible for verifying that anti-collision lighting is operational, visible for 3 SM, and has a flash rate sufficient to avoid a collision at the operating location.

SU 1: Regulations

    b. During night operations, the small unmanned aircraft must be equipped with anti-collision lighting that is visible for at least 3 SM.

        1) However, the rPIC may reduce the intensity of the light if the rPIC determines it is in the interest of safety to do so.

            a) For example, a bright light or a bright strobe light on the small unmanned aircraft in very close proximity to the remote pilot could cause the pilot to lose the ability to observe the UA location, speed, attitude, or altitude with accuracy.

            b) The remote pilot maintains the discretion to reduce the intensity of the anti-collision lighting when they determine it would be in the best interest of safety to do so.

                i) Discretion is an important component of 14 CFR 107.19, which states that the rPIC is directly responsible for the operation of the UA.

                ii) The rPIC must ensure the operation of the UA complies with all regulations of Part 107, including the requirement to maintain the capability of visually observing the UA.

                iii) 14 CFR 107.29 does not require small unmanned aircraft operating during the day to have illuminated UA anti-collision lighting. Lighting is generally not effective for mitigating risk of collision during daytime operations. Remote pilots may exercise their discretion, however, and elect to have lighting on during all daytime operations.

    c. An rPIC or operator may request a waiver of the anti-collision lighting requirement for operations at night and during civil twilight. The process for requesting a waiver is two-fold:

        1) The requester must fully describe the proposed operation and
        2) Establish that the operation can be safely conducted under the terms of a CoW.

25. **Transportation of property** by small unmanned aircraft for compensation or hire must be conducted within a confined area and in compliance with the operating restrictions of Part 107. The transport must occur wholly within the bounds of a single state.

    a. As with other operations in Part 107, sUAS operations involving transportation of property must be conducted within VLOS of the remote pilot.

        1) Although the VLOS limitation can be waived for some operations under the rule, it cannot for transportation of property.

        2) Additionally, Part 107 does not allow the operation of an sUAS from a moving vehicle or aircraft if the small unmanned aircraft is being used to transport property for compensation or hire. This limitation cannot be waived.

        3) The maximum total weight of the small unmanned aircraft (including any property being transported) is limited to under 55 lb.

        4) Other provisions of Part 107 require the remote pilot to know the UA location; to determine the UA attitude, altitude, and direction; to yield the right-of-way to other aircraft; and to maintain the ability to see and avoid other aircraft.

26. **ATC transponder equipment** may not be on as part of an sUAS operation unless otherwise authorized by the Administrator.

27. **ADS-B Out** may not be in transmit mode as part of an sUAS operation unless otherwise authorized by the Administrator.

1.3 REMOTE PILOT CERTIFICATION WITH AN sUAS RATING

1. **Offenses involving alcohol or drugs** are covered under 14 CFR 107.57.
    a. A conviction for the violation of any federal or state statute relating to the growing, processing, manufacture, sale, disposition, possession, transportation, or importation of narcotic drugs, marijuana, or depressant or stimulant drugs or substances is grounds for
        1) Denial of an application for a remote pilot certificate with an sUAS rating for a period of up to 1 year after the date of final conviction or
        2) Suspension or revocation of a remote pilot certificate with an sUAS rating.
    b. 14 CFR 91.17 states that no person may act or attempt to act as a crewmember of a civil aircraft within 8 hours after the consumption of any alcoholic beverage; while under the influence of alcohol; while using any drug that affects the person's faculties in any way contrary to safety; or with a blood-alcohol concentration of 0.04 or greater.
    c. 14 CFR 91.19 states that no person may operate a civil aircraft within the United States with knowledge that narcotic drugs, marijuana, and depressant or stimulant drugs or substances as defined in federal or state statutes are carried in the aircraft.
    d. Committing an act prohibited by 14 CFR 91.17(a) or 91.19(a) is grounds for
        1) Denial of an application for a remote pilot certificate with an sUAS rating for a period of up to 1 year after the date of that act; or
        2) Suspension or revocation of a remote pilot certificate with an sUAS rating.

2. Under 14 CFR 107.59, **refusing to submit to a drug or alcohol test** when requested by a law enforcement officer in accordance with 14 CFR 91.17(c) or **refusing to furnish or authorize the release of the test results** requested by the Administrator in accordance with 14 CFR 91.17(c) or (d) is grounds for
    a. Denial of an application for a remote pilot certificate with an sUAS rating for a period of up to 1 year after the date of that refusal or
    b. Suspension or revocation of a remote pilot certificate with an sUAS rating.

3. The **eligibility requirements for a remote pilot certificate** with an sUAS rating are listed under 14 CFR 107.61.
    a. An applicant for a remote pilot certificate with an sUAS rating must meet and maintain the following eligibility requirements, as applicable:
        1) Be at least 16 years of age.
        2) Be able to read, speak, write, and understand the English language.
        3) Be in a physical and mental condition that would not interfere with the safe operation of an sUAS.
        4) Pass the initial aeronautical knowledge test at an FAA-approved knowledge testing center (KTC).
    b. **Application process.** A person who does not have a Part 61 pilot certificate or a Part 61 certificate holder who has not completed a Part 61 flight review in the previous 24 calendar months must use the following process. A Part 61 pilot who has completed a flight review within the previous 24 calendar months may also elect to use this process.
        1) Pass an initial aeronautical knowledge test administered at an approved KTC.
        2) Complete and submit the Remote Pilot Certificate and/or Rating Application for a remote pilot certificate (FAA Form 8710-13).

SU 1: Regulations

3) **Option 1 (online form):** This is the fastest and simplest method. The FAA Form 8710-13 application should be completed online using the electronic FAA Integrated Airman Certificate and/or Rating Application (IACRA) system (https://iacra.faa.gov).

   a) The applicant must have already passed the initial Remote Pilot aeronautical knowledge test. Once registered with IACRA, they will log in with their username and password.

   b) Click "Start New Application." Then select "Pilot" under Application Type, "Initial Remote Pilot" under Certifications, "Other Path Information," and "Start Application."

   c) Continue through the application process, and select the knowledge test information provided or enter the 17-digit Knowledge Test Exam ID from the knowledge test in IACRA when prompted.

   d) Knowledge Test Reports upload immediately to the IACRA system. This allows processing the application for certification without any delay after passing the test.

   e) The KTC test proctor verifies the identity of the applicant.

   f) Upon completing the online application in IACRA, sign the application electronically and submit it to the Airman Registry for processing. No FAA representative will be required to sign the application if the applicant was able to self-certify.

   NOTE: When the applicant uses this online option, the application will be transmitted electronically to the Airman Registry. The only electronic signature that will be reflected on the IACRA application will be the applicant's. They will receive a confirmation email once the application has completed the Transportation Security Administration (TSA) vetting process. The email will provide information that will allow the applicant to log into the IACRA system and print a copy of the temporary certificate.

4) **Option 2 (paper application):** An applicant can also submit a paper application. If the applicant chooses the paper method, the original initial aeronautical knowledge test report must be mailed with the application to the following address:

   DOT/FAA
   Airmen Certification Branch (AFS-720)
   PO Box 25082
   Oklahoma City, OK 73125

   NOTE: A temporary airman certificate will not be provided to the remote pilot applicant if they do not hold a Part 61 certificate. Thus, it is in the applicant's best interest to utilize Option 1 (IACRA system) instead of the paper method in order to receive a temporary airman certificate once the application has completed the TSA vetting process.

5) The applicant will receive a permanent remote pilot certificate once all other FAA internal processing is complete.

c. **Applicants with Part 61 certificates.** Instead of the process described on the previous page, a person who holds a Part 61 pilot certificate, except a student pilot certificate, and has completed a flight review within the previous 24 calendar months may elect to apply using the following process:

1) Complete the online course [Part 107 Small Unmanned Aircraft Systems (sUAS), ALC-451] located within the FAA Safety Team (FAASTeam) website (www.faasafety.gov) and receive a completion certificate.

2) Complete the Remote Pilot Certificate and/or Rating Application for a remote pilot certificate (FAA Form 8710-13).

   a) **Option 1 (online application):** In almost all cases, the application should be completed online using the FAA IACRA system (https://iacra.faa.gov). The applicant must include verification that they completed the online course or passed an initial aeronautical knowledge test. The applicable official document(s) must be uploaded into IACRA by either the applicant or the certifying official.

   b) **Option 2 (paper):** The application may be completed on paper. Using this method, the certificate of completion for the online course or original initial aeronautical knowledge test report must be included with the application.

      i) A Part 61 pilot, who also meets the requirements of 14 CFR 61.56, may also take the knowledge test for initial certification. If a Part 61 pilot decides to take the knowledge test, the pilot must also include the knowledge test report with the paper application.

      ii) Note that the processing time will be increased if a paper application is used.

3) The applicant should contact a Flight Standards office, a DPE, an ACR, or a CFI to make an appointment to validate the applicant's identification.

   a) The applicant must present the completed FAA Form 8710-13 along with the online course completion certificate or knowledge test report (as applicable) and proof of a current flight review.

      i) The FAA Form 8710-13 application will be signed by the applicant after the Flight Standards office, DPE, ACR, or CFI examines the applicant's photo identification and verifies the applicant's identity. The identification presented must include a photograph of the applicant, the applicant's signature, and the applicant's actual residential address (if different from the mailing address).

SU 1: Regulations

ii) This information may be presented in more than one form of identification. Acceptable methods of identification include, but are not limited to, U.S. drivers' licenses, government identification cards, passports, and military identification cards (refer to AC 107-2A, Appendix D).

iii) Whether using the paper or IACRA method, an appropriate Flight Standards office representative, a DPE, or an ACR will issue the applicant a temporary airman certificate.

NOTE: CFIs are not authorized to issue temporary certificates. The applicant can print his or her own Temporary Airman Certificate after receiving an email from the FAA notifying the applicant that it is available. The FSDO signs and mails the application to the Airmen Certification Branch for the issuance of the permanent certificate. Flight instructors may refer to AC 61-141.

d. **Security disqualification.** After the FAA receives the application, the TSA will automatically conduct a background security screening of the applicant prior to issuance of a remote pilot certificate. If the security screening is successful, the FAA will issue a permanent remote pilot certificate. If the security screening is not successful, the applicant will be disqualified and a temporary pilot certificate will not be issued.

1) Individuals who believe they improperly failed a security threat assessment may appeal the decision to the TSA.

4. **Aeronautical knowledge recency** requirements for a Part 107 remote pilot certificate with a small UAS rating are listed below. The remote pilot must complete a recurrent training course within 24 calendar months of passing an initial aeronautical knowledge test.

Recurrent Training Course Cycle Examples

Person passes an initial aeronautical knowledge test on September 13, 2022.	then	Recurrent training course must be completed no later than September 30, 2024, which does not exceed 24 calendar months.
Person does not complete recurrent training course until October 5, 2024.	then	Person may not exercise the privileges of the remote pilot certificate between October 1, 2024, and October 5, 2024, when the course is completed. The next recurrent training course must be completed no later than October 31, 2026, which does not exceed 24 calendar months.
Person elects to complete recurrent training course prior to September 30, 2024. The recurrent training course is taken and completed on July 15, 2026.	then	The next recurrent training course must be completed no later than July 31, 2026, which does not exceed 24 calendar months.

a. The training courses can be taken online at www.faasafety.gov.

1.4 WAIVERS

1. **Waiver policy and requirements** are listed under 14 CFR 107.200.

    a. The Administrator may issue a Certificate of Waiver (CoW) authorizing a deviation from any regulation specified in 14 CFR 107.205 if the Administrator finds that a proposed sUAS operation can safely be conducted under the terms of that CoW.

    b. A request for a CoW must contain a complete description of the proposed operation and justification that establishes that the operation can safely be conducted under the terms of a CoW.

    c. The Administrator may prescribe additional limitations that the Administrator considers necessary.

    d. A person who receives a CoW issued under this section

        1) May deviate from the regulations of this part to the extent specified in the CoW and
        2) Must comply with any conditions or limitations that are specified in the CoW.

    e. Part 107 includes the option to apply for a CoW. A list of the waivable sections of Part 107 can be found in 14 CFR 107.205 and are listed below:

        1) 14 CFR 107.25, operation from a moving vehicle or aircraft.
        2) 14 CFR 107.29(a)(2) and (b), anti-collision light required for operations at night and during periods of civil twilight.
        3) 14 CFR 107.31, visual line of sight aircraft operation. However, no waiver of this provision will be issued to allow the carriage of property of another by aircraft for compensation or hire.
        4) 14 CFR 107.33, visual observer.
        5) 14 CFR 107.35, operation of multiple small unmanned aircraft systems.
        6) 14 CFR 107.37, yielding the right of way.
        7) 14 CFR 107.39, operation over people.
        8) 14 CFR 107.41, operation in certain airspace.
        9) 14 CFR 107.51, operating limitations for small unmanned aircraft.
        10) 14 CFR 107.145, operations over moving vehicles.

    f. **Applying for a CoW** under 14 CFR 107.200 requires an application to be submitted using the FAA's DroneZone portal located at https://faadronezone.faa.gov.

        1) The FAA will issue waivers/authorizations to certain requirements of Part 107 if an applicant demonstrates the ability to fly safely under the waiver without endangering people or property on the ground or in the air.

    g. The **application process** requires a complete description of the proposed operation and a justification, including supporting data and documentation (as necessary), that establishes the proposed operation can be safely conducted under the terms of a waiver.

        1) A complete listing of Waiver Safety Explanation Guidelines is posted to the FAA's website to assist waiver applicants in preparing their proposals and justifications for waiver applications.

            a) They can be found at www.faa.gov/uas/commercial_operators/part_107_waivers/waiver_safety_explanation_guidelines.

        2) Although not required by Part 107, the FAA encourages applicants to submit their application at least 90 days prior to the start of the proposed operation.

SU 1: Regulations

    3) The FAA strives to complete review and adjudication of waivers within 90 days; however, the time required for the FAA to make a determination regarding waiver requests varies based on the complexity of the request.

    4) First responders and other entities responding to emergency situations may be eligible for expedited approval through the Special Governmental Interest (SGI) process at www.faa.gov/uas/advanced_operations/emergency_situations/.

    5) The amount of data and analysis required as part of the application will be proportional to the specific relief requested.

        a) For example, a request to waive several sections of Part 107 for an operation that takes place in a congested metropolitan area with heavy air traffic will likely require significantly more data and analysis than a request to waive a single section for an operation that takes place in a sparsely populated area with minimal air traffic.

    6) If a CoW is granted, it may include specific special provisions designed to ensure that the sUAS operation may be conducted as safely as one conducted under the provisions of Part 107. A listing of standard special provisions for Part 107 waivers will be available at www.faa.gov/uas/beyond_the_basics/#waiver.

    7) Step-by-step application guidance is available at www.faa.gov/uas/request_waiver.

2. Requests to fly in **controlled airspace** (Class B, C, D, or surface area E) require an application for an airspace authorization or airspace waiver.

    a. **Airspace authorizations** are the most direct and efficient way to request access to controlled airspace. Authorizations can be for a specific location or for broad areas governed by a single ATC jurisdiction, thus accommodating the vast majority of requests for airspace access under 14 CFR 107.41.

        1) An airspace authorization is the mechanism under which a proponent may seek ATC approval for his or her operation. Do not contact an ATC facility directly.

        2) The Low Altitude Authorization and Notification Capability (LAANC) system provides access to controlled airspace near airports through near-real-time processing of airspace authorizations below approved altitudes in controlled airspace.

            a) LAANC automates airspace authorization application and approval through applications developed by FAA-approved UAS service suppliers.

            b) Requests are checked against airspace data in the FAA UAS Data Exchange, such as temporary flight restrictions, NOTAMs, and the UAS Facility Maps.

            c) LAANC also provides information to ATC about where and when planned drone operations will take place.

            d) A list of FAA-approved LAANC UAS service suppliers can be found at www.faa.gov/uas/programs_partnerships/data_exchange.

    b. **Airspace waivers** may be issued when the proponent can demonstrate that the UAS can operate safely in controlled airspace without having to seek prior ATC authorization.

        1) Applicants for this waiver should demonstrate safety mitigations through equipage, technology, and/or other operational parameters in accordance with 14 CFR 107.200.

        2) Processing times for airspace waivers are significantly longer compared to airspace authorizations and require additional safety justification.

    NOTE: If you intend to use a non-airspace Part 107 waiver in controlled airspace (for example, night operations in Class B airspace), you should obtain your non-airspace waiver prior to requesting an airspace authorization or airspace waiver.

1.5 OPERATIONS OVER PEOPLE

1. **Remote pilot responsibilities when operating over people** are regulated under 14 CFR 107.39 and 14 CFR Part 107, Subpart D.

    a. Operation of a small unmanned aircraft (sUA) is prohibited over any person who is not under a safe cover, such as a protective structure or a stationary vehicle, unless the operation is conducted in accordance with one of the four categories listed in Subpart D.

    b. A remote pilot may operate an sUA over a person who is directly participating in the operation of the sUA.

     1) Direct participants include the remote pilot in command (rPIC), another person who may be manipulating the controls, a visual observer (VO), or crewmembers necessary for the safety of the small unmanned aircraft operation.

     2) A direct participant should be directly involved in the small unmanned aircraft flight operation. The remote pilot assigns and briefs the direct participants in preparation for the operation.

     3) The remote pilot may comply with the requirements prohibiting operation over people in several ways, for example,

        a) Selecting an operational location where there are no people and none are expected to be present for the duration of the operation. If the remote pilot selects a location where people are present, the remote pilot should have a plan of action to ensure human beings remain clear of the operating area. The remote pilot may be able to direct people to remain indoors or remain under safe cover until the small unmanned aircraft flight operation has ended.

            i) Safe cover is a structure or stationary vehicle that protects a person from harm if the sUA impacts that structure or vehicle.

        b) Maintaining a safe distance from people who are not directly participating in the operation of the sUA.

        c) Ensuring the sUA will not be operated over any moving vehicles.

    NOTE: The remote pilot should consider risk mitigations and take into account the small unmanned aircraft's course, speed, and trajectory, including the possibility of a failure, to determine whether the sUA would go over or strike a person who is not directly participating in the flight operation.

2. **Operating over people at night** does not alter the categories and their respective restrictions for operations over people.

    a. The risk mitigation measures apply equally to day and night operations when operating over people, with specific requirements for both the manufacturer of the sUA and the remote pilot.

     1) The test methods, analyses, or manner of inspection an applicant uses for determining that an sUA meets the performance-based safety requirements are time-of-day neutral.

b. If the sUA used in an operation at night is eligible to operate in any category for operations over people listed in 14 CFR Part 107, Subpart D, the remote pilot may operate the sUA over human beings at night pursuant to the requirements of 14 CFR 107.29 and 14 CFR 107.39.

   1) In declaring any sUA eligible for operations in Category 2 or 3, manufacturers who produce sUA eligible to operate over people at night will most likely need to consider the mass of an anti-collision light when declaring that the sUA fulfills the safety requirements set forth in either 14 CFR 107.120(a) or 14 CFR 107.130(a).

3. 14 CFR Part 107 establishes **four categories of permissible operations over people**.

   a. **Category 1** covers operations over people using small unmanned aircraft that weigh 0.55 lb. (250 g) or less on takeoff and throughout the duration of flight, including everything that is on board or otherwise attached to the aircraft.

      1) In addition to weight limits, Category 1 UA must not contain any exposed rotating parts that would lacerate human skin upon impact.

      2) Remote pilots are prohibited from operating as a Category 1 operation in sustained flight over open-air assemblies unless the operation meets the requirements of 14 CFR 89.110 or 14 CFR 89.115(a). This prohibition is subject to waiver.

   b. **Category 2** operations over people must meet the requirements of 14 CFR 107.120. To confirm such eligibility, the UA must be listed on an FAA-accepted declaration of compliance (DOC).

      1) To be eligible for use in Category 2 operations, the UA must be designed, produced, or modified such that it

         a) Will not cause injury to a human being that is equivalent to or greater than the severity of injury caused by a transfer of 11 foot-pounds of kinetic energy upon impact from a rigid object,

         b) Does not contain any exposed rotating parts that would lacerate human skin upon impact with a human being, and

         c) Does not contain any safety defects.

      2) It is the remote pilot's responsibility to ensure that the UA is listed on an FAA-accepted DOC as eligible for Category 2 operations and labeled as eligible to conduct Category 2 operations.

         a) A remote pilot can accomplish this by checking online at https://uasdoc.faa.gov to see if the DOC is valid and by visually inspecting the aircraft to ensure a label identifying the aircraft as Category 2 is affixed to the aircraft.

      3) Additionally, the UA must display a label indicating eligibility to conduct Category 2 operations, have current remote pilot operating instructions that apply to the operation of the UA, and be subject to a product support and notification process.

         a) The applicant must submit the DOC containing specific information to affirm that the aircraft meets the safety requirements through an FAA-accepted means of compliance (MOC).

      4) Remote pilots are prohibited from operating as a Category 2 operation in sustained flight over open-air assemblies unless the operation meets the requirements of 14 CFR 89.110 or 14 CFR 89.115(a). This prohibition is subject to waiver.

c. **Category 3** operations over people must meet the safety requirements of 14 CFR 107.130. To confirm such eligibility, the UA must be listed on an FAA-accepted DOC.
   1) To be eligible for use in Category 3 operations, the UA must be designed, produced, or modified such that it
      a) Will not cause injury to a human being that is equivalent to or greater than the severity of the injury caused by a transfer of 25 foot-pounds of kinetic energy upon impact from a rigid object,
      b) Does not contain any exposed rotating parts that would lacerate human skin upon impact with a human being, and
      c) Does not contain any safety defects.
   2) It is the remote pilot's responsibility to ensure the UA is listed on an FAA-accepted DOC and labeled as eligible to conduct Category 3 operations.
      a) A remote pilot can accomplish this by checking online at https://uasdoc.faa.gov to see if the DOC is valid and by visually inspecting the UA to ensure the label identifying it as Category 3 is affixed.
   3) Additionally, the UA must display a label identifying eligibility to conduct Category 3 operations, have current remote pilot operating instructions that apply to the operation of the UA, and be subject to a product support and notification process.
      a) The applicant must submit the DOC containing specific information to affirm that the aircraft meets the safety requirements through an FAA-accepted MOC.

d. **Category 4** eligible UA must have an airworthiness certificate issued by the FAA under 14 CFR Part 21 and must be operated in accordance with the operating limitations specified in the FAA-approved flight manual or as otherwise specified by the Administrator.
   1) The airworthiness certificate allows UA operations for compensation and hire.
   2) The remote pilot conducting Category 4 operations over people must use an eligible UA.
      a) To operate over people in accordance with 14 CFR 107.140 and over moving vehicles in accordance with 14 CFR 107.145(c), the remote pilot must operate the UA in accordance with all operating limitations that apply to the UA, as specified by the Administrator. These operating limitations must not prohibit operations over people.
   3) Remote pilots are prohibited from operating as a Category 4 operation in sustained flight over open-air assemblies unless the operation meets the requirements of 14 CFR 89.110 or 14 CFR 89.110 89.115(a). This prohibition is subject to waiver.

4. **Selecting an operational area** requires practicing risk assessment skills by analyzing the likelihood and severity of the hazards occurring.
   a. Consider whether the operational area can be considered an open-air assembly of persons.
      1) If so, ensure the small unmanned aircraft system (sUAS) is appropriately configured for the category of operation.
   b. Consider remote identification capabilities of the sUAS.
      1) If the sUAS is not fitted with standard remote identification or a broadcast module, verify that the selected operational area is an FAA-recognized identification area (FRIA).

SU 1: Regulations

5. **Minimum distances from a person.** 14 CFR Part 107 does not impose a specific stand-off distance requirement from people when operating a small unmanned aircraft. However, the remote pilot may elect to observe a minimum stand-off distance to ensure the safety of the operation.

    a. When determining an appropriate stand-off distance, the remote pilot should consider the following factors:

        1) The small unmanned aircraft's performance, including course, speed, trajectory, and maneuverability

        2) Environmental conditions such as wind, including gusts, precipitation, and visibility

        3) Operational area conditions such as the location and movement of people, vessels, or vehicles, as well as terrain features, including structures or any other item that could affect the operational area where the sUA is being maneuvered

        4) Probable failures and the ability to perform emergency maneuvers, including emergency landings

        5) The remote pilot's familiarity with and ability to maneuver the sUA

    NOTE: When conducting the small unmanned aircraft operation, the remote pilot should evaluate and make adjustments to this minimum distance from people as conditions change.

6. **Operations over people inside moving vehicles** with an sUA that meets the eligibility requirements for a Category 1, 2, 3, or 4 operation are subject to one of the following conditions:

    a. For Categories 1, 2, and 3 small unmanned aircraft, the operation must be conducted within or over a closed- or restricted-access site. Any person located inside a moving vehicle within the closed- or restricted-access site must be on notice that a small unmanned aircraft may fly over them.

    b. If the operation is not conducted within or over a closed- or restricted-access site, the small unmanned aircraft must not maintain sustained flight over any moving vehicle.

    NOTE: Category 4 small unmanned aircraft may be eligible to operate over moving vehicles as long as the operating limitations specified in the FAA-approved flight manual, or as otherwise specified by the Administrator, do not prohibit such operation.

7. **Modifications to an sUAS** may be allowable according to the remote pilot operating instructions.

    a. Modifications not allowed by the remote pilot operating instructions may render the small unmanned aircraft ineligible for operations over people.

        1) Such modifications would require submission of a new declaration of compliance (DOC).

            a) Additionally, the small unmanned aircraft may need to be relabeled to reflect the category of operations it is eligible to conduct.

    b. In the case of the sale or transfer of the small unmanned aircraft, or use of the aircraft by someone other than the applicant, the applicant must provide remote pilot operating instructions that reflect the aircraft's eligible category and acceptable modifications.

        1) Therefore, the FAA encourages manufacturers of small unmanned aircraft to keep track of modifications that would require an update to the remote pilot operating instructions.

8. Category 3 operations may take place over or within **closed- or restricted-access sites** where everyone located within the site are on notice that a small unmanned aircraft may fly over them, as long as the operational area is not considered an open-air assembly.

   a. People who are not directly participating in the operation of the UA but who are performing functions at the closed- or restricted-access site must be on notice of potential UA operations and should be advised of precautions or other recommended actions to take, if necessary.

   b. Remote pilots are responsible for ensuring no inadvertent or unauthorized access to the site occurs.

      1) Adequate assurance could include physical barriers such as barricading and fencing or monitoring personnel to ensure inadvertent or unauthorized access to the site does not occur.

      2) Geographical boundaries, such as rivers, canals, cliffs, and heavily wooded areas, may serve as effective barriers to restrict access.

Operations Over People – Over or Within Closed/Restricted Access Site

	Category 1	Category 2	***Category 3	Category 4
Directly Participating	Allowed	Allowed	Allowed	Allowed
Not Directly Participating	*Allowed	**Allowed	Must be on Notice	****Operating Limitations

Operations Over People – Not Over or Within Closed/Restricted Access Site

	Category 1	Category 2	***Category 3	Category 4
Directly Participating	Allowed	Allowed	Allowed	Allowed
Not Directly Participating	*Allowed	**Allowed	Transit Only, No Sustained Flight	****Operating Limitations

*Remote pilots are prohibited from operating as a Category 1 operation in sustained flight over open-air assemblies, unless the operation meets the requirements of 14 CFR 89.110 or 14 CFR 89.115(a). This prohibition is subject to waiver.

**Remote pilots are prohibited from operating as a Category 2 operation in sustained flight over open-air assemblies, unless the operation meets the requirements of 14 CFR 89.110 or 14 CFR 89.115(a). This prohibition is subject to waiver.

***Category 3 eligible UA must not operate over open-air assemblies of human beings [14 CFR 107.125(b)].

****Category 4 eligible UA may conduct operations over human beings if not prohibited by the operating limitations specified in the FAA-approved flight manual or otherwise prescribed by the FAA. Remote pilots are prohibited from operating as a Category 4 operation in sustained flight over open-air assemblies, unless the operation meets the requirements of 14 CFR 89.110 or 14 CFR 89.115(a). This prohibition is subject to waiver.

9. **Remote pilot operating instructions** are required for a small unmanned aircraft eligible to conduct Category 2 or 3 operations upon sale or transfer of the small unmanned aircraft or use of the small unmanned aircraft by someone other than the applicant. In addition, the applicant should keep the instructions up-to-date to account for any changes it makes to a small unmanned aircraft.

   a. The remote pilot operating instructions must include, at a minimum, the following information:

      1) General information, system description, and system limitations, including the category or categories of operations over people that the small unmanned aircraft is eligible to conduct

         a) This information must describe whether the small unmanned aircraft must include a specific component on the aircraft to fulfill the performance-based safety requirements of Category 2, 3, or both, for which the small unmanned aircraft applicant has declared compliance. For example, if an applicant has designed the small unmanned aircraft to have a parachute system or other device affixed to the aircraft and that component is provided separately, the remote pilot operating instructions must clearly identify the component that must be attached. Similarly, the remote pilot operating instructions must list components that are eligible or necessary for inclusion on the aircraft.

      2) A statement describing allowable modifications to the small unmanned aircraft

         a) If modifications are allowed, the remote pilot operating instructions must include a complete description of modifications the applicant has determined do not change the eligibility for the category or categories of operations over people for which the small unmanned aircraft has been declared compliant. Such descriptions of modifications include descriptions of the small unmanned aircraft itself as well as any payload any person may include on the aircraft.

         b) Modifications the applicant describes in the remote pilot operating instructions must be consistent with the basis for the FAA's acceptance of the DOC. Any person, however, who modifies a small unmanned aircraft in a way that will affect the eligibility of the small unmanned aircraft to operate over people under Category 2 or 3 is required to submit a new DOC for FAA acceptance before the small unmanned aircraft is eligible to operate over people.

      3) A statement regarding whether the small unmanned aircraft has variable modes or configurations

         a) For a small unmanned aircraft that has such variable modes or configurations, the instructions must describe how a remote pilot can verify what mode or configuration the small unmanned aircraft is in and how to switch between modes or configurations. This information assists the remote pilot in verifying that the small unmanned aircraft is in the correct mode or configuration to conduct a certain category of operations over people.

         b) Similarly, if a remote pilot chooses to operate in a different category of operations over people, or in a mode or configuration that is not permitted for operations over people but is permitted under Part 107, that person must be able to discern the necessary information from the remote pilot operating instructions. The remote pilot should not be able to inadvertently change the mode or configuration.

b. The remote pilot operating instructions must be specific to the particular small unmanned aircraft design. An applicant may update existing instructions to include the required information with the small unmanned aircraft, or the applicant may create a new set of instructions that are specific to operations over people.

1) The FAA does not require the applicant to provide the remote pilot operating instructions in a particular format. An applicant could choose to provide the operating instructions as part of the packaging of a small unmanned aircraft, by making them available electronically, or by any other means.

    a) Regardless of the manner in which the applicant transmits the instructions to remote pilots, the applicant should ensure the instructions remain up-to-date.

    b) Remote PICs should be able to discern clearly the set of operating instructions that are in effect at the time of the intended operation of the small unmanned aircraft over people.

2) Information contained in the remote pilot operating instructions should provide enough detail to enable remote pilots to understand clearly how to configure the small unmanned aircraft to ensure compliance with applicable requirements for operating over people. This information informs the remote pilot and aids in decision making.

    a) While the remote pilot operating instructions can aid a remote pilot in operating safely, it is ultimately the responsibility of the rPIC to determine the safe operational parameters for the operation.

3) 14 CFR Part 107 currently requires remote pilots to conduct a preflight inspection and ensure that the small unmanned aircraft is in a condition for safe operation. These requirements do not change for operations over people. In fact, a preflight assessment for operations over people should be more complex to account for the additional risk inherent in those operations. For example, the rPIC should consider the following:

    a) The location of the people over whom the small unmanned aircraft would fly

    b) The weather and other factors that may play a role in the performance of the small unmanned aircraft

    c) The environment and airspace in which the operation is being conducted

    d) The remote pilot operating instructions to consider the characteristics of small unmanned aircraft, for example, the expected battery life of the small unmanned aircraft

4) The FAA anticipates the remote pilot operating instructions, which are required for small unmanned aircraft eligible to operate in Category 2 or 3 of Part 107, Subpart D, will assist the remote pilot in conducting the preflight check and ensuring the aircraft is in a condition for safe operation prior to conducting the operation.

5) Although the FAA does not require the remote pilot operating instructions to contain information in addition to the items on the previous page, the FAA encourages small unmanned aircraft manufacturers to provide additional operational information to remote pilots. This information will assist remote pilots in planning operations, decision making throughout the flight, and the overall safe conduct of operations of their small unmanned aircraft by providing valuable operating information about the specific small unmanned aircraft design and capabilities.

   a) Manufacturers may wish to develop voluntary standards regarding the information provided in the remote pilot operating instructions. These would provide consistency across small unmanned aircraft remote pilot operating instructions, and the remote pilots would have a clearer understanding of what information would accompany a small unmanned aircraft. Information that a small unmanned aircraft manufacturer may wish to consider providing includes, but is not limited to, the following factors:

Performance, Limitations, and Operating Characteristics	
• Operating temperature limits (high and low limits) • Weather limitations, including wind, precipitation, and maximum wind gusts • Altitude limitations, including maximum operating altitude • Range limitations • Maximum weights	• Airspeed limitations • Power source, including endurance, power setting, and consumption levels appropriate to the type of propulsion system (fuel, battery, etc.) • Prohibited maneuvers • Other limitations necessary for safe operations over people
Normal, Abnormal, and Emergency Operating Procedures	**Weight and Balance**
• Preflight inspection • Emergency or abnormal procedures	• Information regarding the weight and balance of the small unmanned aircraft

10. **Required components and category declaration.** The FAA requires applicants to provide remote pilot operating instructions for a small unmanned aircraft eligible to conduct Category 2 or 3 operations upon sale or transfer of the small unmanned aircraft or use of the small unmanned aircraft by someone other than the applicant.

    a. The operating instructions should include required components for Category 2 and 3 operations, respectively.

11. **Optional components.** The operating instructions may also include optional components and the requirements to affix the optional component onto a UA if intending to operate over people in accordance with Category 2 or 3.

12. **Applicant produced, designed, or modified sUAS for operations over people.** An applicant includes any person who produces, designs, or modifies a small unmanned aircraft eligible to operate over people within the United States.

    a. Someone who builds a small unmanned aircraft from separate components and parts not from a kit is an applicant.

       1) For example, someone may purchase the parts of a small unmanned aircraft separately and build the small unmanned aircraft.

          a) An applicant is required to submit a DOC in order to conduct Category 2 or 3 operations.

    b. An applicant may produce many small unmanned aircraft, sell kits from which to build small unmanned aircraft, or modify a small unmanned aircraft in a way that affects the eligibility of the small unmanned aircraft to conduct a different category of operations over people than it was previously eligible to conduct.

    c. An applicant who manufactures and sells a kit that contains all the components and parts from which to build an operable small unmanned aircraft must comply with the requirements of Part 107, Subpart D, if the aircraft is intended for operations over people.

       1) The kit must contain all the components necessary to build an operable small unmanned aircraft and must not require the owner to purchase any additional materials.

       2) Before the kit is sold, the applicant must ensure the completely assembled small unmanned aircraft, not only its individual component parts, complies with the performance-based safety requirements to determine eligibility using an FAA-accepted means of compliance (MOC) and declare compliance.

          a) This will ensure the small unmanned aircraft meets the requirements of Part 107, Subpart D.

    d. An applicant may be a person who modifies a small unmanned aircraft listed on an existing DOC, resulting in noncompliance with the original declaration.

       1) Noncompliance means the small unmanned aircraft has been altered and is no longer in the same configuration as originally declared.

       2) If the sUA is changed so that it is no longer eligible for operations over people, a new DOC must be submitted prior to conducting operations over people or moving vehicles within that category.

       3) An applicant should specify allowable modifications in the remote pilot operating instructions.

          a) This ensures a remote pilot who may replace parts or otherwise modify the sUA is aware of which modifications would be allowable for the category of operation.

       4) An applicant may develop updates for a small unmanned aircraft after the remote pilot takes possession of it, e.g., a software or hardware update.

          a) To communicate these updates to remote pilots, the manufacturer should make operating instructions for the new capabilities of the small unmanned aircraft available.

e. Any person who makes a modification not permissible by the remote pilot operating instructions to a small unmanned aircraft eligible for Category 2 or 3 operations over people renders that small unmanned aircraft ineligible.

   1) If the person making the modification intends to conduct Category 2 or 3 operations over people with the modified sUA, that person is required to take on the responsibilities of an applicant.

      a) In such a case, the applicant is required to determine that the modified sUA meets the performance-based safety requirements for Category 2 or 3, or both, using an FAA-accepted MOC and to submit a new DOC.

         i) This principle applies to any person who modifies an existing ineligible small unmanned aircraft with the intention of conducting Category 2 or 3, or both, operations over people.

13. A **declaration of compliance (DOC)** is required in order to be eligible to conduct Category 2 or 3 operations over people. The person who designs, produces, or modifies the sUA must declare compliance with the appropriate performance-based safety requirements through use of an FAA-accepted MOC. The FAA will receive such DOCs via an electronic form available at https://uasdoc.faa.gov.

    a. **Submission of a DOC** involves the applicant declaring the following information:

       1) The applicant has demonstrated that the small unmanned aircraft meets the performance-based safety requirements for the category or categories of operation through an FAA-accepted MOC;

       2) The applicant maintains a process to notify owners of small unmanned aircraft and the FAA of any unsafe conditions that render those small unmanned aircraft noncompliant with 14 CFR Part 107, Subpart D;

       3) The applicant verifies that the small unmanned aircraft does not contain any safety defects; and

       4) The applicant will allow the FAA to access its facilities, technical documents, records, or reports as required or to witness any test necessary to determine compliance with the DOC.

    b. **Contents of a DOC.** A completed DOC includes information required by the FAA (1) for determining that a small unmanned aircraft complies with the applicable safety requirements and (2) that is a means of tracking models of small unmanned aircraft that were declared compliant. In accordance with 14 CFR 107.160, applicants will declare they have met the requirements through an FAA-accepted MOC and include the following information:

       1) FAA-accepted MOC used
       2) Name of the applicant
       3) Physical address of the applicant
       4) Email address of the applicant (used for correspondence with the FAA)
       5) Small unmanned aircraft make and model, and series, if applicable
       6) Serial number or range of serial numbers for the small unmanned aircraft subject to the DOC (open-ended are permitted)
       7) Whether the DOC is an initial or an amended DOC, and if amended, the reason for the resubmittal

8) Declaration that the applicant

   a) Has demonstrated the sUA meets the injury severity limits of Category 2 or 3, or both, and the prohibition on exposed rotating parts that would cause lacerations;

   b) Has verified the sUA does not have any safety defects;

   c) Has satisfied the requirement to maintain a product support and notification process; and

   d) Will, upon request, allow the Administrator to inspect its facilities and its technical data.

9) Any other information as required by the Administrator

c. Additionally, if an applicant resubmits an FAA-accepted DOC, the applicant must include the reason for the amendment. For example, the amendment could include additional serial numbers, document the correction of a safety defect, correct the misspelling of the applicant's name, or correct an address.

   1) The FAA will maintain a list of FAA-accepted DOCs and make them publicly available on its website. This allows the FAA and the public to determine which makes and models, and series, if applicable, of small unmanned aircraft are eligible to conduct Category 2 and 3 operations over people.

d. After an applicant declares that a specific small unmanned aircraft meets the requirements of a particular category, the applicant should ensure the sUA continues to comply with the applicable requirements. By submitting the DOC to the FAA for acceptance, the applicant attests it meets the requirements for 14 CFR Part 107, Subpart D, including the following:

   1) The applicant declares it has established and maintains a support and notification process to the public applicable to the small unmanned aircraft that are listed on the DOC.

      a) The product support and notification process exists to notify sUA owners, the public, and the FAA of safety issues that result in noncompliance with regulatory requirements. Notification to the sUA owners could take the form of a notice on a website or electronic notification to owners.

         i) Owners may register their sUA with the manufacturer through a warranty program or to update the sUA's software. Manufacturer registration may be used to advise the remote pilot that the sUA does not fulfill the safety requirements for eligibility in one or more categories of operations over people.

      b) The person who holds the FAA-accepted DOC should exercise due diligence to ensure the communications involving potential noncompliant conditions are communicated to the responsible individual.

      c) Manufacturers are encouraged to design and utilize a system to facilitate communication between the applicant and the owners of sUA. Their product support and notification system should be implemented to communicate corrective actions for safety defects.

         i) When the manufacturer can confirm the safety defects have been corrected for specific serial numbers, a new DOC may be submitted. The manufacturer must verify that those serial numbered aircraft have no safety defects prior to submitting a new DOC.

2) The DOC includes an agreement indicating that the person who holds the FAA-accepted DOC will allow the Administrator to inspect its facilities, technical data, and any manufactured sUA when a safety issue warrants that level of FAA involvement. Prior to inspecting the facilities, the FAA will coordinate with the holder of the DOC to explain the safety concerns. Upon receipt of the FAA notification, the responsible person should be prepared to discuss production and safety procedures, including engineering and quality systems, procedures manuals, and handbooks, when practical. The FAA will expect the responsible person who holds the DOC to be prepared to discuss an evaluation of, and a proposed solution to, the safety concerns. This may include a review of

   a) Critical processes (including special processes) and critical suppliers
   b) Recent design changes
   c) Significant changes in manufacturing personnel, procedures, or inspections
   d) Quality issues or escapes
   e) Any tests necessary to determine compliance with 14 CFR Part 107, Subpart D
   f) Any additional relevant correspondence or data pertaining to issues discovered in the course of new product deliveries or acceptance
   g) Service history data and service difficulties

   NOTE: The FAA expects the responsible person to be prepared with any necessary information regarding the items above and other relevant quality data, procedures, or records available to evaluate the safety concern.

   e. **FAA acceptance of a DOC.** If the FAA determines the applicant has demonstrated compliance with the requirements of 14 CFR Part 107, Subpart D, it will notify the applicant that it has accepted the DOC. All FAA-accepted DOCs will be made available on the FAA website.

14. **Maintenance of an sUAS that is eligible for operations over people** does not require a new DOC to be submitted if the maintenance actions performed on the eligible Category 2 or 3 aircraft do not change the configuration or characteristics of the aircraft.

   a. For example, if replacing propellers is listed as an allowed modification in the remote pilot operating instructions, a new DOC is not required.

      1) However, if replacing propellers is not covered in the remote pilot operating instructions, submission of a new DOC to conduct Category 2 or 3 operations over people is required.

   b. Remote pilot operating instructions should include a list of allowed modifications for the small unmanned aircraft to remain eligible.

15. A **means of compliance (MOC)** is a method of showing that a small unmanned aircraft does not exceed the applicable injury severity limit upon impact with a human being, does not contain any exposed rotating parts that would lacerate human skin, and does not contain any safety defects. An MOC must be accepted by the FAA before an applicant can rely on it to declare compliance with the safety requirements for operations over people.

    a. Anyone may submit an MOC to the FAA for acceptance if it fulfills Category 2 or 3 safety requirements. An individual or a voluntary consensus standards body (e.g., ASTM International or SAE) could develop an acceptable MOC. The MOC must demonstrate through test, analysis, or inspection that the small UA is eligible for operations over people in Category 2 or 3, or both. The MOC may include consensus standards.

        1) Once the FAA accepts an MOC, any person submitting a DOC could use it to establish that a small unmanned aircraft fulfills the requirements of the rule. An applicant requesting FAA acceptance of an MOC must submit certain information to the FAA in a manner the Administrator specifies.

        2) When reviewing an MOC, the FAA utilizes a comprehensive set of criteria to determine whether the testing, analysis, or inspection described in the MOC demonstrates that a small UA meets the appropriate regulatory requirements. An MOC must address the injury severity limits, the prohibition on exposed rotating parts that would cause lacerations, and verification that there are no safety defects.

            a) The FAA determines whether the proposed MOC aligns with accepted methods used by the medical industry, consumer safety groups, or other peer-reviewed test methods. In addition, the FAA considers whether the proposed MOC relies on mitigations that require exceptional remote pilot skill or excessive workload to satisfy the requirements.

    b. An FAA-accepted MOC is subject to an ongoing review by the FAA to ensure the MOC remains valid. If the FAA determines the MOC no longer meets any or all of the requirements to demonstrate compliance with 14 CFR Part 107, Subpart D, the FAA may rescind acceptance. If the FAA elects to rescind an MOC, it will publish a notice of rescission in the Federal Register.

    c. The MOC options an applicant may use are as follows:

        1) An FAA-provided MOC, discussed in item 15.d. beginning below.

        2) An FAA-accepted MOC developed by a voluntary consensus standards body or other entity or an FAA-accepted MOC developed independent of the FAA.

            a) An MOC developed by an individual applicant requires the same level of FAA review as an MOC developed by a voluntary consensus standards body. The FAA generally works with voluntary consensus standards bodies in the development of these standards. As a result, such an MOC will already have gone through a comprehensive review process during development.

    d. **FAA-provided MOC.** Without prejudice to any other MOC that an applicant may propose and the FAA may accept, the FAA offers one already-accepted MOC for both the impact kinetic energy and exposed rotating parts requirements provided in 14 CFR 107.120(a)(1) and (2) (Category 2) and 14 CFR 107.130(a)(1) and (2) (Category 3).

        1) The FAA-provided MOC for the injury severity limitations is developed through an applicant's calculation of the small UA's maximum kinetic energy. This MOC does not account for impact dynamics or other factors but consists of using only the formula the FAA describes to calculate the small UA's maximum kinetic energy.

SU 1: Regulations

      2) The FAA-accepted MOC provides manufacturers with at least one method to demonstrate their small unmanned aircraft would meet the requirements to operate over people. As a result, the MOC involves confirming that (a) the impact of an sUA does not exceed a certain kinetic energy limit, (b) the sUA does not contain any exposed rotating parts, and (c) the sUA does not contain any safety defects.

16. The applicant must demonstrate understanding of **impact kinetic energy** and may use the FAA-provided MOC to do so by confirming the impact of the sUA does not exceed the applicable injury severity limits during a typical failure mode at the aircraft's maximum performance capabilities.

    a. To test a small unmanned aircraft using this MOC, an applicant would first determine the maximum forward airspeed the sUA is capable of attaining at full power in level flight.

        1) This would be done using a reliable and accurate airspeed measurement method under typical environmental conditions.

        2) For example, an applicant could measure the maximum speed using a global positioning system (GPS) groundspeed indicator, a radar gun, or a tape measure and stop watch.

    b. Next, an applicant would determine the ground impact speed resulting from an unpowered free-fall from the highest altitude the sUA is capable of attaining at full power.

        1) The ground impact speed could be determined by performing a drop test from the altitude determined in the previous step using a reliable and accurate vertical speed measurement method under typical environmental conditions.

    c. Once the applicant determines the maximum speeds associated with a horizontal and vertical impact, the applicant would determine the highest combination of these speeds the aircraft could achieve as a result of a typical failure in order to determine the maximum impact kinetic energy.

        1) The applicant should identify and assess typical failures caused by system or equipment loss of function or malfunction as well as those that could be caused by pilot error.

    d. In consideration of the maximum speeds and typical failures described above, the applicant should determine the maximum impact kinetic energy using the following equation:

$$KE_{impact} = 0.0155 \times w \times v^2$$

      KE_{impact} = Maximum impact kinetic energy in foot-pounds (ft.-lb.)
      w = Weight of sUA measured in pounds (lb.)
      v = Maximum impact speed measured in feet per second (ft./sec.)

    1) For example, a small unmanned aircraft that weighs 1.0 lb. and has a maximum impact speed of 26 ft./sec. has a maximum impact kinetic energy calculated as follows:

$$KE_{impact} = 0.0155 \times 1.0 \text{ lb.} \times (26 \text{ ft./sec.})^2 = 10.5 \text{ ft.-lb.}$$

    2) Similarly, a small unmanned aircraft that weighs 1.0 lb. and has a maximum impact speed of 40 ft./sec. has an impact kinetic energy calculated as follows:

$$KE_{impact} = 0.0155 \times 1.0 \text{ lb.} \times (40 \text{ ft./sec.})^2 = 24.8 \text{ ft.-lb.}$$

e. The two tables below provide examples of maximum impact speeds, rounded to whole numbers, associated with the impact kinetic energy thresholds of the different categories and the weight of the small unmanned aircraft.

   1) One table provides speeds in feet per second, and the other table provides speeds in miles per hour (mph).
   2) Applicants may use these tables when following this MOC based on the maximum performance of the sUA.
   3) These tables do not consider any energy absorbing characteristics of a small unmanned aircraft that may reduce the amount of energy that is transferred to a person during a collision.

Maximum Impact Speeds (ft./sec.) for a Given Weight and Impact Kinetic Energy under FAA-Provided MOC

Weight (lb.)	Maximum speed (ft./sec.)	
	Category 2 (11 ft.-lb.)	Category 3 (25 ft.-lb.)
1.0	26	40
1.5	22	33
2.0	19	28
2.5	17	25
3.0	15	23

Maximum Impact Speeds (mph) for a Given Weight and Impact Kinetic Energy under FAA-Provided MOC

Weight (lb.)	Maximum speed (mph)	
	Category 2 (11 ft.-lb.)	Category 3 (25 ft.-lb.)
1.0	18	27
1.5	15	22
2.0	13	19
2.5	11	17
3.0	10	16

17. **Exposed rotating parts** may require testing and analysis to determine that the parts could not become exposed as a result of a typical impact with a person.

   a. If the forces on the sUA during an impact with a person are likely to cause structural failures that cause the rotating parts to become exposed, the design does not satisfy this requirement.
   b. One means, but not the only means, of complying with the requirement would be to manufacture the small unmanned aircraft so that it does not contain any exposed rotating parts.
      1) For example, if the propellers that provide lift and thrust for the sUA are internal to the aircraft, such as in a ducted fan configuration, and would not make contact with a person as a result of a typical impact, the parts would not be exposed. Therefore, the sUA would satisfy the requirement.

SU 1: Regulations

1.6 REMOTE IDENTIFICATION (RID)

1. **Remote identification (RID or remote ID)** is the ability of a drone in flight to provide identification and location information that can be received by other parties.

    a. Remote ID helps the FAA, law enforcement, and other federal agencies find the control station when a drone appears to be flying in an unsafe manner or where it is not allowed to fly.

    b. Remote ID also lays the foundation of the safety and security groundwork needed for more complex drone operations.

    c. Only for Category 1, 2, and 4 operations, sustained flight over open-air assemblies is restricted to sUAS that meet the remote ID requirements under 14 CFR 89.110 or 14 CFR 89.115(a).

2. **Standard remote identification** is required after September 16, 2023, for most small UA that are registered or required to be registered.

    a. The serial number of a standard remote identification UA, or of the remote identification broadcast module, if one is installed on the UA, must be listed on the Certificate of Aircraft Registration.

    1) The serial number may only be listed on one Certificate of Aircraft Registration at a time.

    2) The remote identification broadcast module may be moved from one UA operated under Part 107 to another, but the serial number must also be moved from the first aircraft's Certificate of Aircraft Registration to the second aircraft's certificate prior to operation.

    b. UA that are not required to be registered under 14 CFR Part 48, such as those where the UA weighs 0.55 lb. or less, must comply with remote identification requirements when operated under any operating part for which registration is required.

    1) For example, UA that weigh less than 0.55 lb. are excepted from remote ID requirements, unless they are operated under Part 107, in which case they must be registered regardless of weight.

    c. Remote identification provides data regarding the location and identification of small unmanned aircraft operating in the national airspace system (NAS).

    1) It also provides airspace awareness to the FAA, national security agencies, and law enforcement entities that can be used to distinguish compliant airspace users from those potentially posing a safety or security risk.

    2) A list of UA by make and model that are compliant with remote identification will be found at www.faa.gov/uas when developed.

d. Standard remote identification of UA broadcasts certain message elements over radio frequency (RF) spectrum.

1) These message elements include

   a) Unmanned aircraft identification (either the UA serial number or session ID)
   b) Latitude, longitude, and geometric altitude of both the CS and the UA
   c) The velocity of the UA (including horizontal and vertical speed and direction)
   d) A time mark
   e) An emergency status code

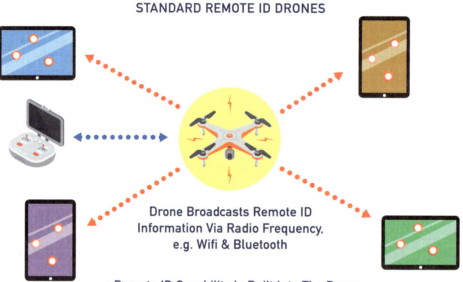

f) The rPIC must ensure the UA or module is broadcasting the remote ID messages "from takeoff to shutdown." In the event of a malfunction, the rPIC must land the UA as soon as practicable.

SU 1: Regulations

3. **Remote Identification Alternatives**

   a. Small unmanned aircraft that are not standard remote identification UA may operate in one of two ways:

      1) The UA may be equipped with a remote identification broadcast module, or
      2) The UA may be operated within an FAA-recognized identification area (FRIA).

   b. UA equipped with remote identification modules may be integrated by the manufacturer (e.g., if a manufacturer upgraded or retrofit the aircraft) or a standalone broadcast module installed by the user secured to the UA prior to takeoff.

   c. The remote identification broadcast module broadcasts certain message elements directly from the UA over RF spectrum.

      1) These message elements include

         a) The UA identification
         b) The UA serial number
         c) Latitude, longitude, and geometric altitude of the UA
         d) Latitude, longitude, and geometric altitude of the takeoff location
         e) Velocity of the UA (including horizontal and vertical speed and direction)
         f) A time mark

      2) UA using a remote identification broadcast module must be operated within VLOS.

   d. A person operating a UA that is not a standard remote identification UA may also operate within VLOS within an FRIA, regardless of the type of operation conducted (e.g., 14 CFR Part 91, 107, or other).

      1) A list of FRIAs will be accessible at www.faa.gov/uas when available.

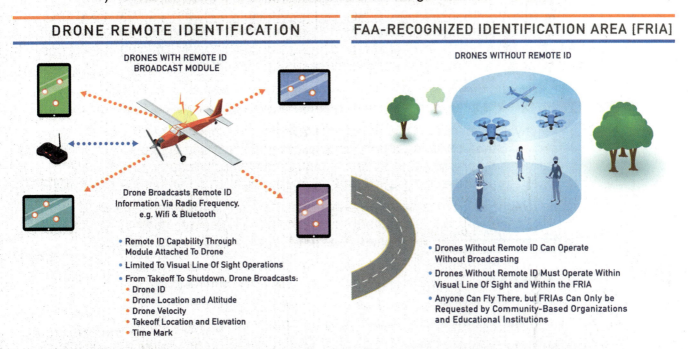

4. An operation without remote identification that is solely for the purpose of **aeronautical research** or to show compliance with regulations may be authorized by the Administrator according to 14 CFR 89.120.

5. **ADS-B Out** works by broadcasting information about an aircraft's GPS location, altitude, groundspeed, and other data to ground stations and other aircraft once per second.
    a. Air traffic controllers and aircraft equipped with ADS-B In can immediately receive this information. This allows more precise tracking of aircraft compared to radar technology, which sweeps for position information every 5 to 12 sec.
    b. ADS-B stands for Automatic Dependent Surveillance-Broadcast.
        1) Automatic -- it periodically transmits information with no pilot or operator involvement required.
        2) Dependent -- the position and velocity vectors are derived from the global positioning system (GPS) or other suitable navigation systems.
        3) Surveillance -- it provides a method of determining three-dimensional position and identification of aircraft, vehicles, or other assets.
        4) Broadcast -- it transmits the available information to anyone with the appropriate receiving equipment.
    c. Radio waves are limited to line of sight, meaning radar signals cannot travel long distances or penetrate mountains and other solid objects. ADS-B ground stations are smaller and more adaptable than radar towers and can be placed in locations not possible with radar. With ground stations in place throughout the country, even in hard to reach areas, ADS-B provides better visibility regardless of the terrain or other obstacles.
    d. 14 CFR 89.125 states that ADS-B Out equipment cannot be used to comply with remote identification requirements.

6. **Notice of Identification and Confirmation of Identification**
    a. No person may operate a foreign-registered civil unmanned aircraft with remote identification in the airspace of the United States unless, prior to the operation, the person submits a **notice of identification** in a form and manner acceptable to the Administrator. The notice of identification must include all of the following:
        1) The name of the person operating the foreign-registered civil unmanned aircraft in the United States, and, if applicable, the person's authorized representative.
        2) The physical address of the person operating the foreign-registered civil unmanned aircraft in the United States, and, if applicable, the physical address for the person's authorized representative. If the operator or authorized representative does not receive mail at the physical address, a mailing address must also be provided.
        3) The telephone number(s) where the person operating the foreign-registered civil unmanned aircraft in the United States, and, if applicable, the person's authorized representative, can be reached while in the United States.
        4) The email address of the person operating the foreign-registered civil unmanned aircraft in the United States, and, if applicable, the email address of the person's authorized representative.
        5) The unmanned aircraft manufacturer and model name.
        6) The serial number of the unmanned aircraft or remote identification broadcast module.
        7) The country of registration of the unmanned aircraft.
        8) The registration number.

SU 1: Regulations

b. The FAA will issue a **Confirmation of Identification** upon completion of the notification requirements.
   1) The filing of a notification and the Confirmation of Identification do not have the effect of United States aircraft registration.
   2) Proof of notification. No person may operate a foreign-registered civil unmanned aircraft with remote identification in the United States unless the person obtains a Confirmation of Identification, maintains such confirmation at the unmanned aircraft's control station, and produces the confirmation when requested by the FAA or a law enforcement officer.
   3) Requirement to maintain current information. The holder of a Confirmation of Identification must ensure the information provided remains accurate and must update the information prior to operating a foreign-registered civil unmanned aircraft in the United States.

7. **Minimum Message Elements Broadcast for Remote Identification**
   a. A standard remote identification unmanned aircraft must be capable of broadcasting over radio frequency (RF) spectrum the following remote identification message elements:
      1) The identity of the unmanned aircraft, consisting of
         a) A serial number assigned to the unmanned aircraft by the person responsible for the production of the standard remote identification unmanned aircraft or
         b) A session ID
      2) An indication of the latitude and longitude of the control station
      3) An indication of the geometric altitude of the control station
      4) An indication of the latitude and longitude of the unmanned aircraft
      5) An indication of the geometric altitude of the unmanned aircraft
      6) An indication of the velocity of the unmanned aircraft
      7) A time mark identifying the Coordinated Universal Time (UTC)
      8) An indication of the emergency status of the unmanned aircraft
   b. Remote identification broadcast modules must be capable of broadcasting the following remote identification message elements:
      1) The identity of the unmanned aircraft, consisting of the serial number assigned to the remote identification broadcast module by the person responsible for the production of the remote identification broadcast module
      2) An indication of the latitude and longitude of the unmanned aircraft
      3) An indication of the geometric altitude of the unmanned aircraft
      4) An indication of the velocity of the unmanned aircraft
      5) An indication of the latitude and longitude of the takeoff location of the unmanned aircraft
      6) An indication of the geometric altitude of the takeoff location of the unmanned aircraft
      7) A time mark identifying the UTC time

8. **Product Labeling**
    a. Category 1
        1) The FAA does not require labeling of small unmanned aircraft eligible for Category 1 operations. However, marking the retail packaging with the weight of the aircraft, or with a general statement that the aircraft weighs 0.55 lb. or less, would be helpful to the consumer.
        2) The manufacturer may also provide information to assist the pilot in determining that the small unmanned aircraft does not have any exposed rotating parts that would lacerate human skin upon impact. This type of packaging would also serve to promote the aircraft to consumers wishing to buy a small unmanned aircraft that has minimal operating restrictions.
        3) The FAA expects applicants to provide this type of information on the packaging of a small unmanned aircraft for easy identification purposes; however, such packaging is not required.
        4) It is the responsibility of the remote pilot to ensure the small unmanned aircraft meets the applicable requirements.
            a) Before conducting Category 1 operations, the remote pilot must determine the small unmanned aircraft weighs 0.55 lb. or less, including everything that is on board or otherwise attached to the aircraft at the time of takeoff and throughout the duration of each operation.
            b) Additionally, the remote pilot is responsible for determining the small unmanned aircraft does not contain any exposed rotating parts that would lacerate human skin upon impact.
    b. Category 2 and Category 3
        1) To be eligible for operations over people in accordance with Category 2 or 3, the small unmanned aircraft must display a label indicating the category or categories for which the small unmanned aircraft is eligible to conduct operations.
        2) Because operating limitations apply to operations under Category 3, the label on the small unmanned aircraft indicating eligibility for operations under Category 3 also serves to inform the remote pilot of the operating limitations (s)he is required to observe.
        3) The FAA does not provide a prescriptive labeling requirement that specifies exactly how an applicant must label an aircraft, what size font to use, specific location, etc.
            a) Due to the large variety of small unmanned aircraft models that exist, a prescriptive requirement would be inappropriate.
            b) Instead, the FAA allows the small unmanned aircraft to be labeled by any means as long as the label is in English, legible, prominent, and permanently affixed to the aircraft before conducting any operations over people.
                i) For example, an applicant may use the following labels: "Category 2," "Category 3," "Cat. 2," or "Cat. 3."
                ii) The label could be painted, etched, or affixed to the aircraft by any permanent means.

c) The label should be located externally, where it can easily be seen.

　　i) The FAA does not prescribe a specific location for label placement because of the design variations of small unmanned aircraft.

　　ii) In the case of very small unmanned aircraft, an applicant may need to exercise creativity in determining the location best suited to satisfying the labeling requirement. Locating a label on a non-critical surface will likely prevent wear and removal during normal operations.

4) If a Category 2 or 3 label affixed to a small unmanned aircraft is damaged, destroyed, or missing, an rPIC must label the aircraft in English such that the label is legible, prominent, and will remain on the small unmanned aircraft for the duration of the operation before conducting operations over human beings.

　　a) The label must correctly identify the category or categories of operation over human beings that the small unmanned aircraft is eligible to conduct.

5) In order to comply with labeling requirements, a remote pilot must ensure the small unmanned aircraft is properly labeled before conducting any operations over people.

　　a) A clear and legible label enables a remote pilot, an inspector, or a member of the public to identify the types of operations a small unmanned aircraft is eligible to conduct.

　　b) An aircraft without a clearly legible label would not be eligible to operate over people.

　　c) If a label degrades and is no longer legible or attached to the aircraft, the remote pilot is responsible for providing a new label before operating over people.

6) The labeling requirement applies regardless of whether a small unmanned aircraft is obtained directly from an applicant or as a subsequent transfer.

　　a) No pilot may operate the small unmanned aircraft unless the pilot verifies that the label meets the requirements of 14 CFR 107.120(b)(1) and 14 CFR 107.130(b)(1), as applicable.

　　b) If the small unmanned aircraft was manufactured before the effective date of this rule, or the small unmanned aircraft was otherwise not labeled, the remote pilot is responsible for determining whether the small unmanned aircraft is listed on an FAA-accepted declaration of compliance (DOC).

　　c) If the small unmanned aircraft is eligible to operate over people, the remote pilot is responsible for labeling the aircraft in accordance with 14 CFR 107.135.

7) A label will need to be changed if a small unmanned aircraft is modified for operation in a different or additional category.

　　a) If the small unmanned aircraft has been modified and is no longer eligible to operate in its previously labeled category, the label must identify the category the small unmanned aircraft is eligible to operate within.

　　b) The person who performed the modification would have to remove or cover the previous label so only the label with the new eligible category is visible on the aircraft.

QUESTIONS

1.1 General

1. According to 14 CFR Part 107, what is required to operate a small UA within 30 minutes after official sunset?

  A. Use of anti-collision lights.
  B. Must be operated in a rural area.
  C. Use of a transponder.

Answer (A) is correct. (14 CFR 107.29)
DISCUSSION: When small UA operations are conducted during civil twilight or within 30 min. after official sunset, the sUA must be equipped with anti-collision lights that are capable of being visible for at least 3 SM.
Answer (B) is incorrect. There is no requirement during civil twilight to operate an sUA in a rural area. **Answer (C) is incorrect.** There is no transponder requirement during civil twilight to operate an sUA.

2. To avoid a possible collision with a manned airplane, you estimate that your small UA climbed to an altitude greater than 600 feet AGL. To whom must you report the deviation?

  A. Air Traffic Control.
  B. The National Transportation Safety Board.
  C. Upon request of the Federal Aviation Administration.

Answer (C) is correct. (14 CFR 107.21)
DISCUSSION: A remote PIC who exercises his or her emergency power to deviate from the rules of Part 107, upon FAA request, is required to send a written report to the FAA explaining the deviation.
Answer (A) is incorrect. Upon request from the FAA, you must report a deviation to the FAA, not Air Traffic Control. **Answer (B) is incorrect.** Upon request from the FAA, you must report a deviation to the FAA, not the National Transportation Safety Board.

3. In accordance with 14 CFR Part 107, you may operate a small UA from a moving vehicle when no property is carried for compensation or hire

  A. Over suburban areas.
  B. Over a sparsely populated area.
  C. Over a parade or other social events.

Answer (B) is correct. (14 CFR 107.25)
DISCUSSION: Part 107 permits operation of a small UA from a moving land or water-borne vehicle over a sparsely populated area. Additionally, transporting another person's property for compensation or hire may not be operated from any moving vehicle.
Answer (A) is incorrect. Part 107 permits operation of a small UA from a moving land or water-borne vehicle over a sparsely populated area, not over a suburban area. **Answer (C) is incorrect.** Part 107 permits operation of a small UA from a moving land or water-borne vehicle over a sparsely populated area, not over a parade or other social events.

4. In accordance with 14 CFR Part 107, except when within a 400' radius of a structure, at what maximum altitude can you operate small UA?

  A. 500 feet AGL.
  B. 400 feet AGL.
  C. 600 feet AGL.

Answer (B) is correct. (14 CFR 107.51)
DISCUSSION: A small UA cannot be flown higher than 400 ft. above ground level (AGL), unless it is flown within a 400-ft. radius of a structure and does not fly higher than 400 ft. above the structure's immediate uppermost limit.
Answer (A) is incorrect. Except when within a 400-ft. radius of a structure, the maximum altitude you can operate a small UA is 400 ft. AGL, not 500 ft. AGL. **Answer (C) is incorrect.** Except when within a 400-foot radius of a structure, the maximum altitude you can operate sUAS is 400 ft. AGL, not 600 ft. AGL.

5. Under what condition would a small UA not have to be registered before it is operated in the United States?

  A. When the aircraft weighs less than .55 pounds on takeoff, including everything that is on-board or attached to the aircraft.
  B. When the aircraft has a takeoff weight that is more than .55 pounds, but less than 55 pounds, not including fuel and necessary attachments.
  C. All small UA need to be registered regardless of the weight of the aircraft before, during, or after the flight.

Answer (A) is correct. (14 CFR 107.13)
DISCUSSION: You need to register your aircraft if it weighs between 0.55 lb. and up to 55 lb.
Answer (B) is incorrect. Aircraft weighing between 0.55 lb. and up to 55 lb. must be registered. **Answer (C) is incorrect.** A small UA does not need to be registered if it weighs less than 0.55 lb.

SU 1: Regulations

6. According to 14 CFR Part 107, the remote pilot in command (rPIC) of a small unmanned aircraft planning to operate within Class C airspace

A. must use a visual observer.
B. is required to file a flight plan.
C. is required to receive ATC authorization.

Answer (C) is correct. (14 CFR 107.41)
DISCUSSION: Operations in Class B, C, or D airspace or within the lateral boundaries of the surface area of Class E airspace designated for an airport are not allowed unless that person has prior authorization from ATC. It is the responsibility of the rPIC of the sUAS to receive this prior authorization.
Answer (A) is incorrect. The rPIC of an sUAS planning to operate within Class C airspace is required to receive prior authorization from ATC, not use a visual observer. **Answer (B) is incorrect.** The rPIC of an sUAS planning to operate within Class C airspace is required to receive prior authorization from ATC, not file a flight plan.

7. Which of the following operations would be regulated by 14 CFR Part 107?

A. Flying for enjoyment with family and friends.
B. Operating your sUAS for an imagery company.
C. Conducting public operations during a search mission.

Answer (B) is correct. (14 CFR 107.1)
DISCUSSION: Part 107 covers the rules for non-hobbyist small unmanned aircraft (sUAS) operations, which include a broad spectrum of commercial uses for drones weighing less than 55 lb. Operating your sUAS for an imagery company would be a commercial operation and therefore would be regulated by Part 107.
Answer (A) is incorrect. Flying for enjoyment with family and friends would not be a commercial operation; therefore, Part 107 would not apply. **Answer (C) is incorrect.** Part 107 does not apply to public aircraft operations; therefore, conducting public operations during a search mission would not be regulated by it.

8. Personnel at an outdoor concert venue use a small UA to drop promotional t-shirts and CDs over the audience. Is this sUAS operation in compliance with 14 CFR Part 107?

A. Compliant with Part 107.
B. Not compliant with Part 107.
C. Part 107 does not apply to this scenario.

Answer (B) is correct. (14 CFR 107.39)
DISCUSSION: This operation is not in compliance with Part 107, which prohibits a person from flying a small UA over anyone who is not directly participating in the operation, not under a covered structure, or not inside a covered stationary vehicle. In addition, no items may be dropped from a small UA in a manner that creates an undue hazard to persons or property.
Answer (A) is incorrect. This small UA operation is not in compliance with Part 107. **Answer (C) is incorrect.** Part 107 includes the rules for non-hobbyist small UA operations, which include a broad spectrum of commercial uses for drones weighing less than 55 lb.; therefore, this scenario would be regulated by Part 107.

9. A professional wildlife photographer operates a small UA from a moving truck to capture aerial images of migrating birds in remote wetlands. The driver of the truck does not serve any crewmember role in the operation. Is this operation in compliance with 14 CFR Part 107?

A. Compliant with Part 107.
B. Not compliant with Part 107.
C. Part 107 does not apply to this scenario.

Answer (A) is correct. (14 CFR 107.25)
DISCUSSION: This small UA operation is in compliance with Part 107, which permits operation of a small UA from a moving land or water-borne vehicle over a sparsely populated area. In addition, this scenario is also compliant because the driver of the truck does not serve any crewmember role in the operation.
Answer (B) is incorrect. This operation is being conducted over a sparsely populated area, and the driver of the truck does not serve any crewmember role in the operation, therefore this operation is in compliance with Part 107. **Answer (C) is incorrect.** This is a commercial operation; therefore, Part 107 applies to this scenario.

10. You have accepted football tickets in exchange for using your sUAS to videotape the field before and after the game. Is this operation subject to 14 CFR Part 107?

A. Yes, this operation is subject to Part 107.
B. No, this operation is not subject to Part 107.
C. Yes, Part 107 allows flight directly over people to capture video.

Answer (A) is correct. (14 CFR 107.1)
DISCUSSION: You have accepted football tickets as a form of compensation for sUAS services; therefore, this is a commercial operation and is subject to Part 107. Part 107 rules are for non-hobbyist small unmanned aircraft (sUA) operations covering a broad spectrum of commercial uses.
Answer (B) is incorrect. Compensation has been received for services; therefore, this scenario is a commercial operation and is subject to Part 107. **Answer (C) is incorrect.** Operations are prohibited over persons not directly involved in the operation of the UA unless under safe cover.

60   SU 1: Regulations

11. You plan to operate a 33 lb. UA to capture aerial imagery over real estate for use in sales listings. Is this operation subject to 14 CFR Part 107?

    A. Yes, this operation is subject to Part 107.

    B. No, this operation is not subject to Part 107.

    C. No, this operation requires a Section 333 exemption.

Answer (A) is correct. (14 CFR 107.1)
    DISCUSSION: Part 107 contains the rules for non-hobbyist small unmanned aircraft (sUA) operations, which cover a broad spectrum of commercial uses for drones weighing less than 55 lb. This scenario is a commercial operation, and the UA weighs less than 55 lb.; therefore, it is subject to Part 107.
    Answer (B) is incorrect. This is a commercial operation, and the UA weighs less than 55 lb.; therefore, it is subject to Part 107. **Answer (C) is incorrect.** This is a routine commercial operation that does not require an exemption or waiver.

12. You are operating a 1280 g (2.8 lb.) quadcopter for your own enjoyment. Is this operation subject to 14 CFR Part 107?

    A. Yes, this operation is subject to Part 107.

    B. No, this operation is not subject to Part 107.

    C. Yes, all aircraft weighing over .55 lb. are subject to Part 107.

Answer (B) is correct. (14 CFR 107.1)
    DISCUSSION: This sUAS operation is not subject to Part 107 because it is being operated for recreational or hobby purposes. Part 107 rules are for non-hobbyist sUAS operations, and cover a broad spectrum of commercial uses for small UA (sUA) weighing less than 55 lb.
    Answer (A) is incorrect. Part 107 covers non-hobbyist sUA operations, including a broad spectrum of commercial uses for drones weighing less than 55 lb.; therefore, this operation is not subject to Part 107. **Answer (C) is incorrect.** An sUA weighing over .55 lb. must be registered, but it is not subject to Part 107 if operated for recreation or hobby.

13. According to 14 CFR Part 107, the responsibility to inspect the small UA to ensure it is in a safe operating condition rests with the

    A. remote pilot in command.

    B. visual observer.

    C. owner of the small UAS.

Answer (A) is correct. (14 CFR 107.49)
    DISCUSSION: The remote pilot in command (rPIC) has the final authority and responsibility for the operation and safety of an sUAS operation conducted under Part 107, which includes checks and inspection of the sUAS.
    Answer (B) is incorrect. It is the responsibility of the rPIC (not the visual observer) to inspect the sUAS to ensure it is in a safe operating condition. **Answer (C) is incorrect.** It is the responsibility of the rPIC (not the owner of the sUAS) to inspect the sUAS to ensure it is in a safe operating condition.

14. Who is responsible for ensuring that there are enough crewmembers for a given sUAS operation?

    A. Remote pilot in command (rPIC).

    B. Person manipulating the controls.

    C. Visual observer.

Answer (A) is correct. (14 CFR 107.19)
    DISCUSSION: The rPIC has the final authority and responsibility for the operation and safety of an sUAS operation conducted under Part 107, which includes ensuring that there are enough crewmembers for a given operation.
    Answer (B) is incorrect. The rPIC, not the person manipulating the controls, has the responsibility to ensure there are enough crewmembers for a given sUAS operation. The person manipulating the controls is under the supervision of the rPIC. **Answer (C) is incorrect.** The rPIC, not the visual observer, has the responsibility to ensure there are enough crewmembers for a given sUAS operation.

15. Unmanned aircraft means an aircraft operated

    A. Without the possibility of direct human intervention from within or on the aircraft.

    B. For hobby and recreational use when not certificated.

    C. During search and rescue operations other than public.

Answer (A) is correct. (14 CFR 107.3)
    DISCUSSION: The term unmanned aircraft (UA) means an aircraft operated without the possibility of direct human intervention from within or on the aircraft.
    Answer (B) is incorrect. The type of operation for a UA does not determine whether or not the aircraft is a UA. **Answer (C) is incorrect.** The type of operation for a UA does not determine whether or not the aircraft is a UA.

16. According to 14 CFR Part 107, an sUA is a small unmanned aircraft weighing

    A. Less than 55 lb.

    B. 55 kg or less.

    C. 55 lb. or less.

Answer (A) is correct. (14 CFR 107.3)
    DISCUSSION: Part 107 defines an sUA as a small unmanned aircraft weighing less than 55 lb., including everything that is onboard or otherwise attached to the aircraft.
    Answer (B) is incorrect. Part 107 defines an sUA as a small unmanned aircraft weighing less than 55 lb., not 55 kg or less. **Answer (C) is incorrect.** Part 107 defines an sUA as a small unmanned aircraft weighing less than 55 lb., not 55 lb. or less.

SU 1: Regulations

17. While operating a small unmanned aircraft system (sUAS), you experience a flyaway and several people suffer injuries. Which of the following injuries requires reporting to the FAA?

- A. Scrapes and cuts bandaged on site.
- B. Minor bruises.
- C. An injury requiring an overnight hospital stay.

Answer (C) is correct. (14 CFR 107.9)
DISCUSSION: The remote pilot in command (rPIC) is required to report an accident if it is considered a serious injury; an example of "serious injury" is if a person required hospitalization.
Answer (A) is incorrect. Scrapes and cuts bandaged on site do not require the rPIC to file an accident report to the FAA.
Answer (B) is incorrect. Minor bruises do not require the rPIC to file an accident report to the FAA.

18. A person without a Part 107 remote pilot certificate may operate an sUAS for commercial operations:

- A. Under the direct supervision of a remote PIC.
- B. Alone, if operating during daylight hours.
- C. Only when visual observers participate in the operation.

Answer (A) is correct. (14 CFR 107.12)
DISCUSSION: Under Part 107, which governs sUAS commercial operations, a person may operate an sUAS under the direct supervision of the remote pilot in command (rPIC); this person is called the "person manipulating the controls."
Answer (B) is incorrect. A person without a remote pilot certificate may not operate an sUAS for commercial operations without direct supervision from a certificated rPIC. **Answer (C) is incorrect.** A person without a remote pilot certificate may operate an sUAS for commercial operations only when an rPIC is supervising the operation, not when visual observers participate.

19. Which of the following types of operations are excluded from the requirements in Part 107?

- A. Quadcopter capturing aerial imagery for crop monitoring.
- B. Model aircraft for hobby use.
- C. UA used for motion picture filming.

Answer (B) is correct. (14 CFR 107.1)
DISCUSSION: Model aircraft for hobby use is excluded from the requirements in Part 107.
Answer (A) is incorrect. A quadcopter capturing aerial imagery for crop monitoring is regulated by Part 107.
Answer (C) is incorrect. UA used for motion picture filming would be regulated by Part 107.

20. A person whose sole task is watching the sUAS to report hazards to the rest of the crew is called:

- A. Remote PIC.
- B. Visual observer.
- C. Person manipulating the controls.

Answer (B) is correct. (14 CFR 107.3)
DISCUSSION: The visual observer is defined as a person acting as a flightcrew member who assists the remote pilot in command (rPIC) and the person manipulating the controls to see and avoid other air traffic or objects aloft or on the ground.
Answer (A) is incorrect. The rPIC is the person who holds a remote pilot certificate and has the final authority and responsibility for the operation; they are not the visual observer.
Answer (C) is incorrect. The person manipulating the controls is a person other than the rPIC who is operating the control station, but is not a visual observer.

21. Who holds the responsibility to ensure all crewmembers who are participating in the operation are not impaired by drugs or alcohol?

- A. Remote pilot in command.
- B. Contractor.
- C. Site supervisor.

Answer (A) is correct. (14 CFR 107.19)
DISCUSSION: It is the responsibility of the remote pilot in command (rPIC) to ensure all crewmembers are not participating in the operation while impaired.
Answer (B) is incorrect. It is the responsibility of the rPIC, not the contractor, to ensure crewmembers are not participating in the operation while impaired. **Answer (C) is incorrect.** It is the responsibility of the rPIC, not a site supervisor, to ensure crewmembers are not participating in the operation while impaired.

22. Who is ultimately responsible for preventing a hazardous situation before an accident occurs?

- A. Remote pilot in command (rPIC).
- B. Person manipulating the controls.
- C. Visual observer.

Answer (A) is correct. (14 CFR 107.19)
DISCUSSION: The rPIC has the final authority and responsibility for the operation and safety of an sUAS operation conducted under Part 107.
Answer (B) is incorrect. The rPIC, not the person manipulating the controls, is responsible for preventing hazardous situations. **Answer (C) is incorrect.** The rPIC, not the visual observer, is responsible for preventing hazardous situations.

23. Power company employees use an sUAS to inspect a long stretch of high voltage powerlines. Due to muddy conditions, their vehicle must stay beside the road and the crew uses binoculars to maintain visual line of sight with the aircraft. Is this operation in compliance with 14 CFR Part 107?

A. Compliant with Part 107.
B. Not compliant with Part 107.
C. Compliant with Part 107 when used with a first-person view (FPV) camera system.

Answer (B) is correct. (14 CFR 107.31)
DISCUSSION: Visual line of sight (VLOS) must be accomplished and maintained by unaided vision, except vision that is corrected by the use of eyeglasses (spectacles) or contact lenses.
Answer (A) is incorrect. Part 107 operations must be accomplished by unaided vision; therefore, binoculars cannot be used. **Answer (C) is incorrect.** An FPV camera system does not provide adequate see-and-avoid capabilities. VLOS must be accomplished and maintained by unaided vision.

24. Which crewmember is required to be under the direct supervision of the remote PIC when operating an sUAS?

A. Remote pilot in command (rPIC).
B. Person manipulating the controls.
C. Visual observer.

Answer (B) is correct. (14 CFR 107.12)
DISCUSSION: The person manipulating the controls is a person other than the rPIC who is controlling the flight of an sUAS and is under the direct supervision of the rPIC when operating the sUAS.
Answer (A) is incorrect. The person manipulating the controls is a person other than the rPIC who is operating the control station. **Answer (C) is incorrect.** The visual observer does not have to be in direct supervision of the rPIC if communication is maintained.

25. Which crewmember must hold a remote pilot certificate with an sUAS rating?

A. Remote pilot in command (rPIC).
B. Person manipulating the controls.
C. Visual observer.

Answer (A) is correct. (14 CFR 107.12)
DISCUSSION: The rPIC must hold a remote pilot certificate with an sUAS rating.
Answer (B) is incorrect. The rPIC, not the person manipulating the controls, must hold a remote pilot certificate with an sUAS rating. **Answer (C) is incorrect.** The rPIC, not the visual observer, must hold a remote pilot certificate with an sUAS rating.

26. According to 14 CFR Part 48, when would a small UA owner not be permitted to register it?

A. If the owner is less than 13 years of age.
B. All persons must register their small UA.
C. If the owner does not have a valid United States driver's license.

Answer (A) is correct. (14 CFR 48.25)
DISCUSSION: The owner must be at least 13 years of age to register a small UA.
Answer (B) is incorrect. A small UA weighing less than .55 lb. does not need registered. **Answer (C) is incorrect.** A driver's license is not required to register a small UA.

27. Whose sole task during an sUAS operation is to watch the sUAS and report potential hazards to the rest of the crew?

A. Remote pilot in command (rPIC).
B. Person manipulating the controls.
C. Visual observer.

Answer (C) is correct. (14 CFR 107.3)
DISCUSSION: The visual observer is a person acting as a flight crew member who sole task is to watch the sUAS and report potential hazards to the rest of the crew.
Answer (A) is incorrect. The visual observer, not the rPIC, has the sole task of watching the sUAS and reporting potential hazards to the rest of the crew. **Answer (B) is incorrect.** The visual observer, not the person manipulating the controls, has the sole task of watching the sUAS and reporting potential hazards to the rest of the crew.

28. According to 14 CFR Part 48, when must a person register a small UA with the Federal Aviation Administration?

A. All civilian small UAs weighing greater than .55 pounds must be registered regardless of its intended use.
B. When the small UA is used for any purpose other than as a model aircraft.
C. Only when the operator will be paid for commercial services.

Answer (A) is correct. (14 CFR 107.13)
DISCUSSION: All civilian sUAS weighing more than 0.55 lb. must be registered with the FAA regardless of its intended use.
Answer (B) is incorrect. An sUAS weighing more than 0.55 lb. must be registered even when used solely as a model aircraft. **Answer (C) is incorrect.** Weight of the sUAS, not the type of operation, determines if an sUAS must be registered.

SU 1: Regulations

29. Within how many days must an sUAS accident be reported to the FAA?

A. 90 days.
B. 30 days.
C. 10 days.

Answer (C) is correct. (14 CFR 107.9)
   DISCUSSION: The rPIC of the sUAS is required to report an accident to the FAA within 10 days if it meets any of the required thresholds.
   Answer (A) is incorrect. An sUAS accident must be reported to the FAA in 10 days, not 90 days. **Answer (B) is incorrect.** An sUAS accident must be reported to the FAA in 10 days, not 30 days.

30. You are part of a news crew, operating an sUAS to cover a breaking story. You experience a flyaway during landing. The unmanned aircraft strikes a vehicle, causing approximately $800 worth of damage. When must you report the accident to the FAA?

A. Any time.
B. Within 10 days.
C. Not to exceed 30 days.

Answer (B) is correct. (14 CFR 107.9)
   DISCUSSION: An accident costing more than $500 to repair or replace damage to property, other than the sUAS, must be reported to the FAA within 10 days.
   Answer (A) is incorrect. The report must be made within 10 days, not any time. **Answer (C) is incorrect.** The report must be made within 10 days, not within 30 days.

31. Before each flight, the rPIC must ensure that

A. Objects carried on the sUAS are secure.
B. The site supervisor has approved the flight.
C. ATC has granted clearance.

Answer (A) is correct. (14 CFR 107.49)
   DISCUSSION: Ensure that any object attached or carried by the small UA is secure and does not adversely affect the flight characteristics or controllability of the aircraft.
   Answer (B) is incorrect. A site supervisor is not required under Part 107. **Answer (C) is incorrect.** ATC clearance is required before flights in controlled airspace, not before every flight.

32. Which operations must comply with 14 CFR Part 107?

A. Civil and public aircraft operations.
B. Public and military operations.
C. Civil operations.

Answer (C) is correct. (14 CFR 107.11)
   DISCUSSION: According to 14 CFR 107.11, this subpart applies to the operation of all civil sUAS subject to this part.
   Answer (A) is incorrect. Part 107 applies to civil sUAS operations, not public aircraft operations. "Public" refers to aircraft used by the government. **Answer (B) is incorrect.** Part 107 applies to civil sUAS operations, not public or military aircraft operations.

33. While operating your small UA, it accidentally strikes your crewmember in the head, causing loss of consciousness. When should this accident be reported?

A. No accidents need to be reported.
B. When requested by the UA owner.
C. Within 10 days of the accident.

Answer (C) is correct. (14 CFR 107.9)
   DISCUSSION: The remote PIC of the sUAS is required to report an accident to the FAA within 10 days if it causes at least serious injury to any person or any loss of consciousness.
   Answer (A) is incorrect. An accident causing a loss of consciousness must be reported to the FAA. **Answer (B) is incorrect.** The accident must be reported to the FAA within 10 days, not when requested by the UA owner.

34. Your surveying company is a title sponsor for a race team at the Indianapolis 500. To promote your new aerial surveying department, you decide to video part of the race using a small UA. The FAA has issued a Temporary Flight Restriction (TFR) for the race in the area you plan to fly. In this situation

A. you may fly your drone in the TFR since your company is sponsoring a team at the race.
B. the TFR applies to all aircraft; you may not fly in the area without a Certificate of Waiver or Authorization.
C. flying your drone is allowed if you notify all non-participating people of the closed course UA operation.

Answer (B) is correct. (AC 107-2A)
   DISCUSSION: You are not authorized to fly within a TFR without a Certificate of Waiver or Authorization.
   Answer (A) is incorrect. You are not authorized to fly within a TFR without a Certificate of Waiver or Authorization. **Answer (C) is incorrect.** You are not authorized to fly within a TFR without a Certificate of Waiver or Authorization.

1.2 Operating Rules

35. Responsibility for collision avoidance in an alert area rests with

A. the controlling agency.
B. the remote pilot in command (rPIC).
C. Air Traffic Control.

Answer (B) is correct. (AIM Para 3-4-6)
DISCUSSION: Alert areas may contain a high volume of pilot training or other unusual activity. The rPIC is responsible for collision avoidance.
Answer (A) is incorrect. The rPIC, not the controlling agency, is responsible for collision avoidance. Answer (C) is incorrect. The rPIC, not ATC, is responsible for collision avoidance.

36. Under what conditions may objects be dropped from a small UA?

A. Only in an emergency.
B. If precautions are taken to avoid injury or damage to persons or property on the surface.
C. If prior permission is received from the Federal Aviation Administration.

Answer (B) is correct. (14 CFR 107.23)
DISCUSSION: No pilot in command of a small UA may allow any object to be dropped from that aircraft in flight that creates a hazard to persons or property. However, this section does not prohibit the dropping of any object if reasonable precautions are taken to avoid injury or damage to persons or property.
Answer (A) is incorrect. Objects may be dropped from a small UA if precautions are taken to avoid injury or damage to persons or property on the surface, not only in an emergency. Answer (C) is incorrect. Objects may be dropped from a small UA if precautions are taken to avoid injury or damage to persons or property on the surface. Prior permission from the FAA is not required.

37. No person may attempt to act as a crewmember of a small UA with

A. .008 percent by weight or more alcohol in the blood.
B. .004 percent by weight or more alcohol in the blood.
C. .04 percent by weight or more alcohol in the blood.

Answer (C) is correct. (14 CFR 107.27)
DISCUSSION: No person may act or attempt to act as a crewmember of a small UA while having a .04% by weight or more alcohol in the blood.
Answer (A) is incorrect. No person may attempt to act as a crewmember of a small UA with .04% (not .008%) by weight or more alcohol in the blood. Answer (B) is incorrect. No person may attempt to act as a crewmember of a small UA with .04% (not .004%) by weight or more alcohol in the blood.

38. A person may not act as a crewmember of a small UA if alcoholic beverages have been consumed by that person within the preceding

A. 8 hours.
B. 12 hours.
C. 24 hours.

Answer (A) is correct. (14 CFR 107.27)
DISCUSSION: No person may act as a crewmember of a small UA if alcoholic beverages have been consumed by that person within the preceding 8 hr.
Answer (B) is incorrect. No person may act as a crewmember of a small UA within 8 hr. (not 12 hr.) after the consumption of any alcoholic beverage. Answer (C) is incorrect. No person may act as a crewmember of a small UA within 8 hr. (not 24 hr.) after the consumption of any alcoholic beverage.

39. Under what condition, if any, may remote pilots fly through a restricted area?

A. When flying on airways.
B. With the controlling agency's authorization.
C. Regulations do not allow this.

Answer (B) is correct. (14 CFR 107.45)
DISCUSSION: A small UA may not be operated within a restricted area unless permission has been obtained from the controlling agency. Frequently, the ATC within the area acts as the controlling agent's authorization.
Answer (A) is incorrect. No person may operate a small UA within a restricted area unless permission has been granted by the using or controlling agency. Answer (C) is incorrect. Restricted areas may be entered with proper authorization.

40. The cloud ceiling is reported at 800 ft. What is the highest altitude you can operate a small UA?

A. 200 ft. AGL.
B. 300 ft. AGL.
C. 800 ft. AGL.

Answer (B) is correct. (14 CFR 107.51)
DISCUSSION: 14 CFR 107.51(d) requires a small UA to be flown no closer than 500 ft. below the clouds.

800 ft. − 500 ft. = 300 ft. AGL

Answer (A) is incorrect. You may operate no less than 500 ft., not 600 ft., below the clouds. Answer (C) is incorrect. You may not operate closer than 500 ft. below the clouds.

SU 1: Regulations

41. According to 14 CFR Part 107, how may a remote pilot operate an unmanned aircraft in Class C airspace?

A. The remote pilot must have prior authorization from the Air Traffic Control (ATC) facility having jurisdiction over that airspace.

B. The remote pilot must monitor the Air Traffic Control (ATC) frequency from launch to recovery.

C. The remote pilot must contact the Air Traffic Control (ATC) facility after launching the unmanned aircraft.

Answer (A) is correct. (AIM Para 3-2-6)
DISCUSSION: Operations in controlled airspace designated for an airport are not allowed unless that person has prior authorization from ATC.
Answer (B) is incorrect. An ATC facility may require the remote pilot to monitor the ATC frequency, but only on a case by case basis. **Answer (C) is incorrect.** Prior authorization must be obtained from ATC prior to operating in the controlled airspace, not after launching the unmanned aircraft.

42. When using a small unmanned aircraft in a commercial operation, who is responsible for informing the participants about emergency procedures?

A. The remote pilot in command.

B. The FAA Inspector-in-Charge.

C. The lead visual observer.

Answer (A) is correct. (14 CFR 107.49)
DISCUSSION: As part of the FAA requirement for the sUAS to be in a condition for safe operation, prior to flight, the remote pilot in command (rPIC) must ensure that all persons directly participating in the UA operation are informed about emergency procedures.
Answer (B) is incorrect. It is the responsibility of the rPIC, not the FAA inspector-in-charge, to ensure that all persons directly participating in the UA operation are informed about emergency procedures. **Answer (C) is incorrect.** It is the responsibility of the rPIC, not the lead visual observer, to ensure that all persons directly participating in the UA operation are informed about emergency procedures.

43. When can someone with a marijuana conviction apply for a remote pilot certificate?

A. Never.

B. 1 year.

C. 18 months.

Answer (B) is correct. (14 CFR 107.57)
DISCUSSION: A conviction for the violation of any federal or state statute relating to the growing, processing, manufacture, sale, disposition, possession, transportation, or importation of narcotic drugs, marijuana, or depressant or stimulant drugs or substances is grounds for denial of an application for a remote pilot certificate with a small UAS rating for a period of up to 1 year after the date of final conviction.
Answer (A) is incorrect. A person with a marijuana conviction may apply for a remote pilot certificate after 1 year. **Answer (C) is incorrect.** A person with a marijuana conviction may apply for a remote pilot certificate after 1 year, not 18 months.

44. Sunrise is at 0645 and the UA is without appropriate lighted anti-collision lighting. When can you launch your sUAS?

A. 0615

B. 0645

C. 0715

Answer (A) is correct. (14 CFR 107.29)
DISCUSSION: No person may operate an sUAS during night without appropriate lighted anti-collision lighting. Night is defined as the period between the end of the evening civil twilight and the beginning of the morning civil twilight. Morning civil twilight is the period of time that begins 30 min. before official sunrise and ends at official sunrise. Therefore, you can launch at 0615 (0645 − 0030 = 0615).
Answer (B) is incorrect. This is the time of sunrise, not the beginning of the morning civil twilight. **Answer (C) is incorrect.** This is 30 min. after sunrise, not 30 min. before sunrise.

45. After having dinner and wine, your client asks you to go outside to demonstrate the small UAs capabilities. You must

A. pass a self-administered sobriety test before operating a small UA.

B. not operate a small UA within 8 hours of consuming any alcoholic beverage.

C. ensure that your visual observer has not consumed any alcoholic beverage in the previous 12 hours.

Answer (B) is correct. (14 CFR 91.17 and 107.17)
DISCUSSION: No person may act or attempt to act as a crewmember of a small UA within 8 hr. after the consumption of any alcoholic beverage.
Answer (A) is incorrect. You may not operate a small UA within the previous 8 hr. of consuming any amount of alcohol. **Answer (C) is incorrect.** You as the pilot, or any crewmember may not have consumed any alcoholic beverage within the previous 8 hr.

46. To whom must your remote pilot certificate be presented, if requested?

A. An FAA Inspector.
B. A person of authority.
C. A Department of State representative.

Answer (A) is correct. (14 CFR 107.7)
DISCUSSION: A remote pilot in command, owner, or person manipulating the flight controls of an sUAS must, upon request, make available to the Administrator (1) the remote pilot certificate with a small UAS rating and (2) any other document, record, or report required.
Answer (B) is incorrect. Your remote pilot certificate must be presented to the FAA (Administrator). A "person of authority" is not defined in the regulations. **Answer (C) is incorrect.** Your remote pilot certificate must be presented to the FAA (Administrator), not a Department of State representative.

47. A small UA must be operated in a manner which

A. does not endanger the life or property of another.
B. requires more than one visual observer.
C. never exceeds 200 feet AGL.

Answer (A) is correct. (14 CFR 107.15)
DISCUSSION: 14 CFR 107.15 prohibits anyone from operating a small UA unless it is in a condition for safe operation. A flight may not continue when the operator knows or has reason to know that the small unmanned aircraft system is no longer in a condition for safe operation.
Answer (B) is incorrect. A visual observer is not required to operate an sUAS. **Answer (C) is incorrect.** Part 107 generally allows a small UA operation up to 400 ft. AGL, not 200 ft. AGL.

48. You plan to release golf balls from your small UA at an altitude of 100 feet AGL. You must ensure the objects being dropped will

A. not create an undue hazard to persons or property.
B. land within 10 feet of the expected landing zone.
C. not cause property damage in excess of $300.

Answer (A) is correct. (14 CFR 107.23)
DISCUSSION: 14 CFR 107.23 states that items may not be dropped from a small UA in a manner that creates an undue hazard to persons or property.
Answer (B) is incorrect. There is no provision in the regulations for dropping objects within a specified distance of a landing zone. **Answer (C) is incorrect.** Any amount of property damage implies that an undue hazard was created.

49. During a flight of your small UA, you observe a hot air balloon entering the area. You should

A. yield the right-of-way to the hot air balloon.
B. ensure the UA passes below, above, or ahead of the balloon.
C. expect the hot air balloon to climb above your altitude.

Answer (A) is correct. (14 CFR 107.37)
DISCUSSION: Each small UA must yield the right of way to all aircraft, airborne vehicles, and launch and reentry vehicles.
Answer (B) is incorrect. Yielding the right of way means that the small UA must give way to the aircraft or vehicle and may not pass over, under, or ahead of it unless well clear. **Answer (C) is incorrect.** The remote PIC must maneuver the small UA to avoid a collision as well as prevent other aircraft from having to take action to avoid the small UA.

50. According to 14 CFR Part 107, what is the maximum groundspeed for a small UA?

A. 87 knots.
B. 87 mph.
C. 100 knots.

Answer (A) is correct. (14 CFR 107.51)
DISCUSSION: The groundspeed of the small UA may not exceed 87 kt. (100 mph).
Answer (B) is incorrect. The maximum groundspeed is 87 kt., not 87 mph. **Answer (C) is incorrect.** The maximum groundspeed is 87 kt. (100 mph), not 100 kt.

51. (Refer to Figure 78 on page 67.) You have been contracted to inspect towers located approximately 4 NM southwest of the Sioux Gateway (SUX) airport operating an unmanned aircraft. What is the maximum altitude above ground level (AGL) that you are authorized to operate over the top of the towers?

A. 400 feet AGL.
B. 402 feet AGL.
C. 802 feet AGL.

Answer (C) is correct. (14 CFR 107.51, Sectional Chart Legend)
DISCUSSION: The height of the towers is 402 ft. AGL. The sUAS may be flown no higher than 400 ft. above the structure's immediate uppermost limit, within a 400-ft. radius of a structure.

402 ft. AGL + 400 ft. = 802 ft. AGL

Answer (A) is incorrect. The sUAS may be flown up to 400 ft. higher than the height of the towers, not 400 ft. AGL. **Answer (B) is incorrect.** The height of the towers is 402 ft. AGL. The sUAS may be flown 400 ft. higher than the structure.

SU 1: Regulations

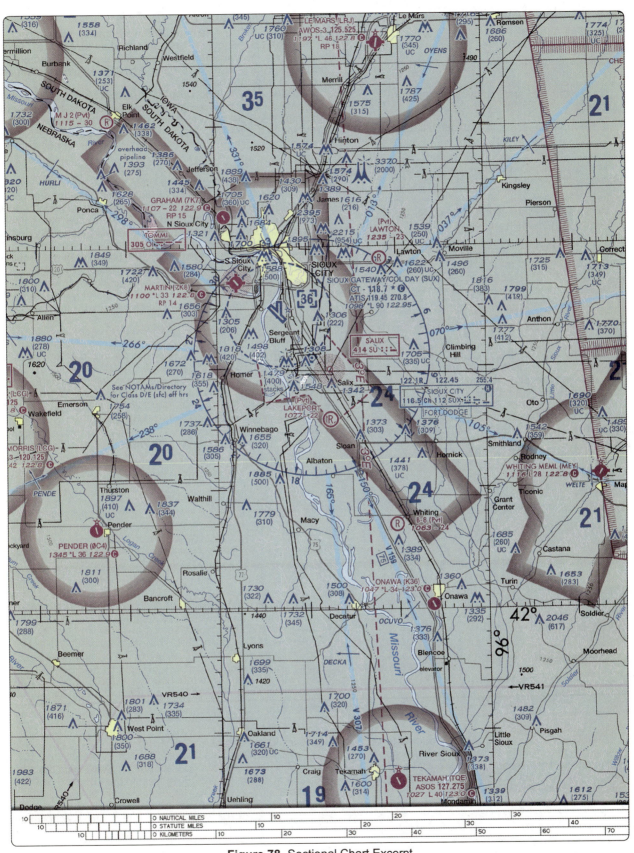

Figure 78. Sectional Chart Excerpt.
NOTE: Chart is not to scale and should not be used for navigation. Use associated scale.

52. Upon request by the FAA, the remote pilot-in-command must provide

A. a logbook documenting small UA landing currency.
B. a remote pilot certificate with a small UAS rating.
C. any employer issued photo identification.

Answer (B) is correct. (14 CFR 107.7)
DISCUSSION: A remote pilot in command, owner, or person manipulating the flight controls of an sUAS must, upon request, make available to the Administrator (1) the remote pilot certificate with a small UAS rating and (2) any other document, record, or report required.
Answer (A) is incorrect. There is no requirement to document small UA landing currency. **Answer (C) is incorrect.** An employer-issued photo identification is not required to be provided to the FAA.

53. When may a remote pilot reduce the intensity of an aircraft's lights during a night flight?

A. At no time may the lights of an sUAS be reduced in intensity at night.
B. When a manned aircraft is in the vicinity of the sUAS.
C. When it is in the interest of safety to dim the aircraft's lights.

Answer (C) is correct. (14 CFR 107.29)
DISCUSSION: The remote pilot in command may reduce the intensity of, but may not extinguish, the anti-collision lighting if they determine that, because of operating conditions, it would be in the interest of safety to do so.
Answer (A) is incorrect. The remote pilot in command may reduce the intensity of, but may not extinguish, the anti-collision lighting if they determine that, because of operating conditions, it would be in the interest of safety to do so. **Answer (B) is incorrect.** The remote pilot in command must determine that it would be in the interest of safety to reduce the intensity of the lights; the intensity should not be reduced only if a manned aircraft is in the vicinity.

54. A company hires a UAS operator to film construction progress on a new headquarters building. The remote pilot in command (rPIC) wants to capture sunrise footage and begins aerial photography about 15 minutes before sunrise. Most of the operation will be conducted after sunrise, though, so the UA is not equipped with anti-collision or position lighting. Is this sUAS operation in compliance with 14 CFR Part 107?

A. Compliant with Part 107.
B. Not compliant with Part 107.
C. Part 107 does not apply in this scenario.

Answer (B) is correct. (14 CFR 107.29)
DISCUSSION: This scenario is not compliant with Part 107. The operation falls within morning civil twilight (e.g., 30 min. prior to sunrise in the contiguous United States). Therefore, the sUAS must be equipped with anti-collision lights that are visible for at least 3 SM from the control station.
Answer (A) is incorrect. This scenario is not compliant with Part 107. **Answer (C) is incorrect.** Part 107 does apply to this scenario.

55. A remote PIC is operating an sUAS at night. A nearby homeowner complains about the ultra-bright LED strobe anti-collision lights. The remote pilot in command (rPIC) reduces the intensity of the light to avoid a confrontation. Is this sUAS operation in compliance with 14 CFR Part 107?

A. Compliant with Part 107.
B. Not compliant with Part 107.
C. Part 107 does not apply in this scenario.

Answer (B) is correct. (14 CFR 107.29)
DISCUSSION: This scenario is not compliant with Part 107. Anti-collision lights must be visible for at least 3 SM from the control station (CS) and have a flash rate sufficient to avoid a collision. The rPIC may only reduce the intensity of the lighting in the interest of operational safety.
Answer (A) is incorrect. This sUAS operation is not in compliance with Part 107. **Answer (C) is incorrect.** 14 CFR 107.29 describes the requirements for operations at night. Anti-collision lights must be visible for at least 3 SM from the control station (CS) and have a flash rate sufficient to avoid a collision.

56. A remote pilot in command (rPIC) is operating an sUAS at night to survey a structure using aerial thermal imagery. The sUAS is equipped with high-visibility position and anti-collision lighting. Though the lighting would be visible for 3 statute miles, the rPIC has also greatly reduced the operational area of the sUAS for night maneuvers. Is this sUAS operation in compliance with 14 CFR Part 107?

A. Compliant with Part 107.
B. Not compliant with Part 107.
C. Part 107 does not apply in this scenario.

Answer (A) is correct. (AC 107-2A)
DISCUSSION: This scenario is compliant with Part 107. The lighting and reduced operational range will help the rPIC keep the sUAS within VLOS and within the intended area of operation.
Answer (B) is incorrect. This scenario is compliant with Part 107. **Answer (C) is incorrect.** Part 107 does apply to this scenario.

SU 1: Regulations

1.3 Remote Pilot Certification with an sUAS Rating

57. After receiving a Part 107 remote pilot certificate with an sUAS rating, how often must you satisfy recurrent training requirements?

A. Every 12 months.
B. Every 8 months.
C. Every 24 months.

Answer (C) is correct. (14 CFR 107.65)
DISCUSSION: A remote pilot must retain and update their aeronautical knowledge to operate in the NAS by completing either an initial knowledge test or recurrent training that has been updated to include night operations.
Answer (A) is incorrect. A remote pilot must complete and satisfy recurrent training requirements every 24 calendar months, not 12 months. **Answer (B) is incorrect.** A remote pilot must complete and satisfy recurrent training requirements every 24 calendar months, not 8 months.

58. Which of the following individuals may process an application for a Part 107 remote pilot certificate with an sUAS rating?

A. Remote pilot in command.
B. Commercial balloon pilot.
C. Designated pilot examiner.

Answer (C) is correct. (14 CFR 107.63, 61.56)
DISCUSSION: An FAA designated pilot examiner (DPE), a Flight Standards office, an airmen certification representative (ACR), or an FAA certificated flight instructor (CFI), may process an application for a Part 107 remote pilot certificate with an sUAS rating.
Answer (A) is incorrect. A remote pilot in command is not authorized to process an application for a Part 107 remote pilot certificate with an sUAS rating. **Answer (B) is incorrect.** A commercial balloon pilot is not authorized to process an application for a Part 107 remote pilot certificate with an sUAS rating.

59. The refusal of a remote pilot in command (rPIC) to submit to a blood alcohol test when requested by a law enforcement officer

A. is grounds for suspension or revocation of their remote pilot certificate.
B. can be delayed for a period up to 8 hours after the request.
C. has no consequences to the remote pilot certificate.

Answer (A) is correct. (14 CFR 107.59)
DISCUSSION: A refusal to submit to a test to indicate the percentage by weight of alcohol in the blood, when requested by a law enforcement officer, or a refusal to furnish or authorize the release of the test results requested by the Administrator is grounds for (1) denial of an application for a remote pilot certificate with an sUAS rating for a period of up to 1 year after the date of that refusal or (2) suspension or revocation of a remote pilot certificate with an sUAS rating.
Answer (B) is incorrect. The rPIC may not delay submitting to a blood alcohol test. **Answer (C) is incorrect.** Refusing to submit to a blood alcohol test may result in a suspension or revocation of the remote pilot certificate.

1.4 Waivers

60. When requesting a waiver, the required documents should be presented to the FAA at least how many days prior to the planned operation?

A. 30 days.
B. 10 days.
C. 90 days.

Answer (C) is correct. (AC 107-2A Chap 5)
DISCUSSION: Although not required by Part 107, the FAA encourages applicants to submit their application at least 90 days prior to the start of the proposed operation.
Answer (A) is incorrect. When requesting a waiver, the required documents should be presented 90 days, not 30 days, prior to the planned operation. **Answer (B) is incorrect.** When requesting a waiver, the required documents should be presented 90 days, not 10 days, prior to the planned operation.

61. The FAA may approve your application for a waiver of provisions in Part 107 only when it has been determined that the proposed operation

A. Involves public aircraft or air carrier operations.
B. Will be conducted outside of the United States.
C. Can be safely conducted under the terms of that certificate of waiver.

Answer (C) is correct. (14 CFR 107.200)
DISCUSSION: The Administrator may issue a certificate of waiver authorizing a deviation from any regulation specified in 14 CFR 107.205 if the Administrator finds that a proposed sUAS operation can safely be conducted under the terms of that certificate of waiver.
Answer (A) is incorrect. Public aircraft or air carrier operations are not covered by Part 107. **Answer (B) is incorrect.** Operations outside the United States are not covered by Part 107.

1.5 Operations over People

62. To conduct Category 1 operations, a remote pilot in command must use a small UA that weighs

A. 0.55 pounds or less.
B. 0.65 pounds or less.
C. 0.75 pounds or less.

Answer (A) is correct. (14 CFR 107.110)
DISCUSSION: To conduct Category 1 operations, a remote pilot in command must use a small UA that weighs 0.55 lb. or less on takeoff and throughout the duration of each operation under Category 1.
Answer (B) is incorrect. To conduct Category 1 operations, a remote pilot in command must use a small UA that weighs 0.55 lb. or less on takeoff and throughout the duration of each operation under Category 1. **Answer (C) is incorrect.** To conduct Category 1 operations, a remote pilot in command must use a small UA that weighs 0.55 lb. or less on takeoff and throughout the duration of each operation under Category 1.

63. Which Category of small UA must have an airworthiness certificate issued by the FAA?

A. 4
B. 3
C. 2

Answer (A) is correct. (14 CFR 107.140)
DISCUSSION: To be eligible to operate over human beings under Category 4 operations, the sUAS must have an airworthiness certificate issued under 14 CFR Part 21.
Answer (B) is incorrect. Category 3 sUAS operations do not require an airworthiness certificate. **Answer (C) is incorrect.** Category 2 sUAS operations do not require an airworthiness certificate.

64. Which Category of operations over people requires that the small UA will not cause injury equivalent to or greater than the impact of 11 foot-pounds of kinetic energy?

A. Category 1.
B. Category 2.
C. Category 4.

Answer (B) is correct. (14 CFR 107.120)
DISCUSSION: To be eligible for use in Category 2 operations, the small UA must be designed, produced, or modified such that it will not cause injury to a human being that is equivalent to or greater than the severity of injury caused by a transfer of 11 foot-pounds of kinetic energy upon impact from a rigid object.
Answer (A) is incorrect. Category 1 sUAS operations do not include impact kinetic energy requirements. **Answer (C) is incorrect.** Category 4 sUAS operations do not include impact kinetic energy requirements.

65. Which Category of operations over people requires that the small UA will not cause injury equivalent to or greater than the impact of 25 foot-pounds of kinetic energy?

A. Category 1.
B. Category 2.
C. Category 3.

Answer (C) is correct. (14 CFR 107.130)
DISCUSSION: To be eligible for use in Category 3 operations, the small UA must be designed, produced, or modified such that it will not cause injury to a human being that is equivalent to or greater than the severity of injury caused by a transfer of 25 foot-pounds of kinetic energy upon impact from a rigid object.
Answer (A) is incorrect. Category 1 sUAS operations do not include impact kinetic energy requirements. **Answer (B) is incorrect.** Category 2 sUAS operations must not cause injury to a human being that is equivalent to or greater than the severity of injury caused by a transfer of 11 foot-pounds of kinetic energy upon impact from a rigid object.

66. Which Category of operations over people is allowed for operations conducted over a closed or restricted-access site?

A. Category 1.
B. Category 2.
C. Category 3.

Answer (C) is correct. (14 CFR 107.125)
DISCUSSION: Category 3 operations are allowed (1) at a closed- or restricted-access site when everyone is notified or (2) when not within a closed- or restricted-access site and the sUAS does not sustain flight over people not directly involved in the operation.
Answer (A) is incorrect. Category 1 sUAS operations are not bound by closed- or restricted-access sites. **Answer (B) is incorrect.** Category 2 sUAS operations are not bound by closed- or restricted-access sites.

SU 1: Regulations

67. Which Category of operations over people is limited to sUAS that weigh 0.55 pounds or less, including everything that is on board or attached?

A. Category 1.
B. Category 2.
C. Category 3.

Answer (A) is correct. (14 CFR 107.110)
   DISCUSSION: To conduct Category 1 operations, a remote pilot in command must use a small UA that weighs 0.55 lb. or less including everything that is on board or otherwise attached to the aircraft.
   Answer (B) is incorrect. To conduct Category 1 operations, a remote pilot in command must use a small UA that weighs 0.55 lb. or less including everything that is on board or otherwise attached to the aircraft. **Answer (C) is incorrect.** To conduct Category 1 operations, a remote pilot in command must use a small UA that weighs 0.55 lb. or less including everything that is on board or otherwise attached to the aircraft.

1.6 Remote Identification (RID)

68. Where must a small UA serial number be listed when using either standard remote identification or a broadcast module?

A. The aircraft's Document of Compliance.
B. The manufacturer's Method of Compliance.
C. The Certificate of Aircraft Registration.

Answer (C) is correct. (AC 107-2A)
   DISCUSSION: The serial number of a standard remote identification UA, or of the remote identification broadcast module, if one is installed on the UA, must be listed on the Certificate of Aircraft Registration.
   Answer (A) is incorrect. A small UA serial number must be listed on the Certificate of Aircraft Registration. **Answer (B) is incorrect.** A small UA serial number must be listed on the Certificate of Aircraft Registration.

69. Which of the following UA may only operate in "FAA-recognized identification areas"?

A. A new UA produced after the compliance date with standard Remote ID capabilities.
B. An existing or home-built UA that is later equipped with a Remote ID broadcast module.
C. Any UA that does not have Remote ID capabilities.

Answer (C) is correct. (14 CFR 89.115)
   DISCUSSION: UA without remote ID capabilities may only operate at FAA-recognized identification areas and are also limited to VLOS. New UA produced with standard remote ID capabilities and UA equipped after production with a remote ID broadcast module are both limited to VLOS.
   Answer (A) is incorrect. A new UA produced after the compliance date with standard remote ID capabilities is not limited to operations within FAA-recognized identification areas. **Answer (B) is incorrect.** A UA that is later equipped with a remote ID broadcast module is not limited to operations within FAA-recognized identification areas.

70. In which category of operations is sustained flight over open-air assemblies not restricted to sUAS that meet remote ID requirements?

A. Category 2.
B. Category 3.
C. Category 4.

Answer (B) is correct. (AC 107-2A)
   DISCUSSION: Only for Category 1, 2, and 4 operations, sustained flight over open-air assemblies is restricted to sUAS that meet the remote ID requirements under 14 CFR 89.110 or 14 CFR 89.115(a).
   Answer (A) is incorrect. Category 2 sUAS operations are required to meet the remote ID requirements under 14 CFR 89.110 or 14 CFR 89.115(a). **Answer (C) is incorrect.** Category 4 sUAS operations are required to meet the remote ID requirements under 14 CFR 89.110 or 14 CFR 89.115(a).

71. When operated under 14 CFR Part 107, small UA that weigh less than 0.55 lb.

A. must comply with remote ID requirements.
B. need not comply with remote ID requirements.
C. must be registered under 14 CFR Part 48.

Answer (A) is correct. (AC 107-2A)
   DISCUSSION: UA that weigh less than 0.55 lb. are excepted from remote ID requirements, unless they are operated under Part 107, in which case they must be registered regardless of weight.
   Answer (B) is incorrect. When operated under Part 107, UA must comply with remote ID requirements regardless of weight. **Answer (C) is incorrect.** A UA that is operated solely for recreational purposes and weighs under 0.55 lb. is not required to be registered under Part 48 (14 CFR 48.15). However, small UA that are not required to be registered under Part 48 must still comply with remote ID requirements when operated under Part 107.

72. If the UA or Remote ID broadcast module indicates that the equipment is not functioning properly while the UA is in flight, the Remote PIC must

A. Land the UA as soon as practicable.
B. Transfer control of the UA to a visual observer.
C. Immediately report the malfunction to the FAA.

Answer (A) is correct. (14 CFR 89.110)
DISCUSSION: The remote PIC must ensure the UA or module is broadcasting the remote ID messages "from takeoff to shutdown" and must land the UA as soon as practicable in the event of a malfunction.
Answer (B) is incorrect. The remote PIC must land the UA as soon as practicable in the event of a malfunction. **Answer (C) is incorrect.** The malfunction need not be reported to the FAA.

73. What must a person, who is manipulating the controls of a small UA, do if the standard remote identification fails during a flight?

A. Land the aircraft as soon as practicable.
B. Notify the nearest FAA Air Traffic facility.
C. Activate the aircraft's navigation lights.

Answer (A) is correct. (14 CFR 89.110)
DISCUSSION: The person manipulating the flight controls of the sUAS must land the UA as soon as practicable if the standard remote identification of the UA is no longer broadcasting.
Answer (B) is incorrect. FAA Air Traffic facilities need not be notified. **Answer (C) is incorrect.** The UA lights need not be activated if the standard remote identification fails during flight.

STUDY UNIT TWO

AIRSPACE CLASSIFICATION AND OPERATING REQUIREMENTS

(17 pages of outline)

2.1	Airspace Classification	(24 questions)	73, 90
2.2	Airspace Operational Requirements	(6 questions)	83, 104

2.1 AIRSPACE CLASSIFICATION

1. Understanding **general airspace** is essential to unmanned aircraft (UA) operations within certain airspace areas. Restrictions are required for **safety reasons**.

   a. The complexity or density of aircraft movements in other airspace areas may result in additional aircraft and pilot requirements for operation within such airspace.

      1) It is important to be familiar with the operational requirements for the various airspace segments.

   b. The federal airspace system is classified into six class designations. The objectives of this airspace classification are to

      1) Simplify the airspace designations
      2) Increase standardization of equipment and pilot requirements for operations in various classes of airspace
      3) Promote pilot understanding of ATC services available
      4) Achieve international commonality and satisfy our responsibilities as a member state of ICAO (International Civil Aviation Organization)

   c. The diagram below shows the airspace classification and summarizes the classifications with regard to the requirements and services available in each class of airspace.

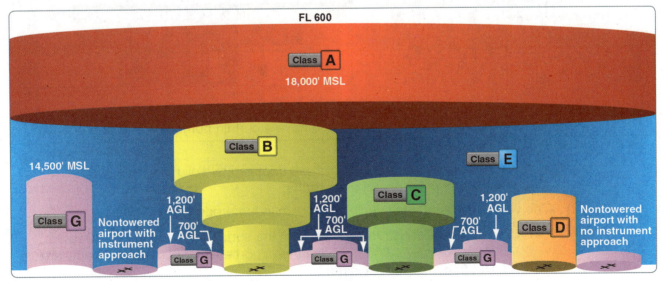

Airspace profile.

d. **Class B airspace** is generally the airspace from the surface to 10,000 ft. MSL surrounding the nation's busiest airports in terms of IFR operations or passenger enplanements (e.g., Atlanta, Chicago, etc.).

1) The configuration of each Class B airspace area is individually tailored and consists of a surface area and two or more layers.

2) The lateral limits of Class B airspace are depicted by heavy blue lines on a sectional or terminal area chart.

    a) The vertical limits of each section of Class B airspace are shown in hundreds of feet MSL.

3) The 30-NM veil, within which an altitude-reporting transponder (Mode C) is required by manned aircraft regardless of aircraft altitude, is depicted by a thin magenta circle.

4) Class B airspace is shown on the sectional chart (below left) and on the diagram (below right).

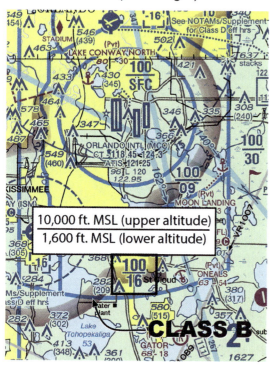
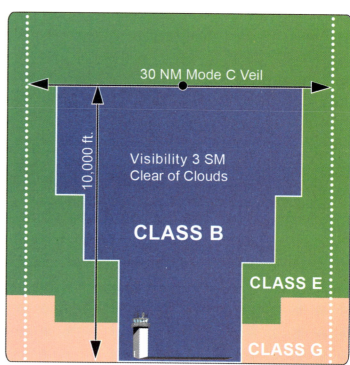

e. **Class C airspace** surrounds those airports that have an operational control tower, are serviced by a radar approach control, and have a certain number of IFR operations or passenger enplanements.

1) The lateral limits of Class C airspace are depicted by solid magenta lines on sectional and some terminal area charts.

2) The vertical limits of each circle are shown in hundreds of feet MSL.

    a) The inner surface area extends from the surface upward to the indicated altitude (usually 4,000 ft. above the airport elevation). It extends outward 5 NM from the primary airport.

    b) The shelf area extends from the indicated altitude (usually 1,200 ft. above the airport elevation) to the same upper altitude limit as the surface area.

SU 2: Airspace Classification and Operating Requirements 75

3) Class C airspace is shown on the sectional chart (below left) and on the diagram (below right).

   a) Class C airspace vertical limits in the example extend
      i) From the surface (SFC) to 4,000 ft. MSL (40) in the surface area
      ii) From 1,200 ft. MSL (12) to 4,000 ft. MSL in the shelf area

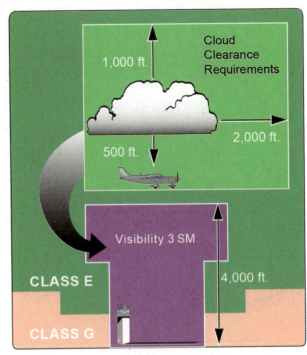

f. **Class D airspace** surrounds those airports that have both an operating control tower and weather services available and that are not associated with Class B or C airspace.

   1) Airspace at an airport with a part-time control tower is classified as Class D airspace only when the control tower is operating.

      a) When a tower ceases operation, the Class D airspace reverts to Class E or a combination of Class G and E airspace.

   2) Class D airspace is depicted by a blue segmented (dashed) circle on a sectional chart.

   3) Class D airspace normally extends from the surface up to and including 2,500 ft. AGL.

   4) The lateral limits of Class D airspace are depicted by dashed blue lines on a sectional or terminal area chart.

      a) The ceiling (usually 2,500 ft. above the airport elevation) is shown within the circle in hundreds of feet MSL.

      b) The radius of airspace area is usually 5 NM.

      c) The lateral dimensions of Class D airspace are based on the instrument procedures for which the controlled airspace is established.

5) Class D airspace is shown on the sectional chart (below left) and on the diagram (below right).

   a) The ceiling of Class D airspace in the examples is 2,700 ft. MSL.
   b) If depicted, a dashed magenta line (see bottom left of sectional chart below) illustrates an area of Class E airspace extending upward from the surface.

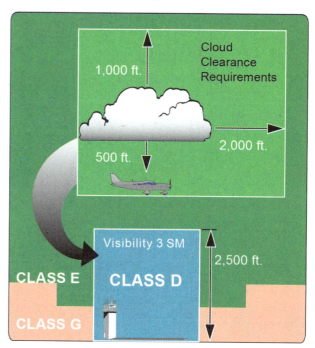

g. **Class E airspace** is any controlled airspace that is not Class A, B, C, or D airspace.

   1) Except for 18,000 ft. MSL (the floor of Class A airspace), Class E airspace has no defined vertical limit but extends upward from either the surface or a designated altitude to the overlying or adjacent controlled airspace.

   2) In most areas, the Class E airspace base is 1,200 ft. AGL. In many other areas, the Class E airspace base is either the surface or 700 ft. AGL. Some Class E airspace begins at an MSL altitude depicted on the charts instead of an AGL altitude.

   3) A dashed magenta line around an airport indicates Class E airspace extending upward from the surface.

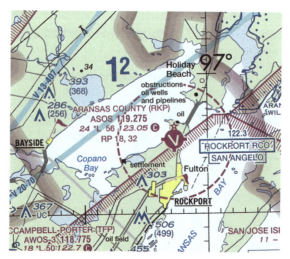

4) A light magenta-shaded line indicates Class E airspace extending upward from 700 ft. AGL within the area enclosed by the line. Outside the line, Class E airspace begins at 1,200 ft. AGL.

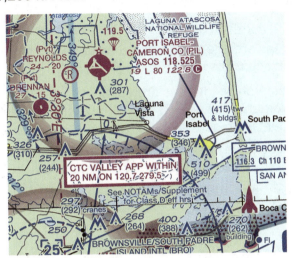

5) Types of Class E Airspace

Class E airspace beginning at the surface.

Class E airspace beginning 700 feet AGL.

Class E airspace beginning 1,200 feet AGL.

Class E airspace begins at the altitude defined by the zipper line.

Federal Airways, Class E airspace begins at 1,200 feet AGL.

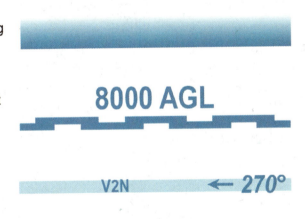

h. **Class G airspace** is that airspace that has not been designated as Class A, B, C, D, or E airspace (i.e., it is uncontrolled airspace).

1) Class G airspace exists beneath the floor of controlled airspace in areas where the controlled airspace does not extend down to the surface.

2) Class G airspace vertical limit is up to, but not including, 14,500 ft. MSL.

3) Class G airspace is not shown. It is implied to exist everywhere controlled airspace does not exist.

a) Class G airspace extends upward from the surface to the floor of overlying controlled airspace.

2. **Special-Use Airspace**

    a. **Prohibited areas** are airspace within which flight is prohibited. Such areas are established for security or other reasons of national welfare.

       1) Prohibited areas protect government interests as well as ecologically sensitive areas.

       2) Prohibited areas are often surrounded by large Temporary Flight Restrictions (TFRs) when certain situations exist.

          a) Because prohibited areas protect areas the President often visits, pilots must be aware that large TFRs will be implemented around those areas when the President is present.

       3) Prohibited areas have varied ceilings but all begin at the surface. Depending on the area protected, prohibited area ceilings range from 1,000 ft. MSL to 18,000 ft. MSL.

       4) Notices of new, uncharted prohibited areas are disseminated via the Notice to Air Missions (NOTAM) system.

    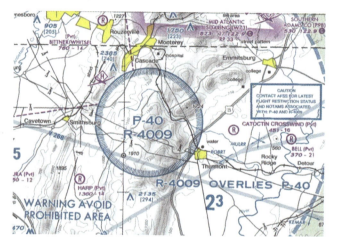

    b. **Restricted areas** are airspace within which flight, while not wholly prohibited, is subject to restrictions. Restricted areas denote the existence of unusual, often invisible hazards to aircraft, such as artillery firing, aerial gunnery, or guided missiles.

       1) Restricted areas are charted with an "R" followed by a number (e.g., R-4401).

       2) The size and shape of restricted airspace areas vary based on the operation areas they restrict.

       3) Restricted areas are often placed next to, or stacked on top of, each other.

          a) The altitudes of restricted areas vary based on the operations conducted within them.

       4) If a restricted area is active, a pilot must receive prior permission of the controlling agency before attempting to fly through it.

          a) Times and altitudes of operation as well as the name of the controlling agency can be found on the sectional aeronautical chart.

SU 2: Airspace Classification and Operating Requirements 79

- c. **Warning areas** are airspace of defined dimensions, extending from 3 NM outward from the coast of the U.S., that contain activity that may be hazardous to nonparticipating aircraft. The purpose of a warning area is to warn nonparticipating pilots of the potential danger (such as the hazards in restricted areas).
    1) A warning area may be located over domestic or international waters or both.
    2) Warning areas should be thought of exactly as restricted areas are.
        a) Because they are outside the 3 NM airspace boundary of U.S. airspace, they cannot be regulated as restricted areas are.
    3) Times and altitudes of operation can be found on the sectional aeronautical chart.
- d. **Military operations areas (MOAs)** are airspace established to separate certain military training activities from IFR traffic.
    1) Pilots should exercise extreme caution while flying within an MOA when military activity is being conducted.
        a) Before beginning a flight that crosses an MOA, contact any FSS within 100 NM of the area to obtain accurate real-time information concerning the MOA hours of operation.
        b) Prior to entering an active MOA, contact the controlling agency for traffic advisories.
    2) MOAs are often placed next to, or stacked on top of, each other.
        a) The altitudes of MOAs vary based on the operations conducted within them.
        b) Times and altitudes of operation as well as the name of the controlling agency can be found on the sectional aeronautical chart.
    3) MOAs are often found in conjunction with restricted areas.
        a) Pay careful attention to such airspace when planning crossing flights to ensure you do not violate active restricted airspace.
- e. **Alert areas** are depicted on aeronautical charts to inform nonparticipating pilots of areas that may contain a high volume of pilot training or an unusual type of aerial activity.
    1) All activity within an alert area is conducted in accordance with Federal Aviation Regulations.
        a) There is no specific controlling agency for an alert area, and crossing clearance is not required or given.
- f. **National security areas (NSAs)** consist of defined vertical and lateral dimensions established at locations where there is a requirement for increased security and safety of ground facilities.
- g. **Controlled firing areas** contain activities that, if not conducted in a controlled environment, could be hazardous to nonparticipating aircraft.
    1) The activities are suspended immediately when spotter aircraft, radar, or ground lookout positions indicate an aircraft might be approaching the area.
    2) These areas are not depicted on charts because the pilot is not required to take action.

3. **Other Airspace Areas**

   a. **Airport advisory areas** encompass the areas within 10 SM of airports that have no operating control towers but where FSSs are located. At such locations, the FSS provides advisory service to arriving and departing aircraft. Participation in the Local Airport Advisory (LAA) program is recommended but not required.

   b. **Military training routes (MTRs)** are developed for use by the military for the purpose of conducting low-altitude (below 10,000 ft. MSL), high-speed training (more than 250 kt.).

      1) The routes above 1,500 ft. AGL are flown, to the maximum extent possible, under IFR.

         a) The routes at 1,500 ft. AGL and below are flown under VFR.

      2) Extreme vigilance should be exercised when flying through or near these routes.

      3) MTRs will be identified and charted as follows:

         a) MTRs with no segment above 1,500 ft. AGL must be identified by four-number characters, e.g., IR1206, VR1207.

         b) MTRs that include one or more segments above 1,500 ft. AGL must be identified by three-number characters, e.g., IR206, VR207.

         c) Alternate IR/VR routes or route segments are identified by using the basic/principal route designation followed by a letter suffix, e.g., IR008A, VR1007B, etc.

   c. **Temporary flight restrictions (TFRs)** contain airspace where the flight of aircraft is prohibited without advanced permission and/or an FAA waiver. This restriction exists because the area inside the TFR is often of key importance to national security or national welfare. TFRs may also be put into effect in the vicinity of any incident or event that by its nature may generate such a high degree of public interest that hazardous congestion of air traffic is likely.

      1) TFRs are very different from other forms of airspace because they are often created, canceled, moved, and/or changed.

         a) The temporary nature of TFRs can make keeping track of their locations and durations challenging.

      2) TFRs protect government interests as well as the general public.

      3) TFRs often surround other forms of airspace when extra security is necessary.

         a) Because TFRs protect the President, pilots must be aware that large TFRs will be implemented around any area where the President is present.

      4) A NOTAM implementing temporary flight restrictions will contain a description of the area in which the restrictions apply.

         a) The size and shape of TFRs vary based on the areas they protect.

            i) Most TFRs are in the shape of a circle and are designed to protect the center of that circle.

            ii) TFRs always have defined vertical and lateral boundaries as indicated in the NOTAMs.

d. Flight limitations in the proximity of space flight operations are designated in a NOTAM.
e. Flight restrictions in the proximity of Presidential and other parties are put into effect by a regulatory NOTAM to establish flight restrictions.
   1) Restrictions are required because numerous aircraft and large assemblies of persons may be attracted to areas to be visited or traveled by the President or Vice President, heads of foreign states, and other public figures.
      a) In addition, restrictions are imposed in the interest of providing protection to these public figures.
   2) Presidential TFRs are issued with as much advanced notice as possible, given security concerns.
      a) The President is always surrounded by a 10-NM no-fly zone from the surface to 18,000 ft. MSL.
         i) No aircraft may operate in this area without a waiver or the advanced permission of the FAA.
      b) The President is also surrounded by a 30-NM TFR.
         i) Certain limited operations are allowed in this area.
f. Tabulations of **parachute jump areas** in the U.S. are contained in the Chart Supplement.
g. **VFR corridor** is airspace through Class B airspace, with defined vertical and lateral boundaries, in which aircraft may operate without an ATC clearance or communication with ATC. A VFR corridor is, in effect, a hole through the Class B airspace.
h. **Class B airspace VFR transition route** is a specific flight course depicted on a VFR terminal area chart for transiting a specific Class B airspace.
   1) These routes include specific ATC-assigned altitudes, and pilots must obtain an ATC clearance prior to entering the Class B airspace.
i. **Terminal Radar Service Area (TRSA)**
   1) TRSAs are not controlled airspace from a regulatory standpoint (i.e., they do not fit into any of the airspace classes) because TRSAs were never subject to the rulemaking process.
      a) TRSAs are areas where participating pilots can receive additional radar services known as TRSA Service.
   2) The primary airport(s) within the TRSA are Class D airspace.
      a) The remaining portion of the TRSA normally overlies Class E airspace beginning at 700 or 1,200 ft. AGL.
j. Published VFR Routes
   1) Published VFR routes are for transitioning around, under, or through some complex airspace.
   2) Terms such as VFR flyway, VFR corridor, Class B airspace VFR transition route, and terminal area VFR route have been applied to such routes.
   3) These routes are generally found on VFR terminal area planning charts.

k. Wildlife Areas/Wilderness Areas/National Parks
  1) These are depicted as blue dotted outlined areas.
  2) Pilots of all aircraft are requested to operate above 2,000 ft. AGL in these areas.
  3) Because this altitude is above 400 ft. AGL, remote pilots should not consider operating in these areas.

l. National Oceanic and Atmospheric Administration (NOAA) Marine Areas
  1) These are depicted off the coast as magenta dotted outlined areas.
  2) Pilots of all aircraft are required to operate above a minimum altitude as charted, usually 1,000 to 2,000 ft. AGL in these areas.
  3) Because this altitude is above 400 ft. AGL, remote pilots should not consider operating in these areas.

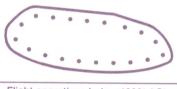

4. The **National Airspace System (NAS)** can be divided into two categories of airspace: regulatory and nonregulatory.
  a. Within these two categories, there are four types:
    1) Controlled
    2) Uncontrolled
    3) Special use
    4) Other airspace
  b. Controlled airspace is defined as an area within which ATC service is provided to IFR and VFR flights in accordance with the airspace classification.
    1) Controlled airspace is designated as Class A, B, C, D, and E airspace.
    2) Uncontrolled airspace is designated as Class G airspace.
  c. The distinction between uncontrolled airspace and the various types of controlled airspace relates to the following factors:
    1) ATC clearance requirements
    2) Pilot qualification requirements (as it relates to manned aircraft)
    3) VFR flight visibility and distance from clouds requirements

2.2 AIRSPACE OPERATIONAL REQUIREMENTS

1. Understanding of **basic weather minimums** begins for the remote pilot with minimum visibility, as observed from the location of the control station (CS), which may be no less than 3 SM.

    a. Minimum distance from clouds may be no less than 500 feet below a cloud and no less than 2,000 feet horizontally from the cloud.

    1) For example, if the cloud bases are reported at 800 ft. AGL, the maximum altitude at which an unmanned aircraft (UA) may be operated is 300 ft. AGL.

    b. One way to ensure adherence to the minimum visibility and cloud clearance requirements is to obtain local aviation weather reports that include current and forecast weather conditions.

    1) If there is more than one local aviation reporting station near the operating area, the remote pilot in command (rPIC) should choose the closest one that is also the most representative of the terrain surrounding the operating area.

    2) If local aviation weather reports are not available, then the rPIC may not operate the UA if unable to determine the required visibility and cloud clearances by other reliable means.

    3) It is imperative that the UA not be operated above any cloud, and that there are no obstructions to visibility, such as smoke or a cloud, between the UA and the rPIC.

    c. Manned aircraft are subject to the minimum visibility and cloud clearance requirements set forth in the table below.

Airspace	Flight Visibility	Distance from Clouds
Class A	Not Applicable	Not applicable
Class B	3 SM	Clear of Clouds
Class C	3 SM	500 ft. below 1,000 ft. above 2,000 ft. horiz.
Class D	3 SM	500 ft. below 1,000 ft. above 2,000 ft. horiz.
Class E:		
Less than 10,000 ft. MSL	3 SM	500 ft. below 1,000 ft. above 2,000 ft. horiz.
At or above 10,000 ft. MSL	5 SM	1,000 ft. below 1,000 ft. above 1 SM horiz.

Airspace	Flight Visibility	Distance from Clouds
Class G: 1,200 ft. or less above the surface (regardless of MSL altitude)		
Day	1 SM	Clear of clouds
Night	3 SM	500 ft. below 1,000 ft. above 2,000 ft. horiz.
More than 1,200 ft. above the surface but less than 10,000 ft. MSL		
Day	1 SM	500 ft. below 1,000 ft. above 2,000 ft. horiz.
Night	3 SM	500 ft. below 1,000 ft. above 2,000 ft. horiz.
More than 1,200 ft. above the surface and at or above 10,000 ft. MSL	5 SM	1,000 ft. below 1,000 ft. above 1 SM horiz.

2. Understanding **ATC authorizations and related operating limitations** is important to Part 107 operators even though their sUAS will not be subject to Part 91. The equipage and communications requirements outlined in Part 91 were designed to provide safety and efficiency in controlled airspace.

   a. Although sUAS operations under Part 107 are not subject to Part 91, as a practical matter, ATC authorization or clearance may depend on operational parameters similar to those found in Part 91.

   b. The FAA has the authority to approve or deny aircraft operations based on traffic density, controller workload, communication issues, or any other type of operations that could potentially impact the safe and expeditious flow of air traffic in that airspace.

      1) Those planning sUAS operations in controlled airspace are encouraged to become familiar with the UAS Data Exchange and utilize the Low Altitude Authorization and Notification Capability (LAANC).

3. **Operations near airports** require that remote pilots operate in a manner that will not interfere with operations and traffic patterns at any airport, heliport, or seaplane base.

4. Understanding **potential flight hazards** is vital to remote pilot integration into the existing manned aircraft environment.

   a. The following are seven high priority flight hazard items:

      1) **Common accident causal factors** are often associated with pilot errors, lack of proficiency, and faulty knowledge.

         a) The 10 most frequent causal factors for general aviation accidents that involve the PIC are

            i) Inadequate preflight preparation and/or planning
            ii) Failure to obtain and/or maintain flying speed
            iii) Failure to maintain direction control
            iv) Improper level off
            v) Failure to see and avoid objects or obstructions
            vi) Mismanagement of fuel
            vii) Improper inflight decisions or planning
            viii) Misjudgment of distance and speed
            ix) Selection of unsuitable terrain
            x) Improper operation of flight controls

         b) The PIC should be alert at all times. Strangely, air collisions almost invariably occur under ideal weather conditions. Unlimited visibility encourages a sense of security that is not at all justified.

         c) If another aircraft is too close, the PIC should give way instead of waiting for the other pilot.

      2) Avoid **flight beneath unmanned balloons**, as many of those will have, extending below them, either a suspension device to which the payload or instrument package is attached, or a trailing wire antenna, or both.

         a) In many instances these balloon subsystems may be invisible to the pilot until the sUAS is close to the balloon, thereby creating a potentially dangerous situation.

         b) Therefore, good judgment on the part of the remote pilot dictates that sUAS should remain well clear of all unmanned free balloons and flight below them should be avoided at all times.

3) **Emergency airborne inspection of other aircraft** may involve flying in very close proximity to that aircraft. Most pilots receive little, if any, formal training or instruction in this type of flying activity. Close proximity flying without sufficient time to plan (i.e., in an emergency situation), coupled with the stress involved in a perceived emergency, can be hazardous.

   a) The pilot in the best position to assess the situation should take the responsibility of coordinating the airborne intercept and inspection and take into account the unique flight characteristics and differences of the category(s) of aircraft involved.

   b) Some of the safety considerations are

   i) Area, direction, and speed of the intercept

   ii) Aerodynamic effects (e.g., rotorcraft downwash)

   iii) Minimum safe separation distances

   iv) Communications requirements, lost communications procedures, and coordination with ATC

   v) Suitability of diverting the distressed aircraft to the nearest safe airport

   vi) Emergency actions to terminate the intercept

   c) Close proximity, in-flight inspection of another aircraft is uniquely hazardous. The PIC of the aircraft experiencing the emergency must not relinquish control of the situation and/or jeopardize the safety of his or her aircraft. The maneuver must be accomplished with minimum risk to both aircraft.

4) **Precipitation static (P-static)** is caused by aircraft in flight coming in contact with uncharged particles. These particles can be rain, snow, fog, sleet, hail, volcanic ash, dust, or any solid or liquid particles.

   a) When the aircraft strikes these neutral particles the positive element of the particle is reflected away from the aircraft and the negative particle adheres to the skin of the aircraft. In a very short period of time, a substantial negative charge will develop on the skin of the aircraft.

   b) If the aircraft is not equipped with static dischargers, or has an ineffective static discharger system, when a sufficient negative voltage level is reached, the aircraft may go into "CORONA." That is, it will discharge the static electricity from the extremities of the aircraft, such as the wing tips, horizontal stabilizer, vertical stabilizer, antenna, propeller tips, etc.

   c) This discharge of static electricity can cause certain radio frequencies to become unreliable. This can lead to loss of control of the sUAS or interfere with other communication devices, such as first-person-view video systems or telemetry monitoring systems.

5) **Light amplification by stimulated emission of radiation (laser) operations** can create significant hazards to pilots of manned aircraft, resulting in temporary crewmember blindness.

   a) For sUAS operators, lasers can interfere with camera operations and remote optical equipment used to monitor surroundings.

   b) FAA regulations prohibit the disruption of aviation activity by any person on the ground or in the air. The FAA and the Food and Drug Administration (the federal agency that has the responsibility to enforce compliance with federal requirements for laser systems and laser light show products) are working together to ensure that operators of these devices do not pose a hazard to aircraft operators.

   c) In cooperation with federal, state, and local law enforcement agencies, the FAA requests everyone's help in reporting laser incidents. If you are the victim of or a witness to a laser incident, please report it to the FAA at www.faa.gov/aircraft/safety/report/laserinfo.

6) Avoid **flight in the vicinity of thermal plumes,** such as smoke stacks and cooling towers.

   a) Thermal plumes are defined as visible or invisible emissions from power plants, industrial production facilities, or other industrial systems that release large amounts of vertically directed unstable gases.

      i) High-temperature exhaust plumes may cause significant air disturbances such as turbulence and vertical shear. Other identified potential hazards include, but are not necessarily limited to, reduced visibility, engine particulate contamination, and/or icing.

      ii) Results of encountering a plume may include airframe damage, aircraft upset, and/or engine damage or failure.

      iii) These hazards are most critical during low altitude flight, especially during takeoff and landing.

   b) Thermal plumes may be associated with power plants or other sensitive properties and should be avoided. Failure to avoid these areas could be considered operating in a careless or reckless manner.

7) **Flying in the wire environment** affects nearly all sUAS operations given the altitudes flown.

   a) Below 1,000 ft. AGL, wires, towers, utility poles, guy wires, etc., create often invisible hazards to remote pilots.

      i) Obstacles, such as towers and obstructions, are depicted on the sectional chart using a blue upside-down V and a dot. The top number is the height of the obstruction in feet above mean sea level (MSL). The bottom number in parentheses is the height of the obstruction in feet above ground level (AGL).

      ii) Obstacles 1,000 ft. and higher are depicted using an elongated upside-down V with a taller point.

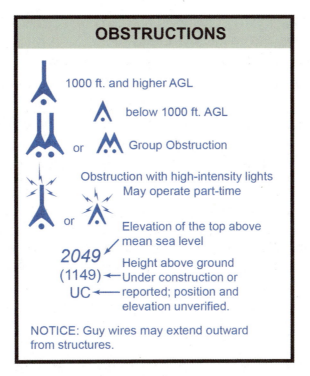

- b) Many of the hazards are often visible to pilots; however, due to a focus on flying the sUAS and other distractions, the hazards can become invisible.
- c) Most skeletal structures are supported by guy wires that are very difficult to see in good weather and can be invisible at dusk or during periods of reduced visibility. These wires can extend about 1,500 ft. horizontally from a structure; therefore, all skeletal structures should be avoided horizontally by at least 2,000 ft.
- d) Overhead transmission and utility lines often span approaches to runways; natural flyways, such as lakes, rivers, gorges, and canyons; and cross other landmarks pilots frequently follow, such as highways, railroad tracks, etc.
    - i) As with antenna towers, these high voltage/power lines or the supporting structures of these lines may not always be readily visible and the wires may be virtually impossible to see under certain conditions.
    - ii) Many power lines do not require notice to the FAA and therefore are not marked and/or lighted. Many of those that do require notice do not exceed 200 ft. AGL or meet the Obstruction Standard of 14 CFR Part 77 and therefore are not marked and/or lighted.
    - iii) All pilots are cautioned to remain extremely vigilant for these power lines or their supporting structures.
- e) Man-made obstacles and obstructions are typically depicted on sectional charts if they are over 200 ft. AGL. Consult the legend on your sectional chart for more details.

5. Understanding the **NOTAM system**, including how to obtain established NOTAMs, is the key to effective flight preparation and operational safety.

   a. NOTAMs are time-critical aeronautical information either temporary in nature or not sufficiently known in advance to permit publication on aeronautical charts or in other operational publications.

   b. The information is disseminated immediately via the Federal NOTAM System (FNS).

   c. NOTAMs contain current notices to air missions that are considered essential to the safety of flight, as well as supplemental data affecting other operational publications.

   d. NOTAMs are classified into various types:

      1) **NOTAM (D)** includes information such as airport or primary runway closures; changes in the status of navigational aids; radar service availability; and other information essential to planned en route, terminal, or landing operations. Also included is information on airport taxiways, aprons, ramp areas, and associated lighting.

      2) **FDC NOTAMs** are issued by the Flight Data Center and contain regulatory information such as amendments to published instrument approach charts and other current aeronautical charts.

      3) **Pointer NOTAMs** reduce total NOTAM volume by pointing to other NOTAM (D) and FDC NOTAMs rather than duplicating potentially unnecessary information for an airport or NAVAID. They allow pilots to reference NOTAMs that might not be listed under a given airport or NAVAID identifier.

      4) **SAA NOTAMs** are issued when Special Activity Airspace (SAA) will be active outside the published schedule times and when required by the published schedule, although pilots must still check published schedule times for SAA as well as any other NOTAMs for that airspace.

      5) **Military NOTAMs** reference military airports and NAVAIDs and are rarely of any interest to civilian pilots.

   e. NOTAMs should be checked prior to each flight. To check NOTAMs, the remote PIC should obtain a briefing.

   f. There are several methods for checking NOTAMs.

      1) FAA NOTAM retrieval: https://notams.aim.faa.gov/notamSearch/nsapp.html#/

         a) This website allows the NOTAM database to be searched for a radius around a specific location(s), within a radius of a known latitude/longitude, or along a flight path.

      2) Flight Service (online): www.1800wxbrief.com

         a) The main menu provides access to a pilot dashboard, weather, flight planning and briefing, airport information, UAS planning tools, account, links, and help information.

            i) The UAS planning tools allow users to easily define UAS operating areas.

         b) A user guide and videos with extensive instructions are available under the Help menu.

3) Flight Service (phone): 1-800-WX-BRIEF (800-992-7433)

   a) A Flight Service specialist may be accessed by following the menu prompts to speak with a briefer.

   b) Identify yourself as a remote pilot and the area within which you are operating. You should reference an official aviation fix, such as an airport or navigational aid, if known. You can also identify your location using latitude and longitude.

      i) A standard briefing should be requested to obtain complete weather and NOTAMs for your area, for a flight within 6 hours.

      ii) An abbreviated briefing should be requested if only checking NOTAMs or obtaining an update following a previous briefing.

      iii) An outlook briefing should be requested for a flight more than 6 hours in the future.

4) Contractions are used extensively in NOTAMs. Most are known from common usage or can be deciphered phonetically.

6. **UAS Data Exchange** is a joint initiative between government and private industry through which airspace data is shared in order to support UAS integration into the airspace.

   a. Low Altitude Authorization and Notification Capability **(LAANC)** is a product of this initiative that facilitates data sharing between the FAA and FAA-approved UAS Service Suppliers. These suppliers provide the desktop and mobile applications that allow pilots to utilize LAANC.

   b. LAANC automates the airspace authorization application and approval process. Requests are checked against multiple airspace data sources such as NOTAMs, TFRs, facility maps, special use airspace sources, and airports and airspace classes.

      1) Often, approval can be received almost immediately, allowing flight into towered airspace without notifying control for operations under 400 ft.

      2) LAANC is currently offered at nearly 600 airports nationally.

QUESTIONS

2.1 Airspace Classification

1. When a control tower located on an airport within Class D airspace ceases operation for the day, what happens to the airspace designation?

   A. The airspace designation normally will not change.
   B. The airspace remains Class D airspace as long as a weather observer or automated weather system is available.
   C. The airspace reverts to Class E or a combination of Class E and G airspace during the hours the tower is not in operation.

Answer (C) is correct. (AIM Para 3-2-5)
   DISCUSSION: When a tower ceases operation, the Class D airspace reverts to Class E or a combination of Class G and E.
   Answer (A) is incorrect. Class D airspace is designated when there is an operating control tower. When the tower ceases operation for the day, the airspace reverts to Class E or a combination of Class G and E airspace. **Answer (B) is incorrect.** The airspace reverts to Class E, not Class D, when the tower ceases operation for the day and an approved weather observer or automated weather system is available.

2. (Refer to Figure 20 on page 91.) (Refer to Area 5.) How would a remote PIC "CHECK NOTAMS" as noted in the CAUTION box regarding the unmarked balloon?

   A. By utilizing the B4UFLY mobile application.
   B. By contacting the FAA district office.
   C. By obtaining a briefing via an online source such as: 1800WXBrief.com.

Answer (C) is correct. (AIM Para 5-1-3)
   DISCUSSION: NOTAMs should be checked prior to each flight. To check NOTAMs, the remote PIC should obtain an official briefing online or over the phone.
   Answer (A) is incorrect. The B4UFLY mobile application does not provide NOTAMs. **Answer (B) is incorrect.** NOTAMs can be obtained from Flight Service or online sources, not the FAA district office.

3. (Refer to Figure 20 on page 91.) (Refer to Area 1.) The Fentress NALF Airport (NFE) is in what type of airspace?

   A. Class C.
   B. Class E.
   C. Class G.

Answer (B) is correct. (ACUG)
   DISCUSSION: The NALF Fentress (NFE) Airport is surrounded by a dashed magenta line, indicating Class E airspace from the surface.
   Answer (A) is incorrect. Class C airspace is surrounded by a solid magenta line. The line surrounding NFE airport is dashed magenta. **Answer (C) is incorrect.** The dashed magenta line surrounding NFE Airport indicates Class E begins at the surface. A shaded magenta line would be required to indicate Class G airspace from the surface up to 700 ft. AGL.

4. (Refer to Figure 20 on page 91.) (Refer to Area 4.) What hazards to aircraft may exist in restricted areas such as R-5302A?

   A. Unusual, often invisible, hazards such as aerial gunnery or guided missiles.
   B. High volume of pilot training or an unusual type of aerial activity.
   C. Military training activities that necessitate acrobatic or abrupt flight maneuvers.

Answer (A) is correct. (AIM Para 3-4-3)
   DISCUSSION: See Fig. 20. Restricted areas denote the existence of unusual, often invisible, hazards to aircraft such as military firing, aerial gunnery, or guided missiles.
   Answer (B) is incorrect. A high volume of pilot training or an unusual type of aerial activity describes an alert area, not a warning area. **Answer (C) is incorrect.** Military training activities that necessitate acrobatic or abrupt flight maneuvers are characteristic of MOAs, not restricted areas.

SU 2: Airspace Classification and Operating Requirements

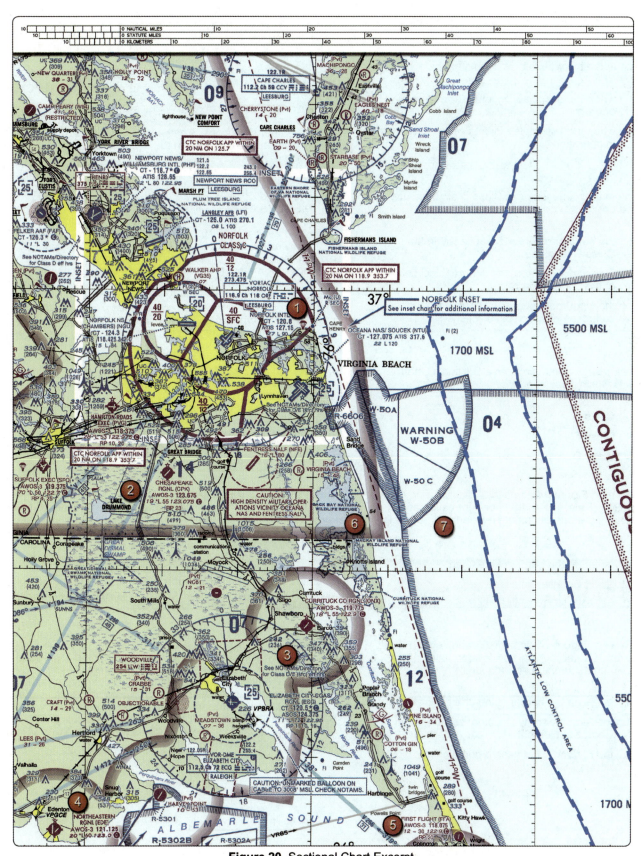

Figure 20. Sectional Chart Excerpt.
NOTE: Chart is not to scale and should not be used for navigation. Use associated scale.

5. Airspace at an airport with a part-time control tower is classified as Class D airspace only

    A. when the weather minimums are below basic VFR.

    B. when the associated control tower is in operation.

    C. when the associated Flight Service Station is in operation.

Answer (B) is correct. (AIM Para 3-2-5)
    DISCUSSION: A Class D airspace area is automatically in effect when and only when the associated part-time control tower is in operation regardless of weather conditions, availability of radar services, or time of day. Airports with part-time operating towers only have a part-time Class D airspace area.
    Answer (A) is incorrect. A Class D airspace area is automatically in effect when the tower is in operation, regardless of the weather conditions. **Answer (C) is incorrect.** A Class D airspace area is in effect when the associated control tower, not FSS, is in operation.

6. The lateral dimensions of Class D airspace are based on

    A. the number of airports that lie within the Class D airspace.

    B. 5 statute miles from the geographical center of the primary airport.

    C. the instrument procedures for which the controlled airspace is established.

Answer (C) is correct. (AIM Para 3-2-5)
    DISCUSSION: The lateral dimensions of Class D airspace are based upon the instrument procedures for which the controlled airspace is established.
    Answer (A) is incorrect. While the FAA will attempt to exclude satellite airports as much as possible from Class D airspace, the major criteria for the lateral dimension will be based on the instrument procedures for which the controlled airspace is established. **Answer (B) is incorrect.** The lateral dimensions of Class D airspace are based on the instrument procedures for which the Class D airspace is established, not a specified radius from the primary airport.

7. A blue segmented circle on a Sectional Chart depicts which class airspace?

    A. Class B.

    B. Class C.

    C. Class D.

Answer (C) is correct. (AIM Para 3-2-5)
    DISCUSSION: A blue segmented circle on a sectional chart depicts Class D airspace.
    Answer (A) is incorrect. Class B airspace is depicted on a sectional chart by a solid, not segmented, blue circle. **Answer (B) is incorrect.** Class C airspace is depicted on a sectional chart by a solid magenta, not a blue segmented, circle.

8. (Refer to Figure 24 on page 93 and Legend 1 on page 95.) (Refer to Area 3.) For information about the parachute operations at Tri-County Airport, refer to

    A. notes on the border of the chart.

    B. Chart Supplements U.S.

    C. the FNS NOTAM search portal online.

Answer (B) is correct. (ACUG)
    DISCUSSION: The miniature parachute near the Tri-County Airport (area 3 on Fig. 24) indicates a parachute jumping area. In Legend 1, the symbol for a parachute jumping area instructs you to see the Airport/Facility Directory section of the Chart Supplement for more information.
    Answer (A) is incorrect. The Chart Supplement U.S. contains information about parachute operations, not the notes on the border of the sectional chart. **Answer (C) is incorrect.** NOTAMs are issued for hazards to flight.

9. (Refer to Figure 24 on page 93 and Legend 1 on page 95.) (Refer to Area 1.) For information about the parachute jumping at Caddo Mills Airport, refer to

    A. notes on the border of the chart.

    B. the Airport/Facility Directory section of the Chart Supplement.

    C. the FNS NOTAM search portal online.

Answer (B) is correct. (ACUG)
    DISCUSSION: The miniature parachute near the Caddo Mills Airport (at 1 on Fig. 24) indicates a parachute jumping area. In Legend 1, the symbol for a parachute jumping area instructs you to see the Airport/Facility Directory section of the Chart Supplement for more information.
    Answer (A) is incorrect. The sectional chart legend identifies symbols only. **Answer (C) is incorrect.** NOTAMs are issued only for hazards to flight.

SU 2: Airspace Classification and Operating Requirements

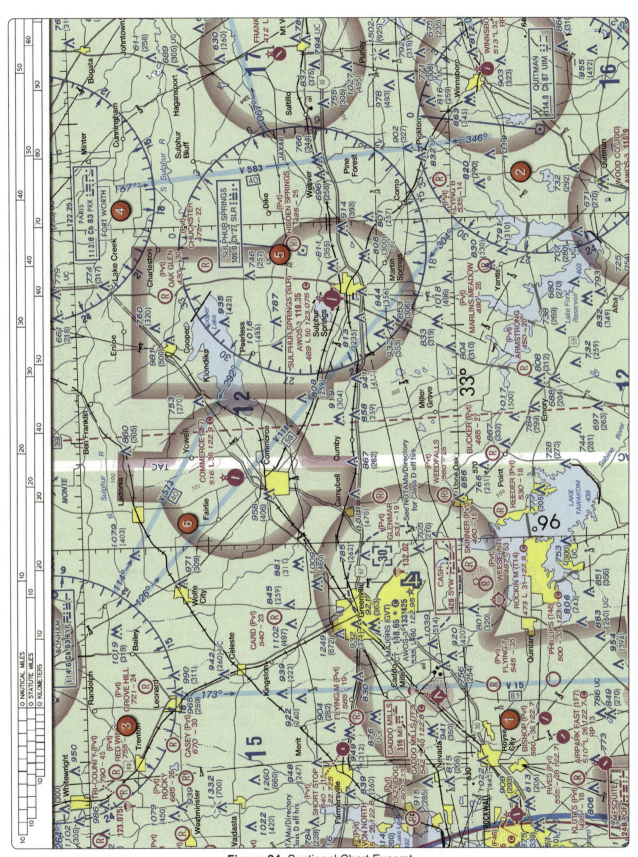

Figure 24. Sectional Chart Excerpt.
NOTE: Chart is not to scale and should not be used for navigation. Use associated scale.

10. (Refer to Figure 23 below, and Legend 1 on page 95.) (Refer to Area 3.) For information about glider operations at Ridgeland Airport, refer to

A. notes on the border of the chart.
B. the Chart Supplement.
C. the FNS NOTAM search portal online.

Answer (B) is correct. (ACUG)
   DISCUSSION: The miniature glider near the Ridgeland Airport (at 3 on Fig. 23) indicates a glider operations area. The Chart Supplement will have information on the glider operations at Ridgeland Airport.
   Answer (A) is incorrect. The sectional chart legend identifies symbols only. **Answer (C) is incorrect.** NOTAMs are issued only for hazards to flight.

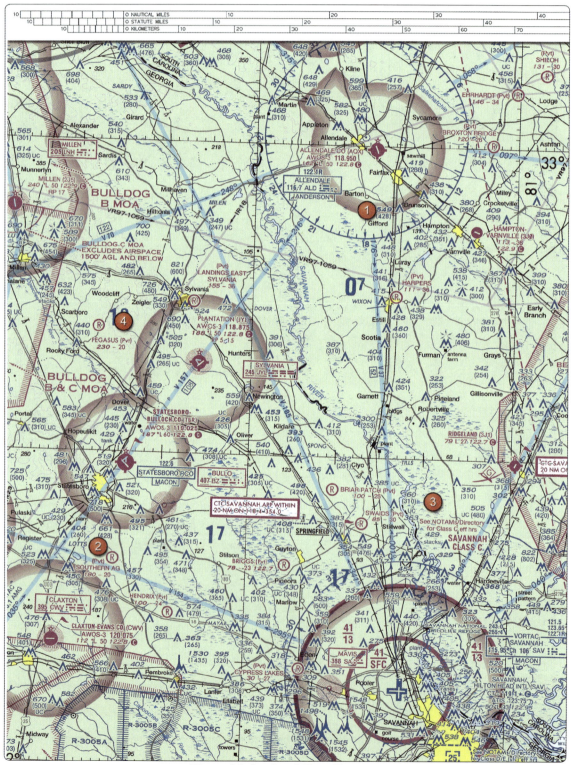

Figure 23. Sectional Chart Excerpt.
NOTE: Chart is not to scale and should not be used for navigation. Use associated scale.

SU 2: Airspace Classification and Operating Requirements

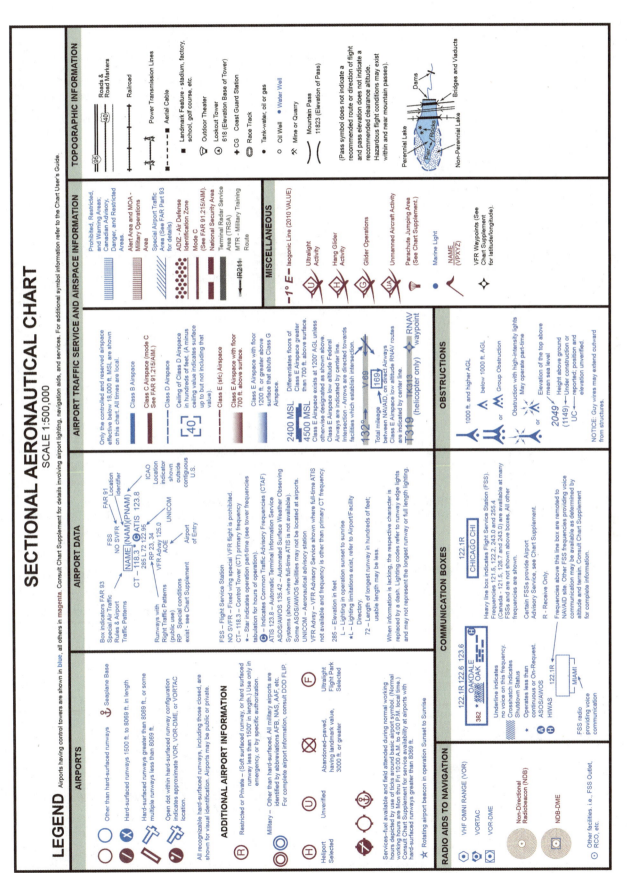

Legend 1. Sectional Aeronautical Chart.

11. Which is true concerning the blue and magenta colors used to depict airports on Sectional Aeronautical Charts?

    A. Airports with control towers underlying Class A, B, and C airspace are shown in blue; Class D and E airspace are magenta.

    B. Airports with control towers underlying Class C, D, and E airspace are shown in magenta.

    C. Airports with control towers underlying Class B, C, D, and E airspace are shown in blue.

Answer (C) is correct. (ACUG)
DISCUSSION: On sectional charts, airports with control towers underlying Class B, C, D, E, or G airspace are shown in blue. Airports with no control towers are shown in magenta.
Answer (A) is incorrect. There are no airports in Class A airspace. Airports with control towers are shown in blue, and all others are in magenta. **Answer (B) is incorrect.** Airports with control towers are shown in blue, not magenta.

12. Information concerning parachute jumping sites may be found in the

    A. NOTAMs.

    B. Chart Supplement.

    C. Graphic Notices and Supplemental Data.

Answer (B) is correct. (Chart Supplement)
DISCUSSION: Information concerning parachute jump sites may be found in the Chart Supplement.
Answer (A) is incorrect. NOTAMs are only issued for special situations, not routine jump sites. **Answer (C) is incorrect.** Graphic Notices and Supplemental Data are no longer published.

13. (Refer to Figure 25 on page 97.) What is the base of Class B airspace at Lakeview (30F) Airport (area 2)?

    A. 4,000

    B. 3,000

    C. 1,700

Answer (B) is correct. (AIM Chap 3)
DISCUSSION: To the southwest of Lakeview Airport, there are numbers 110 over 30 in blue color. This indicates the base of Class B airspace between the blue airspace lines is 3,000 ft. MSL and the top is 11,000 ft. MSL.
Answer (A) is incorrect. The base is indicated at 4,000 ft. MSL beyond the blue line located north of Lakeview Airport. **Answer (C) is incorrect.** A base of 1,700 ft. would be below the maximum elevation figure in that quadrant.

14. (Refer to Figure 25 on page 97.) (Refer to Area 3.) The floor of Class B airspace at Dallas Executive Airport is

    A. at the surface.

    B. 3,000 feet MSL.

    C. 3,100 feet MSL.

Answer (B) is correct. (ACUG, 14 CFR 71.9)
DISCUSSION: Dallas Executive Airport (Fig. 25, area 3) has a segmented blue circle around it depicting Class D airspace. Dallas Executive Airport also underlies Class B airspace as depicted by solid blue lines. The altitudes of the Class B airspace are shown as $\frac{110}{30}$ to the southeast of the airport. The bottom number denotes the floor of the Class B airspace to be 3,000 ft. MSL.
Answer (A) is incorrect. The floor of Class D, not Class B, airspace is at the surface. **Answer (C) is incorrect.** This is not a defined limit of any airspace over Dallas Executive Airport.

15. (Refer to Figure 25 on page 97.) (Refer to Area 4.) The airspace directly overlying Fort Worth Meacham is

    A. Class B airspace to 10,000 feet MSL.

    B. Class C airspace to 5,000 feet MSL.

    C. Class D airspace to 3,200 feet MSL.

Answer (C) is correct. (ACUG)
DISCUSSION: The airspace overlying Fort Worth Meacham (Fig. 25, southeast of 4) is Class D airspace as denoted by the segmented blue lines. The upper limit is depicted in a broken box in hundreds of feet MSL southeast of the airport. Thus, the Class D airspace extends from the surface to 3,200 ft. MSL.
Answer (A) is incorrect. Class D, not Class B, airspace extends from the surface of Ft. Worth Meacham. Class B airspace overlies the airport from 4,000 ft. MSL to 11,000 ft. MSL. **Answer (B) is incorrect.** Class D, not Class C, airspace directly overlies Ft. Worth Meacham from the surface to 3,200 ft. MSL, not 5,000 ft. MSL.

SU 2: Airspace Classification and Operating Requirements

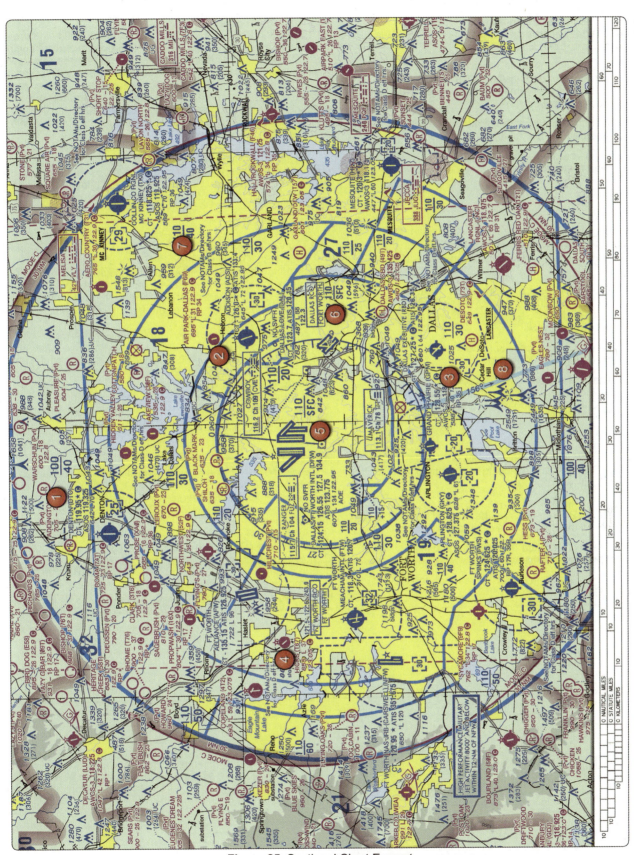

Figure 25. Sectional Chart Excerpt.
NOTE: Chart is not to scale and should not be used for navigation. Use associated scale.

16. (Refer to Figure 26 on page 99.) (Refer to Area 2.) What hazards to aircraft may exist in areas such as Devils Lake East MOA?

A. Unusual, often invisible, hazards to aircraft such as artillery firing, aerial gunnery, or guided missiles.
B. Military training activities that necessitate acrobatic or abrupt flight maneuvers.
C. High volume of pilot training or an unusual type of aerial activity.

Answer (B) is correct. (AIM Para 3-4-5)
   DISCUSSION: Military Operations Areas (MOAs), such as Devils Lake East in Fig. 26 consist of defined lateral and vertical limits that are designated for the purpose of separating military training activities from IFR traffic. Most training activities necessitate acrobatic or abrupt flight maneuvers, i.e., air combat tactics, aerobatics, and formation training. Therefore, the likelihood of a collision is increased inside an MOA. VFR traffic is permitted, but extra vigilance should be exercised in seeing and avoiding military aircraft.
   Answer (A) is incorrect. Unusual, often invisible, hazards to aircraft, such as artillery firing, aerial gunnery, or guided missiles, are characteristic of restricted areas, not MOAs.
   Answer (C) is incorrect. A high volume of pilot training or an unusual type of aerial activity is characteristic of alert areas, not MOAs.

17. (Refer to Figure 26 on page 99.) (Refer to Area 2.) Identify the airspace over Bryn Airport.

A. Class G airspace -- surface up to but not including 1,200 feet AGL; Class E airspace -- 1,200 feet AGL up to but not including 18,000 feet MSL.
B. Class G airspace -- surface up to but not including 18,000 feet MSL.
C. Class G airspace -- surface up to but not including 700 feet MSL; Class E airspace -- 700 feet to 14,500 feet MSL.

Answer (A) is correct. (ACUG)
   DISCUSSION: Bryn Airport is located 1.5 in. south of 2 on Fig. 26. There is no specific airspace designation around Bryn. Therefore, the airspace over the airport is Class G airspace up to the next overlying airspace. Unless the floor is designated otherwise, Class E airspace exists from 1,200 ft. AGL, up to but not including 18,000 ft. MSL.
   Answer (B) is incorrect. The Class G airspace above Bryn Airport ends at 1,200 ft. AGL (the beginning of Class E airspace), not 18,000 ft. MSL. **Answer (C) is incorrect.** Class G airspace above Bryn Airport extends to 1,200 ft. AGL, not 700 ft. AGL. Class G airspace up to 700 ft. AGL (not MSL) would be indicated by magenta shading surrounding Bryn Airport. Additionally, Class E airspace above Bryn Airport extends to 18,000 ft. MSL, not 14,500 ft. MSL.

18. (Refer to Figure 26 on page 99.) (Refer to east of Area 5.) The airspace overlying and within 5 miles of Barnes County Airport is

A. Class D airspace from the surface to the floor of the overlying Class E airspace.
B. Class E airspace from the surface to 1,200 feet MSL.
C. Class G airspace from the surface to 700 feet AGL.

Answer (C) is correct. (ACUG)
   DISCUSSION: The magenta band surrounding Barnes County Airport indicates Class E airspace exists with a floor of 700 feet AGL. Class G airspace is over the airport from the surface up to the base of the Class E airspace within the magenta ring.
   Answer (A) is incorrect. Class D airspace has a control tower and is depicted with dashed blue lines. The Barnes County Airport does not have a control tower because the airport identifier is magenta, not blue. **Answer (B) is incorrect.** An airport located in Class E airspace at the surface would be marked by magenta dashed lines, such as the ones surrounding Jamestown Airport to the left. Barnes has no such lines.

SU 2: Airspace Classification and Operating Requirements

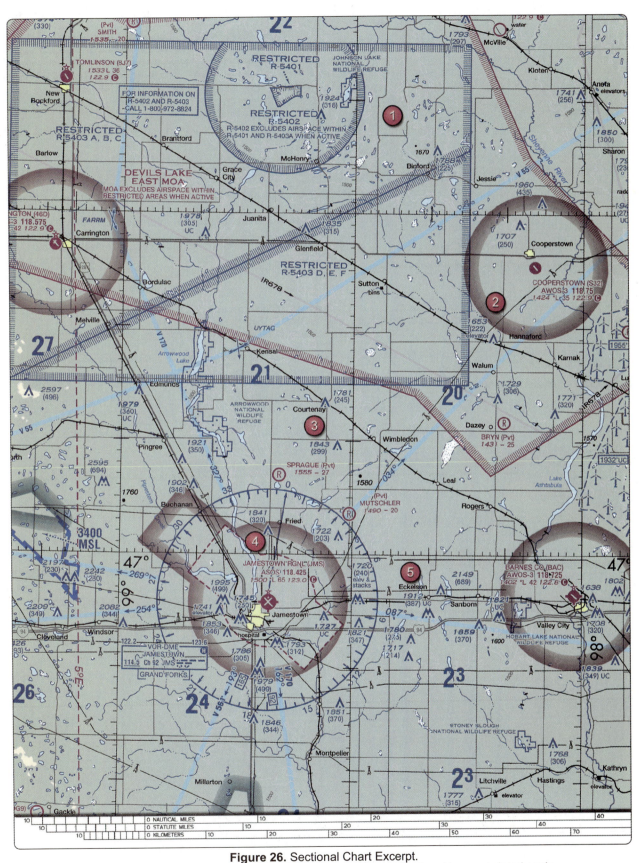

Figure 26. Sectional Chart Excerpt.
NOTE: Chart is not to scale and should not be used for navigation. Use associated scale.

19. (Refer to Figure 75 on page 101.) The airspace surrounding the Gila Bend AF AUX Airport (GXF) (area 6) is classified as Class

A. B.
B. C.
C. D.

Answer (C) is correct. (AIM Chap 3)
DISCUSSION: The GXF airport is surrounded by a dashed blue line, which indicates it is within Class D airspace.
Answer (A) is incorrect. Class B airspace is surrounded by a solid blue line. **Answer (B) is incorrect.** Class C airspace is surrounded by a solid magenta line.

20. (Refer to Figure 75 on page 101.) (Refer to Area 6.) During preflight planning, you plan to operate in R-2305. Where would you find additional information regarding this airspace?

A. In the *Aeronautical Information Manual*.
B. In the Charts Supplements U.S.
C. In the Special Use Airspace area of the chart.

Answer (C) is correct. (FAA-H-8083-25)
DISCUSSION: Restricted areas are charted with an "R" followed by a number (e.g., R-4401). Information about restricted areas can be obtained on the back of the sectional chart.
Answer (A) is incorrect. Information about a specific restricted area can be found on the back of the sectional chart, not the *AIM*. **Answer (B) is incorrect.** Information about a specific restricted area can be found on the back of the sectional chart, not the Chart Supplement U.S.

21. (Refer to Figure 75 on page 101.) What is the dotted outlined area northeast of Gila Bend Airport, near area 3?

A. Restricted airspace.
B. Military operations area.
C. Wilderness area.

Answer (C) is correct. (ACUG)
DISCUSSION: The area just to the west of area 3 represents an area that is a national park, wildlife refuge, primitive and wilderness area, etc. To the northwest of this area is the name, North Maricopa Mountains Wilderness Area.
Answer (A) is incorrect. A restricted area on a sectional chart is outlined with a hashed blue border and labeled with an "R" followed by a numbered (e.g., R-1234). **Answer (B) is incorrect.** A military operations area (MOA) is outlined with a hashed magenta border. MOAs are named rather than numbered (e.g., Snowbird MOA) and further defined on the back of sectional charts.

SU 2: Airspace Classification and Operating Requirements

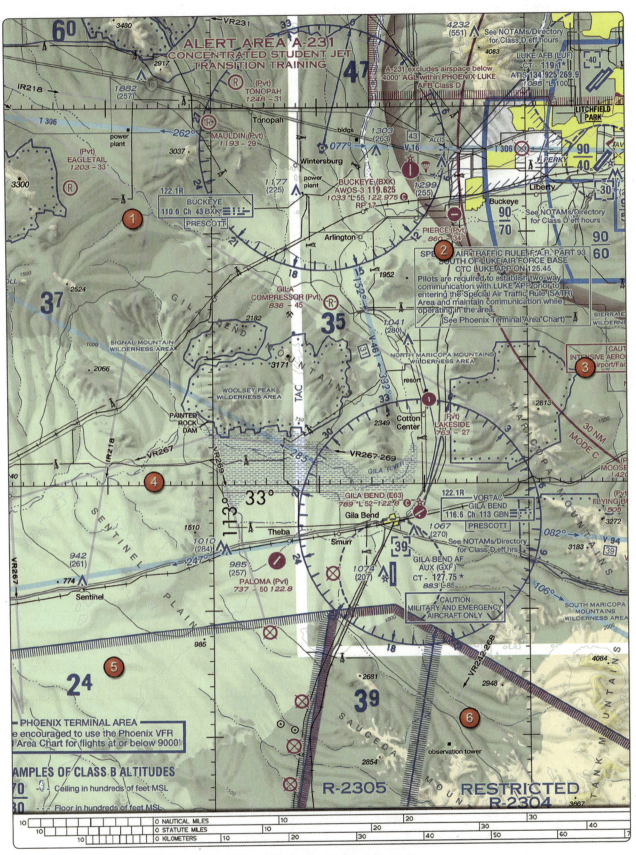

Figure 75. Sectional Chart Excerpt.
NOTE: Chart is not to scale and should not be used for navigation. Use associated scale.

22. (Refer to Figure 78 on page 103.) You have been hired to use your small UAS to inspect the railroad tracks from Blencoe (SE of Sioux City) to Onawa. Will ATC authorization be required?

A. Yes, Onawa is in Class D airspace that is designated for an airport.
B. No, your entire flight is in Class G airspace.
C. Yes, you must contact the Onawa control tower to operate within 5 miles of the airport.

Answer (B) is correct. (Sectional Chart Legend)
DISCUSSION: Refer to Legend 1 on page 95. Blencoe is located about 5 NM south of Onawa. The entire flight will be conducted within Class G airspace; therefore, ATC authorization is not required.
Answer (A) is incorrect. Onawa is located in Class G, not Class D, airspace. **Answer (C) is incorrect.** Onawa is located in Class G airspace and does not have a control tower.

23. (Refer to Figure 78 on page 103.) (Near the center of the figure.) What class of airspace is associated with SIOUX GATEWAY/COL DAY (SUX) Airport?

A. Class B airspace.
B. Class C airspace.
C. Class D airspace.

Answer (C) is correct. (Sectional Chart Legend)
DISCUSSION: Sioux Gateway/Col Day Airport is located in Class D airspace, which is indicated by a blue segmented circle.
Answer (A) is incorrect. Sioux Gateway/Col Day Airport is located in Class D, not Class B, airspace. **Answer (B) is incorrect.** Sioux Gateway/Col Day Airport is located in Class D, not Class C, airspace.

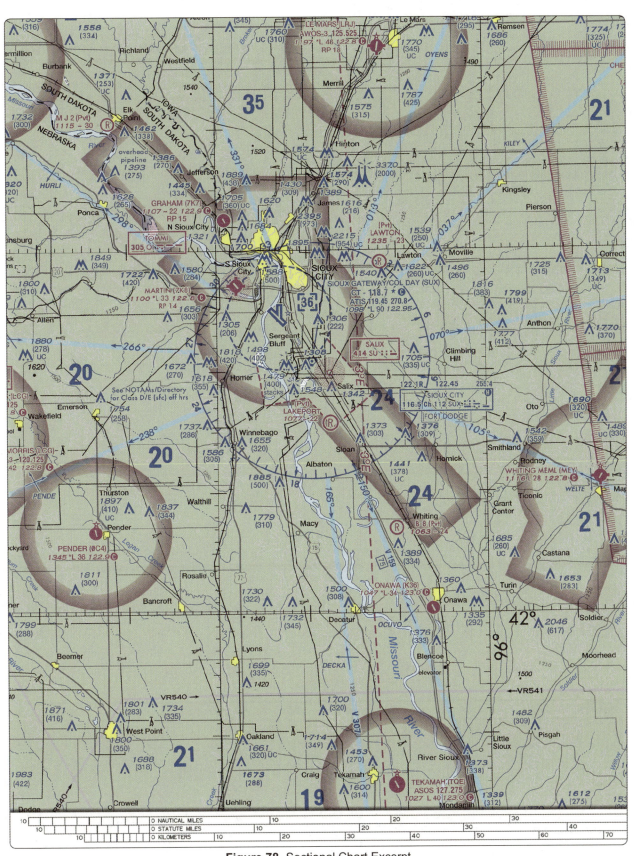

Figure 78. Sectional Chart Excerpt.
NOTE: Chart is not to scale and should not be used for navigation. Use associated scale.

24. (Refer to Figure 59 on page 105.) (Refer to Area 3.) What is the airspace classification around Findlay (FDY) airport?

A. C.
B. D.
C. E.

Answer (C) is correct. (ACUG and Sectional Chart)
DISCUSSION: A magenta dashed line surrounding an airport identifies it as Class E airspace that extends to the surface. The presence of this dashed magenta line indicates that this airport offers a precision instrument approach.
Answer (A) is incorrect. Class C airspace is identified by two solid magenta lines surrounding the airport. **Answer (B) is incorrect.** Class D airspace is surrounded by dashed blue lines.

2.2 Airspace Operational Requirements

25. (Refer to Figure 59 on page 105.) (Refer to Area 2.) The chart shows a gray line with "VR1667, VR1617, VR1638, and VR1668." Could this area present a hazard to the operations of a small UA?

A. No, all operations will be above 400 feet.
B. Yes, this is a Military Training Route from the surface to 1,500 feet AGL and below.
C. Yes, the defined route provides traffic separation to manned aircraft.

Answer (B) is correct. (AIM Para 3-5-2)
DISCUSSION: Military training routes (MTRs) are developed for use by the military for the purpose of conducting low-altitude (below 10,000 ft. MSL), high-speed training (more than 250 kt.). MTRs with no segment above 1,500 ft. AGL must be identified by four number characters; e.g., IR1206, VR1207.
Answer (A) is incorrect. Operations on these MTRs could also exist below 400 ft., not just above 400 ft. **Answer (C) is incorrect.** Manned aircraft operating in VFR conditions are expected to see-and-avoid to prevent collisions.

SU 2: Airspace Classification and Operating Requirements

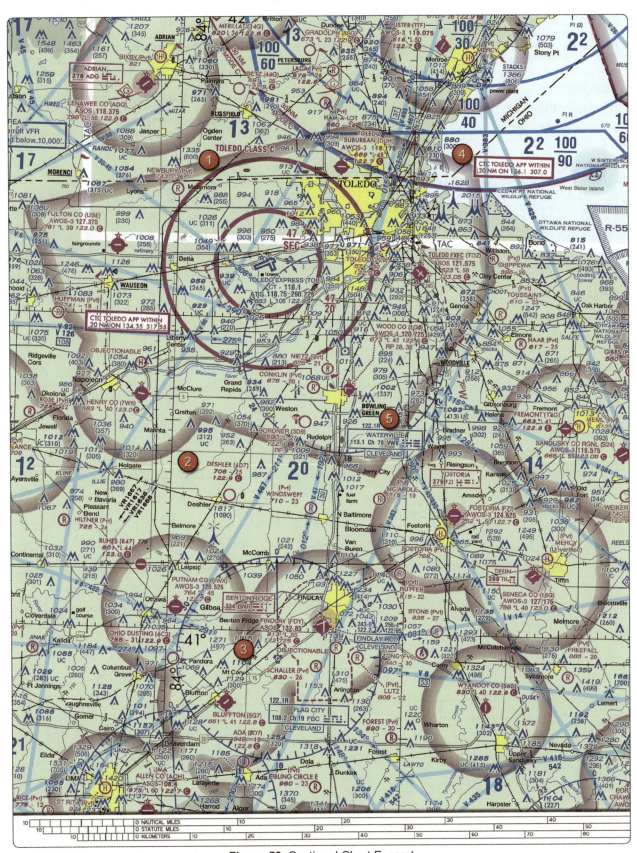

Figure 59. Sectional Chart Excerpt.
NOTE: Chart is not to scale and should not be used for navigation. Use associated scale.

26. (Refer to Figure 20 on page 107.) (Refer to Area 4.) A small UA is being launched 2 NM northeast of the town of Hertford. What is the height of the highest obstacle?

A. 399 feet MSL.
B. 500 feet MSL.
C. 500 feet AGL.

Answer (C) is correct. (ACUG)
DISCUSSION: Obstacles, such as towers and obstructions, are depicted on the sectional chart using a blue upside-down V and a dot. The top number is the height of the obstruction in feet above mean sea level (MSL). The bottom number in parentheses is the height of the obstruction in feet above ground level (AGL). The highest obstacle 2 NM northeast of Hertford is 500 ft. AGL.
Answer (A) is incorrect. This highest obstacle is 500 ft. AGL, not 399 ft. MSL. **Answer (B) is incorrect.** This highest obstacle is 500 ft. AGL, not 500 ft. MSL.

27. (Refer to Figure 20 on page 107.) (Refer to Area 3.) With ATC authorization, you are operating your small unmanned aircraft approximately 4 SM southeast of Elizabeth City Regional Airport (ECG). What hazard is indicated to be in that area?

A. High density military operations in the vicinity.
B. Unmarked balloon on a cable up to 3,008 feet AGL.
C. Unmarked balloon on a cable up to 3,008 feet MSL.

Answer (C) is correct. (ACUG)
DISCUSSION: On Fig. 20, northwest of 5, find "CAUTION: UNMARKED BALLOON ON CABLE TO 3,008 MSL." This is self-explanatory.
Answer (A) is incorrect. High density military operations are noted in the caution box south of Fentress NALF, not Elizabeth City. **Answer (B) is incorrect.** The balloon extends to 3,008 ft. MSL, not AGL.

SU 2: Airspace Classification and Operating Requirements

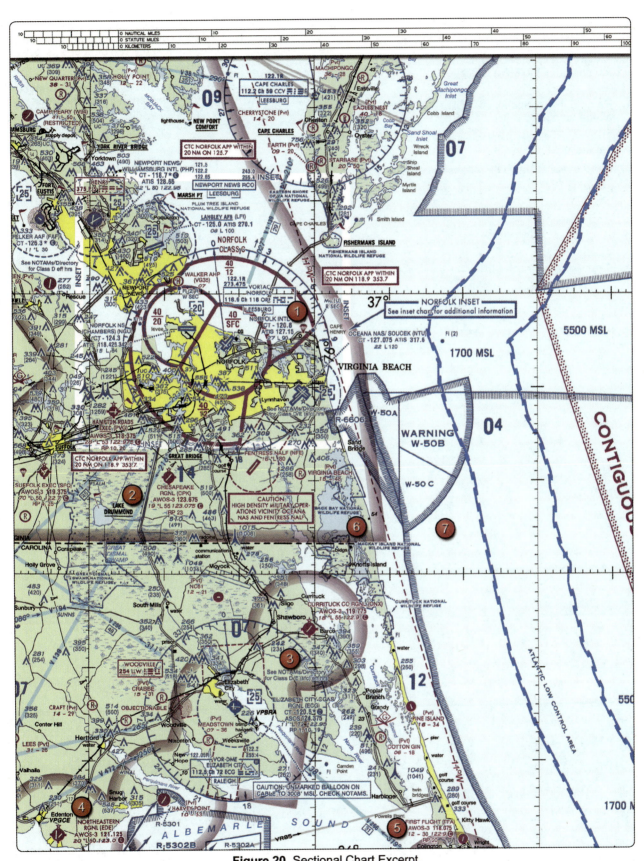

Figure 20. Sectional Chart Excerpt.
NOTE: Chart is not to scale and should not be used for navigation. Use associated scale.

28. (Refer to Figure 21 on page 109.) You have been hired by a farmer to use your small UA to inspect his crops. The area that you are to survey is in the Devil's Lake West MOA, east of area 2. How would you find out if the MOA is active?

A. Refer to the legend for special use airspace phone number.
B. This information is available in the Small UAS database.
C. Refer to the Military Operations Directory.

Answer (A) is correct. (AIM Para 3-4-5)
DISCUSSION: Times and altitudes of operation as well as the name of the controlling agency can be found on the sectional aeronautical chart legend.
Answer (B) is incorrect. MOA activity is found on the sectional chart legend, not a Small UAS database. **Answer (C) is incorrect.** MOA activity is found on the sectional chart legend, not the Military Operations Directory.

SU 2: Airspace Classification and Operating Requirements

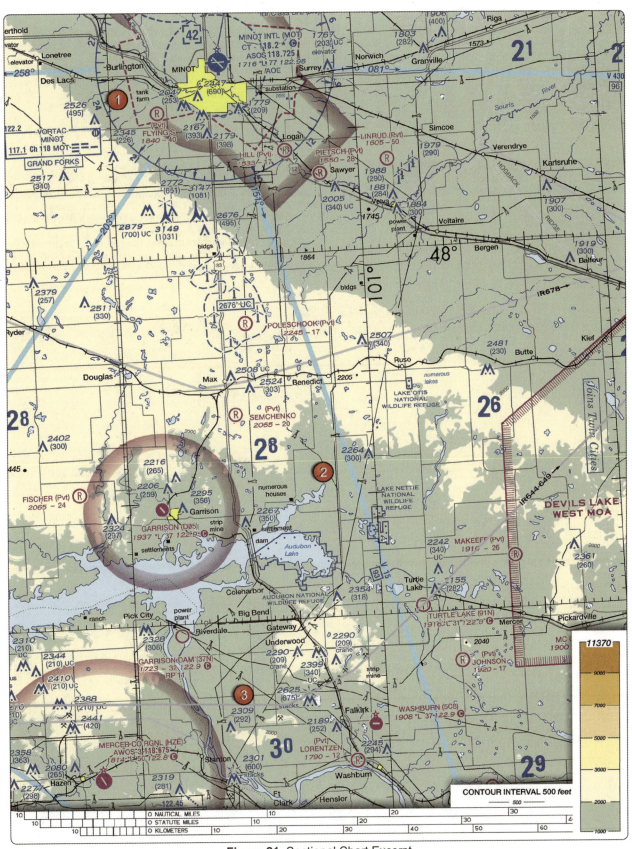

Figure 21. Sectional Chart Excerpt.
NOTE: Chart is not to scale and should not be used for navigation. Use associated scale.

29. (Refer to Figure 23 on page 111.) (Refer to Area 4.) What is the required flight visibility for a remote pilot operating an unmanned aircraft near the Plantation Airport (JYL)?

A. 5 statute miles.
B. 1 statute mile.
C. 3 statute miles.

Answer (C) is correct. (14 CFR 107.51)
DISCUSSION: Regardless of the location, the minimum flight visibility, as observed from the location of the control station, must be no less than 3 SM.
Answer (A) is incorrect. The minimum flight visibility must be 3 SM, not 5 SM. **Answer (B) is incorrect.** The minimum flight visibility must be 3 SM, not 1 SM.

30. (Refer to Figure 23 on page 111.) (Refer to Area 3.) What is the floor of the Savannah Class C airspace at the shelf area (outer circle)?

A. 1,300 feet AGL.
B. 1,300 feet MSL.
C. 1,700 feet MSL.

Answer (B) is correct. (AIM Para 3-2-4)
DISCUSSION: Savannah Class C (Fig. 23, area 3) has a magenta circle around it depicting Class C airspace. The altitudes of the Class C airspace shelf area are shown as 41/13 in the outer circle. The bottom number denotes the floor of the Class C airspace to be 1,300 ft. MSL.
Answer (A) is incorrect. The floor of the shelf area is charted in feet above MSL, not AGL. **Answer (C) is incorrect.** The floor of the shelf area is 1,300 ft. MSL, not 1,700 ft. MSL.

SU 2: Airspace Classification and Operating Requirements

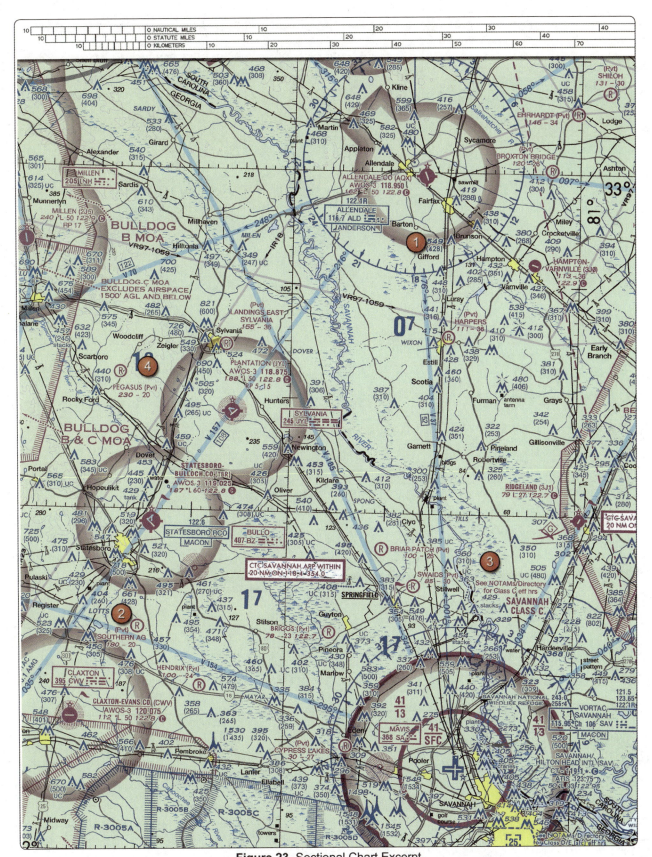

Figure 23. Sectional Chart Excerpt.
NOTE: Chart is not to scale and should not be used for navigation. Use associated scale.

STUDY UNIT THREE
AVIATION WEATHER SERVICES

(20 pages of outline)

| 3.1 | Sources of Weather | (22 questions) 113, 133 |

3.1 SOURCES OF WEATHER

1. **Internet weather briefing** and sources of weather available for flight planning purposes should be retrieved using official aviation weather sources, such as Flight Service.

   a. **Flight Service (online)** can be accessed without signing up or logging in; however, official briefings may be accessed only after logging in to an account at www.1800wxbrief.com.

      1) The main menu provides access to a pilot dashboard, weather, and flight planning and briefing information, along with some UAS planning tools.

         a) The UAS planning tools allow users to easily define UAS operating areas (UOA).

   b. **Flight Service (phone)** is available at 1-800-WX-BRIEF (800-992-7433), where a specialist may be reached by following the menu prompts to speak with a briefer.

      1) Identify yourself as a remote pilot and the area you are operating in. You should reference an official aviation fix, such as an airport or navigational aid if known, or use latitude and longitude.

      2) **Types of briefings** vary by time window and nature of the operation.

         a) A standard briefing should be requested to obtain complete weather and NOTAMs for your area for a flight within 6 hours.

         b) Traditionally, an abbreviated briefing should be requested only if requesting specific information or obtaining an update to a previous briefing. However, these are often the most requested remote pilot briefings and supply ample information for most applications.

         c) An outlook briefing should be requested for operations planned more than 6 hours in the future.

            i) Outlook briefings will usually not contain the same information as a standard briefing, such as current conditions.

c. Aviation Weather Center at www.aviationweather.gov provides weather products such as SIGMETs, AIRMETs, weather depiction, surface analysis, PROG charts, METARs, TAFs, winds aloft forecasts, and radar imagery.

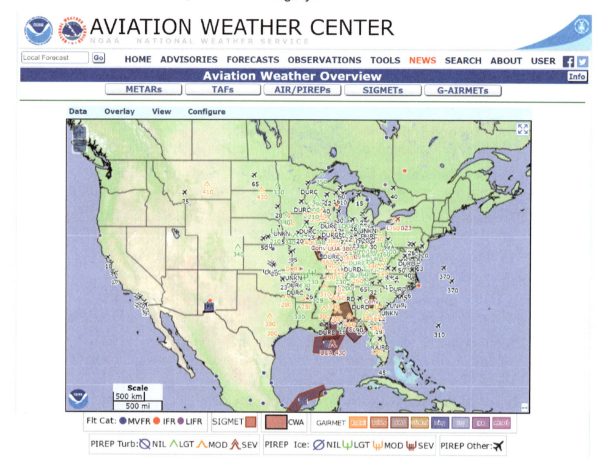

SU 3: Aviation Weather Services 115

d. National Weather Service at www.weather.gov contains local and national forecast products and maps.

1) Many products are interactive, allowing the user to quickly zoom to specific regions and display a wide range of user-selected weather products including hazards, temperature, winds, sky cover, precipitation, etc.

2. **METAR (Aviation Routine Weather Report)**

   a. A METAR contains the elements below and on the following pages in order. Consider the example METAR below for reference.

   > METAR KGNV 201953Z 24015KT 3/4SM R28/2400FT +TSRA
   > BKN008 OVC015CB 26/25 A2985 RMK TSB32RAB32

METAR	KGNV	201953Z	____	24015KT	3/4SM	R28/2400FT	+TSRA
1.	2.	3.	4.	5.	6.	7.	8.

BKN008 OVC015CB	26/25	A2985	RMK TSB32RAB32
9.	10.	11.	12.

   1) **Type of report**. The type of report will always appear as the lead element of the report. There are two types of reports:

      a) **METAR** -- an aviation routine weather report
      b) **SPECI** -- a nonroutine aviation weather report

   2) **ICAO station identifier**. The METAR uses the ICAO four-letter station identifier.

      a) In the contiguous 48 states, the three-letter domestic location identifier is prefixed with a "K."

         i) EXAMPLE: The identifier for San Francisco, CA, is KSFO.

   3) **Date and time of report** shows the observation date and time transmitted as a six-digit date/time group appended with the letter **Z** to denote Coordinated Universal Time (UTC).

      a) The first two digits are the date followed with two digits for the hour and two digits for minutes.

   4) **Modifiers** classify the reporting source.

      a) **AUTO** identifies the report as an automated weather report with no human intervention, and the type of sensor (A01, A02) used at the automated station is encoded in the remarks section of the report.

      b) **COR** identifies the report as a corrected report to replace an earlier report with an error.

5) **Wind** follows the date/time or modifier element.
   a) The average 2-minute direction and speed are reported in a five- or six-digit format.
      i) The first three digits are the direction FROM which the wind is blowing. The direction is to the nearest 10-degree increment referenced to TRUE north.
      ii) The last two or three digits are the wind speed in knots -- two digits for speeds less than 100 kt., three digits for speeds greater than 100 kt.
      iii) The abbreviation **KT** is appended to denote the use of knots for wind speed.
   b) EXAMPLES:
      i) 24015KT means the wind is from 240° true at 15 kt.
      ii) VRB04KT means the wind is variable in direction at 4 kt.
      iii) 210103G130KT means the wind is from 210° true at 103 kt. with gusts to 130 kt.
      iv) 00000KT means the wind is calm (i.e., less than 1 kt.).
6) **Visibility** is reported as **prevailing visibility** and considered representative of the visibility conditions at the observing site. This representative visibility is the greatest distance at which objects can be seen and identified through at least 180° of the horizon circle, which need not be continuous.
   a) Visibility is reported in statute miles (SM) with a space and then fractions of statute miles, as needed, with **SM** appended to it.
   b) EXAMPLE: **1 1/2SM** means visibility is one and one-half statute miles.
   c) Automated reporting stations will show visibility less than 1/4 SM as **M1/4SM** and visibility of 10 SM and greater as **10SM**.
7) **Runway visual range (RVR)** is reported whenever the prevailing visibility is 1 SM or less and/or the RVR for the designated instrument runway is 6,000 ft. or less.
   a) RVR is reported in the following format: **R** identifies the group, followed by the runway heading and parallel designator if needed, a solidus (/), and the visual range in feet (meters in other countries) followed with **FT**.
      i) EXAMPLE: **R28/1200FT** means Runway 28 visual range is 1,200 ft.

8) **Weather** groups are constructed by considering, in sequence, the intensity or proximity, followed by the descriptor and the weather phenomenon; e.g., heavy rain shower is coded as +SHRA. The weather phenomenon represented by UP means unknown precipitation (automated stations only).

   a) **Intensity** may be shown with most precipitation types, including those of a showery nature.

Symbol	Meaning
+	Heavy
(no symbol)	Moderate
−	Light

   i) Intensity levels may be shown with obscurations, such as blowing dust, sand, or snow.

   ii) When more than one type of precipitation is present, the intensity refers to the first precipitation type (most predominant).

   b) **Proximity** is applied to and reported only for weather occurring in the vicinity of the airport (between 5 and 10 SM of the usual point of observation) and is denoted by **VC**.

   i) VC will replace the intensity symbol; i.e., intensity and VC will never be shown in the same group.

   c) **Descriptors** further identify weather phenomena and are used with certain types of precipitation and obscurations.

Coded	Meaning	Coded	Meaning
TS	Thunderstorm	DR	Low Drifting
SH	Showers	MI	Shallow
FZ	Freezing	BC	Patchy
BL	Blowing	PR	Partial

   i) Although **TS** and **SH** are used with precipitation and may be preceded with an intensity symbol, the intensity applies to the precipitation and not the descriptor.

   ii) EXAMPLE: **+SHRA** means heavy rain showers.

   d) **Precipitation** is any form of water particles, whether solid or liquid, that fall from the atmosphere and reach the ground.

Coded	Meaning	Coded	Meaning
RA	Rain	GR	Hail (1/4 in. or greater)
DZ	Drizzle	GS	Small Hail/Snow Pellets
SN	Snow	PL	Ice Pellets
SG	Snow Grains	IC	Ice Crystals
UP	Unknown Precipitation		

   i) **GS** is used to indicate hail less than 1/4 in. in diameter.

   ii) For **IC** to be reported, the visibility must be reduced by ice crystals to 6 SM or less.

e) **Obscurations** are any phenomena in the atmosphere, other than precipitation, that reduce horizontal visibility.

Coded	Meaning	Coded	Meaning
FG	Fog (visibility less than 5/8 SM)	PY	Spray
BR	Mist (visibility 5/8 to 6 SM)	SA	Sand
FU	Smoke	DU	Dust
HZ	Haze	VA	Volcanic Ash

   i) **FG** is used to indicate fog restricting visibility to less than 5/8 SM.
   ii) **BR** is used to indicate mist restricting visibility from 5/8 to 6 SM and is never coded with a descriptor.
   iii) **BCFG** and **PRFG** are used to indicate patchy fog or partial fog only if the prevailing visibility is 7 SM or greater.

f) **Other** weather phenomena are reported when they occur.

Coded	Meaning	Coded	Meaning
SQ	Squall	SS	Sandstorm
DS	Duststorm	PO	Well-Developed Dust/Sand Whirls
FC	Funnel Cloud	+FC	Tornado or Waterspout

   i) A **squall** (**SQ**) is a sudden increase in wind speed of at least 16 kt., with the speed rising to 22 kt. or more and lasting at least 1 min.
   ii) **+FC** is used to denote a tornado, waterspout, or well-developed funnel cloud with the type indicated in the remarks.

g) **Examples of Reported Weather Phenomena**
   i) **TSRA** means thunderstorm with moderate rain.
   ii) **+SN** means heavy snow.
   iii) **–RA FG** means light rain and fog.
   iv) **VCSH** means showers in the vicinity.

9) **Sky condition** is reported in eighths of sky cover, using the following contractions:

Contraction	Meaning	Summation Amount
SKC or CLR*	Clear	0 or 0 below 12,000 ft.
FEW	Few	>0 to 2/8
SCT	Scattered	3/8 to 4/8
BKN	Broken	5/8 to 7/8
OVC	Overcast	8/8
VV	Vertical Visibility (indefinite ceiling)	8/8
CB	Cumulonimbus	When present
TCU	Towering Cumulus	When present

*__SKC__ will be reported at manual stations. **CLR** will be used at automated stations when no clouds below 12,000 ft. are reported.

   a) A **ceiling** is defined as the lowest broken or overcast layer aloft or vertical visibility into a surface-based obstruction.

b) **Heights** of cloud bases are reported with three digits in hundreds of feet above ground level (AGL).

   i) When more than one layer is reported, layers are given in ascending order of height. For each layer above a lower layer(s), the sky cover contraction for that layer will be the **total sky cover**, which includes that layer and all lower layers.

   ii) EXAMPLE: **SCT010 BKN025 OVC080** reports three layers:
   - A scattered layer at 1,000 ft.
   - A broken layer (ceiling) at 2,500 ft.
   - A top layer at 8,000 ft. In this case, it is assumed that the total sky covered by all the layers is 8/8. Thus, the upper layer is reported as overcast.

c) **Vertical visibility** is the distance one may see vertically into an obscuring phenomena.

   i) If **towering cumulus clouds (TCU)** or cumulonimbus clouds **(CB)** are present, they are reported after the height that represents their base.
   - EXAMPLES:

     SCT025TCU BKN080 BKN250 means 2,500 ft. scattered towering cumulus, ceiling 8,000 ft. broken, 25,000 ft. broken.

     SCT008 OVC012CB means 800 ft. scattered, ceiling 1,200 ft. overcast cumulonimbus clouds.

   ii) Height into an indefinite ceiling is preceded with **VV** (vertical visibility) followed by three digits indicating the vertical visibility in hundreds of feet. The layer is spoken of as an "indefinite ceiling" and indicates total obscuration.
   - EXAMPLE: **1/8SM FG VV006** means visibility 1/8 SM, fog, indefinite ceiling 600 ft.

10) **Temperature/dew point group** items are reported in a two-digit form in whole degrees Celsius (C) separated by a solidus (/) with temperatures below zero prefixed with **M**.

   a) EXAMPLES:
      i) **15/08** means temperature is 15°C and dew point is 8°C.
      ii) **00/M02** means temperature is 0°C and dew point is –2°C.
      iii) **M05/** means temperature is –5°C and dew point is missing.

   b) An air mass with a 3°C or less temperature/dew point spread is considered saturated.

11) The **altimeter** is reported in a four-digit format representing tens, units, tenths, and hundredths of inches of mercury prefixed with **A**. The decimal point is not reported.

   a) EXAMPLE: **A2995** means the altimeter setting is 29.95 inches of mercury.

12) **Remarks** will be included in all observations, when appropriate, and are preceded by the contraction **RMK**.

   a) Time entries are shown as minutes past the hour if the time reported occurs during the same hour the observation is taken.

- b) Location of phenomena within 5 SM of the station will be reported as at the station.
    - i) Phenomena between 5 and 10 SM will be reported in the vicinity, **VC**.
    - ii) Phenomena beyond 10 SM will be reported as distant, **DSNT**.
- c) **Automated, manual, and plain language** remarks may be generated from either manual or automated weather reporting stations, and they generally elaborate on parameters reported in the body of the report. Some of these remarks include
    - i) **Station type.** This remark is shown only if the **AUTO** modifier was used.
        - **AO1** means the automated weather station is without a precipitation discriminator.
        - **AO2** means the automated weather station has a precipitation discriminator.
        - A precipitation discriminator can determine the difference between liquid and frozen/freezing precipitation.
    - ii) **Beginning and/or ending times for precipitation and thunderstorms.**
        - When precipitation begins or ends, remarks will show the type of precipitation as well as the beginning and/or ending time(s) of occurrence.
        - Types of precipitation may be combined if beginning or ending at the same time.
        - EXAMPLE: **RAB05E30SNB20E55** means that rain began at 5 min. past the hour and ended at 30 min. past the hour, and snow began at 20 min. past the hour and ended at 55 min. past the hour.
        - When thunderstorms begin or end, remarks will show the thunderstorm as well as the beginning and/or ending time(s) of occurrence.
        - EXAMPLE: **TSB05E40** means the thunderstorm began at 5 min. past the hour and ended at 40 min. past the hour.
- d) **Additive** data groups are reported only at designated stations, and **maintenance** data groups are reported only from automated weather reporting stations. Some of these remarks include
    - i) **Sensor status indicators.** If automated weather reporting station sensors are not working, the following remarks will appear:
        - **PWINO** -- present weather identifier not available
        - **PNO** -- precipitation amount not available
        - **FZRANO** -- freezing rain information indicator not available
        - **TSNO** -- thunderstorm information not available
        - **VISNO** -- visibility sensor information not available
        - **CHINO** -- cloud height indicator information not available
    - ii) **Maintenance indicator.** A maintenance indicator (dollar) sign ($) is included when an automated weather reporting system detects that maintenance is needed on the system.

3. **Terminal Aerodrome Forecasts (TAF)**

   a. A TAF is a concise statement of the expected weather at a specific airport during a 24- or 30-hour period.

   b. The TAF covers an area within a 5-SM radius of the center of the airport and is prepared four times daily at 0000Z, 0600Z, 1200Z, and 1800Z.

   1) Many of the weather codes used in the METAR are also used in the TAF.

   2) The 32 largest airports in the U.S. offer 30-hour forecasts. Every other site provides a 24-hour forecast.

   c. A TAF contains the elements in items 1)-9) below and on the next page in order. Forecast change indicators (items 10)-12)) and probability forecast (item 13)) are used as appropriate. Consider the example TAF below for reference.

   ```
   TAF
   KOKC 051130Z 0512/0612 14008KT 5SM BR BKN030 WS018/32030KT
     TEMPO 0513/0516 1SM BR
     FM051600 16010KT P6SM SKC
     BECMG 0522/0624 20013G20KT 4SM SHRA OVC020
     PROB40 0600/0606 2SM TSRA OVC008CB=
   ```

TAF	KOKC	051130Z	0512/0612	14008KT	5SM	BR	BKN030
1.	2.	3.	4.	5.	6.	7.	8.

WS018/32030KT	TEMPO 0513/0516 1SM BR	FM051600 16010KT P6SM SKC
9.	10.	11.

   BECMG 0522/0624 20013G20KT 4SM SHRA OVC020
   12.

   PROB40 0600/0606 2SM TSRA OVC008CB=
   13.

   1) **Type of report.** There are two types of TAF issuance:

      a) **TAF** means a routine forecast.
      b) **TAF AMD** means an amended forecast.

   2) **ICAO station identifier.** The TAF uses the ICAO four-letter station identifier.

   3) **Date and time of origin** is the date and time (UTC) that the forecast is actually prepared. The format is a two-digit date and a four-digit time followed by the letter **Z**.

   4) **Valid period date and time** is the UTC valid period of the forecast in a two-digit date followed by the two-digit beginning hour, a solidus, and the two-digit date and two-digit ending hour.

      a) Valid periods beginning at 0000 UTC will be indicated as **00**, and valid periods ending at 0000 UTC will be indicated as **24**.

   5) **Wind** is a five- or six-digit group with the forecast surface wind direction (first three digits) referenced to true north and the speed (last two digits or three digits if 100 kt. or greater).

      a) The abbreviation **KT** is appended to denote the use of knots for wind speed.
      b) A calm wind (0 kt.) is forecast as **00000KT**.

   6) **Visibility** is forecast in statute miles with a space and then fractions of statute miles, as needed, with **SM** appended to it.

      a) Forecast visibility greater than 6 SM is coded **P6SM**.

7) **Weather** phenomenon or phenomena are coded in TAF reports using the same format, qualifiers, and phenomena contractions as METAR reports, except **UP** (unknown precipitation).
   a) Obscurations to vision will be forecast whenever the prevailing visibility is forecast to be 6 SM or less.
   b) If no significant weather is expected to occur during a specific time period in the forecast, the weather group is omitted for that time period.
      i) If, after a time period in which significant weather has been forecast, a change to a forecast of no significant weather occurs, the contraction **NSW** (No Significant Weather) will appear as the weather included in becoming (BECMG) or temporary (TEMPO) groups.
      ii) NSW will not be used in the initial time period of a TAF or in from (FM groups).
8) **Sky conditions** use the METAR format, except that cumulonimbus clouds (CB) are the only cloud type forecast in TAFs.
9) **Wind shear** (optional data) is the forecast of nonconvective low-level winds (up to 2,000 ft. AGL) and is entered after the sky conditions when wind shear is expected. The wind shear element is omitted if not expected to occur.
   a) The forecast includes the height of the wind shear followed by the wind direction and wind speed at the indicated height.
   b) Wind shear is encoded with the contraction **WS**, followed by a three-digit height and winds at the height indicated in the same format as surface winds.
      i) Height is given in hundreds of feet AGL up to and including 2,000 ft.
10) **Temporary (TEMPO) group** is used for any conditions in wind, visibility, weather, or sky condition expected to last for generally less than 1 hour at a time (occasional) and to occur during less than half the time period.
    a) The **TEMPO** indicator is followed by a four-digit group, a solidus, and another four-digit group giving the beginning day/hour and the ending day/hour of the time period during which the temporary conditions are expected.
    b) Only the changing forecast meteorological conditions are included in **TEMPO** groups.
       i) The omitted conditions are carried over from the previous time group.
11) **From (FM) group** is used when a rapid change, usually occurring in less than 1 hour, is expected.
    a) Typically, a rapid change of prevailing conditions to a new set of conditions is associated with a synoptic feature (i.e., cold or warm front) passing through the terminal area.
    b) Appended to the **FM** indicator is the two-digit date and the four-digit hour and minute when the change is expected to begin and continue until the next change group or until the end of the current forecast.
    c) A **FM** group will always mark the beginning of a new line in a TAF report.
    d) Each **FM** group contains all the required elements, i.e., wind, visibility, weather, and sky condition.
       i) Weather and wind shear will be omitted in **FM** groups when it is not significant to aviation.
       ii) **FM** groups will not include the contraction **NSW**.

12) **Becoming (BECMG) group** is used when a gradual change in conditions is expected over a longer time period, but no longer than 2 hours.

   a) Appended to the **BECMG** indicator is a four-digit group, a solidus, and another four-digit group with the beginning day/hour and the ending day/hour of the change period.

   i) The gradual change will occur within this time period.

   b) Only the changing forecast meteorological conditions are included in **BECMG** groups.

   i) The omitted conditions are carried over from the previous time group.

13) **Probability (PROB) forecast** indicates the chance of thunderstorms or other precipitation events occurring, along with associated weather conditions (wind, visibility, and sky conditions).

   a) A probability forecast will not be used during the first 6 hr. of a TAF.

   b) Appended to the **PROB** contraction is the probability value.

   i) EXAMPLES:

   PROB40 means there is a 40-49% probability.
   PROB30 means there is a 30-39% probability.

   c) Appended to the **PROB** indicator is a four-digit group giving the beginning day/hour and another four-digit group giving the ending day/hour of the time period during which the precipitation or thunderstorms are expected.

4. **Understanding of weather charts** allows a big-picture overview useful in flight planning and weather briefing before departure and in monitoring weather for prolonged operations.

   a. The surface analysis chart is generated to show areas of high and low pressure, fronts, temperatures, dew points, wind directions and speeds, local weather, and visual obstructions.

   1) This chart is transmitted every 3 hours and covers the contiguous 48 states and adjacent areas.

   b. Surface weather observations for reporting points are also depicted on this chart.

   1) Each reporting point is illustrated by a station model, which includes the following: Type of Observation, Sky Cover, Clouds, Sea Level Pressure, Pressure Change/Tendency, Precipitation, Dew Point, Present Weather, Temperature, and Wind.

2) The figure below shows weather chart symbols for a sample station model.

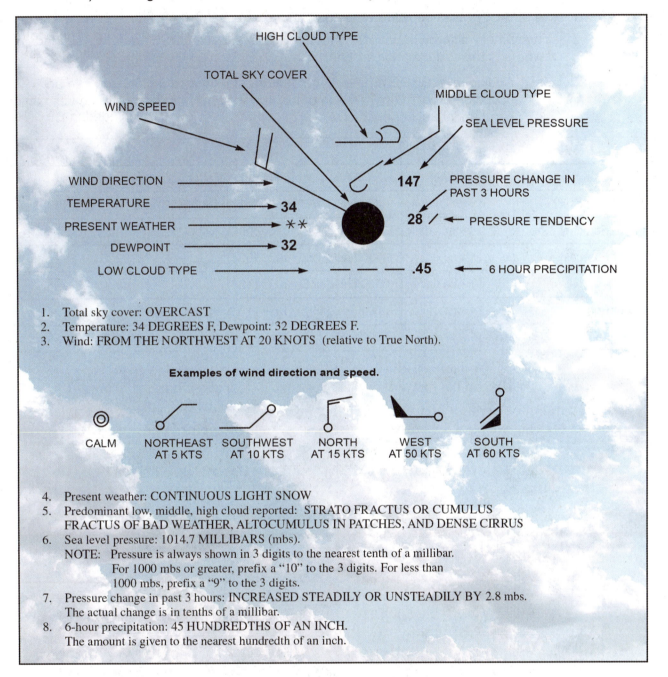

c. Short-Range Surface Prognostic (PROG) Charts provide a forecast of surface pressure systems, fronts, and precipitation for a 2 1/2-day (60-hr.) period with additional daily forecasts from days 3 through 7.

1) The forecast area covers the 48 contiguous states, the coastal waters, and portions of Canada and Mexico.

2) The forecasted conditions are divided into five forecast periods: 12, 24, 36, 48, and 60 hours.

a) Each chart depicts a "snapshot" of weather elements expected at the specified valid time.

d. PROGs are very similar to surface analysis charts.

1) All of the symbols depicted on both charts are the same.

2) The primary difference between the two charts is that PROGs are forecast charts, whereas the surface analysis chart is a "current conditions" chart.

a) Additionally, PROG charts do not feature station model plots and can be considered a "future" version of the surface analysis chart with the valid times and update schedule below.

Product	Frequency	Times
Current Analysis	3 hours	every 3 hours about 90 minutes after valid time
12 hour Forecast	4 times daily	~0200 (valid 12Z), 0400 (18Z), 1300 (00Z), and 1430 (06Z)
24 hour Forecast	4 times daily	~0430 (valid 00Z), 0700 (06Z), 1330 (12Z), and 1930 (18Z)
36 hour Forecast	Twice daily	~0730 (valid 12Z), 1930 (00Z)
48 hour Forecast	Twice daily	~0730 (valid 00Z), 1930 (12Z)
60 hour Forecast	Twice daily	~0730 (valid 00Z), 1930 (12Z)
3, 4, 5, 6 and 7 day Forecasts	Once daily	~1400 (valid 12Z). The 3 day forecast is actually a 3 1/2 day forecast

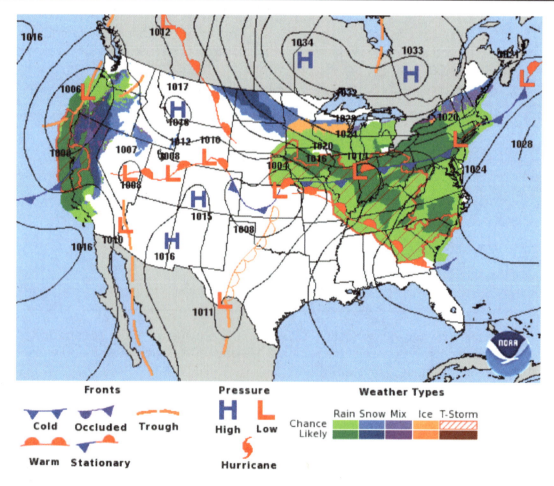

SU 3: Aviation Weather Services

e. Plotted data on the chart includes

1) **Pressure systems**, which are depicted by pressure centers, troughs, isobars, drylines, tropical waves, tropical storms, and hurricanes using standard symbols.

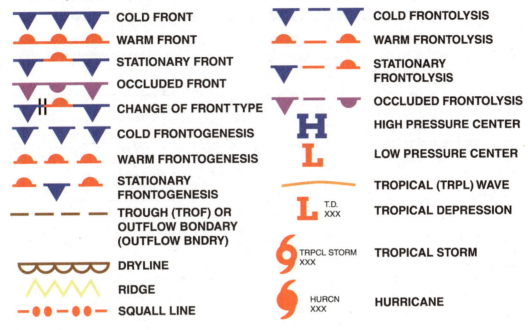

a) Isobars are denoted by solid, thin gray lines that join areas of equal pressure and are labeled in intervals of 4 millibars (mb) (992 mb, 996 mb, 1,000 mb, 1,004 mb, etc.).

b) The central pressure is plotted near the respective pressure center.

2) **Fronts**, which are depicted to show their forecast position at the chart valid time, using the standard chart symbols above.

a) Because frontal movement causes significant changes in weather, pressure, and wind, pilots should carefully consider the forecasted frontal depictions and plan their flight accordingly.

3) **Precipitation** areas, which are enclosed by thick, solid green lines.

   a) Standard precipitation symbols are used to identify precipitation types and are positioned within or adjacent to the associated area of precipitation.

   i) If adjacent to the area, an arrow will point to the area with which they are associated.

   b) A mix of precipitation is indicated by the use of two pertinent symbols separated by a slash.

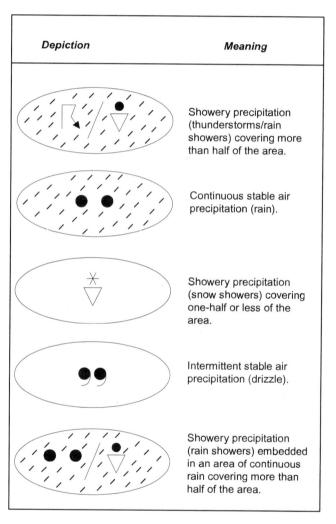

   c) A bold, dashed gray line is used to separate precipitation within an outlined area with contrasting characteristics.

   i) EXAMPLE: A dashed line would be used to separate an area of snow from an area of rain.

   d) Precipitation characteristics are further described by the use of shading.

   i) Shading or lack of shading indicates the expected coverage of the precipitation.

   ii) Shaded areas indicate the precipitation is expected to have more than 50% (broken) coverage.

   iii) Unshaded areas indicate 30-50% (scattered) coverage.

SU 3: Aviation Weather Services

f. The Low-Level Significant Weather (SIGWX) Chart provides a forecast of aviation weather hazards.

1) The charts are primarily intended to be used as guidance products for preflight briefings.
2) Each chart depicts a "snapshot" of weather expected at the specified valid time.
3) The forecast domain covers the 48 contiguous states and the coastal waters for altitudes below 24,000 ft. MSL (FL240 or 400 millibars).
4) SIGWX charts are issued four times per day by the Aviation Weather Center (AWC).
    a) Two charts are issued: a 12-hour and a 24-hour chart.

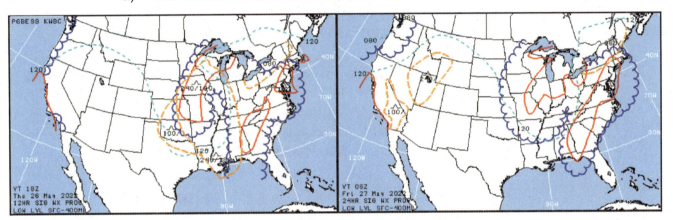

5) Low-Level SIGWX Charts depict weather flying categories, turbulence, and freezing levels. Icing is not specifically forecast.
    a) See the chart symbol legend below.

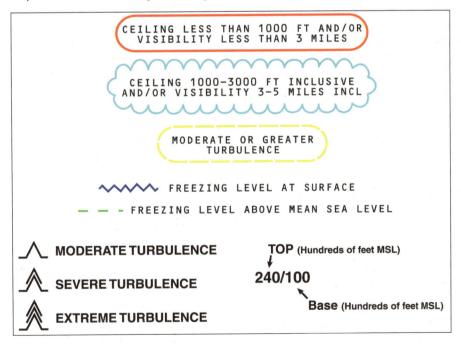

6) **Flying Categories**

   a) Instrument Flight Rules (IFR) areas are outlined with a solid red line.

   b) Marginal Visual Flight Rules (MVFR) areas are outlined with a scalloped blue line.

   c) Visual Flight Rules (VFR) areas are implied and therefore not depicted.

7) **Turbulence**

   a) Areas of moderate or greater turbulence are enclosed by bold, dashed yellow lines.

   b) Turbulence intensities are identified by standard symbols, as shown in the turbulence figure on the previous page.

   c) Turbulence height is depicted by two numbers separated by a solidus (/).

      i) EXAMPLE: An area on the chart with turbulence indicated as **240/100** indicates the turbulence can be expected from the top at FL240 to the base at 10,000 feet MSL.

      ii) When the base height is omitted, the turbulence is forecast to reach the surface. For example, an indication of **080/** identifies a turbulence layer from the surface to 8,000 feet MSL.

      iii) Turbulence associated with thunderstorms is not depicted on the chart.

   d) The intensity symbols and height information may be located within or adjacent to the forecast areas of turbulence.

      i) If located adjacent to an area, an arrow will point to the associated area.

8) **Freezing Levels**

   a) If the freezing level is at the surface, it is depicted by a blue saw-toothed symbol.

   b) Freezing levels above the surface are depicted by fine, green dashed lines labeled in hundreds of feet MSL beginning at 4,000 feet using 4,000 foot intervals. If multiple freezing levels exist, these lines are drawn to the highest freezing level.

      i) For example, **80** identifies the 8,000-foot freezing level contour.
      ii) The lines are discontinued where they intersect the surface.

   c) The freezing level for locations between lines is determined by interpolation.

      i) EXAMPLE: The freezing level midway between the 4,000- and 8,000-foot lines is 6,000 feet.

SU 3: Aviation Weather Services   131

g. **Radar observations** provide information about the location and intensity of precipitation.

  1) NEXRAD (**Nex**t Generation **Rad**ar) obtains weather information based upon returned energy. The radar emits a burst of energy. If the energy strikes an object, such as precipitation, the energy is scattered in all directions. A small fraction of that scattered energy is directed back toward the radar.

  2) **WSR-88D NEXRAD**, commonly called Doppler radar, provides in-depth observations that inform surrounding communities of impending weather. It has two operational modes: clear air and precipitation.

    a) In clear air mode, the radar is in its most sensitive operational mode because a slow antenna rotation allows the radar to sample the atmosphere longer. Images are updated about every 10 minutes in this mode.

    b) Precipitation mode is used when precipitation is present. These images update approximately every 4 to 6 minutes.

    c) Intensity values are measured in dBZ (decibels of Z) and are depicted in color on the radar image.

    d) Intensities are correlated to intensity terminology (phraseology) for ATC purposes.

Example of a weather radar scope.   WSR-88D Weather Radar Echo Intensity Legend.

Reflectivity (dBZ) Ranges	Weather Radar Echo Intensity
<30 dBZ	Light
30–40 dBZ	Moderate
>40–50 dBZ	Heavy
50+ dBZ	Extreme

WSR-88D Weather Radar Precipitation Intensity Terminology.

5. **Automated surface observing systems (ASOS) and automated weather observing systems (AWOS)** consist of various sensors, a processor, a computer-generated voice subsystem, and a transmitter to broadcast local, minute-by-minute weather data directly to the pilot. These systems provide information that can be used in remote pilot operations and by the National Weather Service to generate METARs.

   a. **Automated Weather Observing System (AWOS)**

      1) Transmits on a discrete VHF radio frequency

      2) Engineered to be receivable to a maximum of 25 NM from the site and a maximum altitude of 10,000 feet above ground level

         a) At many locations, AWOS signals may be received on the surface of the airport, but local conditions may limit the maximum AWOS reception distance and/or altitude.

      3) Transmits a 20 to 30 second weather message updated each minute

         a) Pilots monitor the designated frequency for the automated weather broadcast.
         b) There is no two-way communication capability.

   b. **Automated Surface Observing System (ASOS)/Automated Weather Sensor System (AWSS)**

      1) Primary surface weather observing system of the U.S.

         a) AWSS is a follow-on program that provides identical data as ASOS.
         b) ASOS/AWSS is more sensitive and provides more information than AWOS.

      2) Designed to support aviation operations and weather forecast activities

         a) ASOS/AWSS will provide continuous minute-by-minute observations and perform the basic observing functions necessary to generate a METAR and other aviation weather information.

      3) Transmitted and received by the pilot in exactly the same way as AWOS

   c. The following table explains what information is provided by each automated weather reporting system type:

Weather Reporting Systems

Element Reported	AWOS-A	AWOS-1	AWOS-2	AWOS-3	ASOS
Altimeter	X	X	X	X	X
Wind		X	X	X	X
Temperature/Dew Point		X	X	X	X
Density Altitude		X	X	X	X
Visibility			X	X	X
Clouds/Ceiling				X	X
Precipitation					X
Remarks					X

QUESTIONS
3.1 Sources of Weather

1. To get a complete weather overview for the planned flight, the Remote Pilot in Command should obtain

A. an outlook briefing.
B. an abbreviated briefing.
C. a standard briefing.

Answer (C) is correct. (AC 00-45H Chap 1)
DISCUSSION: A standard briefing should be requested to obtain complete weather and NOTAMs for your area.
Answer (A) is incorrect. An outlook briefing should be requested for a flight more than 6 hours in the future.
Answer (B) is incorrect. An abbreviated briefing should be requested when the user needs to supplement mass disseminated data, to update a previous briefing, or to obtain specific information.

2. To get a complete weather briefing for the planned flight, the pilot should request

A. a general briefing.
B. an abbreviated briefing.
C. a standard briefing.

Answer (C) is correct. (AC 00-45H Chap 1)
DISCUSSION: To get a complete briefing before a planned flight, the pilot should request a standard briefing. This will include all pertinent information needed for a safe flight.
Answer (A) is incorrect. A general briefing is not standard terminology for any type of weather briefing. **Answer (B) is incorrect.** An abbreviated briefing is provided as a supplement to mass disseminated data or a previous briefing. It can also be used to obtain specific information.

3. Which type of weather briefing should a pilot request to supplement mass disseminated data?

A. An outlook briefing.
B. A supplemental briefing.
C. An abbreviated briefing.

Answer (C) is correct. (AC 00-45H Chap 1)
DISCUSSION: An abbreviated briefing will be provided when the user requests information to supplement mass disseminated data, to update a previous briefing, or to obtain specific information.
Answer (A) is incorrect. An outlook briefing should be requested if the proposed departure time is 6 hr. or more in the future. **Answer (B) is incorrect.** A supplemental briefing is not a standard type of briefing.

4. A weather briefing that is provided when the information requested is 6 or more hours in advance of the proposed departure time is

A. an outlook briefing.
B. a forecast briefing.
C. a prognostic briefing.

Answer (A) is correct. (AC 00-45H Chap 1)
DISCUSSION: An outlook briefing is given when the briefing is 6 or more hours before the proposed departure time.
Answer (B) is incorrect. A forecast briefing is not a type of weather briefing. **Answer (C) is incorrect.** A prognostic briefing is not a type of weather briefing.

5. To update a previous weather briefing, a pilot should request

A. an abbreviated briefing.
B. a standard briefing.
C. an outlook briefing.

Answer (A) is correct. (AC 00-45H Chap 1)
DISCUSSION: An abbreviated briefing will be provided when the user requests information (1) to supplement mass disseminated data, (2) to update a previous briefing, or (3) to be limited to specific information.
Answer (B) is incorrect. A standard briefing is a complete preflight briefing to include all (not update) information pertinent to a safe flight. **Answer (C) is incorrect.** An outlook briefing is for a flight at least 6 hr. in the future.

6. (Refer to Figure 12 below.) Which of the reporting stations have VFR weather?

A. All.
B. KINK, KBOI, and KJFK.
C. KINK, KBOI, and KLAX.

Answer (C) is correct. (AC 00-45H Chap 3)
 DISCUSSION: KINK is reporting visibility of 15 SM and sky clear (15SM SKC); KBOI is reporting visibility of 30 SM and a scattered cloud layer base at 15,000 ft. (30SM SCT150); and KLAX is reporting visibility of 6SM in mist (foggy conditions > 5/8 SM visibility) with a scattered cloud layer at 700 ft. and another one at 25,000 ft. (6SM BR SCT007 SCT250). All of these conditions are above VFR weather minimums of 1,000-ft. ceiling and/or 3-SM visibility.
 Answer (A) is incorrect. KMDW is reporting a visibility of 1 1/2 SM in rain and a ceiling of 700 ft. overcast (1 1/2SM RA OVC007), and KJFK is reporting a visibility of 1/2SM in fog and a ceiling of 500 ft. overcast (1/2SM FG OVC005). Both of these are below VFR weather minimums of 1,000-ft. ceiling and/or 3-SM visibility. *Answer (B) is incorrect.* KJFK is reporting a visibility of 1/2 SM in fog and a ceiling of 500 ft. overcast (1/2SM FG OVC005), which is below the VFR weather minimums of 1,000-ft. ceiling and/or 3-SM visibility.

```
METAR KINK 121845Z 11012G18KT 15SM SKC 25/17 A3000

METAR KBOI 121854Z 13004KT 30SM SCT150 17/6 A3015

METAR KLAX 121852Z 25004KT 6SM BR SCT007 SCT250 16/15 A2991

SPECI KMDW 121856Z 32005KT 1 1/2SM RA OVC007 17/16 A2980 RMK RAB35

SPECI KJFK 121853Z 18004KT 1/2SM FG R04/2200 OVC005 20/18 A3006
```

Figure 12. Aviation Routine Weather Reports (METAR).

7. (Refer to Figure 12 above.) What are the wind conditions at Wink, Texas (KINK)?

A. Calm.
B. 110° at 12 knots, gusts 18 knots.
C. 111° at 2 knots, gusts 18 knots.

Answer (B) is correct. (AC 00-45H Chap 3)
 DISCUSSION: The wind group at KINK is coded as 11012G18KT. The first three digits are the direction the wind is blowing from referenced to true north. The next two digits are the wind speed in knots. If the wind is gusty, it is reported as a "G" after the speed followed by the highest (or peak) gust reported. Thus, the wind conditions at KINK are 110° true at 12 kt., peak gust at 18 kt.
 Answer (A) is incorrect. A calm wind would be reported as 00000KT, not 11012G18KT. *Answer (C) is incorrect.* The wind conditions at KINK are 110°, not 111°, at 12 kt., not 2 kt.

8. (Refer to Figure 12 above.) The remarks section for KMDW has RAB35 listed. This entry means

A. blowing mist has reduced the visibility to 1-1/2 SM.
B. rain began at 1835Z.
C. the barometer has risen .35" Hg.

Answer (B) is correct. (AC 00-45H Chap 3)
 DISCUSSION: In the remarks (RMK) section for KMDW, RAB35 means that rain began at 35 min. past the hour. Because the report was taken at 1856Z, rain began at 35 min. past the hour, or 1835Z.
 Answer (A) is incorrect. RAB35 means that rain began at 35 min. past the hour, not that blowing mist has reduced the visibility to 1 1/2 SM. *Answer (C) is incorrect.* RAB35 means that rain began at 35 min. past the hour, not that the barometer has risen .35 in. Hg.

9. (Refer to Figure 12 above.) The wind direction and velocity at KJFK is from

A. 180° true at 4 knots.
B. 180° magnetic at 4 knots.
C. 040° true at 18 knots.

Answer (A) is correct. (AC 00-45H Chap 3)
 DISCUSSION: The wind group at KJFK is coded as 18004KT. The first three digits are the direction the wind is blowing from referenced to true north. The next two digits are the speed in knots. Thus, the wind direction and speed at KJFK are 180° true at 4 kt.
 Answer (B) is incorrect. Wind direction is referenced to true, not magnetic, north. *Answer (C) is incorrect.* The wind direction is 180° true at 4 kt., not 040° true at 18 kt.

SU 3: Aviation Weather Services

10. (Refer to Figure 12 on page 134.) What are the current conditions for Chicago Midway Airport (KMDW)?

A. Sky 700 feet overcast, visibility 1-1/2SM, rain.
B. Sky 7000 feet overcast, visibility 1-1/2SM, heavy rain.
C. Sky 700 feet overcast, visibility 11, occasionally 2SM, with rain.

Answer (A) is correct. (AC 00-45H Chap 3)
 DISCUSSION: At KMDW, a special METAR (SPECI) taken at 1856Z reported wind 320° at 5 kt., visibility 1 1/2 SM in moderate rain, overcast clouds at 700 ft., temperature 17°C, dew point 16°C, altimeter 29.80" Hg, remarks follow, and rain began at 35 min. past the hour.
 Answer (B) is incorrect. The intensity of the rain is moderate, not heavy. Heavy rain would be coded +RA.
 Answer (C) is incorrect. Visibility is 1 1/2 SM, not 11 SM with an occasional 2 SM.

11. For aviation purposes, ceiling is defined as the height above the Earth's surface of the

A. lowest reported obscuration and the highest layer of clouds reported as overcast.
B. lowest broken or overcast layer or vertical visibility into an obscuration.
C. lowest layer of clouds reported as scattered, broken, or thin.

Answer (B) is correct. (AC 00-45H Chap 3)
 DISCUSSION: A ceiling layer is not designated in the METAR code. For aviation purposes, the ceiling is the lowest broken or overcast layer, or vertical visibility into an obscuration.
 Answer (A) is incorrect. A ceiling is the lowest, not highest, broken or overcast layer, or the vertical visibility into an obscuration, not the lowest obscuration. **Answer (C) is incorrect.** A ceiling is the lowest broken or overcast, not scattered, layer. Also, there is no provision for reporting thin layers in the METAR code.

12. When requesting weather information for the following morning, a pilot should request

A. an outlook briefing.
B. a standard briefing.
C. an abbreviated briefing.

Answer (A) is correct. (AC 00-45H Chap 1)
 DISCUSSION: An outlook briefing should be requested when the briefing is 6 or more hours in advance of the proposed departure.
 Answer (B) is incorrect. A standard briefing should be requested if the proposed departure time is less than 6 hr. in the future and if you have not received a previous briefing or have received information through mass dissemination media. **Answer (C) is incorrect.** An abbreviated briefing is provided as a supplement to mass disseminated data, to update a previous briefing, or to obtain specific information.

13. Radar weather reports are of special interest to pilots because they indicate

A. large areas of low ceilings and fog.
B. location of precipitation along with type, intensity, and cell movement of precipitation.
C. location of precipitation along with type, intensity, and trend.

Answer (B) is correct. (AC 00-45H Chap 3)
 DISCUSSION: Radar weather reports are of special interest to pilots because they report the location of precipitation along with type, intensity, and cell movement.
 Answer (A) is incorrect. Weather radar cannot detect clouds or fog, only precipitation size particles. **Answer (C) is incorrect.** Radar weather reports no longer include trend information.

14. (Refer to Figure 15 on page 137.) In the TAF for KMEM, what does "SHRA" stand for?

A. Rain showers.
B. A shift in wind direction is expected.
C. A significant change in precipitation is possible.

Answer (A) is correct. (AC 00-45H Chap 5)
DISCUSSION: SHRA is a coded group of forecast weather. SH is a descriptor that means showers. RA is a type of precipitation that means rain. Thus, SHRA means rain showers.
Answer (B) is incorrect. SHRA means rain showers, not that a shift in wind direction is expected. A change in wind direction would be reflected by a forecast wind. **Answer (C) is incorrect.** SHRA means rain showers, not that a significant change in precipitation is possible.

15. (Refer to Figure 15 on page 137.) During the time period from 0600Z to 0800Z, what visibility is forecast for KOKC?

A. Greater than 6 statute miles.
B. Possibly 6 statute miles.
C. Not forecasted.

Answer (A) is correct. (AC 00-45H Chap 5)
DISCUSSION: At KOKC, between 0600Z and 0800Z, conditions are forecast to become wind 210° at 15 kt., visibility greater than 6 SM (P6SM), scattered clouds at 4,000 ft. with conditions continuing until the end of the forecast (1200Z).
Answer (B) is incorrect. Between 0600Z and 0800Z, the visibility is forecast to be greater than, not possibly, 6 statute miles. **Answer (C) is incorrect.** Between 0600Z and 0800Z, the visibility is forecast to be greater than 6 statute miles (P6SM).

16. (Refer to Figure 15 on page 137.) In the TAF from KOKC, the clear sky becomes

A. overcast at 2,000 feet during the forecast period between 2200Z and 2400Z.
B. overcast at 200 feet with a 40 percent probability of becoming overcast at 600 feet during the forecast period between 2200Z and 2400Z.
C. overcast at 200 feet with the probability of becoming overcast at 400 feet during the forecast period between 2200Z and 2400Z.

Answer (A) is correct. (AC 00-45H Chap 5)
DISCUSSION: In the TAF for KOKC, from 2200Z to 2400Z, the conditions are forecast to gradually become wind 200° at 13 kt. with gusts to 20 kt., visibility 4 SM in moderate rain showers, overcast clouds at 2,000 feet. Between the hours of 0000Z and 0600Z, a chance (40 percent) exists of visibility 2 SM in thunderstorm with moderate rain, and 800 ft. overcast, cumulus clouds.
Answer (B) is incorrect. Between 2200Z and 2400Z, the coded sky condition of OVC020 means overcast clouds at 2,000 ft., not 200 feet. **Answer (C) is incorrect.** Between 2200Z and 2400Z, the coded sky condition of OVC020 means overcast clouds at 2,000 ft., not 200 feet.

17. (Refer to Figure 15 on page 137.) What is the valid period for the TAF for KMEM?

A. 1200Z to 1800Z.
B. 1200Z to 1200Z.
C. 1800Z to 2400Z.

Answer (C) is correct. (AC 00-45H Chap 5)
DISCUSSION: The valid period of a TAF follows the four-letter location identifier and the six-digit issuance date/time. The valid period group is a two-digit date followed by the two-digit beginning hour and the two-digit ending hour. The valid period of the TAF for KMEM is 1218/1324, which means the forecast is valid from the 12th day at 1800Z until the 13th at 2400Z.
Answer (A) is incorrect. The valid period of the TAF for KOKC, not KMEM, is from 1200Z to 1800Z. **Answer (B) is incorrect.** The valid period of the TAF for KMEM is from the 12th day, not 1200Z, at 1800Z until the 13th at 2400Z, not 1200Z.

SU 3: Aviation Weather Services 137

18. (Refer to Figure 15 below.) Between 1000Z and 1200Z the visibility at KMEM is forecast to be?

    A. 1/2 statute mile.
    B. 3 statute miles.
    C. 6 statute miles.

Answer (B) is correct. (AC 00-45H Chap 5)
    DISCUSSION: Between 1000Z and 1200Z, the conditions at KMEM are forecast to gradually become wind calm, visibility 3 SM in mist, sky clear with temporary (occasional) visibility 1/2 SM in fog between 1200Z and 1400Z. Conditions are expected to continue until 1600Z.
    Answer (A) is incorrect. Between the hours of 1200Z and 1400Z, not between 1000Z and 1200Z, the forecast is for temporary (occasional) visibility of 1/2 SM in fog. **Answer (C) is incorrect.** Between 1000Z and 1200Z, the forecast visibility for KMEM is 3 SM, not 6 SM.

19. (Refer to Figure 15 below.) In the TAF from KOKC, the "FM (FROM) Group" is forecast for the hours from 1600Z to 2200Z with the wind from

    A. 160° at 10 knots.
    B. 180° at 10 knots.
    C. 180° at 10 knots, becoming 200° at 13 knots.

Answer (B) is correct. (AC 00-45H Chap 5)
    DISCUSSION: The FM group states that, from 1600Z until 2200Z (time of next change group), the forecast wind is 180° at 10 knots.
    Answer (A) is incorrect. The forecast wind is 180°, not 160°, at 10 knots. **Answer (C) is incorrect.** The BECMG (becoming) group is a change group and is not part of the FM forecast group. The wind will gradually become 200° at 13 kt. with gusts to 20 kt., between 2200Z and 2400Z.

20. (Refer to Figure 15 below.) The only cloud type forecast in TAF reports is

    A. nimbostratus.
    B. cumulonimbus.
    C. scattered cumulus.

Answer (B) is correct. (AC 00-45H Chap 5)
    DISCUSSION: Cumulonimbus clouds are the only cloud type forecast in TAFs. If cumulonimbus clouds are expected at the airport, the contraction CB is appended to the cloud layer that represents the base of the cumulonimbus cloud(s).
    Answer (A) is incorrect. The only cloud type forecast in TAFs is cumulonimbus, not nimbostratus, clouds. **Answer (C) is incorrect.** The only cloud type forecast in TAFs is cumulonimbus, not scattered cumulus, clouds.

```
TAF

KMEM  121720Z 1218/1324 20012KT 5SM HZ BKN030 PROB40 1220/1222 1SM TSRA OVC008CB
      FM122200 33015G20KT P6SM BKN015 OVC025 PROB40 1220/1222 3SM SHRA
      FM120200 35012KT OVC008 PROB40 1202/1205 2SM-RASN BECMG 1306/1308 02008KT BKN012
      BECMG 1310/1312 00000KT 3SM BR SKC TEMPO 1212/1214 1/2SM FG
      FM131600 VRB06KT P6SM SKC=

KOKC  051130Z 0512/0618 14008KT 5SM BR BKN030 TEMPO 0513/0516 1 1/2SM BR
      FM051600 18010KT P6SM SKC BECMG 0522/0524 20013G20KT 4SM SHRA OVC020
      PROB40 0600/0606 2SM TSRA OVC008CB BECMG 0606/0608 21015KT P6SM SCT040=
```

Figure 15. Terminal Aerodrome Forecasts (TAF).

21. (Refer to Figure 19 on page 139.) Interpret the weather symbol depicted in Utah on the 12-hour Significant Weather Prognostic Chart.

A. Moderate turbulence, surface to 18,000 feet.
B. Thunderstorm tops at 18,000 feet.
C. Base of clear air turbulence, 18,000 feet.

Answer (A) is correct. (AC 00-45H Chap 5)
    DISCUSSION: Refer to the upper panel of the Significant Weather Prognostic Chart in Fig. 19. In Utah, the weather symbol indicates moderate turbulence as designated by the symbol of a small peaked hat. Note that the broken line indicates moderate or greater turbulence. The peaked hat is the symbol for moderate turbulence. The 180 means the moderate turbulence extends from the surface upward to 18,000 feet.
    Answer (B) is incorrect. The peaked hat symbol denotes moderate turbulence, not thunderstorms. The symbol for thunderstorms is shown by what looks like the letter "R."
    Answer (C) is incorrect. This is not the base of the clear air turbulence. A line over a number indicates a base.

22. (Refer to Figure 19 on page 139.) You are planning a flight in southern Georgia at 1300Z. What condition should you expect?

A. Ceiling 1,000 to 3,000 ft. and/or visibility 3 to 5 mi. with moderate turbulence.
B. Ceiling 1,000 to 3,000 ft. and/or visibility 3 to 5 mi. and temperatures below freezing.
C. Ceiling less than 1,000 ft. and/or visibility less than 3 mi. and temperatures above freezing.

Answer (C) is correct. (AC 00-45H Chap 5)
    DISCUSSION: Refer to the bottom panel of the significant weather prognostic chart in Fig. 19 because the flight occurs during the forecast period following 06Z. The weather in southern Georgia is forecast to have ceilings less than 1,000 ft. and/or visibility less than 3 mi. (as indicated by the solid red line) and temperatures above freezing (as indicated by the dashed green line).
    Answer (A) is incorrect. The ceiling is forecast to be less than 1,000 ft. and/or visibility less than 3 mi. at the time of the flight (refer to the bottom panel). Turbulence is not forecast in the area. **Answer (B) is incorrect.** The ceiling is forecast to be less than 1,000 ft. and/or visibility less than 3 mi. at the time of the flight (refer to the bottom panel). Temperatures are forecast to be above freezing (as indicated by the dashed green line).

SU 3: Aviation Weather Services 139

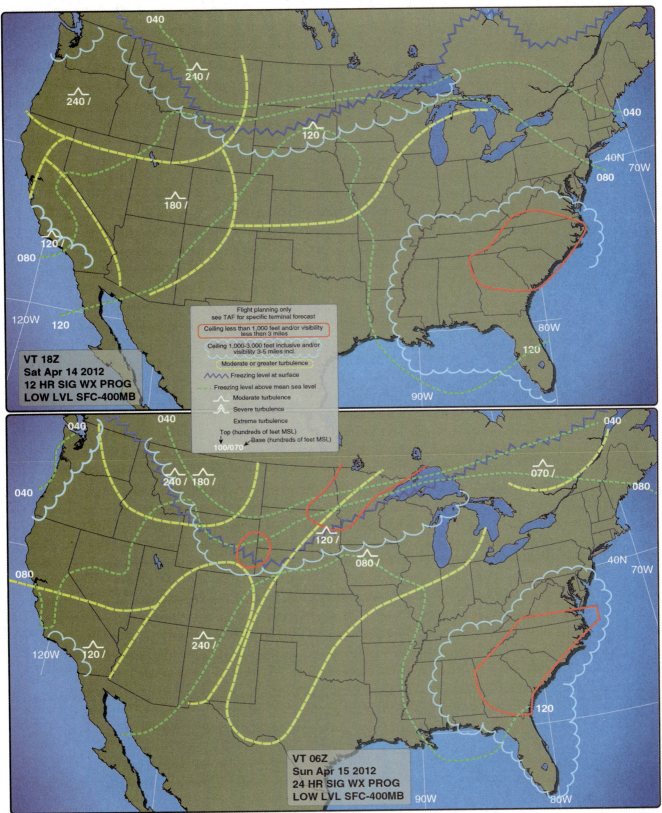

Figure 19. Low-Level Significant Weather (SIGWX) Prognostic Charts.

Notes

STUDY UNIT FOUR
WEATHER EFFECTS ON PERFORMANCE

(21 pages of outline)

4.1 Effects of Weather on Performance	(55 questions) 141, 162

4.1 EFFECTS OF WEATHER ON PERFORMANCE

1. **Understanding weather factors** and their effects on unmanned aircraft (UA) performance is essential even though UA operations are often conducted at very low altitudes. Weather factors can greatly influence performance and safety of flight.

    a. As with any flight, the remote pilot in command (rPIC) should check and consider the weather conditions prior to and during every operation. Factors that affect UA performance and risk management include

    1) Atmospheric pressure and stability
    2) Wind and currents
    3) Uneven surface heating
    4) Visibility and cloud clearance

    b. **Density altitude** is a measurement of the density of the air that accounts for variations in non-standard pressures and non-standard temperature in the atmosphere.

    1) As air density decreases, density altitude is said to increase.

        a) Density altitude is used in determining UA performance potential.

    2) Because of the inescapable influence density altitude has on an aircraft and performance, every pilot should understand its effects. Air density is affected by pressure, temperature, and humidity.

        a) The density of air is directly proportional to pressure. Since air is a gas, it can be compressed or expanded.

            i) When air is compressed (resulting in increased pressure), a greater amount of air occupies a given volume; thus, the density of air is increased.

            ii) When pressure is decreased on a given volume of air, the air expands and occupies a greater space; thus, the density of air is decreased.

        b) The density of air varies inversely with temperature. Thus, a given volume holds less air, and air density is decreased.

            i) As the temperature of the air increases, the air expands, occupying more volume.

            ii) As air temperature decreases, the air contracts and density is increased.

- c) Humidity is the amount of water vapor in the air and is not generally considered a major factor in density altitude computation because the effect of humidity is related more to combustion engine power than to aerodynamic efficiency.
    - i) Because water vapor weighs less than dry air, any given volume of moist air weighs less (i.e., is less dense) than an equal volume of dry air.
    - ii) Warm, moist air is less dense (i.e., has a higher density altitude) than cold, dry air.
    - iii) Humidity affects engine power because the water vapor uses airspace that is available for vaporized fuel.
    - iv) As humidity increases, less air enters the cylinders, causing a slight increase in density altitude.
- d) In the atmosphere, both temperature and pressure decrease with altitude and have conflicting effects on density. However, the fairly rapid drop in pressure as altitude is increased usually has a dominating effect over the decrease in temperature.
    - i) Thus, we can expect the air density to decrease with altitude.
- e) At higher elevation locations, such as those in the western U.S., high temperatures sometimes have such an effect on density altitude that safe operations may be impossible.
    - i) Even at lower elevations with excessively high temperature or humidity, aircraft performance can become marginal, and it may be necessary to reduce the airplane's weight for safe operations.

c. **Wind and currents** are generated in part by differences in temperature creating differences in pressure. These pressure differences contribute to the movement of air masses.
  1) The horizontal movement of air is called wind, and the vertical movement of air is called convection.
  2) A cooler surface area would create a high-pressure area, while a warmer surface area would create a low-pressure area. (Recall the effect of temperature on air pressure.)
  3) Whenever a pressure difference develops, a force is created that moves the air from the higher pressure to the lower pressure. This force is called the **pressure gradient force**.
     - a) The strength of the pressure gradient force is determined by the amount of pressure difference and the distance between the high- and low-pressure areas. (See the isobar image under item 1.d.8)a) on page 151.)
        - i) The pressure gradient force increases as the pressure difference increases and/or the distance between the two pressure areas decreases.

SU 4: Weather Effects on Performance

4) Since the Earth rotates, the air does not flow directly from high- to low-pressure areas. In the Northern Hemisphere, it is deflected to the right by what is called the **Coriolis force**.
   a) In the Northern Hemisphere, the wind blows clockwise around a high and counterclockwise around a low due to the Coriolis force.
   b) The strength of the Coriolis force is directly proportional to wind speed. The faster the wind, the stronger the Coriolis force.
5) At approximately 3,000 ft. AGL and below, friction between the wind and the Earth's surface slows the wind. This reduces the Coriolis force but does not affect the pressure gradient force.
6) Since friction does not affect upper-level winds, the pressure gradient force and the Coriolis force are equal, which causes the wind to flow around, but not into, the low-pressure area.
   a) Near the surface, friction slows the wind speed, reducing the Coriolis force but not the pressure gradient force. Thus, the wind flows into the low-pressure area.
      i) Surface winds are slower and from a different direction than upper-level winds.
7) At the surface when air converges into a low, it cannot go outward against the pressure gradient nor can it go downward into the ground. It must go upward. Therefore, a low or a trough is an area of rising air.
   a) Rising air is conducive to cloud development and precipitation. Thus, low-pressure areas are generally associated with bad weather.
   b) Conversely, air moving out from a high or a ridge depletes the quantity of air and is an area of descending air.
      i) Descending air tends to dissipate clouds, so highs are usually associated with good weather.
8) Wind and currents can affect UA performance and maneuverability during all phases of flight. Be vigilant when operating UA at low altitudes, in confined areas, near buildings or other structures, and near natural obstructions (such as mountains, bluffs, or canyons).
   a) Consider the following effects of wind on performance:
      i) Obstructions on the ground affect the flow of wind, may create rapidly changing wind gusts, and can be an unseen danger.
      ii) The intensity of the turbulence associated with ground obstructions depends on the size of the obstacle and the primary velocity of the wind.
      iii) Even when operating in an open field, wind blowing against surrounding trees can create significant low-level turbulence.

- b) High winds may make it difficult to maintain a geographical position in flight and may consume more battery power.
- c) Remember that local conditions, geological features, and other anomalies can change the wind direction and speed close to the Earth's surface.
    - i) For example, when operating close to a building, winds blowing against the building could cause strong updrafts that can result in ballooning or a loss of positive control. On the other hand, winds blowing over the building from the opposite side can cause significant downdrafts that can have a dramatic sinking effect on the unmanned aircraft.
- d) Different surfaces radiate heat in varying amounts. The resulting uneven heating of the air creates small areas of local circulation called convective currents.
    - i) Convective currents can cause bumpy, turbulent air that can dramatically affect the remote PIC's ability to control unmanned aircraft at lower altitudes.
    - ii) For example, plowed ground, rocks, sand, and barren land give off a large amount of heat and are likely to result in updrafts. Water, trees, and other areas of vegetation tend to absorb and retain heat and are likely to result in downdrafts.

9) **Types of wind** are primary, secondary, and local winds that greatly impact weather.
   - a) A **jet stream** is a narrow band of strong winds (50 kt. or more) moving generally from west to east at a level near the tropopause.
   - b) A **valley wind** occurs when colder, denser air in the surroundings settles downward and forces the warmer air near the ground up the mountain slope.
   - c) A **mountain wind** occurs at night when the air near the mountain slope is cooled by terrestrial radiation, becomes heavier than the surrounding air, and sinks along the slope.
   - d) A **katabatic wind** is a wind blowing down an incline, where the incline itself has been a factor in causing the wind. A mountain wind is a good example of a katabatic wind.

SU 4: *Weather Effects on Performance*   145

e) **Sea and land breezes** vary due to temperature changes between day and night. During the day, the land is warmer than the sea; at night, the wind reverses from the cool land to the warmer water.

　i) Daylight sea breezes are caused by cooler and denser air moving inland off the water. Once over the warmer land, the air heats up and rises. Currents push the air out over the water, where it cools and descends, starting the process over again.

　ii) At night, the wind reverses from the cool land to the warmer water called a land breeze.

　iii) These breezes occur only when the overall pressure gradient is weak.

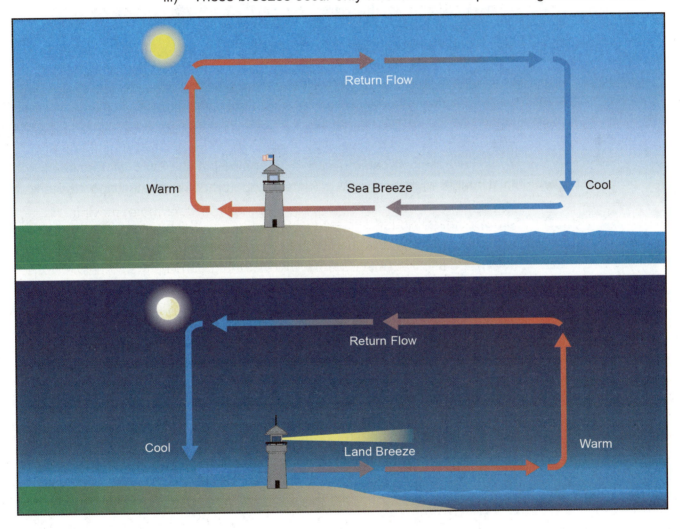

d. **Atmospheric stability, pressure, and temperature** are valuable indicators of upcoming weather and overall trend.
   1) Stability of air masses.
      a) Stable air characteristics
         i) Stratiform clouds
         ii) Smooth air
         iii) Fair-to-poor visibility in haze and smoke
         iv) Continuous precipitation
      b) Unstable air characteristics
         i) Cumuliform clouds
         ii) Turbulent air
         iii) Good visibility
         iv) Showery precipitation
      c) When air is warmed from below, it rises and causes instability.
      d) The lapse rate is the decrease in temperature with increase in altitude. As the lapse rate increases (i.e., air cools more with increases in altitude), air is more unstable.
         i) The lapse rate can be used to determine the stability of air masses.
      e) Moist, stable air moving up a mountain slope produces stratus type clouds as it cools.
      f) Turbulence and clouds with extensive vertical development result when unstable air rises.
      g) Steady precipitation preceding a front is usually an indication of a warm front, which results from warm air being cooled from the bottom by colder air.
         i) This results in stable air with stratiform clouds and little or no turbulence.
   2) Temperature inversions occur when temperature increases as altitude increases.
      a) Normally, temperature decreases as altitude increases.
      b) Temperature inversions usually result in a stable layer of air.
      c) A temperature inversion often develops near the ground on clear, cool nights when the wind is light.
         i) It is caused by terrestrial radiation.
      d) Smooth air with restricted visibility is usually found beneath a low-level temperature inversion.
   3) Two commonly used temperature scales are Celsius (C) and Fahrenheit (F).
      a) The Celsius scale is used in most aviation weather reports, forecasts, and charts.
      b) Two common temperature references are the melting point of pure ice and the boiling point of pure water at sea level.
         i) The boiling point of water is 100°C or 212°F.
         ii) The melting point of ice is 0°C or 32°F.
      c) Most flight computers provide for direct conversion of temperature from one scale to the other.

d) The simple formulas below demonstrate how to mathematically convert from one unit of measure to the other.

$$°C = \frac{5}{9}(F - 32) \quad \text{or} \quad °F = \frac{9}{5}C + 32$$

4) Heat is a form of energy. When a substance contains heat, it exhibits the property we measure as temperature, which is the degree of a substance's warmth or coldness.

   a) A specific amount of heat added to or removed from a substance will raise or lower its temperature a definite amount. Each substance has a unique temperature change per specific change in heat.

      i) EXAMPLE: If a land surface and a water surface have the same temperature and an equal amount of heat is added, the land surface becomes hotter than the water surface. Conversely, with equal heat loss, the land becomes colder than the water.

   b) Every physical process of weather either is accompanied by or is the result of heat exchanges.

5) Five main types of temperature variations affect weather:

   a) **Diurnal variation.** This change in temperature from day to night and night to day is brought about by the rotation of the Earth.

   b) **Seasonal variation.** Since the Earth's axis is tilted with respect to its orbit, the angle at which a particular spot or region receives solar radiation varies throughout the year. This phenomenon accounts for the temperature variations of the four seasons.

   c) **Variation with latitude.** The sun is nearly overhead in the equatorial regions. Since the Earth is spherical, the sun's rays reach the higher latitudes at an angle. For this reason, the equatorial regions receive the most radiant energy and are the warmest.

   d) **Variations with topography.** Since land heats and cools at a faster rate than water, air temperatures over land vary more widely than those over large bodies of water, which tend to have more minimal temperature changes. Wet soil, swamps, and thick vegetation also help to control temperature fluctuations.

   e) **Temperature variation with altitude.** The amount of temperature decrease with increases in altitude is defined as the **lapse rate**.

      i) Standard sea level temperature is 15°C. The average standard lapse rate in the troposphere is 2°C per 1,000 ft.

      ii) An increase in temperature with an increase in altitude is called an **inversion** because the lapse rate is inverted.

      iii) An inversion may occur when the ground cools faster than the air over it. Air in contact with the ground becomes cold, while only a few hundred feet higher, the temperature has changed very little. Thus, the temperature increases with altitude.

      iv) Inversions may occur at any altitude.

6) Atmospheric pressure is the force per unit area exerted by the weight of the atmosphere. It is measured per unit area, e.g., pounds per square inch (psi).

   a) The instrument designed for measuring atmospheric pressure is the barometer, with the aneroid barometer being the most common.

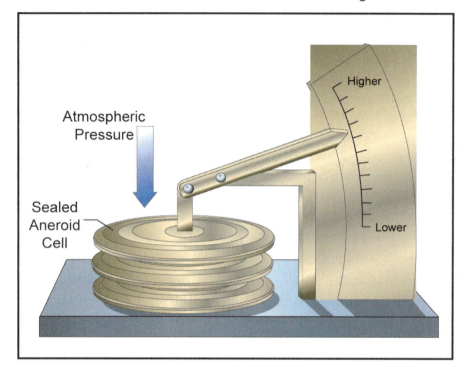

   i) The aneroid barometer consists of a partially evacuated flexible metal cell connected to a registering mechanism. As the atmospheric pressure changes, the metal cell expands or contracts, which drives a needle along a scale calibrated in pressure units.

   b) The commonly used pressure units are inches of mercury (in. Hg.), millibars (mb), and hectoPascal (hPa).

   i) Inches of mercury notation is used in automated weather report broadcasts, and millibar notation is commonly used (interchangeably with hectoPascal notation) on weather charts.

   c) The pressure measured at a station is called the **station pressure**.

   d) Standard atmospheric pressure at sea level is 29.92 in. Hg.

7) **Pressure variation** is due to changes in altitude and temperature of the air. Other factors also affect pressure, but their effects are negligible.

   a) **Altitude.** At higher altitudes, the weight of the air above decreases.

      i) This decrease in pressure from air above results in a lower atmospheric pressure. The amount of air remains constant as altitude increases, but the pressure exerted on it is less.

      ii) A volume of air at 18,000 ft. above the surface weighs only half of the same volume at sea level.

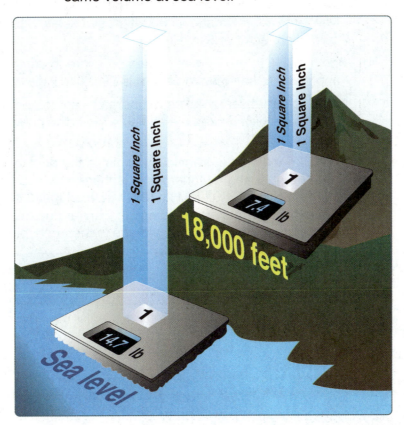

      iii) Within the lower few thousand feet of the troposphere (i.e., near the Earth's surface), pressure decreases at a rate of roughly 1 in. Hg per 1,000 ft. of altitude. As one goes higher, this rate of decrease slows.

   b) The **temperature** of air is constantly in a state of flux. Like most substances, air expands as it becomes warmer and shrinks as it cools.

      i) When air is warm and expands, pressure decreases because the same amount of air exists in a larger area.

      ii) When air is cooled, it contracts. The pressure is greater than that of the warm air because the same amount of air takes up a smaller area.

c) **Sea-level pressure** is the atmospheric pressure at sea level at a given location. Since pressure varies with altitude, you cannot accurately compare pressures between airports or weather stations at different altitudes unless you adjust those pressures to a common reference point. The standardized measurement used in aviation is mean sea level (MSL). An example follows:

   i) Denver, CO, is approximately 5,000 ft. above sea level. If the station pressure in Denver is 24.92 in. Hg, you can determine the sea level pressure with a simple calculation.

   ii) The standard pressure lapse rate is 1 in. Hg per 1,000 ft. of altitude. Denver is approximately 5,000 ft. above sea level, which equates to a correction factor of 5 in. Hg.

   iii) Add 5 in. Hg to the Denver station pressure to determine the approximate sea-level pressure is 29.92 in. Hg.

   iv) The weather observer takes temperature and other factors into account, but this simplified example explains the basic principle of sea-level pressure.

   v) The following image graphically explains the pressure variation changes by showing that a "standard atmosphere" day in Denver occurs when the pressure is 24.92 in. Hg. (Bear in mind that the temperature would be 5°C on a standard day in Denver due to a corresponding temperature lapse rate with altitude in the troposphere.)

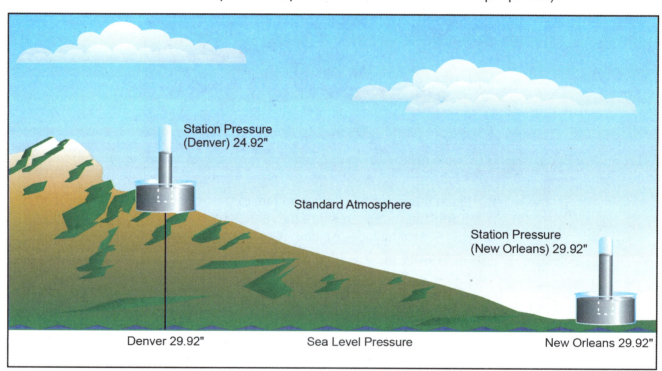

8) **Pressure** areas on various weather charts are depicted by lines that connect points of equal pressure. These lines are called **isobars**.

   a) Weather charts depicting isobars allow you to see identifiable, organized pressure patterns.

   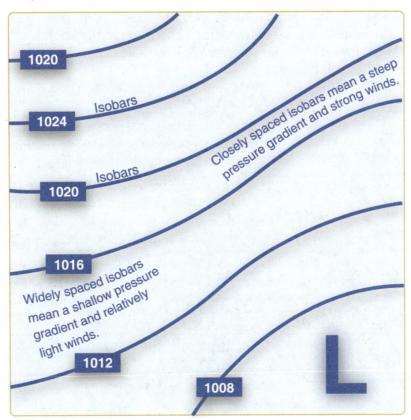

   b) The pressure systems shown on these charts are defined as follows:

   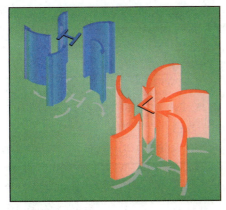

   i) **Low** -- an area of pressure surrounded on all sides by higher pressure, also called a cyclone. In the Northern Hemisphere, a cyclone, or low pressure system, is a mass of air that rotates counterclockwise when viewed from above.

   ii) **High** -- a center of pressure surrounded on all sides by lower pressure, also called an anticyclone. In the Northern Hemisphere, an anticyclone, or high-pressure system, is a mass of air that rotates clockwise when viewed from above.

   iii) **Trough** -- an elongated area of low pressure, with the lowest pressure along a line marking maximum cyclonic curvature.

   iv) **Ridge** -- an elongated area of high pressure, with the highest pressure along a line marking maximum anticyclonic curvature.

   v) **Col** -- the neutral area between two highs or two lows. It also is the intersection of a trough and a ridge. The col on a pressure surface is analogous to a mountain pass on a topographic surface.

e. **Air Masses and Fronts**

1) **Air masses** come to rest or move slowly over an extensive area having uniform properties of temperature and moisture, causing the body of air to take on the same properties.

   a) The area over which the air mass acquires its properties of temperature and moisture is its **source region**. There are many source regions, the best examples being large polar regions, cold northern and warm tropical oceans, and large desert areas.

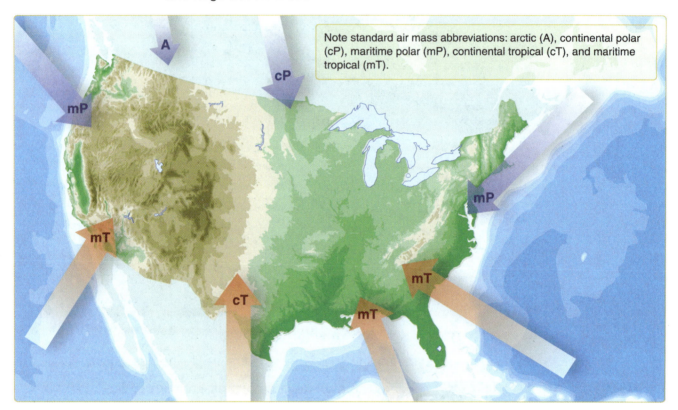

Note standard air mass abbreviations: arctic (A), continental polar (cP), maritime polar (mP), continental tropical (cT), and maritime tropical (mT).

   b) An air mass tends to take on properties of the underlying surface when it moves away from its source region, thus becoming modified. Some ways in which air masses are modified include the following:

   i) Cool air moving over a warm surface is heated from below, generating instability and increasing the possibility of showers.

   ii) Warm air moving over a cool surface is cooled from below, increasing stability. If air is cooled to its dew point, stratus clouds and/or fog forms.

   iii) Evaporation from water surfaces and falling precipitation adds water vapor to the air. When the water is warmer than the air, evaporation can raise the dew point sufficiently to saturate the air and form stratus clouds or fog.

   iv) Water vapor is removed by condensation and precipitation.

2) **Fronts** describe the frontal zone between two different air masses. Across this zone, temperature, humidity, and wind often change rapidly over short distances.
    a) Discontinuities. When you pass through a frontal zone, these changes may be abrupt, indicating a narrow front. A more subtle change indicates a broad and diffused front.
        i) The most easily recognizable indication that you are passing through a front will be a temperature change.
        ii) Temperature-dew point spread usually differs across a front.
        iii) Wind always changes across a front. Direction, speed, or both will change.
        iv) Pressure may change abruptly as you move from one air mass to another. It is important to keep a current altimeter setting when in the vicinity of a front.
    b) Types of fronts. There are four principal types of fronts:
        i) Cold front -- the leading edge of an advancing cold air mass. At the surface, cold air overtakes and replaces warm air. Cold fronts tend to precede high-pressure systems.
        ii) Warm front -- the leading edge of an advancing mass of warm air. Since cold air is more dense, it hugs the ground. Warm air slides up and over the cold mass. This elongates the frontal zone making it more diffuse. Warm fronts generally move about half as fast as cold fronts under the same wind conditions. Warm fronts tend to precede low-pressure systems.
        iii) Stationary front -- occurs when neither air mass is replacing the other and there is little or no movement. Surface winds tend to blow parallel to the front.
        iv) Occluded front -- occurs when a fast-moving cold front catches up with a slow-moving warm front. The difference in temperature within each frontal system is a major factor in determining whether a cold or warm front occlusion (i.e., which will be dominant) occurs.
    c) Frontolysis and Frontogenesis
        i) As adjacent air masses converge and as temperature and pressure differences equalize, the front dissipates. This dissipation is called frontolysis.
        ii) When two air masses come together and form a front, the process is called frontogenesis.
    d) Weather occurring with a front depends on the
        i) Amount of moisture available
        ii) Degree of stability of the air that is forced upward
        iii) Slope of the front
        iv) Speed of the frontal movement
        v) Upper wind flow

f. **Moisture, cloud formation, and precipitation** occur in the atmosphere out of the gaseous phase.

1) Water vapor is invisible, like the other atmospheric gases, but its quantity in the air can still be measured. It is generally expressed as follows:

   a) Relative humidity is a ratio of how much actual water vapor is present to the amount that could be present. At 100% relative humidity, the air is saturated.

   b) Dew point is the temperature to which air must be cooled to become saturated by the water vapor that is already present in that air.

      i) Dew point is compared to air temperature to determine how close the air is to saturation. This difference is referred to as the temperature-dew point spread.

      ii) As the temperature and dew point converge, fog, clouds, or rain should be anticipated.

   c) The following image explains relative humidity and dew point:

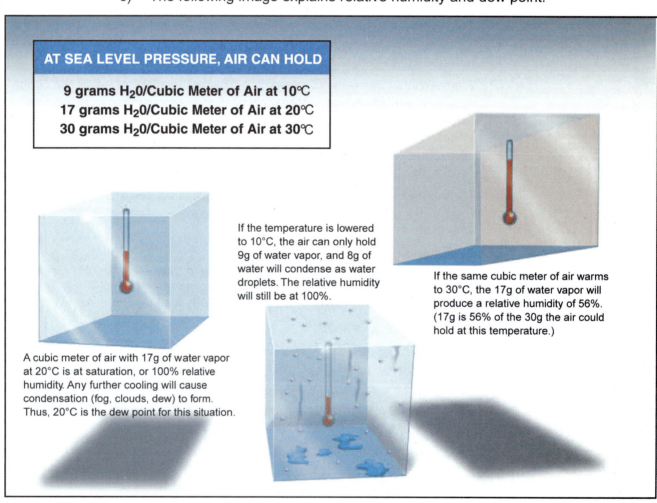

2) The phase changes of water are designated by the following terms:

   a) **Condensation** -- the change of water vapor to liquid water
   b) **Evaporation** -- the change of liquid water to water vapor
   c) **Freezing** -- the change of liquid water to ice
   d) **Melting** -- the change of ice to liquid water
   e) **Sublimation** -- the change of ice to water vapor
   f) **Deposition** -- the change of water vapor to ice

3) Supercooled water consists of water droplets existing at temperatures below freezing.
   a) Supercooled water is dangerous because it immediately forms into heavy, clear ice when it strikes an airplane's surface.
4) Dew forms when the Earth's surface cools to below the dew point of adjacent air as a result of heat radiation. Moisture forms (condenses) on leaves, grass, and exposed objects. This is the same process that causes a cold glass of water to "sweat" in warm, humid weather.
5) Frost forms in much the same way as dew. The difference is that the dew point of surrounding air must be colder than freezing. Water vapor changes directly to ice crystals or frost (deposition) rather than condensing as dew.
6) **Clouds** are a visible collection of minute water or ice particles suspended in air. A cloud may be composed entirely of liquid water, ice crystals, or a mixture of the two.
   a) Cloud formation. Normally, air must become saturated for condensation to occur. Saturation may result from cooling the temperature, increasing the dew point, or both. Cooling is far more predominant. There are three ways to cool air to saturation:
      i) Air moving over a colder surface
      ii) Stagnant air lying over a cooling surface
      iii) Expansional cooling in upward-moving air (the major cause of cloud formation)
   b) If the cloud is on the ground, it is fog.
   c) When entire layers of air cool to the point of saturation, fog or sheet-like stratus clouds result.
   d) Saturation of a localized updraft produces a towering cumulus cloud.
7) **Precipitation** is an all-inclusive term denoting drizzle, rain, snow, ice pellets, hail, and ice crystals. Precipitation occurs when any of these particles grow in size and weight until the atmosphere can no longer suspend them and they fall.
   a) Precipitation can change its state as the temperature of its environment changes.
   b) Falling snow may melt to form rain in warmer layers of air at lower altitudes.
   c) Rain falling through colder air may become supercooled, freezing on impact as freezing rain.
      i) Freezing rain always indicates warmer air at higher altitudes.
      ii) It may freeze during its descent, falling as ice pellets.
      iii) Ice pellets always indicate freezing rain at higher altitudes.
   d) Hailstones form when water droplets are lifted above the freezing level by updrafts of a thunderstorm, where they freeze solid. They may be circulated up and down within the storm, increasing in size and weight until they become too heavy to remain aloft and fall to the surface or are ejected through the anvil.
      i) Hail may be encountered up to 20 miles from a strong thunderstorm cell.
   e) To produce significant precipitation, clouds must be at least 4,000 ft. thick.

g. **Thunderstorms and microbursts** are weather conditions an unmanned aircraft operator should consider hazardous.

1) For a thunderstorm to form, the air must have

   a) Sufficient water vapor
   b) An unstable lapse rate
   c) An initial upward boost (lifting) to start the storm process in motion

      i) Surface heating, converging winds, sloping terrain, a frontal surface, or any combination of these can provide the necessary lifting.

2) A thunderstorm cell progresses through three stages during its life cycle:

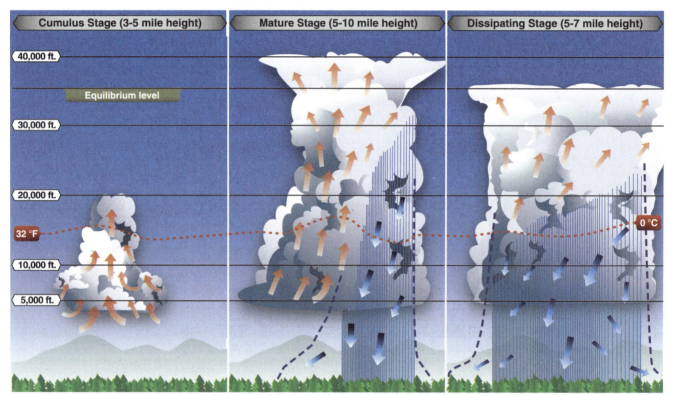

   a) The **cumulus stage**. Although most cumulus clouds do not grow into thunderstorms, every thunderstorm begins as a cumulus. The key feature in the cumulus stage is the updraft.

      i) Early during the cumulus stage, water droplets are quite small but grow to raindrop size as the cloud grows.
      ii) As the raindrops grow still heavier, they fall. This cold rain drags air with it, creating a cold downdraft coexisting with the updraft.

   b) The **mature stage**. Precipitation beginning to fall from the cloud base is the sign that a downdraft has developed and a cell has entered the mature stage.

      i) Cold rain in the downdraft retards compressional (adiabatic) heating, and the downdraft remains cooler than the surrounding air. Thus, its downward speed is accelerated.

SU 4: Weather Effects on Performance   157

   ii) The downrushing air spreads outward at the surface, producing strong gusty surface winds, a sharp temperature drop, and a rapid rise in pressure.

   iii) Updrafts and downdrafts in close proximity create strong vertical shear and a very turbulent environment.

   iv) All thunderstorm hazards reach their greatest intensity during the mature stage. Hazards include tornadoes, turbulence, icing, hail, lightning, low visibility and ceiling, and effects on an airplane's altimeter.

  c) The **dissipating stage**. Downdrafts characterize the dissipating stage of the thunderstorm cell, and the storm dies.

 3) **Thunderstorms** can be single-cell, multi-cell, squall line, or supercell.

  a) Air mass thunderstorms most often result from surface heating and last only about 20 to 90 min.

  b) Steady state thunderstorms are usually associated with weather systems.

   i) Fronts, converging winds, and troughs aloft force air upwards to initiate the storms.

   ii) They may last for several hours.

 4) A **squall line** is a nonfrontal narrow band of steady state thunderstorms.

  a) Squall lines often form in front of cold fronts in moist unstable air, but they may also develop in unstable air far removed from any fronts.

  b) Squall lines generally produce the most severe thunderstorm conditions (e.g., heavy hail, destructive winds, tornadoes, etc.).

h. **Tornadoes** can emanate from the most violent thunderstorms drawing air into their cloud bases with great vigor. If the incoming air has any initial rotating motion, it often forms an extremely concentrated vortex from the surface well into the cloud. Meteorologists have estimated that wind in such a vortex can exceed 200 knots with quite low pressure inside the vortex.

 1) The strong winds gather dust and debris and the low pressure generates a funnel-shaped cloud extending downward from the cumulonimbus base.

  a) If the cloud does not reach the surface, it is a funnel cloud.
  b) If the cloud touches a land surface, it is a tornado.
  c) If the cloud touches water, it is a waterspout.

 2) Tornadoes occur with both isolated and squall-line thunderstorms.

  a) Reports for forecasts of tornadoes indicate that atmospheric conditions are favorable for violent turbulence.

  b) An aircraft entering a tornado vortex is almost certain to suffer loss of control and structural damage.

  c) Since the vortex extends well into the cloud, any aircraft inadvertently caught in a severe thunderstorm could encounter a hidden vortex.

 3) Families of tornadoes have been observed as appendages of the main cloud extending several miles outward from the area of lightning and precipitation. Thus, any cloud connected to a severe thunderstorm carries a threat of violence.

i. **Icing** is a cumulative hazard to aircraft. When ice builds up on the surface of an aircraft, it increases weight and drag while reducing lift and thrust. These factors tend to slow the aircraft and/or force it to descend. Icing can also seriously impair UA and rotor performance.

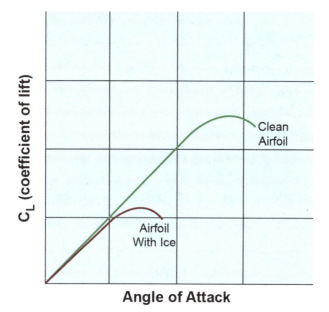
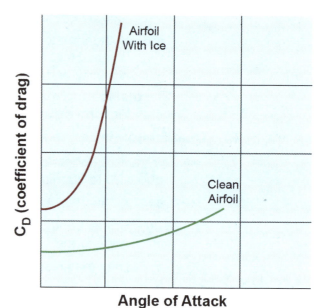

1) Structural icing will occur if two conditions are met:

   a) The UA is flying through visible moisture, such as rain or cloud droplets.
   b) The air temperature where the moisture strikes the aircraft is 0°C or cooler.

      i) Aerodynamic cooling can lower the temperature of an airfoil to 0°C even though ambient temperature is slightly higher.

2) Various types of ice can form on UA surfaces.

   a) **Clear ice** forms when water droplets that touch the airplane flow across the surface before freezing. Clear ice will accumulate as a smooth sheet. This type of ice forms when the water droplets are large, such as in rain or cumuliform clouds.

      i) Clear ice is very heavy and difficult to remove.
      ii) It can substantially increase the gross weight of an airplane.

SU 4: Weather Effects on Performance

      b) **Rime ice** forms when water droplets are small, such as those in stratiform clouds or light drizzle, and freeze on impact without spreading. Rime ice is rough and opaque, similar to frost in your home freezer.

          i) Its irregular shape and rough surface greatly decrease the aerodynamic efficiency of an airplane's wings, thus reducing lift and increasing drag.

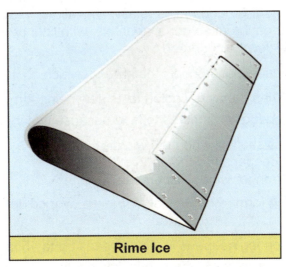

Rime Ice

      c) **Mixed ice** is a combination of clear and rime ice. It forms when water droplets vary in size. Some freeze on impact and some spread before freezing. Mixed ice is opaque and has a very rough surface.

   3) Frost, ice, and/or snow may accumulate on parked airplanes. All frost, ice, and/or snow should be removed before takeoff.

j. **Hail** competes with turbulence as the greatest thunderstorm hazard to aircraft. Supercooled drops above the freezing level begin to freeze.

   1) Once a drop has frozen, other drops latch on and freeze to it, so the hailstone grows—sometimes into a huge ice ball.

      a) Large hail occurs with severe thunderstorms with strong updrafts that have built to great heights. Eventually, the hailstones fall, possibly some distance from the storm core.

      b) Hail may be encountered in clear air several miles from thunderstorm clouds.

   2) As hailstones fall through air whose temperature is above 0°C, they begin to melt and precipitation may reach the ground as either hail or rain.

      a) Rain at the surface does not mean the absence of hail aloft.

      b) Possible hail should be anticipated with any thunderstorm, especially beneath the anvil of a large cumulonimbus.

          i) Hailstones larger than one-half inch in diameter can significantly damage larger aircraft in a few seconds.

          ii) Hailstones of any size should be considered a significant hazard to UA.

k. **Fog** is a surface-based cloud composed of either water droplets or ice crystals and is one of the most persistent weather hazards encountered in aviation. A small temperature-dew point spread is essential for fog to form, while abundant condensation nuclei, such as may be found in industrial areas, enhance the formation of fog.

1) Fog is classified by the way it forms.
2) **Radiation fog**, or ground fog, is relatively shallow. It forms almost exclusively at night or near daybreak under a clear sky, with little or no wind, and with a small temperature-dew point spread.
   a) Terrestrial radiation cools the ground, which cools the air in contact with it.
      i) When the air is cooled to its dew point, fog forms.
   b) Radiation fog is restricted to land because water cools little at night.
      i) It is shallow when the wind is calm.
      ii) It deepens in wind up to 5 kt.
      iii) Stronger winds disperse the fog.
3) **Advection fog** forms when moist air moves over colder ground or water. At sea, it is called sea fog.
   a) Advection fog deepens in wind speeds up to 15 kt.
   b) Wind much stronger than 15 kt. lifts the fog into a layer of low clouds.
   c) Advection fog is more persistent and extensive than radiation fog and can appear during day or night.
4) **Upslope fog** forms as a result of moist, stable air being cooled adiabatically as it moves up sloping terrain.
   a) Once the upslope wind ceases, the fog dissipates.
   b) Upslope fog is often quite dense and extends to high altitudes.
5) **Precipitation-induced fog** forms when relatively warm rain falls through cool air; evaporation from the precipitation saturates the cool air and forms fog.
   a) Precipitation-induced fog can become quite dense and continue for a long time.
   b) It is most commonly associated with warm fronts.
   c) It occurs near other possible hazards, such as icing, turbulence, and thunderstorms.
6) **Steam fog** forms in winter when cold, dry air passes from land areas over comparatively warm ocean waters.
   a) It is composed entirely of water droplets that often freeze quickly.
   b) Low-level turbulence and hazardous icing can occur.

7) When operating UA for imaging or survey purposes, be especially alert for development of fog in the following conditions:
   a) The following morning when at dusk temperature-dew point spread is 10°C (15°F) or less, skies are clear, and winds are light
   b) When moist air is flowing from a relatively warm surface to a colder surface
   c) When temperature-dew point spread is 3°C (5°F) or less and decreasing
   d) When a moderate or stronger moist wind is blowing over an extended upslope
      i) Temperature and dew point converge at about 2°C (4°F) for every 1,000 ft. the air is lifted.
   e) When air is blowing from a cold surface (either land or water) over warmer water
      i) This would produce steam fog.
   f) When rain or drizzle falls through cool air
      i) This is especially prevalent during winter ahead of a warm front and behind a stationary front or stagnating cold front.

l. **Ceiling and visibility** will be a concern for remote operation beyond line of sight.
   1) Cloud height above ground level is entered under the station circle in hundreds of feet, the same as coded in the METAR.
      a) If total sky cover is scattered, the cloud height entered is the base of the lowest layer.
      b) If total sky cover is broken or greater, the cloud height entered is the ceiling.
      c) A totally obscured sky is shown by the sky cover symbol "X."
         i) A totally obscured sky always has a height entry of the ceiling (vertical visibility into the obscuration).

m. **Lightning**
   1) NEVER operate the small unmanned aircraft system (sUAS) when lightning is in the area.
      a) NO PLACE outside is safe when thunderstorms are in the area!
      b) If you hear thunder, lightning is close enough to strike you.
      c) When you hear thunder, immediately move to safe shelter. A safe shelter is a substantial building with electricity or plumbing or an enclosed, metal-topped vehicle with windows up.
      d) Stay in a safe shelter at least 30 minutes after you hear the last sound of thunder.
   2) Lightning strikes the United States about 25 million times a year. Although most lightning occurs in the summer, people can be struck at any time of year.
      a) According to the National Weather Service, lightning kills an average of 49 people in the United States each year, and hundreds more are severely injured.
   3) Lightning strikes can interfere with communications on low and medium frequencies and sUAS equipment.

QUESTIONS

4.1 Effects of Weather on Performance

1. How would high density altitude affect the performance of a small unmanned aircraft?

A. Decreased performance.
B. No change in performance.
C. Increased performance.

Answer (A) is correct. (FAA-H-8083-25B Chap 11)
DISCUSSION: Takeoff and climb performance are reduced by high density altitude. High density altitude is a result of high temperatures and high relative humidity.
Answer (B) is incorrect. High density altitude decreases performance. **Answer (C) is incorrect.** High density altitude decreases performance.

2. You have received an outlook briefing from flight service through 1800wxbrief.com. The briefing indicates you can expect a low-level temperature inversion with high relative humidity. What weather conditions would you expect?

A. Smooth air, poor visibility, fog, haze, or low clouds.
B. Light wind shear, poor visibility, haze, and light rain.
C. Turbulent air, poor visibility, fog, low stratus type clouds, and showery precipitation.

Answer (A) is correct. (FAA-H-8083-25B Chap 12)
DISCUSSION: A low-level inversion is usually associated with stable air. Characteristics of a stable air mass include stratiform clouds, continuous precipitation, smooth air, and fair to poor visibility in haze and smoke.
Answer (B) is incorrect. Smooth air, not light wind shear is a characteristic of stable (not unstable) air. **Answer (C) is incorrect.** Smooth air and steady precipitation, not turbulence and showery precipitation, is a characteristic of stable (not unstable) air.

3. What effect does high density altitude have on the efficiency of a UA propeller?

A. Propeller efficiency is increased.
B. Propeller efficiency is decreased.
C. Density altitude does not affect propeller efficiency.

Answer (B) is correct. (FAA-H-8083-25B Chap 11)
DISCUSSION: The propeller produces thrust in proportion to the mass of air being accelerated through the rotating propeller. If the air is less dense, the propeller efficiency is decreased. A higher density altitude means less dense air.
Answer (A) is incorrect. Propeller efficiency is decreased, not increased. **Answer (C) is incorrect.** The propeller exerts less force on the air at higher density altitudes.

4. An air mass moving inland from the coast in winter is likely to result in

A. rain.
B. fog.
C. frost.

Answer (B) is correct. (FAA-H-8083-25B Chap 12)
DISCUSSION: Advection fog forms when moist air moves over colder ground or water. It is most common in coastal areas.
Answer (A) is incorrect. Fog (not rain) is most likely to result from an air mass moving inland from the coast in the winter. **Answer (C) is incorrect.** Frost additionally requires freezing temperatures.

5. What are the standard temperature and pressure values for sea level?

A. 15°C and 29.92" Hg.
B. 59°C and 1013.2 millibars.
C. 59°F and 29.92 millibars.

Answer (A) is correct. (FAA-H-8083-25B Chap 4)
DISCUSSION: The standard temperature and pressure values for sea level are 15°C and 29.92" Hg. This is equivalent to 59°F and 1013.2 millibars of mercury.
Answer (B) is incorrect. Standard temperature is 59°F (not 59°C). **Answer (C) is incorrect.** Standard pressure is 29.92" Hg (not 29.92 millibars).

6. What effect does high density altitude, as compared to low density altitude, have on propeller efficiency and why?

A. Efficiency is increased due to less friction on the propeller blades.
B. Efficiency is reduced because the propeller exerts less force at high density altitudes than at low density altitudes.
C. Efficiency is reduced due to the increased force of the propeller in the thinner air.

Answer (B) is correct. (AC 00-6B Chap 5)
DISCUSSION: The propeller produces thrust in proportion to the mass of air being accelerated through the rotating propeller. If the air is less dense, the propeller efficiency is decreased. Remember, higher density altitude refers to less dense air.
Answer (A) is incorrect. There is decreased, not increased, efficiency. **Answer (C) is incorrect.** The propeller exerts less (not more) force on the air when the air is thinner, i.e., at higher density altitudes.

SU 4: Weather Effects on Performance

7. What effect, if any, does high humidity have on aircraft performance?

A. It increases performance.
B. It decreases performance.
C. It has no effect on performance.

Answer (B) is correct. (FAA-H-8083-25B Chap 4)
DISCUSSION: As the air becomes more humid, it becomes less dense. This is because a given volume of moist air weighs less than the same volume of dry air. Less dense air reduces aircraft performance.
Answer (A) is incorrect. High humidity reduces (not increases) performance. **Answer (C) is incorrect.** The three factors that affect aircraft performance are pressure, temperature, and humidity.

8. Which factor would tend to increase the density altitude at a given airport?

A. An increase in barometric pressure.
B. An increase in ambient temperature.
C. A decrease in relative humidity.

Answer (B) is correct. (AC 00-6B Chap 5)
DISCUSSION: When air temperature increases, density altitude increases because, at a higher temperature, the air is less dense.
Answer (A) is incorrect. Density altitude decreases as barometric pressure increases. **Answer (C) is incorrect.** Density altitude decreases as relative humidity decreases.

9. Which combination of atmospheric conditions will reduce aircraft takeoff and climb performance?

A. Low temperature, low relative humidity, and low density altitude.
B. High temperature, low relative humidity, and low density altitude.
C. High temperature, high relative humidity, and high density altitude.

Answer (C) is correct. (FAA-H-8083-25B Chap 11)
DISCUSSION: Takeoff and climb performance are reduced by high density altitude. High density altitude is a result of high temperatures and high relative humidity.
Answer (A) is incorrect. Low temperature, low relative humidity, and low density altitude all improve airplane performance. **Answer (B) is incorrect.** Low relative humidity and low density altitude both improve airplane performance.

10. Every physical process of weather is accompanied by, or is the result of, a

A. movement of air.
B. pressure differential.
C. heat exchange.

Answer (C) is correct. (FAA-H-8083-25B Chap 12)
DISCUSSION: Every physical process of weather is accompanied by, or is the result of, a heat exchange. A heat differential (difference between the temperatures of two air masses) causes a differential in pressure, which in turn causes movement of air. Heat exchanges occur constantly, e.g., melting, cooling, updrafts, downdrafts, wind, etc.
Answer (A) is incorrect. Movement of air is a result of heat exchange. **Answer (B) is incorrect.** Pressure differential is a result of heat exchange.

11. What causes variations in altimeter settings between weather reporting points?

A. Unequal heating of the Earth's surface.
B. Variation of terrain elevation.
C. Coriolis force.

Answer (A) is correct. (FAA-H-8083-25B Chap 12)
DISCUSSION: Unequal heating of the Earth's surface causes differences in air pressure, which is reflected in differences in altimeter settings between weather reporting points.
Answer (B) is incorrect. Variations in altimeter settings between stations is a result of unequal heating of the Earth's surface, not variations of terrain elevations. **Answer (C) is incorrect.** Variations in altimeter settings between stations is a result of unequal heating of the Earth's surface, not the Coriolis force.

12. The wind at 5,000 feet AGL is southwesterly while the surface wind is southerly. This difference in direction is primarily due to

A. stronger pressure gradient at higher altitudes.
B. friction between the wind and the surface.
C. stronger Coriolis force at the surface.

Answer (B) is correct. (AC 00-6B Chap 7)
DISCUSSION: Winds aloft at 5,000 ft. are largely affected by the Coriolis force, which deflects wind to the right, in the Northern Hemisphere. But at the surface, the winds will be more southerly (they were southwesterly aloft) because the Coriolis force has less effect at the surface where the wind speed is slower. The wind speed is slower at the surface due to the friction between the wind and the surface.
Answer (A) is incorrect. Pressure gradient is a force that causes wind, not the reason for wind direction differences. **Answer (C) is incorrect.** The Coriolis force at the surface is weaker (not stronger) with slower wind speed.

13. The development of thermals depends upon

  A. a counterclockwise circulation of air.
  B. temperature inversions.
  C. solar heating.

Answer (C) is correct. (AC 00-6B Chap 4)
  DISCUSSION: Thermals are updrafts in small-scale convective currents. Convective currents are caused by uneven heating of the Earth's surface. Solar heating is the means of heating the Earth's surface.
  Answer (A) is incorrect. A counterclockwise circulation describes an area of low pressure in the Northern Hemisphere. **Answer (B) is incorrect.** A temperature inversion is an increase in temperature with height, which hinders the development of thermals.

14. Convective circulation patterns associated with sea breezes are caused by

  A. warm, dense air moving inland from over the water.
  B. water absorbing and radiating heat faster than the land.
  C. cool, dense air moving inland from over the water.

Answer (C) is correct. (AC 00-6B Chap 9)
  DISCUSSION: Sea breezes are caused by cool and more dense air moving inland off the water. Once over the warmer land, the air heats up and rises. Thus the cooler, more dense air from the sea forces the warmer air up. Currents push the hot air over the water where it cools and descends, starting the cycle over again. This process is caused by land heating faster than water.
  Answer (A) is incorrect. The air over the water is cooler (not warmer). **Answer (B) is incorrect.** Water absorbs and radiates heat slower (not faster) than land.

15. The boundary between two different air masses is referred to as a

  A. frontolysis.
  B. frontogenesis.
  C. front.

Answer (C) is correct. (AC 00-6B Chap 10)
  DISCUSSION: A front is a surface, interface, or transition zone of discontinuity between two adjacent air masses of different densities. It is the boundary between two different air masses.
  Answer (A) is incorrect. Frontolysis is the dissipation of a front. **Answer (B) is incorrect.** Frontogenesis is the initial formation of a front or frontal zone.

16. One weather phenomenon which will always occur when flying across a front is a change in the

  A. wind direction.
  B. type of precipitation.
  C. stability of the air mass.

Answer (A) is correct. (AC 00-6B Chap 10)
  DISCUSSION: The definition of a front is the zone of transition between two air masses of different air pressure or density, e.g., the area separating high and low pressure systems. Due to the difference in changes in pressure systems, there will be a change in wind.
  Answer (B) is incorrect. Frequently, precipitation will exist or not exist for both sides of the front: rain showers before and after or no precipitation before and after a dry front. **Answer (C) is incorrect.** Fronts separate air masses with different pressures, not stabilities; e.g., both air masses could be either stable or unstable.

17. One of the most easily recognized discontinuities across a front is

  A. a change in temperature.
  B. an increase in cloud coverage.
  C. an increase in relative humidity.

Answer (A) is correct. (AC 00-6B Chap 10)
  DISCUSSION: Of the many changes that take place across a front, the most easily recognized is the change in temperature. When flying through a front, you will notice a significant change in temperature, especially at low altitudes.
  Answer (B) is incorrect. Although cloud formations may indicate a frontal system, they may not be present or easily recognized across the front. **Answer (C) is incorrect.** Precipitation is not always associated with a front.

18. If there is thunderstorm activity in the vicinity of an airport at which you plan to land, which hazardous atmospheric phenomenon might be expected on the landing approach?

  A. Precipitation static.
  B. Wind-shear turbulence.
  C. Steady rain.

Answer (B) is correct. (AC 00-6B Chap 19)
  DISCUSSION: The most hazardous atmospheric phenomenon near thunderstorms is wind shear turbulence.
  Answer (A) is incorrect. Precipitation static is a steady, high level of noise in radio receivers, which is caused by intense corona discharges from sharp metallic points and edges of flying aircraft. This discharge may be seen at night and is also called St. Elmo's fire. **Answer (C) is incorrect.** Thunderstorms are usually associated with unstable air, which would produce rain showers (not steady rain).

SU 4: Weather Effects on Performance

19. A nonfrontal, narrow band of active thunderstorms that often develop ahead of a cold front is known as a

- A. prefrontal system.
- B. squall line.
- C. dry line.

Answer (B) is correct. (AC 00-6B Chap 19)
   DISCUSSION: A nonfrontal, narrow band of active thunderstorms that often develops ahead of a cold front is known as a squall line.
   Answer (A) is incorrect. A prefrontal system is a term that has no meaning. **Answer (C) is incorrect.** A dry line is a front that seldom has any significant air mass contrast except for moisture.

20. What conditions are necessary for the formation of thunderstorms?

- A. High humidity, lifting force, and unstable conditions.
- B. High humidity, high temperature, and cumulus clouds.
- C. Lifting force, moist air, and extensive cloud cover.

Answer (A) is correct. (AC 00-6B Chap 19)
   DISCUSSION: Thunderstorms form when there is sufficient water vapor, an unstable lapse rate, and an initial upward boost (lifting) to start the storm process.
   Answer (B) is incorrect. A high temperature is not required for the formation of thunderstorms. **Answer (C) is incorrect.** Extensive cloud cover is not necessary for the formation of thunderstorms.

21. During the life cycle of a thunderstorm, which stage is characterized predominately by downdrafts?

- A. Cumulus.
- B. Dissipating.
- C. Mature.

Answer (B) is correct. (AC 00-6B Chap 19)
   DISCUSSION: Thunderstorms have three life cycles: cumulus, mature, and dissipating. It is in the dissipating stage that the storm is characterized by downdrafts as the storm rains itself out.
   Answer (A) is incorrect. Cumulus is the building stage when there are updrafts. **Answer (C) is incorrect.** The mature stage is when there are both updrafts and downdrafts, which create dangerous wind shears.

22. Thunderstorms reach their greatest intensity during the

- A. mature stage.
- B. downdraft stage.
- C. cumulus stage.

Answer (A) is correct. (AC 00-6B Chap 19)
   DISCUSSION: Thunderstorms reach their greatest intensity during the mature stage, where updrafts and downdrafts cause a high level of wind shear.
   Answer (B) is incorrect. The downdraft stage is known as the dissipating stage, which is when the thunderstorm rains itself out. **Answer (C) is incorrect.** The cumulus stage is characterized by continuous updrafts and is not the most intense stage of a thunderstorm.

23. What feature is normally associated with the cumulus stage of a thunderstorm?

- A. Roll cloud.
- B. Continuous updraft.
- C. Frequent lightning.

Answer (B) is correct. (AC 00-6B Chap 19)
   DISCUSSION: The cumulus stage of a thunderstorm has continuous updrafts that build the storm. The water droplets are carried up until they become too heavy. Once they begin falling and creating downdrafts, the storm changes from the cumulus to the mature stage.
   Answer (A) is incorrect. The roll cloud is the cloud on the ground, which is formed by the downrushing cold air pushing out from underneath the bottom of the thunderstorm. **Answer (C) is incorrect.** Frequent lightning is associated with the mature stage, where there is a considerable amount of wind shear and static electricity.

24. Which weather phenomenon signals the beginning of the mature stage of a thunderstorm?

- A. The appearance of an anvil top.
- B. Precipitation beginning to fall.
- C. Maximum growth rate of the clouds.

Answer (B) is correct. (AC 00-6B Chap 19)
   DISCUSSION: The mature stage of a thunderstorm begins when rain begins falling. This means that the downdrafts are occurring sufficiently to carry water all the way through the thunderstorm.
   Answer (A) is incorrect. The appearance of an anvil top normally occurs during the dissipating stage when the upper winds blow the top of the cloud downwind. **Answer (C) is incorrect.** The maximum growth rate of clouds is later in the mature stage and does not necessarily mark the start of the mature stage.

166 SU 4: Weather Effects on Performance

25. Which weather phenomenon is always associated with a thunderstorm?

A. Lightning.
B. Heavy rain.
C. Hail.

Answer (A) is correct. (AC 00-6B Chap 19)
DISCUSSION: A thunderstorm, by definition, has lightning because lightning causes the thunder.
Answer (B) is incorrect. Although heavy rain showers usually occur, hail may occur instead. **Answer (C) is incorrect.** Hail is produced only when the lifting action extends above the freezing level and the supercooled water begins to freeze.

26. One in-flight condition necessary for structural icing to form is

A. small temperature/dewpoint spread.
B. stratiform clouds.
C. visible moisture.

Answer (C) is correct. (AC 00-6B Chap 18)
DISCUSSION: Two conditions are necessary for structural icing while in flight. First, the airplane must be flying through visible moisture, such as rain or cloud droplets. Second, the temperature at the point where the moisture strikes the airplane must be freezing or below.
Answer (A) is incorrect. The temperature dew point spread is not a factor in icing as it is in the formation of fog or clouds. **Answer (B) is incorrect.** No special cloud formation is necessary for icing as long as visible moisture is present.

27. In which environment is aircraft structural ice most likely to have the highest accumulation rate?

A. Cumulus clouds with below freezing temperatures.
B. Freezing drizzle.
C. Freezing rain.

Answer (C) is correct. (AC 00-6B Chap 18)
DISCUSSION: Freezing rain usually causes the highest accumulation rate of structural icing because of the nature of the supercooled water striking the airplane.
Answer (A) is incorrect. While icing potential is great in cumulus clouds with below freezing temperatures, the highest accumulation rate is in an area with large, supercooled water drops (i.e., freezing rain). **Answer (B) is incorrect.** Freezing drizzle will not build up ice as quickly as freezing rain.

28. The presence of ice pellets at the surface is evidence that there

A. are thunderstorms in the area.
B. has been cold frontal passage.
C. is a temperature inversion with freezing rain at a higher altitude.

Answer (C) is correct. (AC 00-6B Chap 14)
DISCUSSION: Rain falling through colder air may freeze during its descent, falling as ice pellets. Ice pellets always indicate freezing rain at a higher altitude.
Answer (A) is incorrect. Ice pellets form when rain freezes during its descent, which may or may not be as a result of a thunderstorm. **Answer (B) is incorrect.** Ice pellets only indicate that rain is freezing at a higher altitude, not that a cold front has passed through an area.

29. Where does wind shear occur?

A. Only at higher altitudes.
B. Only at lower altitudes.
C. At all altitudes, in all directions.

Answer (C) is correct. (AC 00-6B Chap 17)
DISCUSSION: Wind shear is the eddies in between two wind currents of differing velocities, direction, or both. Wind shear may be associated with either a wind shift or a wind speed gradient at any level in the atmosphere.
Answer (A) is incorrect. A wind shear may occur at any (not only higher) altitudes. **Answer (B) is incorrect.** A wind shear may occur at any (not only lower) altitudes.

30. When may hazardous wind shear be expected?

A. When stable air crosses a mountain barrier where it tends to flow in layers forming lenticular clouds.
B. In areas of low-level temperature inversion, frontal zones, and clear air turbulence.
C. Following frontal passage when stratocumulus clouds form indicating mechanical mixing.

Answer (B) is correct. (AC 00-6B Chap 17)
DISCUSSION: Wind shear is the abrupt rate of change of wind velocity (direction and/or speed) per unit of distance and is normally expressed as vertical or horizontal wind shear. Hazardous wind shear may be expected in areas of low-level temperature inversion, frontal zones, and clear air turbulence.
Answer (A) is incorrect. A mountain wave forms when stable air crosses a mountain barrier where it tends to flow in layers forming lenticular clouds. Turbulence, not wind shear, is expected in this area. **Answer (C) is incorrect.** Mechanical turbulence (not wind shear) may be expected following frontal passage when clouds form, indicating mechanical mixing.

SU 4: Weather Effects on Performance

31. If the temperature/dewpoint spread is small and decreasing, and the temperature is 62°F, what type weather is most likely to develop?

   A. Freezing precipitation.
   B. Thunderstorms.
   C. Fog or low clouds.

Answer (C) is correct. (AC 00-6B Chap 3)
DISCUSSION: The difference between the air temperature and dew point is the temperature/dew point spread. As the temperature/dew point spread decreases, fog or low clouds tend to develop.
Answer (A) is incorrect. There cannot be freezing precipitation if the temperature is 62°F. Answer (B) is incorrect. Thunderstorms have to do with unstable lapse rates, not temperature/dew point spreads.

32. What is meant by the term "dewpoint"?

   A. The temperature at which condensation and evaporation are equal.
   B. The temperature at which dew will always form.
   C. The temperature to which air must be cooled to become saturated.

Answer (C) is correct. (AC 00-6B Chap 3)
DISCUSSION: Dew point is the temperature to which air must be cooled to become saturated or have 100% humidity.
Answer (A) is incorrect. Evaporation is the change from water to water vapor and is not directly related to the dew point. Answer (B) is incorrect. Dew forms only when heat radiates from an object whose temperature lowers below the dew point of the adjacent air.

33. The amount of water vapor which air can hold depends on the

   A. dewpoint.
   B. air temperature.
   C. stability of the air.

Answer (B) is correct. (AC 00-6B Chap 3)
DISCUSSION: Air temperature largely determines how much water vapor can be held by the air. Warm air can hold more water vapor than cool air.
Answer (A) is incorrect. Dew point is the temperature at which air must be cooled to become saturated by the water vapor already present in the air. Answer (C) is incorrect. Air stability is the state of the atmosphere at which vertical distribution of temperature is such that air particles will resist displacement from their initial level.

34. What are the processes by which moisture is added to unsaturated air?

   A. Evaporation and sublimation.
   B. Heating and condensation.
   C. Supersaturation and evaporation.

Answer (A) is correct. (AC 00-6B Chap 3)
DISCUSSION: Evaporation is the process of converting a liquid to water vapor, and sublimation is the process of converting ice to water vapor.
Answer (B) is incorrect. Heating alone does not add moisture. Condensation is the change of water vapor to liquid water. Answer (C) is incorrect. Supersaturation is a nonsense term in this context.

35. Which conditions result in the formation of frost?

   A. The temperature of the collecting surface is at or below freezing when small droplets of moisture fall on the surface.
   B. The temperature of the collecting surface is at or below the dewpoint of the adjacent air and the dewpoint is below freezing.
   C. The temperature of the surrounding air is at or below freezing when small drops of moisture fall on the collecting surface.

Answer (B) is correct. (AC 00-6B Chap 3)
DISCUSSION: Frost forms when both the collecting surface is below the dew point of the adjacent air and the dew point is below freezing. Frost is the deposition of water vapor to ice crystals.
Answer (A) is incorrect. If small droplets of water fall on the collecting surface, which is at or below freezing, ice (not frost) will form. Answer (C) is incorrect. If small droplets of water fall while the surrounding air is at or below freezing, ice (not frost) will form.

36. Clouds, fog, or dew will always form when

   A. water vapor condenses.
   B. water vapor is present.
   C. relative humidity reaches 100 percent.

Answer (A) is correct. (AC 00-6B Chap 3)
DISCUSSION: As water vapor condenses, it becomes visible as clouds, fog, or dew.
Answer (B) is incorrect. Water vapor is usually always present but does not form clouds, fog, or dew without condensation. Answer (C) is incorrect. Even at 100% humidity, water vapor may not condense, e.g., sufficient condensation nuclei may not be present.

37. Low-level turbulence can occur and icing can become hazardous in which type of fog?

A. Rain-induced fog.
B. Upslope fog.
C. Steam fog.

Answer (C) is correct. (AC 00-6B Chap 16)
DISCUSSION: Steam fog forms in winter when cold, dry air passes from land areas over comparatively warm ocean waters and is composed entirely of water droplets that often freeze quickly. Low-level turbulence can occur, and icing can become hazardous.
Answer (A) is incorrect. Precipitation- (rain-) induced fog is formed when relatively warm rain or drizzle falls through cool air and evaporation from the precipitation saturates the cool air and forms fog. While the hazards of turbulence and icing may occur in the proximity of rain-induced fog, these hazards occur as a result of the steam fog formation process. **Answer (B) is incorrect.** Upslope fog forms when moist, stable air is cooled as it moves up sloping terrain.

38. In which situation is advection fog most likely to form?

A. A warm, moist air mass on the windward side of mountains.
B. An air mass moving inland from the coast in winter.
C. A light breeze blowing colder air out to sea.

Answer (B) is correct. (AC 00-6B Chap 16)
DISCUSSION: Advection fog forms when moist air moves over colder ground or water. It is most common in coastal areas.
Answer (A) is incorrect. A warm, moist air mass on the windward side of mountains produces rain or upslope fog as it blows upward and cools. **Answer (C) is incorrect.** A light breeze blowing colder air out to sea causes steam fog.

39. What situation is most conducive to the formation of radiation fog?

A. Warm, moist air over low, flatland areas on clear, calm nights.
B. Moist, tropical air moving over cold, offshore water.
C. The movement of cold air over much warmer water.

Answer (A) is correct. (AC 00-6B Chap 16)
DISCUSSION: Radiation fog is shallow fog of which ground fog is one form. It occurs under conditions of clear skies, little or no wind, and a small temperature/dew point spread. The fog forms almost exclusively at night or near dawn as a result of terrestrial radiation cooling the ground and the ground cooling the air on contact with it.
Answer (B) is incorrect. Moist, tropical air moving over cold, offshore water causes advection fog, not radiation fog. **Answer (C) is incorrect.** Movement of cold, dry air over much warmer water results in steam fog.

40. What types of fog depend upon wind in order to exist?

A. Radiation fog and ice fog.
B. Steam fog and ground fog.
C. Advection fog and upslope fog.

Answer (C) is correct. (AC 00-6B Chap 16)
DISCUSSION: Advection fog forms when moist air moves over colder ground or water. It is most common in coastal areas. Upslope fog forms when wind blows moist air upward over rising terrain and the air cools below its dew point. Both advection fog and upslope fog require wind to move air masses.
Answer (A) is incorrect. No wind is required for the formation of either radiation (ground) or ice fog. **Answer (B) is incorrect.** No wind is required for the formation of ground (radiation) fog.

41. The suffix "nimbus," used in naming clouds, means

A. a cloud with extensive vertical development.
B. a rain cloud.
C. a middle cloud containing ice pellets.

Answer (B) is correct. (AC 00-6B Chap 13)
DISCUSSION: The suffix "nimbus" or the prefix "nimbo" means a rain cloud.
Answer (A) is incorrect. Clouds with extensive vertical development are called either towering cumulus or cumulonimbus. **Answer (C) is incorrect.** A middle cloud has the prefix "alto."

42. The conditions necessary for the formation of cumulonimbus clouds are a lifting action and

A. unstable air containing an excess of condensation nuclei.
B. unstable, moist air.
C. either stable or unstable air.

Answer (B) is correct. (AC 00-6B Chap 19)
DISCUSSION: Unstable, moist air, in addition to a lifting action, i.e., convective activity, is needed to form cumulonimbus clouds.
Answer (A) is incorrect. There must be moisture available to produce the clouds and rain; e.g., in a hot, dry dust storm, there would be no thunderstorm. **Answer (C) is incorrect.** The air must be unstable or there will be no lifting action.

SU 4: Weather Effects on Performance

43. What clouds have the greatest turbulence?

A. Towering cumulus.
B. Cumulonimbus.
C. Nimbostratus.

Answer (B) is correct. (AC 00-6B Chap 13)
DISCUSSION: The greatest turbulence occurs in cumulonimbus clouds, which are thunderstorm clouds.
Answer (A) is incorrect. Towering cumulus clouds are an earlier stage of cumulonimbus clouds. **Answer (C) is incorrect.** Nimbostratus is a gray or dark, massive cloud layer diffused by continuous rain or ice pellets. It is a middle cloud with very little turbulence but may pose serious icing problems.

44. What cloud types would indicate convective turbulence?

A. Cirrus clouds.
B. Nimbostratus clouds.
C. Towering cumulus clouds.

Answer (C) is correct. (AC 00-6B Chap 13)
DISCUSSION: Towering cumulus clouds are an early stage of cumulonimbus clouds, or thunderstorms, that are based on convective turbulence, i.e., an unstable lapse rate.
Answer (A) is incorrect. Cirrus clouds are high, thin, featherlike ice crystal clouds in patches and narrow bands that are not based on any convective activity. **Answer (B) is incorrect.** Nimbostratus are gray or dark, massive clouds diffused by continuous rain or ice pellets with very little turbulence.

45. What is a characteristic of stable air?

A. Stratiform clouds.
B. Unlimited visibility.
C. Cumulus clouds.

Answer (A) is correct. (FAA-H-8083-25B Chap 12)
DISCUSSION: Characteristics of a stable air mass include stratiform clouds, continuous precipitation, smooth air, and fair to poor visibility in haze and smoke.
Answer (B) is incorrect. Restricted, not unlimited, visibility is an indication of stable air. **Answer (C) is incorrect.** Fair weather cumulus clouds indicate unstable conditions, not stable conditions.

46. What are characteristics of unstable air?

A. Turbulence and good surface visibility.
B. Turbulence and poor surface visibility.
C. Nimbostratus clouds and good surface visibility.

Answer (A) is correct. (FAA-H-8083-25B Chap 12)
DISCUSSION: Characteristics of an unstable air mass include cumuliform clouds, showery precipitation, turbulence, and good visibility, except in blowing obstructions.
Answer (B) is incorrect. Poor surface visibility is a characteristic of stable (not unstable) air. **Answer (C) is incorrect.** Stratus clouds are characteristic of stable (not unstable) air.

47. A stable air mass is most likely to have which characteristic?

A. Showery precipitation.
B. Turbulent air.
C. Poor surface visibility.

Answer (C) is correct. (FAA-H-8083-25B Chap 12)
DISCUSSION: Characteristics of a stable air mass include stratiform clouds and fog, continuous precipitation, smooth air, and fair to poor visibility in haze and smoke.
Answer (A) is incorrect. Showery precipitation is a characteristic of an unstable (not stable) air mass. **Answer (B) is incorrect.** Turbulent air is a characteristic of an unstable (not stable) air mass.

48. What are characteristics of a moist, unstable air mass?

A. Cumuliform clouds and showery precipitation.
B. Poor visibility and smooth air.
C. Stratiform clouds and showery precipitation.

Answer (A) is correct. (FAA-H-8083-25B Chap 12)
DISCUSSION: Characteristics of an unstable air mass include cumuliform clouds, showery precipitation, turbulence, and good visibility, except in blowing obstructions.
Answer (B) is incorrect. Poor visibility and smooth air are characteristics of stable (not unstable) air. **Answer (C) is incorrect.** Stratiform clouds and continuous precipitation are characteristics of stable (not unstable) air.

49. What would decrease the stability of an air mass?

A. Warming from below.
B. Cooling from below.
C. Decrease in water vapor.

Answer (A) is correct. (AC 00-6B Chap 12)
DISCUSSION: When air is warmed from below, even though cooling adiabatically, it remains warmer than the surrounding air. The colder, more dense surrounding air forces the warmer air upward, and an unstable condition develops.
Answer (B) is incorrect. Cooling from below means the surrounding air is warmer, which would increase (not decrease) the stability of an air mass. **Answer (C) is incorrect.** As water vapor in air decreases, the air mass tends to increase (not decrease) stability.

50. What measurement can be used to determine the stability of the atmosphere?

A. Atmospheric pressure.
B. Actual lapse rate.
C. Surface temperature.

Answer (B) is correct. (AC 00-6B Chap 12)
   DISCUSSION: The stability of the atmosphere is determined by vertical movements of air. Warm air rises when the air above is cooler. The actual lapse rate, which is the decrease of temperature with altitude, is therefore a measure of stability.
   Answer (A) is incorrect. Atmospheric pressure is the pressure exerted by the atmosphere as a consequence of gravitational attraction exerted upon the "column" of air lying directly above the point in question. It cannot be used to determine stability. **Answer (C) is incorrect.** While the surface temperature may have some effect on temperature changes and air movements, it is the actual lapse rate that determines the stability of the atmosphere.

51. What are characteristics of a moist, unstable air mass?

A. Turbulence and showery precipitation.
B. Poor visibility and smooth air.
C. Haze and smoke.

Answer (A) is correct. (FAA-H-8083-25B Chap 12)
   DISCUSSION: Characteristics of an unstable air mass include cumuliform clouds, showery precipitation, turbulence, and good visibility, except in blowing obstructions.
   Answer (B) is incorrect. Poor visibility and smooth air are characteristics of stable (not unstable) air. **Answer (C) is incorrect.** Haze and smoke are characteristics of stable (not unstable) air.

52. What are the characteristics of stable air?

A. Good visibility and steady precipitation.
B. Poor visibility and steady precipitation.
C. Poor visibility and intermittent precipitation.

Answer (B) is correct. (FAA-H-8083-25B Chap 12)
   DISCUSSION: Characteristics of a stable air mass include stratiform clouds, continuous precipitation, smooth air, and fair to poor visibility in haze and smoke.
   Answer (A) is incorrect. Good visibility is a characteristic of unstable (not stable) air. **Answer (C) is incorrect.** Intermittent precipitation is a characteristic of unstable (not stable) air.

53. Which of the following considerations is more relevant to a remote pilot in command (rPIC) when evaluating unmanned aircraft performance?

A. Current weather conditions.
B. The number of available ground crew.
C. The type of UA operation.

Answer (A) is correct. (FAA-H-8083-25B Chap 11)
   DISCUSSION: Even though UA operations are often conducted at very low altitudes, weather factors can greatly influence performance and safety of flight. As with any flight, the rPIC should check and consider the weather conditions prior to and during every UA flight.
   Answer (B) is incorrect. The number of available ground crew is not relevant to the evaluating performance. **Answer (C) is incorrect.** Weather conditions, not the type of UA operation, is the most relevant factor affecting performance.

54. While operating around buildings, the remote pilot in command (rPIC) should be aware of the creation of wind gusts that

A. increase performance of an aircraft.
B. change rapidly in direction and speed causing turbulence.
C. enhance stability and imagery.

Answer (B) is correct. (sUASSG Chap 3)
   DISCUSSION: Wind and currents can affect UA performance and maneuverability during all phases of flight. Be vigilant when operating UA at low altitudes, in confined areas, near buildings or other structures, and near natural obstructions (such as mountains, bluffs, or canyons).
   Answer (A) is incorrect. Wind gusts require more extensive control inputs to counter its effects. This decreases performance and maneuverability. **Answer (C) is incorrect.** Rapidly changing wind gusts can be an unseen danger causing significant low-level turbulence that adversely affects stability and imagery.

55. Which of the following geographical features may create downdrafts that affect UA performance?

A. Rocks or sand.
B. Plowed ground or barren land.
C. Water or vegetation.

Answer (C) is correct. (FAA-H-8083-25B Chap 12)
   DISCUSSION: Water, trees, and other areas of vegetation tend to absorb and retain heat and are likely to result in downdrafts.
   Answer (A) is incorrect. Rocks and sand give off a large amount of heat and are likely to result in updrafts. **Answer (B) is incorrect.** Plowed ground and barren land give off a large amount of heat and are likely to result in updrafts.

STUDY UNIT FIVE

LOADING AND PERFORMANCE

(11 pages of outline)

| 5.1 | Flight Controls and Aerodynamics | (18 questions) 171, 182 |
| 5.2 | Loading and Performance | (10 questions) 175, 186 |

5.1 FLIGHT CONTROLS AND AERODYNAMICS

1. The three **primary flight controls** of a fixed-wing aircraft are the ailerons, the elevator (or stabilator), and the rudder.

    a. Movement of any of these primary flight control surfaces changes the airflow and pressure distribution over and around the airfoil.

    1) These changes affect the lift and drag produced and allow a pilot to control the aircraft about its three axes of rotation.

    b. **Ailerons** are control surfaces attached to each wing that move in the opposite direction from one another to control roll about the longitudinal axis.

    1) EXAMPLE: Moving the control station stick to the right causes the right aileron to deflect upward, resulting in decreased lift on the right wing. The left aileron moves in the opposite direction and increases the lift on the left wing. Thus, the increased lift on the left wing and the decreased lift on the right wing cause the airplane to roll to the right.

    c. The **elevator** is the primary control device for changing the pitch attitude of an airplane, changing the pitch about the lateral axis. It is usually located on the fixed horizontal stabilizer on the tail of the airplane.

    1) EXAMPLE: Pulling back on the control station stick deflects the trailing edge of the elevator up. This position creates a downward aerodynamic force, causing the tail of the aircraft to move down and the nose to pitch up.

    2) A **stabilator** is a one-piece horizontal stabilizer and elevator that pivots from a central hinge point.

    3) A **canard** is similar to the horizontal stabilizer but is located in front of the main wings. An elevator is attached to the trailing edge of the canard to control pitch.

        a) The canard, however, actually creates lift and holds the nose up rather than the aft-tail design that prevents the nose from rotating downward.

    d. The **rudder** controls movement of the aircraft about its vertical axis.

    1) When deflecting the rudder into the airflow, a horizontal force is exerted in the opposite direction; this motion is called yaw.

    e. Flight control effectiveness increases with speed because there is more airflow over the surface of the control device.

2. **Secondary flight controls** may consist of wing flaps, leading edge devices, spoilers, and trim systems.

   a. **Flaps** are attached to the trailing edge of the wing and are used during approach and landing to increase wing lift. This allows an increase in the angle of descent without increasing airspeed.

   b. **Spoilers** are high-drag devices deployed from the wings to reduce lift and increase drag. They are found on gliders and some high-speed aircraft.

   c. **Trim systems** are used to relieve the pilot of the need to maintain constant pressure on the flight controls. They include trim tabs, antiservo tabs, and ground adjustable tabs.

3. The four **aerodynamic forces** acting on an aircraft during flight are lift, the upward-acting force; weight, the downward-acting force; thrust, the forward-acting force; and drag, the rearward-acting force.

   a. These forces are at equilibrium when the airplane is in unaccelerated flight:

   Lift = Weight
   Thrust = Drag

   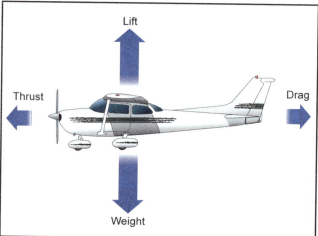

   b. **Bernoulli's Principle** states in part that "the internal pressure of a fluid (liquid or gas) decreases at points where the speed of the fluid increases." In other words, high speed flow is associated with low pressure, and low speed flow is associated with high pressure.

   1) This principle is applicable to an airplane wing because it is designed and constructed with a curve or camber. When air flows along the upper wing surface, it travels faster than the airflow along the lower wing surface.

   2) Therefore, the pressure above the wing is less than it is below the wing. This generates a lift force over the upper curved surface of the wing.

4. The **angle of attack** is the angle between the wing chord line and the relative wind direction.

   a. The wing chord line is an imaginary straight line from the leading edge to the trailing edge of the wing.

   b. The relative wind is the direction of airflow relative to the wing when the wing is moving through the air.

   c. The angle of attack at which a wing stalls remains constant regardless of weight, loading, airspeed, etc.

   1) This is the critical angle of attack.

5. A **stall** is a loss of lift and an increase in drag occurring when an aircraft is flown at an angle of attack greater than the angle for maximum lift. The angle of attack for maximum lift is also called the critical angle of attack.

   a. Thus, a stall occurs whenever the critical angle of attack is exceeded.

SU 5: Loading and Performance

b. Stall speed increases proportionally to the square root of the load factor. Therefore, when an aircraft is in a bank, the stall speed will increase.

c. To understand the stall phenomenon, some basic factors affecting aerodynamics and flight should be reviewed with particular emphasis on their relation to stall speeds. The stall speed is the speed at which the critical angle of attack is exceeded.

   1) When the angle of attack is increased to approximately 18° to 20° on most airfoils, the airstream can no longer follow the upper curvature of the wing because of the excessive change in direction. This is the critical angle of attack.

      a) As the critical angle of attack is approached, the airstream begins separating from the rear of the upper wing surface. As the angle of attack is further increased, the airstream is forced to flow straight back, away from the top surface of the wing and from the area of highest camber. The figure below depicts this.

      b) This causes a swirling or burbling of the air as it attempts to follow the upper surface of the wing. When the critical angle of attack is reached, the turbulent airflow, which appeared near the trailing edge of the wing at lower angles of attack, quickly spreads forward over the entire upper wing surface.

      c) This results in a sudden increase in pressure on the upper wing surface and a considerable loss of lift. Due to both this loss of lift and the increase in form drag (a larger area of the wing and fuselage is exposed to the airstream), the remaining lift is insufficient to support the airplane, and the wing stalls.

      d) To recover from a stall, the angle of attack must be decreased so that the airstream can once again flow smoothly over the wing surface.

         i) Remember that the angle of attack is the angle between the chord line and the relative wind, not between the chord line and the horizon.

         ii) An airplane can be stalled in any attitude of flight with respect to the horizon, at any airspeed, and at any power setting, if the critical angle of attack is exceeded.

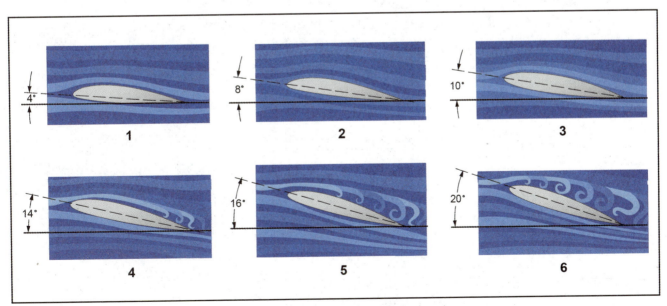

Airflow at various angles of attack.

6. **Ground effect** is the result of the interference of the ground (or water) surface with the airflow patterns about an airplane.
    a. The vertical component of the airflow around the wing is restricted, which alters the wing's upwash, downwash, and wingtip vortices.
    b. The reduction of the wingtip vortices alters the spanwise lift distribution and reduces the induced angle of attack and induced drag.
        1) Thus, the wing will require a lower angle of attack in ground effect to produce the same lift coefficient, or, if a constant angle of attack is maintained, an increase in the lift coefficient will result.
    c. An sUA is affected by ground effect when it is within the length of the sUA's wingspan above the ground. The ground effect is most often recognized when the sUA is less than one-half the wingspan's length above the ground.
    d. Ground effect may cause an sUA to float on landings or permit it to become airborne with insufficient airspeed to stay in flight above the area of ground effect.
    e. Ground effect must be considered during takeoffs and landings.
        1) If a pilot fails to understand the relationship between the aircraft and ground effect during takeoff, a hazardous situation is possible because the recommended takeoff speed may not be achieved.
        2) Due to the reduced drag in ground effect, the aircraft may seem capable of takeoff well below the recommended speed. As the aircraft rises out of ground effect with insufficient speed, the greater induced drag may result in marginal initial performance.
        3) In extreme conditions, the aircraft may become airborne initially with insufficient speed and then settle back to the runway.
7. The horizontal component of lift makes a fixed-wing sUA turn.
    a. To attain this horizontal component of lift, the pilot coordinates rudder, aileron, and elevator.
    b. The rudder controls the yaw, i.e., rotation about the vertical axis, but does not cause the sUA to turn.

SU 5: Loading and Performance

5.2 LOADING AND PERFORMANCE

1. **Understanding the effects of loading changes** is critical to the safety of flight for sUAS. An unmanned aircraft that is loaded out of balance may exhibit unexpected and unsafe flight characteristics.

    a. Before any flight, verify that the unmanned aircraft is correctly loaded by determining the weight and balance condition.

    b. An aircraft's weight and balance restrictions established by the manufacturer or the builder should be closely followed.

    　　1) Compliance with the manufacturer's weight and balance limits is critical to flight safety. The remote pilot in command (rPIC) must consider the consequences of an overweight aircraft if an emergency condition arises.

    c. Although a maximum gross takeoff weight may be specified, the aircraft may not always safely take off with this load under all conditions.

    　　1) Conditions that affect takeoff and climb performance, such as high elevations, high air temperatures, and high humidity (high density altitudes), may require a reduction in weight before flight is attempted.

    　　2) Other factors to consider prior to takeoff are runway/launch area length, surface, slope, surface wind, and the presence of obstacles. These factors may require a reduction in weight prior to flight.

    d. Weight changes during flight also have a direct effect on aircraft performance.

    　　1) Fuel burn is the most common weight change during flight. As fuel is used, the aircraft becomes lighter and performance is improved, but this could have a negative effect on balance.

    　　2) In UAS operations, weight change during flight may occur when expendable items are used on board (e.g., a jettisonable load).

2. **Balance, stability, and center of gravity (CG)** govern the qualities of an inherently stable aircraft that returns to its original condition (position or attitude) after being disturbed. It requires less effort to control.

    a. The location of the CG with respect to the center of lift (or center of pressure) determines the longitudinal stability of an aircraft.

    　　1) Changes in the center of pressure in a wing affect the aircraft's aerodynamic balance and control.

    b. Fixed-wing sUAs (except a T-tail) normally pitch down when power is reduced (and the controls are not adjusted) because the downwash on the elevators from the propeller slipstream is reduced and elevator effectiveness is reduced. This allows the nose to drop.

    c. When the CG in a fixed-wing sUA is located at or rear of the aft CG limit, the sUA

    　　1) Develops an inability to recover from stall conditions and
    　　2) Becomes less stable at all airspeeds.

    d. Adverse balance conditions (i.e., weight distribution) may affect flight characteristics in much the same manner as excess weight conditions.

e. Review any available manufacturer weight and balance data and follow all restrictions and limitations.

1) The CG is a point at which the unmanned aircraft would balance if it were suspended at that point.
2) The CG is not a fixed point marked on the aircraft; its location depends on the distribution of aircraft weight.
3) As variable load items are shifted or expended, there may be a resultant shift in CG location.
4) The rPIC should determine how the CG will shift and the resultant effects on the aircraft.
5) If the CG is not within the allowable limits after loading or does not remain within the allowable limits for safe flight, it will be necessary to relocate or shed some weight before flight is attempted.

f. If the manufacturer does not provide specific weight and balance data, apply general weight and balance principles to determine limits for a given flight.

1) For example, add weight to the unmanned aircraft in a manner that does not adversely affect the aircraft's CG location.

3. **Use of performance data to calculate the sUAS performance** determines the overall efficiency of the operation and whether the sUAS may be able to launch with this load under all conditions.

a. Without an understanding of performance data, if it does become airborne, the unmanned aircraft may exhibit unexpected and unusually poor flight characteristics.

b. Gross weight of an aircraft is the empty weight of the aircraft (sUAS), plus the weight of any fuel, batteries, and payload, i.e., the aircraft and everything it is carrying.

1) Payload usually refers to the weight of optional components or accessories carried by the sUAS that are not required for flight.

   a) Examples of payload equipment may include electro-optical equipment, mounting hardware, and electronics such as

      i) Camera(s) and associated controls, gimbals, and equipment
      ii) Direct mapping equipment, such as LIDAR
      iii) Georeferencing equipment
      iv) See and avoid sensors
      v) Optional batteries
      vi) Data link systems (nonessential)

SU 5: Loading and Performance

2) The empty weight provided for an sUAS may or may not include the weight of the battery or fuel source.

   a) The empty weight will be provided by the manufacturer in the operating handbook or flight manual.

   b) Verify which components are included in the empty weight by studying the notes in the manufacturer's manuals and by weighing the sUAS.

3) Factors that may require a reduction in weight prior to flight include

   a) High density altitude conditions

      i) High elevations.

      ii) High air temperatures.

      iii) High humidity.

      iv) At higher density altitudes, air density actually decreases. Air that is less dense has fewer air molecules and decreases performance.

   b) Runway/launch area length

   c) Surface

   d) Slope

   e) Surface wind

   f) Presence of obstacles

c. Common Performance Deficiencies of Overloaded Aircraft

   1) Excessive weight reduces the flight performance in almost every respect. In addition, operating above the maximum weight limitation can compromise the structural integrity of an unmanned aircraft.

   2) The most common performance deficiencies of an overloaded aircraft are

      a) Reduced rate of climb
      b) Lower maximum altitude
      c) Shorter endurance
      d) Reduced maneuverability

d. Effects of Weight Changes

   1) Weight changes have a direct effect on aircraft performance.

   2) Fuel burn is the most common weight change that takes place during flight.

   3) For battery-powered unmanned aircraft, weight change during flight may occur when expendable items are used on board (e.g., agricultural use).

      a) Changes of mounted equipment between flights, such as the installation of cameras, battery packs, or other instruments, may also affect the weight and balance and performance of an sUAS.

e. Effects of Load Factor

1) Load factor is the ratio of the amount of lift generated to the weight of the aircraft.

   a) In a level turn, the wings must produce additional lift because both a vertical and horizontal component of lift is being generated by the wings.

2) Unmanned airplane performance can be decreased due to an increase in load factor when the airplane is operated in maneuvers other than straight-and-level flight.

3) The load factor increases at a terrific rate after a bank has reached 45° or 50°.

   a) The load factor for any aircraft in a coordinated level turn at 60° bank is 2 Gs.
   b) The load factor in an 80° bank is 5.76 Gs.
   c) The wing must produce lift equal to these load factors to maintain altitude.

4) The rPIC should be mindful of the increased load factor and its possible effects on the aircraft's structural integrity and the results of an increase in stall speed.

   a) As with manned aircraft, an unmanned airplane will stall when critical angle of attack is exceeded.

      i) Due to the low altitude operating environment, consideration should be given to ensure aircraft control is maintained and the aircraft is not operated outside its performance limits.

5) A load factor chart like the example below is given with the amount of bank on the horizontal axis (along the bottom of the graph), and the load factor on the vertical axis (up the left side of the graph). Additionally, a table that provides the load factor corresponding to specific bank angles is found on the left side of the chart. Use this table to answer load factor questions.

   a) Compute the load factor by multiplying the airplane's weight by the load factor that corresponds to the given angle of bank. For example, the wings of a 33-lb. airplane in a 60° bank must support 66 lb. (33 lb. × 2.000).

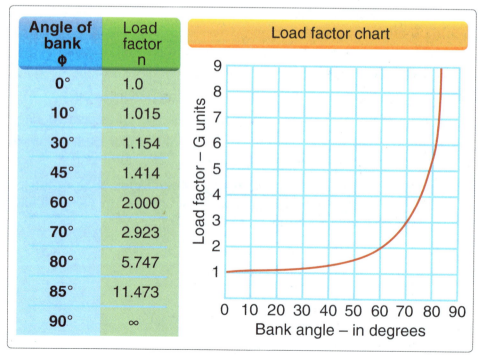

Figure 2. Load Factor Chart.

SU 5: Loading and Performance 179

- f. Performance or operational information may be provided by the manufacturer in the form of an Aircraft Flight Manual (AFM), Pilot's Operating Handbook (POH), or owner's manual. Follow all manufacturer recommendations for evaluating performance to ensure safe and efficient operation.
    1) These charts usually require cross-referencing two or more variables to determine allowable gross weight.
    2) For example, cross reference a given pressure altitude with a known temperature to determine the maximum weight limitation.
        a) Performance tables usually list limitations according to specific temperature or altitude increments, e.g., 0°C, 10°C, 20°C, 30°C, etc. and S.L. (sea level), 1000', 2000', 3000', etc.
        b) Performance limitations can be estimated by using the increments closest to actual conditions but should be interpolated when exact limitations must be known.
            i) EXAMPLE: If the temperature is 25°C, the limitation would be halfway between the limits listed for 20°C and 30°C.
        c) Pay attention to the unit of measurement. If the temperature on the performance charts is listed in Celsius, but the known temperature for your area is reported in Fahrenheit, you will need to convert.
        d) Remember to convert the altitude above sea level to pressure altitude by using the pressure altitude conversion factor on the density altitude chart in Study Unit 4, "Weather Effects on Performance."
            i) You will also need to know the local altimeter setting for this conversion.
            ii) This is obtained from a nearby aviation routine weather report (METAR).
- g. Even when specific performance data is not provided, the rPIC should be familiar with the operating environment and all available information regarding the safe and recommended operation of the sUAS.
    1) The rPIC is responsible for ensuring that every flight can be accomplished safely, does not pose an undue hazard, and does not increase the likelihood of a loss of positive control.
    2) Consider how your decisions affect the safety of flight.
        a) If you attempt flight in windy conditions, the unmanned aircraft may require an unusually high power setting to ascend. This action may cause a rapid depletion of battery power and result in a failure mode.
        b) If you attempt flight in wintery weather conditions, ice may accumulate on the unmanned aircraft's surface. Ice increases the weight and adversely affects performance characteristics of the sUAS.
    3) Due to the diversity and rapidly-evolving nature of sUAS operations, individual rPICs have flexibility to determine what equipage methods, if any, mitigate risk sufficiently to meet performance-based requirements, such as the prohibition on creating an undue hazard if there is a loss of aircraft control.

4) The FAA acknowledges that some manufacturers provide comprehensive operational data and manuals, such as AFM or POH, and others do not.

   a) When operational data is provided, follow the manufacturer's instructions and recommendations.

      i) The chart below shows the effect of higher density altitude on allowable gross weight for the Freefly Alta 8.

      ii) EXAMPLE: At sea level, 10°C, the allowable gross weight is 40.0 lb. At a 10,000-ft. pressure altitude and 30°C, the allowable gross weight is 26.1 lb., a 35% decrease in performance.

Press Alt Ft	0°C Max Gross Weight (lb)	0°C Max Gross Weight (kg)	10°C Max Gross Weight (lb)	10°C Max Gross Weight (kg)	20°C Max Gross Weight (lb)	20°C Max Gross Weight (kg)	30°C Max Gross Weight (lb)	30°C Max Gross Weight (kg)	40°C Max Gross Weight (lb)	40°C Max Gross Weight (kg)
S.L.	40.0	18.1	40.0	18.1	39.3	17.8	38.0	17.2	36.8	16.7
1000	40.0	18.1	39.3	17.8	37.9	17.2	36.7	16.6	35.5	16.1
2000	39.2	17.8	37.8	17.2	36.6	16.6	35.4	16.0	34.2	15.5
3000	37.8	17.2	36.5	16.5	35.2	16.0	34.1	15.5	33.0	15.0
4000	36.4	16.5	35.2	15.9	34.0	15.4	32.8	14.9	31.8	14.4
5000	35.1	15.9	33.9	15.4	32.7	14.8	31.6	14.3	30.6	13.9
6000	33.8	15.3	32.6	14.8	31.5	14.3	30.5	13.8	29.5	13.4
7000	32.6	14.8	31.4	14.2	30.3	13.8	29.3	13.3	28.4	12.9
8000	31.3	14.2	30.2	13.7	29.2	13.2	28.2	12.8	27.3	12.4
9000	30.2	13.7	29.1	13.2	28.1	12.7	27.2	12.3	26.3	11.9
10000	29.0	13.2	28.0	12.7	27.0	12.3	26.1	11.9	25.3	11.5

This chart is from an Alta 8 and is used with permission from Freefly Systems.

   b) Even when operational data is not supplied by the manufacturer, the rPIC can better understand the unmanned aircraft's capabilities and limitations by establishing a process for tracking malfunctions, defects, and flight characteristics in various environments and conditions.

      i) Use this operational data to establish a baseline for determining performance, reliability, and risk assessment for your particular system.

h. Endurance is the approximate flight time before the energy source (fuel or battery power) is depleted. Any operation or factor requiring more use of power reduces endurance times.

   1) Factors affecting endurance include

      a) Gross weight. A higher gross weight requires increased power settings to lift the sUAS and maneuver.

      b) Extensive maneuvering. Constant and abrupt control movements such as quick turns and variations in altitude require higher power consumption.

      c) Wind and gusty conditions require increased power settings to sustain flight. A 10-kt. wind will cause the sUAS to move with the air unless controls are inputted to counter the effects of the wind.

         i) If the mission requires extensive hovering, wind in one direction requires control inputs nearly equal forward flight at the same speed as the wind.

SU 5: Loading and Performance

2) Performance tables, charts, or graphs may be given to approximate flight times versus payload.

   a) Using the performance data requires cross referencing factors such as payload and battery or fuel capacity to determine the approximate flight time for a specified period of time.

   i) Performance tables may include more than one variable for battery capacity. For comparison, a 16Ah battery lasts longer than a 10Ah battery.

   ii) The chart below shows the effect carrying a heavier payload has on endurance for the Freefly Alta 8.

   iii) EXAMPLE: For a given sUAS make and model, a 10-lb. payload using a 16Ah battery may allow approximately 19-min. of endurance. The same 10-lb. payload using a 10Ah battery may only have a 12-min. endurance.

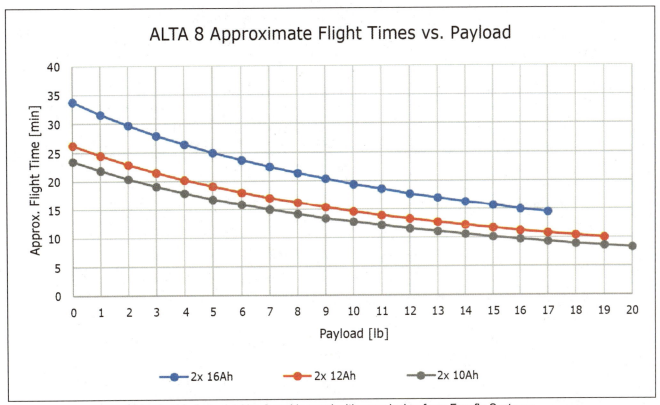

This chart is from an Alta 8 and is used with permission from Freefly Systems.

3) Ensure sufficient reserve power is available to safely operate the sUAS.

   a) As reserve power is depleted, there may not be sufficient power to perform abrupt maneuvers or return the sUAS to the home location.

   b) Voltage by itself is not adequate to determine remaining endurance.

   c) Unlike engines powered by liquid fuel, a minimum voltage is necessary to provide power to all sUAS components.

   i) EXAMPLE: A full charge of 4.2 volts for a specific sUAS may provide 100% power. The same battery at 3.7 volts might only provide 20% of the remaining usable capacity. This is only a 0.5 volt reduction but is an 80% reduction in remaining capacity.

QUESTIONS

5.1 Flight Controls and Aerodynamics

1. What is one purpose of wing flaps?

A. To enable the pilot to make steeper approaches to a landing without increasing the airspeed.
B. To relieve the pilot of maintaining continuous pressure on the controls.
C. To decrease wing area to vary the lift.

Answer (A) is correct. (FAA-H-8083-25B Chap 6)
DISCUSSION: Extending the flaps increases the wing camber and the angle of attack of the wing. This increases wing lift and induced drag, which enables the pilot to make steeper approaches to a landing without an increase in airspeed.
Answer (B) is incorrect. Trim tabs (not wing flaps) help relieve control pressures. **Answer (C) is incorrect.** Wing area usually remains the same, except for certain specialized flaps that increase (not decrease) the wing area.

2. One of the main functions of flaps during approach and landing is to

A. decrease the angle of descent without increasing the airspeed.
B. permit a touchdown at a higher indicated airspeed.
C. increase the angle of descent without increasing the airspeed.

Answer (C) is correct. (FAA-H-8083-25B Chap 6)
DISCUSSION: Extending the flaps increases the wing camber and the angle of attack of the wing. This increases wing lift and induced drag, which enables the pilot to increase the angle of descent without increasing the airspeed.
Answer (A) is incorrect. Extending the flaps increases lift and induced drag, which enables the pilot to increase (not decrease) the angle of descent without increasing the airspeed. **Answer (B) is incorrect.** Flaps increase lift at slow airspeed, which permits touchdown at a lower (not higher) indicated airspeed.

3. What is the purpose of the rudder on an aircraft?

A. To control yaw.
B. To control pitch.
C. To control roll.

Answer (A) is correct. (FAA-H-8083-25B)
DISCUSSION: The rudder is used to control yaw, which is rotation about the fixed-wing sUA's vertical axis.
Answer (B) is incorrect. Pitch is movement about the lateral axis and is controlled by the elevator. **Answer (C) is incorrect.** Roll is movement about the longitudinal axis and is controlled by ailerons.

4. The elevator controls movement around which axis?

A. Longitudinal.
B. Lateral.
C. Vertical.

Answer (B) is correct. (FAA-H-8083-25B Chap 6)
DISCUSSION: The elevator is the primary control device for changing the pitch attitude of a fixed-wing sUA about the lateral axis.
Answer (A) is incorrect. Ailerons are control surfaces attached to each wing that move in the opposite direction from one another to control roll about the longitudinal axis. **Answer (C) is incorrect.** The rudder controls movement of the aircraft about its vertical axis.

5. Which of the following is true concerning flaps?

A. Flaps are attached to the leading edge of the wing and are used to increase wing lift.
B. Flaps allow an increase in the angle of descent without increasing airspeed.
C. Flaps are high drag devices deployed from the wings to reduce lift.

Answer (B) is correct. (FAA-H-8083-25B Chap 6)
DISCUSSION: Flaps are attached to the trailing edge of the wing and are used during approach and landing to increase wing lift. This allows an increase in the angle of descent without increasing airspeed.
Answer (A) is incorrect. Flaps are attached to the trailing edge, not the leading edge, of the wing. **Answer (C) is incorrect.** Spoilers, not flaps, are high-drag devices deployed from the wings to reduce lift and increase drag.

SU 5: Loading and Performance

6. Trim systems are designed to do what?

A. They relieve the pilot of the need to maintain constant pressure on the flight controls.
B. They are used during approach and landing to increase wing lift.
C. They move in the opposite direction from one another to control roll.

Answer (A) is correct. (FAA-H-8083-25B Chap 6)
DISCUSSION: Trim systems are used to relieve the pilot of the need to maintain constant pressure on the flight controls. They include trim tabs, anti-servo tabs, and ground adjustable tabs.
Answer (B) is incorrect. Flaps, not trim systems, are used during approach and landing to increase lift. This allows an increase in the angle of descent without increasing airspeed. **Answer (C) is incorrect.** Ailerons are control surfaces attached to each wing that move in the opposite direction from one another to control roll about the longitudinal axis.

7. The four forces acting on an aircraft in flight are

A. lift, weight, thrust, and drag.
B. lift, weight, gravity, and thrust.
C. lift, gravity, power, and friction.

Answer (A) is correct. (FAA-H-8083-25B Chap 5)
DISCUSSION: Lift is produced by the wings and opposes weight, which is the result of gravity. Thrust is produced by the engine/propeller and opposes drag, which is the resistance of the air as the aircraft moves through it.
Answer (B) is incorrect. Gravity reacts with the aircraft's mass, thus producing weight, which opposes lift. **Answer (C) is incorrect.** Gravity results in weight, power produces thrust, and friction is a cause of drag. Power, gravity, velocity, and friction are not aerodynamic forces in themselves.

8. When are the four forces that act on an aircraft in equilibrium?

A. During unaccelerated level flight.
B. When the aircraft is accelerating.
C. When the aircraft is at rest on the ground.

Answer (A) is correct. (FAA-H-8083-25B Chap 5)
DISCUSSION: The four forces (lift, weight, thrust, and drag) that act on an aircraft are in equilibrium during unaccelerated level flight.
Answer (B) is incorrect. Thrust must exceed drag in order for the aircraft to accelerate. **Answer (C) is incorrect.** When the aircraft is at rest on the ground, there are no aerodynamic forces acting on it other than weight (gravity).

9. What is the relationship of lift, drag, thrust, and weight when the aircraft is in straight-and-level flight?

A. Lift equals weight and thrust equals drag.
B. Lift, drag, and weight equal thrust.
C. Lift and weight equal thrust and drag.

Answer (A) is correct. (FAA-H-8083-25B Chap 5)
DISCUSSION: When the aircraft is in straight-and-level flight (assuming no change of airspeed), it is not accelerating, and therefore lift equals weight and thrust equals drag.
Answer (B) is incorrect. Lift equals weight and drag equals thrust. **Answer (C) is incorrect.** Lift and weight are equal and thrust and drag are equal, but the four are not equal to each other.

10. In a 30° banking turn, a UA will

A. stall at the same airspeed.
B. stall at a lower airspeed.
C. stall at a higher airspeed.

Answer (C) is correct. (FAA-H-8083-25B)
DISCUSSION: Stall speed increases proportionally to the square root of the load factor; therefore, when an aircraft is in a bank, the stall speed will increase.
Answer (A) is incorrect. Stall speed does not stay the same; it increases during a banking turn. **Answer (B) is incorrect.** Stall speed increases, not decreases, during a banking turn.

11. What is ground effect?

A. The result of the interference of the surface of the Earth with the airflow patterns about an airplane.
B. The result of an alteration in airflow patterns increasing induced drag about the wings of an airplane.
C. The result of the disruption of the airflow patterns about the wings of an airplane to the point where the wings will no longer support the airplane in flight.

Answer (A) is correct. (FAA-H-8083-25B Chap 5)
DISCUSSION: Ground effect is due to the interference of the ground (or water) surface with the airflow patterns about the airplane in flight. As the wing encounters ground effect, there is a reduction in the upwash, downwash, and the wingtip vortices. The result is a reduction in induced drag. Thus, for a given angle of attack, the wing will produce more lift in ground effect than it does out of ground effect.
Answer (B) is incorrect. The result of the alteration in airflow patterns about the wing decreases, not increases, the induced drag. **Answer (C) is incorrect.** The disruption of the airflow patterns about the wing decreases induced drag, which causes an increase, not decrease, in lift at a given angle of attack.

12. Floating caused by the phenomenon of ground effect will be most realized during an approach to land when at

    A. less than the length of the wingspan above the surface.

    B. twice the length of the wingspan above the surface.

    C. a higher-than-normal angle of attack.

Answer (A) is correct. (FAA-H-8083-25B Chap 5)
    DISCUSSION: Ground effect is most usually recognized when the airplane is within one-half of the length of its wingspan above the surface. It may extend as high as a full wingspan length above the surface. Due to an alteration of the airflow about the wings, induced drag decreases, which reduces the thrust required at low airspeeds. Thus, any excess speed during the landing flare may result in considerable floating.
    Answer (B) is incorrect. Ground effect generally extends up to only one wingspan length, not two. **Answer (C) is incorrect.** Floating will occur with excess airspeed, which results in a lower-than-normal, not higher-than-normal, angle of attack.

13. What must a pilot be aware of as a result of ground effect?

    A. Wingtip vortices increase creating wake turbulence problems for arriving and departing aircraft.

    B. Induced drag decreases; therefore, any excess speed at the point of flare may cause considerable floating.

    C. A full stall landing will require less up elevator deflection than would a full stall when done free of ground effect.

Answer (B) is correct. (FAA-H-8083-25B Chap 5)
    DISCUSSION: Ground effect reduces the upwash, downwash, and vortices caused by the wings, resulting in a decrease in induced drag. Thus, thrust required at low airspeeds will be reduced, and any excess speed at the point of flare may cause considerable floating.
    Answer (A) is incorrect. Wingtip vortices are decreased, not increased. **Answer (C) is incorrect.** A full stall landing will require more, not less, up elevator deflection since the wing will require a lower angle of attack in ground effect to produce the same amount of lift.

14. An aircraft leaving ground effect during takeoff will

    A. experience a reduction in ground friction and require a slight power reduction.

    B. experience an increase in induced drag and a decrease in performance.

    C. require a lower angle of attack to maintain the same lift coefficient.

Answer (B) is correct. (FAA-H-8083-25B Chap 5)
    DISCUSSION: During the takeoff phase of flight, ground effect produces some important relationships. The airplane leaving ground effect after takeoff encounters just the reverse of the airplane entering ground effect during landing; i.e., the airplane leaving ground effect will (1) require an increase in angle of attack to maintain the same lift coefficient, (2) experience an increase in induced drag and thrust required, (3) experience a decrease in stability and a nose-up change in moment, and (4) produce a reduction in static source pressure and an increase in indicated airspeed.
    Answer (A) is incorrect. While the aerodynamic characteristics of the tail surfaces and the fuselage are altered by ground effects, the principal effects due to proximity of the ground are the changes in the aerodynamic characteristics of the wing, not a reduction in ground friction. As the wing encounters ground effect and is maintained at a constant lift coefficient, there is consequent reduction in the upwash, downwash, and the wingtip vortices. **Answer (C) is incorrect.** The aircraft will require a higher angle of attack to maintain the same lift coefficient as when it was in ground effect.

15. A stall occurs when the smooth airflow over the unmanned airplane's wing is disrupted and the lift degenerates rapidly. This is caused when the wing

    A. exceeds the maximum speed.

    B. exceeds maximum allowable operating weight.

    C. exceeds its critical angle of attack.

Answer (C) is correct. (FAA-H-8083-25B Chap 5)
    DISCUSSION: A stall is a loss of lift and an increase in drag that occurs when an aircraft is flown at an angle of attack greater than the angle for maximum lift. The angle of attack for maximum lift is also called the critical angle of attack.
    Answer (A) is incorrect. Exceeding the maximum speed may cause structural damage, but the critical angle of attack must be exceeded in order to stall. **Answer (B) is incorrect.** Exceeding the maximum allowable operating weight may adversely affect performance, but the critical angle of attack must be exceeded in order to stall.

16. The term "angle of attack" is defined as the angle between the

A. chord line of the wing and the relative wind.
B. airplane's longitudinal axis and that of the air striking the airfoil.
C. airplane's center line and the relative wind.

Answer (A) is correct. (FAA-H-8083-25B Chap 5)
DISCUSSION: The angle of attack is the angle between the wing chord line and the direction of the relative wind. The wing chord line is a straight line from the leading edge to the trailing edge of the wing. The relative wind is the direction of the airflow relative to the wing when the wing is moving through the air.
Answer (B) is incorrect. Angle of attack is the angle between the wing chord line and the relative wind, not the airplane's longitudinal axis. **Answer (C) is incorrect.** The centerline of the airplane and its relationship to the relative wind is not a factor in defining angle of attack. Angle of attack is the relationship between the wing chord line and the relative wind.

17. The angle of attack at which an airplane wing stalls will

A. increase if the CG is moved forward.
B. change with an increase in gross weight.
C. remain the same regardless of gross weight.

Answer (C) is correct. (FAA-H-8083-25B Chap 5)
DISCUSSION: A given airplane wing will always stall at the same angle of attack regardless of airspeed, weight, load factor, or density altitude. Each wing has a particular angle of attack (the critical angle of attack) at which the airflow separates from the upper surface of the wing and the stall occurs.
Answer (A) is incorrect. A change in CG will not change the wing's critical angle of attack. **Answer (B) is incorrect.** The critical angle of attack does not change when gross weight changes.

18. (Refer to Figure 1 below.) The acute angle A is the angle of

A. incidence.
B. attack.
C. dihedral.

Answer (B) is correct. (FAA-H-8083-25B Chap 5)
DISCUSSION: The angle between the relative wind and the wing chord line is the angle of attack. The wing chord line is a straight line from the leading edge to the trailing edge of the wing.
Answer (A) is incorrect. The angle of incidence is the acute angle formed by the chord line of the wing and the longitudinal axis of the airplane. **Answer (C) is incorrect.** The dihedral is the angle at which the wings are slanted upward from the wing root to the wingtip.

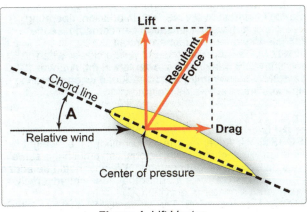

Figure 1. Lift Vector.

5.2 Loading and Performance

19. To ensure that the unmanned aircraft center of gravity (CG) limits are not exceeded, follow the aircraft loading instructions specified in the

 A. Pilot's Operating Handbook or UAS Flight Manual.
 B. *Aeronautical Information Manual (AIM)*.
 C. *Aircraft Weight and Balance Handbook*.

Answer (A) is correct. (FAA-H-8083-1B 4-4-5)
 DISCUSSION: Performance or operational information may be provided by the manufacturer in the form of an Aircraft Flight Manual, Pilot's Operating Handbook, or owner's manual. Follow all manufacturer recommendations for evaluating performance to ensure safe and efficient operation.
 Answer (B) is incorrect. The *AIM* is a guide to basic flight information and ATC procedures. **Answer (C) is incorrect.** The *Aircraft Weight and Balance Handbook* does not contain the limitations for a specific aircraft.

20. According to 14 CFR Part 107, who is responsible for determining the performance of a small unmanned aircraft?

 A. Remote pilot-in-command.
 B. Manufacturer.
 C. Owner or operator.

Answer (A) is correct. (14 CFR 107.49)
 DISCUSSION: Even when specific performance data is not provided, the remote pilot in command (rPIC) should be familiar with the operating environment and all available information regarding the safe and recommended operation of the sUAS.
 Answer (B) is incorrect. Manufacturers do not always provide specific performance data. **Answer (C) is incorrect.** The rPIC, not the owner or operator, is responsible for determining performance. Note that the operator may refer to someone other than the rPIC.

21. When operating an unmanned airplane, the remote pilot should consider that the load factor on the wings may be increased any time

 A. the CG is shifted rearward to the aft CG limit.
 B. the airplane is subjected to maneuvers other than straight and level flight.
 C. the gross weight is reduced.

Answer (B) is correct. (FAA-H-8083-25B Chap 5)
 DISCUSSION: Load factor is the ratio of the amount of lift generated to the weight of the aircraft. In a level turn, the wings must produce additional lift because both a vertical and horizontal component of lift is being generated by the wings.
 Answer (A) is incorrect. An aft CG may affect the handling characteristics, not the load factor. **Answer (C) is incorrect.** Load factor is a ratio that is increased by maneuvers other than straight-and-level flight, not changes in weight.

22. What could be a consequence of operating a small unmanned aircraft above its maximum allowable weight?

 A. Faster speed.
 B. Shorter endurance.
 C. Increased maneuverability.

Answer (B) is correct. (FAA-H-8083-25B Chap 10)
 DISCUSSION: Excessive weight reduces flight performance in almost every respect. In addition, operating above the maximum weight limitation can compromise the structural integrity of an unmanned aircraft.
 Answer (A) is incorrect. Speed will be slower when operating above the maximum allowable weight. **Answer (C) is incorrect.** Maneuverability will be reduced when operating above the maximum allowable weight.

23. When loading cameras or other equipment on an sUAS, mount the items in a manner that

 A. is visible to the visual observer or other crewmembers.
 B. does not adversely affect the center of gravity.
 C. can be easily removed without the use of tools.

Answer (B) is correct. (14 CFR 107.49)
 DISCUSSION: Adverse balance conditions (i.e., weight distribution) may affect flight characteristics in much the same manner as an excess weight condition. Weight should be added to the unmanned aircraft in a manner that does not adversely affect the aircraft's center of gravity (CG).
 Answer (A) is incorrect. The entire sUAS must be visible to visual observers or other crewmembers, not necessarily external equipment. **Answer (C) is incorrect.** External equipment should be securely attached, but it does not need to be easily removable without the use of tools.

SU 5: Loading and Performance

24. (Refer to Figure 2 below.) If an unmanned airplane weighs 33 pounds, what approximate weight would the airplane structure be required to support during a 30° banked turn while maintaining altitude?

A. 34 pounds.
B. 47 pounds.
C. 38 pounds.

Answer (C) is correct. *(FAA-H-8083-25B Chap 5)*
DISCUSSION: Look on the left side of the chart in Fig. 2 to extrapolate that at a 30° bank angle, the load factor is 1.154. Thus, a 33-lb. airplane in a 30° bank would require its wings to support 38 lb. (33 lb. × 1.154).
Answer (A) is incorrect. An airplane supporting a load of 34 lb. in a 30° banked turn would weigh 29.5 lb., not 33 lb.
Answer (B) is incorrect. A 33-lb. airplane supporting a load of 47 lb. would require a 45° banked turn, not a 30° banked turn.

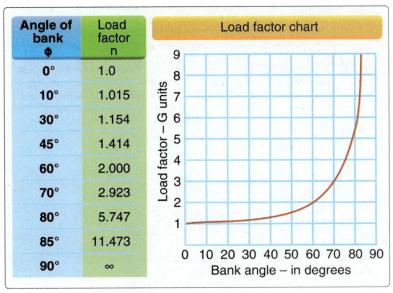

Figure 2. Load Factor Chart.

25. What determines the longitudinal stability of an aircraft?

A. The location of the CG with respect to the center of lift.
B. The effectiveness of the horizontal stabilizer, rudder, and rudder trim tab.
C. The relationship of thrust and lift to weight and drag.

Answer (A) is correct. *(FAA-H-8083-25B Chap 5)*
DISCUSSION: The location of the center of gravity with respect to the center of lift determines, to a great extent, the longitudinal stability of the aircraft. Positive stability is attained by having the center of lift behind the center of gravity. Then the tail provides negative lift, creating a downward tail force, which counteracts the nose's tendency to pitch down.
Answer (B) is incorrect. The rudder and rudder trim tab control the yaw, not the pitch. **Answer (C) is incorrect.** The relationship of thrust and lift to weight and drag affects speed and altitude, not longitudinal stability.

26. An aircraft said to be inherently stable will

A. be difficult to stall.
B. require less effort to control.
C. not spin.

Answer (B) is correct. *(FAA-H-8083-25B Chap 5)*
DISCUSSION: An inherently stable aircraft will usually return to the original condition of flight (except when in a bank) if disturbed by a force such as air turbulence. Thus, an inherently stable aircraft will require less effort to control than an inherently unstable one.
Answer (A) is incorrect. Stability of an aircraft has an effect on stall characteristic, not on the difficulty level of entering a stall. **Answer (C) is incorrect.** An inherently stable aircraft will spin.

27. An airplane has been loaded in such a manner that the CG is located aft of the aft CG limit. One undesirable flight characteristic a pilot might experience with this airplane would be

A. a longer takeoff run.
B. difficulty in recovering from a stalled condition.
C. stalling at higher-than-normal airspeed.

Answer (B) is correct. (FAA-H-8083-25B Chap 10)
DISCUSSION: The recovery from a stall in any airplane becomes progressively more difficult as its center of gravity moves backward. Generally, airplanes become less controllable, especially at slow flight speeds, as the center of gravity is moved backward.
Answer (A) is incorrect. An airplane with an aft CG has less drag, resulting in a shorter, not longer, takeoff run. **Answer (C) is incorrect.** An airplane with an aft CG flies at a lower angle of attack, resulting in a lower, not higher, stall speed.

28. Loading an airplane to the most aft CG will cause the airplane to be

A. less stable at all speeds.
B. less stable at slow speeds, but more stable at high speeds.
C. less stable at high speeds, but more stable at low speeds.

Answer (A) is correct. (FAA-H-8083-25B Chap 10)
DISCUSSION: Airplanes become less stable at all speeds as the center of gravity is moved backward. The rearward center of gravity limit is determined largely by considerations of stability.
Answer (B) is incorrect. An aft CG will cause the airplane to be less stable at all speeds. **Answer (C) is incorrect.** An aft CG will cause the airplane to be less stable at all speeds.

STUDY UNIT SIX
RADIO COMMUNICATIONS PROCEDURES

(7 pages of outline)

6.1	Radio Communications Procedures	(18 questions) 189, 196

6.1 RADIO COMMUNICATIONS PROCEDURES

1. **Airport operations with and without an operating control tower** require equal attention to safety from the unmanned aircraft operator.

    a. Airports with an Operating Control Tower

      1) An airport with an operating control tower normally has

         a) Ground control for control of aircraft taxiing on the surface of the airport (except the runway) and

         b) Tower control for control of aircraft on the active runway and in the vicinity of the airport.

      2) Many busy airports also have approach control and departure control.

         a) The approach or departure controller coordinates arriving and departing traffic, usually for a busy airport with a control tower.

      3) Automatic Terminal Information Service (ATIS) is a continuous airport advisory service also provided at busy airports.

      4) Clearance delivery is a required communication at very busy and medium-density airports. It is used before contacting ground control to obtain departure instructions.

    b. Airports without an Operating Control Tower

      1) At an airport that does not have an operating control tower, there is no air traffic control over movements of aircraft on the ground or around the airport in the air. This may also be referred to as an uncontrolled airport.

         a) It is essential that pilots be alert, look for other traffic, and exchange information when approaching or departing an airport without an operating control tower.

            i) This is of particular importance since other aircraft may not have communication capability, or pilots may not communicate their presence or intentions.

      2) To achieve the greatest degree of safety, it is essential that all radio-equipped aircraft transmit/receive on a common frequency identified for the purpose of airport advisories.

      3) Observing and avoiding other aircraft at an airport without an operating control tower is of paramount importance.

         a) Relatedly, being considerate to the other pilots should have high priority both in the air and on the ground.

         b) Finally, do not assume absence of traffic because few airplanes use an airport.

2. A **Common Traffic Advisory Frequency (CTAF)** is used to monitor manned aircraft communications.

   a. The key to communicating at an airport without an operating control tower is the selection of the correct frequency. The term **CTAF** is synonymous with this program.

      1) CTAF is a frequency designated for the purpose of carrying out airport advisory practices while operating to or from an airport without an operating control tower.

         a) CTAF may be a UNICOM, MULTICOM, FSS, or tower frequency.
         b) The CTAF at an airport is indicated on the sectional chart by a © next to the appropriate frequency.

      2) Pilots of inbound aircraft should monitor and communicate as appropriate on the CTAF 10 NM from the airport.

         a) Pilots of departing aircraft should monitor and communicate on the CTAF from start-up, during taxi, and until 10 NM from the airport unless Federal Aviation Regulations or local procedures require otherwise.

      3) Pilots of aircraft conducting other than arriving or departing operations at altitudes normally used by arriving and departing aircraft should monitor/communicate on the CTAF while within 10 NM of the airport unless Federal Aviation Regulations or local procedures require otherwise.

      4) **MULTICOM** is a frequency (122.9 MHz) used for self-announced procedures at airports without operating control towers that are not served by an FSS or UNICOM.

         a) At such an airport, the MULTICOM frequency will be identified on charts as the CTAF.
         b) Use the same phraseology as explained for UNICOM.

3. Understanding the **recommended traffic advisory procedures** used by manned aircraft pilots, such as self-announcing of position and intentions, is important.

   a. Pilots use radios to

      1) Obtain air traffic control (ATC) clearances

         a) Ground control
         b) Tower control, e.g., takeoffs and landings
         c) Approach and departure control (in the vicinity of the airport)
         d) En route control

      2) Obtain weather briefings, file flight plans, etc., with Flight Service Stations (FSSs)

      3) Communicate with FBOs and each other on CTAF, UNICOM, and MULTICOM frequencies

   b. Airplane communication radios operate on the VHF (very high frequency) band between 118.000 MHz and 136.975 MHz.

      1) VHF radios are limited to line-of-sight transmissions; thus, aircraft at higher altitudes are able to transmit and receive at greater distances.

SU 6: Radio Communications Procedures

c. Radio communications are a critical link in the ATC system. The link can be a strong bond between pilots and controllers, or it can be broken with surprising speed and disastrous results.

   1) The single most important factor in pilot-controller communications is understanding.

      a) Good phraseology enhances safety and is a mark of a professional pilot.
      b) Jargon, chatter, and "CB" slang have no place in ATC communications.

d. In virtually all situations, pilot radio broadcasts can be thought of as

   1) To whom they are talking
   2) Who they are
   3) Where they are
   4) What they want to do
   5) To whom they are talking (when making common traffic advisories in uncontrolled airport areas)

Summary of Recommended Communication Procedures

	FACILITY AT AIRPORT	FREQUENCY USE	COMMUNICATION/BROADCAST PROCEDURES OUTBOUND	COMMUNICATION/BROADCAST PROCEDURES INBOUND
1.	UNICOM (no tower or FSS)	Communicate with UNICOM station on published CTAF frequency (122.7, 122.8, 122.725, 122.975, or 123.0). If unable to contact UNICOM station, use self-announced procedures on CTAF.	Before taxiing and before taxiing on the runway for departure.	10 NM out. Entering downwind, base, and final. Leaving the runway.
2.	No tower, FSS, or UNICOM	Self-announce on MULTICOM frequency 122.9.	Before taxiing and before taxiing on the runway for departure.	10 NM out. Entering downwind, base, and final. Leaving the runway.

4. The remote pilot must understand the **aeronautical advisory communications station (UNICOM) and associated communication procedures** used by manned aircraft pilots.

   a. UNICOM is a nongovernment air/ground radio communication station that may provide airport advisories at airports where there is no tower or FSS. UNICOM stations may provide pilots with weather information, wind direction, the recommended runway, or other necessary information.

      1) If the UNICOM frequency is designated as the CTAF, it will be identified on aeronautical charts and the Chart Supplement.

         a) UNICOM frequencies include 122.8, 122.7, 122.725, 122.975, and 123.0 MHz.

      2) The following practices help identify the location of aircraft in the traffic pattern and enhance safety of flight.

         a) Select the correct UNICOM/CTAF frequency.
         b) Monitor the frequency for these types of communications.
         c) Approximately 10 NM from the airport, pilots report altitude; state the airplane type, airplane identification, location relative to the airport, and the decision to land or overfly; and request wind information and runway in use.
         d) Report on downwind, base, and final approach.
         e) Report leaving the runway.

3) Inbound examples of UNICOM phraseology:
   a) Pilot: JONESVILLE UNICOM CESSNA ONE ZERO TWO FOXTROT, 10 MILES NORTH DESCENDING THROUGH (ALTITUDE) LANDING JONESVILLE, REQUEST WIND AND RUNWAY INFORMATION JONESVILLE.
      i) Response from FBO: CESSNA CALLING JONESVILLE, WIND THREE FOUR ZERO AT SEVEN, RUNWAY THREE SIX IN USE WITH TWO AIRCRAFT IN THE PATTERN.
   b) Pilot: JONESVILLE TRAFFIC CESSNA ONE ZERO TWO FOXTROT ENTERING (DOWNWIND/BASE/FINAL) FOR RUNWAY THREE SIX (FULL STOP/TOUCH-AND-GO) JONESVILLE.
   c) Pilot: JONESVILLE TRAFFIC CESSNA ONE ZERO TWO FOXTROT CLEAR OF RUNWAY THREE SIX JONESVILLE.

4) Outbound examples of UNICOM phraseology:
   a) Pilot: JONESVILLE UNICOM CESSNA ONE ZERO TWO FOXTROT (LOCATION ON AIRPORT) TAXIING TO RUNWAY THREE SIX, REQUEST WIND AND TRAFFIC INFORMATION JONESVILLE.
   b) Pilot: JONESVILLE TRAFFIC CESSNA ONE ZERO TWO FOXTROT DEPARTING RUNWAY THREE SIX. REMAINING IN THE PATTERN/DEPARTING THE PATTERN TO THE (DIRECTION) (AS APPROPRIATE) JONESVILLE.

5. **Automatic Terminal Information Service (ATIS)**
   a. If available, the ATIS frequency is listed on the sectional chart just under the tower control frequency for the airport, e.g., ATIS 125.05. ATIS provides a continuous transmission that provides information for arriving and departing aircraft, including
      1) Time of the latest weather report
      2) Sky conditions, visibility, and obstructions to visibility
         a) The absence of a sky condition or ceiling and/or visibility and obstructions to visibility on ATIS indicates a sky condition of 5,000 ft. or above and visibility of 5 SM or more.
            i) A remark on the broadcast may state, "The weather is better than 5,000 and 5," or the existing weather may be broadcast.
      3) Temperature and dew point (degrees Celsius)
      4) Wind direction (magnetic) and velocity
      5) Altimeter
      6) Other pertinent remarks, instrument approach, and runway in use
         a) The departure runway will be given only if it is different from the landing runway, except at locations having a separate ATIS for departure.
   b. The purpose of ATIS is to relieve the ground controllers' and approach controllers' workload. They need not repeat the same information.
   c. The ATIS broadcast is updated whenever any official weather is received, regardless of content or changes, or when a change is made in other pertinent data, such as a runway change. Each new broadcast is labeled with a letter of the alphabet at the beginning of the broadcast; e.g., "This is information alpha" or "information bravo."

SU 6: Radio Communications Procedures

6. **Aircraft Call Signs and Registration Numbers**
    a. Pilots and controllers use aircraft call signs to direct communication with specific aircraft.
        1) Call signs may consist of an aircraft type and registration number, airline and flight number, and some other call sign and designated number.
            a) EXAMPLES: Bonanza six-six-four-two-one, Delta two-three-eight, Angel flight seven-five-five.
            b) Improper use of call signs can result in pilots executing a clearance intended for another aircraft.
            c) ATC specialists will not abbreviate call signs of air carrier or other civil aircraft having authorized call signs.
                i) ATC specialists may initiate abbreviated call signs of other aircraft by using the prefix and the last three digits/letters of the aircraft identification after communications are established.
                ii) Pilots may use the abbreviated call sign in subsequent contacts with the ATC specialist.

7. **Phonetic Alphabet**
    a. Pilots and ATC use the phonetic alphabet to help differentiate between similar sounding identifications.

Letter	Morse	Word	Pronunciation
A	.-	Alpha	(AL-FAH)
B	-...	Bravo	(BRAH-VOH)
C	-.-.	Charlie	(CHAR-LEE) or (SHAR-LEE)
D	-..	Delta	(DELL-TAH)
E	.	Echo	(ECK-OH)
F	..-.	Foxtrot	(FOKS-TROT)
G	--.	Golf	(GOLF)
H	....	Hotel	(HOH-TEL)
I	..	India	(IN-DEE-AH)
J	.---	Juliett	(JEW-LEE-ETT)
K	-.-	Kilo	(KEY-LOH)
L	.-..	Lima	(LEE-MAH)
M	--	Mike	(MIKE)
N	-.	November	(NO-VEM-BER)
O	---	Oscar	(OSS-CAH)
P	.--.	Papa	(PAH-PAH)
Q	--.-	Quebec	(KEH-BECK)
R	.-.	Romeo	(ROW-ME-OH)
S	...	Sierra	(SEE-AIR-RAH)
T	-	Tango	(TANG-GO)
U	..-	Uniform	(YOU-NEE-FORM)
V	...-	Victor	(VIK-TAH)
W	.--	Whiskey	(WISS-KEY)
X	-..-	Xray	(ECKS-RAY)
Y	-.--	Yankee	(YANG-KEY)
Z	--..	Zulu	(ZOO-LOO)
1	.----	One	(WUN)
2	..---	Two	(TOO)
3	...--	Three	(TREE)
4	....-	Four	(FOW-ER)
5	.....	Five	(FIFE)
6	-....	Six	(SIX)
7	--...	Seven	(SEV-EN)
8	---..	Eight	(AIT)
9	----.	Nine	(NIN-ER)
0	-----	Zero	(ZEE-RO)

    b. The phonetic equivalents is used for single letters and for spelling out groups of letters or difficult words.
    c. Work through the listing of alphabetic phonetic equivalents, saying each out loud to learn it.
        1) Note that the Morse code is also provided, although it is not used as frequently as it once was. You need not learn the Morse code; just keep it handy.

8. **Phraseology: Altitudes, Directions, Speed, and Time**
    a. **Figures**
        1) Figures indicating hundreds and thousands in round numbers, as for ceiling heights and upper wind levels up to 9,900, are spoken in accordance with the following:
            a) EXAMPLES: 500 is "FIVE HUNDRED"
               4,500 is "FOUR THOUSAND FIVE HUNDRED"
        2) Numbers above 9,900 are spoken by separating the digits preceding the word "thousand."
            a) EXAMPLES: 10,000 is "ONE ZERO THOUSAND"
               13,500 is "ONE THREE THOUSAND FIVE HUNDRED"
        3) Airway numbers. Airways are routes between navigational aids, such as VORs (i.e., airways are highways in the sky).
            a) EXAMPLE: V12 is "VICTOR TWELVE"
        4) All other numbers are spoken by pronouncing each digit.
            a) EXAMPLE: 10 is "ONE ZERO"
        5) When a radio frequency contains a decimal point, the decimal point is spoken as "POINT."
            a) EXAMPLE: 122.1 is "ONE TWO TWO POINT ONE"
    b. **Altitudes and Flight Levels**
        1) Up to but not including 18,000 ft. MSL, state the separate digits of the thousands, plus the hundreds, if appropriate.
            a) EXAMPLES: 12,000 is "ONE TWO THOUSAND"
               12,500 is "ONE TWO THOUSAND FIVE HUNDRED"
        2) At and above 18,000 ft. MSL (FL 180), state the words "flight level" followed by the separate digits of the flight level.
            a) EXAMPLE: FL 190 is "FLIGHT LEVEL ONE NINER ZERO" (19,000 ft. MSL).
    c. **Directions**
        1) The three digits of bearing, course, heading, and wind direction should always be magnetic. The word "TRUE" must be added when it applies.
        2) EXAMPLES:
            a) (Magnetic course) 005 is "ZERO ZERO FIVE"
            b) (True course) 050 is "ZERO FIVE ZERO TRUE"
            c) (Magnetic bearing) 360 is "THREE SIX ZERO"
            d) (Magnetic heading) 100 is "ONE ZERO ZERO"
            e) (Wind direction) 220 is "TWO TWO ZERO"
        3) Wind velocity (speed) is always included with wind direction, e.g., "THREE FOUR ZERO AT ONE ZERO."
            a) ATC gives winds in magnetic direction.
            b) FSS gives winds in true direction from weather reports and forecasts.

4) ATC traffic advisories provide information based on the position of other aircraft from your airplane in terms of clock direction in a no-wind condition (i.e., it is based on your ground track, not heading).

   a) 12 o'clock is straight ahead.
   b) 3 o'clock is directly off your right wing.
   c) 6 o'clock is directly behind you.
   d) 9 o'clock is directly off your left wing.
   e) Other positions also may be described according to clock direction, e.g., 2 o'clock or 10 o'clock.

d. **Speeds**

   1) Say the separate digits of the speed followed by the word "knots."

      a) EXAMPLES: 250 is "TWO FIVE ZERO KNOTS"
         185 is "ONE EIGHT FIVE KNOTS"

   2) The controller may omit the word "knots" when using speed adjustment procedures, e.g., "INCREASE SPEED TO ONE FIVE ZERO."

e. **Time**

   1) Aviation uses an international standard time with a 24-hour clock system to establish a common time.

   2) The international standard time is called Coordinated Universal Time (UTC). The term "Zulu" (Z) may be used to denote UTC. This used to be referred to as Greenwich Mean Time (GMT).

      a) UTC is actually the time at the 0° meridian, which passes through the Royal Observatory in Greenwich, England.

   3) The FAA uses UTC or Zulu time for all operations. Use the time conversion table below to find UTC. For daylight savings time, subtract 1 hour.

      a) When converting from UTC or Zulu time to local time, subtract the hours.

Time Zone	UTC
Eastern Standard Time	+5 hr.
Central Standard Time	+6 hr.
Mountain Standard Time	+7 hr.
Pacific Standard Time	+8 hr.
Alaska Standard Time	+9 hr.
Hawaii Standard Time	+10 hr.

   4) The 24-hr. clock system is used in radio transmissions. The hour is indicated by the first two figures and the minutes by the last two figures.

      a) EXAMPLES: 0000 is "ZERO ZERO ZERO ZERO" (midnight)
         0920 is "ZERO NINER TWO ZERO" (9:20 a.m.)
         1850 is "ONE EIGHT FIVE ZERO" (6:50 p.m.)

QUESTIONS

6.1 Radio Communications Procedures

1. Automatic Terminal Information Service (ATIS) is the continuous broadcast of recorded information concerning

    A. pilots of radar-identified aircraft whose aircraft is in dangerous proximity to terrain or to an obstruction.

    B. nonessential information to reduce frequency congestion.

    C. noncontrol information in selected high-activity terminal areas.

Answer (C) is correct. (AIM Para 4-1-13)
DISCUSSION: The continuous broadcast of recorded noncontrol information is known as the ATIS. ATIS includes weather, active runway, and other information that arriving and departing pilots need to know.
Answer (A) is incorrect. A controller who has a radar-identified aircraft under his or her control will issue a terrain or obstruction alert to an aircraft that is in dangerous proximity to terrain or to an obstruction. **Answer (B) is incorrect.** ATIS is considered essential (not nonessential) information, but routine, i.e., noncontrol.

2. Absence of the sky condition and visibility on an ATIS broadcast indicates that

    A. weather conditions are at or above VFR minimums.

    B. the sky condition is clear and visibility is unrestricted.

    C. the ceiling is at least 5,000 feet and visibility is 5 miles or more.

Answer (C) is correct. (AIM Para 4-1-13)
DISCUSSION: The ceiling/sky condition, visibility, and obstructions to vision may be omitted from the ATIS broadcast if the ceiling is above 5,000 ft. with visibility more than 5 statute miles.
Answer (A) is incorrect. The absence of the sky condition and visibility on an ATIS broadcast implies that the ceiling is above 5,000 ft. and the visibility is more than 5 statute miles. **Answer (B) is incorrect.** The absence of the sky condition and visibility on an ATIS broadcast implies that the ceiling is above 5,000 ft., not clear, and the visibility is more than 5 SM, not unrestricted.

3. The correct method of stating the aircraft call sign N169US is

    A. November one six niner uniform sierra.

    B. November one six niner unmanned system.

    C. November one hundred sixty nine uniform sierra.

Answer (A) is correct. (AIM Para 4-2-3)
DISCUSSION: The proper phraseology for aircraft call signs is to state each number and letter individually using the phonetic alphabet.
Answer (B) is incorrect. "Unmanned system" is not the phonetic equivalent for the letters U and S. **Answer (C) is incorrect.** The numbers 169 should be stated individually as one six niner.

4. (Refer to Figure 22 on page 197 and Figure 31 on page 198.) (Refer to Area 2 in Figure 22.) At Coeur D'Alene which frequency should be used as a Common Traffic Advisory Frequency (CTAF) to monitor airport traffic?

    A. 122.05 MHz.

    B. 135.075 MHz.

    C. 122.8 MHz.

Answer (C) is correct. (AIM Para 4-1-9)
DISCUSSION: The common traffic advisory frequency is 122.8. It is given in Fig. 22, after "L74" in the airport information on the sectional chart. Radio frequencies are also given in Fig. 31, the Chart Supplement, under "Communications."
Answer (A) is incorrect. This is the remote communication outlet (RCO) frequency to contact Boise FSS in the vicinity of Coeur D'Alene, not the CTAF. **Answer (B) is incorrect.** This is the AWOS frequency, not the CTAF.

5. (Refer to Figure 22 on page 197 and Figure 31 on page 198.) (Refer to Area 2 in Figure 22.) At Coeur D'Alene, which frequency should be used as a Common Traffic Advisory Frequency (CTAF) to self-announce position and intentions?

    A. 122.05 MHz.

    B. 122.1/108.8 MHz.

    C. 122.8 MHz.

Answer (C) is correct. (Chart Supplement)
DISCUSSION: Fig. 31 is the Chart Supplement excerpt for Coeur D'Alene Air Terminal. Look for the section titled **Communications**. On that same line, it states the CTAF (and UNICOM) frequency is 122.8 MHz.
Answer (A) is incorrect. This is the remote communications outlet (RCO) frequency to contact Boise FSS in the vicinity of Coeur D'Alene, not the CTAF. **Answer (B) is incorrect.** The COE VOR/DME frequency, not the CTAF, is 108.8 MHz.

SU 6: Radio Communications Procedures

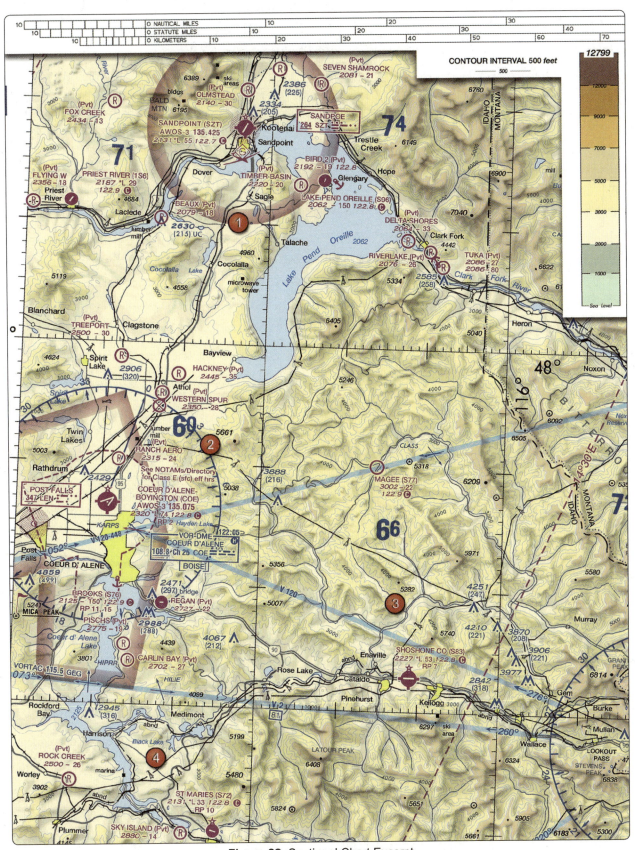

Figure 22. Sectional Chart Excerpt.
NOTE: Chart is not to scale and should not be used for navigation. Use associated scale.

IDAHO 31

COEUR D'ALENE–PAPPY BOYINGTON FLD (COE)   9 NW   UTC−8(−7DT)   GREAT FALLS
  N47°46.46' W116°49.18'
  2320   B   S4   **FUEL** 100, JET A   OX 1, 2, 3, 4   Class IV, ARFF Index A   NOTAM FILE COE   H−1C, L−13B
  RWY 05−23: H7400X100 (ASPH−GRVD)   S−57, D−95, 2S−121, 2D−165   HIRL   0.6% up NE   IAP
    RWY 05: MALSR (NSTD). PAPI(P4R)—GA 3.0° TCH 56'.
    RWY 23: REIL. PAPI(P4R)—GA 3.0° TCH 50'.
  RWY 01−19: H5400X75 (ASPH)   S−50, D−83, 2S−105, 2D−150
    MIRL   0.3% up N
    RWY 01: REIL. PAPI(P2L)—GA 3.0° TCH 39'. Rgt tfc.
    RWY 19: PAPI(P2L)—GA 3.0° TCH 41'. 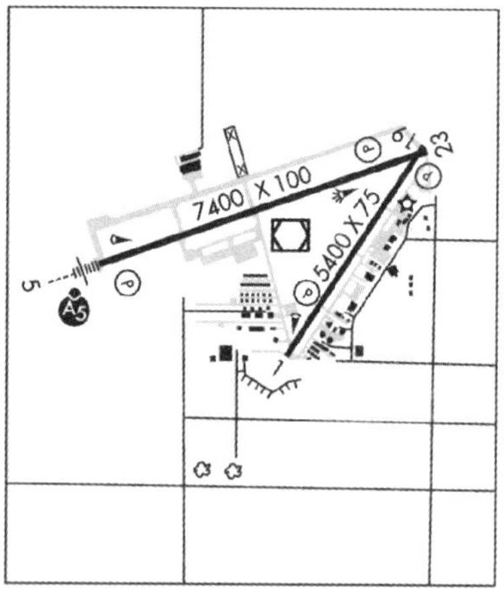
  RUNWAY DECLARED DISTANCE INFORMATION
    RWY 01:   TORA−5400   TODA−5400   ASDA−5400   LDA−5400
    RWY 05:   TORA−7400   TODA−7400   ASDA−7400   LDA−7400
    RWY 19:   TORA−5400   TODA−5400   ASDA−5400   LDA−5400
    RWY 23:   TORA−7400   TODA−7400   ASDA−7400   LDA−7400
  AIRPORT REMARKS: Attended Mon−Fri 1500−0100Z‡. For after hrs fuel-self svc avbl or call 208-772-6404, 208-661-4174, 208-661-7449, 208-699-5433. Self svc fuel avbl with credit card. 48 hr PPR for unscheduled ops with more than 30 passenger seats call arpt manager 208-446-1860. Migratory birds on and invof arpt Oct−Nov. Remote cntl airstrip is 2.3 miles west AER 05. Arpt conditions avbl on AWOS. Rwy 05 NSTD MALSR, thld bar extends 5' byd rwy edge lgts each side. ACTIVATE MIRL Rwy 01−19, HIRL Rwy 05−23, REIL Rwy 01 and Rwy 23, MALSR Rwy 05—CTAF. PAPI Rwy 01, Rwy 19, Rwy 05, and Rwy 23 opr continuously.
  WEATHER DATA SOURCES: AWOS−3 135.075 (208) 772-8215.
    HIWAS 108.8 COE.
  COMMUNICATIONS: CTAF/UNICOM 122.8
    RCO 122.05 (BOISE RADIO)
  ⒭ SPOKANE APP/DEP CON 132.1
  AIRSPACE: CLASS E svc continuous.
  RADIO AIDS TO NAVIGATION: NOTAM FILE COE.
    (T) VORW/DME 108.8   COE   Chan 25   N47°46.42' W116°49.24'   at fld. 2320/19E.   HIWAS.
      DME portion unusable:
        220°−240° byd 15 NM   280°−315° byd 15 NM blo 11,000'.
    POST FALLS NDB (MHW) 347   LEN   N47°44.57' W116°57.66'   053° 6.0 NM to fld.
    ILS 110.7   I−COE   Rwy 05   Class ID.   Localizer unusable 25° left and right of course.

Figure 31. Chart Supplement.

SU 6: Radio Communications Procedures

6. (Refer to Figure 21 below.) (Refer to Area 2.) The CTAF/MULTICOM frequency for Garrison Airport is

- A. 122.8 MHz.
- B. 122.9 MHz.
- C. 123.0 MHz.

Answer (B) is correct. (ACUG)
DISCUSSION: The CTAF for Garrison Municipal Airport (west of area 2 in Fig. 21) is 122.9 MHz, because that frequency is marked with a C.
Answer (A) is incorrect. There is no indication of 122.8 MHz at Garrison. **Answer (C) is incorrect.** There is no indication of 123.0 MHz at Garrison.

Figure 21. Sectional Chart Excerpt.
NOTE: Chart is not to scale and should not be used for navigation. Use associated scale.

7. The correct method of stating 4,500 feet MSL to ATC is

A. "FOUR THOUSAND FIVE HUNDRED."
B. "FOUR POINT FIVE."
C. "FORTY-FIVE HUNDRED FEET MSL."

Answer (A) is correct. (AIM Para 4-2-9)
DISCUSSION: The proper phraseology for altitudes up to but not including 18,000 ft. MSL is to state the separate digits of the thousands, plus the hundreds, if appropriate. It would be "four thousand, five hundred."
Answer (B) is incorrect. Four point five is slang (not correct) phraseology. **Answer (C) is incorrect.** The thousand is spoken separately from the hundreds and not together. A stated altitude is understood to be MSL, unless otherwise stated.

8. The correct method of stating 10,500 feet MSL to ATC is

A. "TEN THOUSAND, FIVE HUNDRED FEET."
B. "TEN POINT FIVE."
C. "ONE ZERO THOUSAND, FIVE HUNDRED."

Answer (C) is correct. (AIM Para 4-2-9)
DISCUSSION: The proper phraseology for altitudes up to but not including 18,000 ft. MSL is to state the separate digits of the thousands, plus the hundreds, if appropriate. It would be one zero thousand, five hundred.
Answer (A) is incorrect. It is one zero, not ten.
Answer (B) is incorrect. Ten point five is slang (not correct) phraseology.

9. (Refer to Figure 26 on page 201.) (Refer to Area 2.) While monitoring the Cooperstown CTAF you hear an aircraft announce that they are midfield left downwind to RWY 13. Where would the aircraft be relative to the runway?

A. The aircraft is East.
B. The aircraft is South.
C. The aircraft is West.

Answer (A) is correct. (AIM Para 4-1-5)
DISCUSSION: Cooperstown Airport shows one runway. Runway numbers and letters are determined from the approach direction. A runway designated at 13 has a magnetic direction of 130°. An aircraft on the midfield left downwind is at the midpoint of the left side of the runway, heading in the opposite direction (310°). This places the aircraft to the east of the runway.
Answer (B) is incorrect. An aircraft south of the runway would be on the left base leg for RWY 31. **Answer (C) is incorrect.** An aircraft west of the runway would be midfield left downwind to RWY 31.

10. (Refer to Figure 26 on page 201.) (Refer to Area 4.) The CTAF/UNICOM frequency at Jamestown Airport is

A. 122.2 MHz.
B. 123.0 MHz.
C. 123.6 MHz.

Answer (B) is correct. (ACUG)
DISCUSSION: The UNICOM frequency is printed in bold italics in the airport identifier. At Jamestown it is 123.0 MHz. The C next to it indicates it as the CTAF.
Answer (A) is incorrect. This is the Flight Service frequency, not UNICOM. **Answer (C) is incorrect.** This is an FSS frequency, not UNICOM.

11. (Refer to Figure 26 on page 201.) (Refer to Area 5.) What is the CTAF/UNICOM frequency at Barnes County Airport?

A. 122.2 MHz.
B. 122.8 MHz.
C. 123.6 MHz.

Answer (B) is correct. (ACUG)
DISCUSSION: In Fig. 26, Barnes County Airport is to the east of area 5. The CTAF at Barnes County Airport is marked as the UNICOM frequency for the airport, i.e., 122.8 MHz.
Answer (A) is incorrect. This is the Flight Service frequency. **Answer (C) is incorrect.** This is an FSS frequency.

12. (Refer to Figure 26 on page 201.) What does the line of latitude at area 4 measure?

A. The degrees of latitude east and west of the Prime Meridian.
B. The degrees of latitude north and south from the equator.
C. The degrees of latitude east and west of the line that passes through Greenwich, England.

Answer (B) is correct. (sUASSG Chap 11)
DISCUSSION: Lines of latitude are parallel to the equator and used to measure degrees of latitude north (N) or south (S) of the Equator.
Answer (A) is incorrect. Lines of longitude, not latitude, measure degrees east and west of the Prime Meridian.
Answer (C) is incorrect. Lines of longitude, not latitude, measure degrees east and west of the line passing through Greenwich, England (Prime Meridian).

SU 6: Radio Communications Procedures

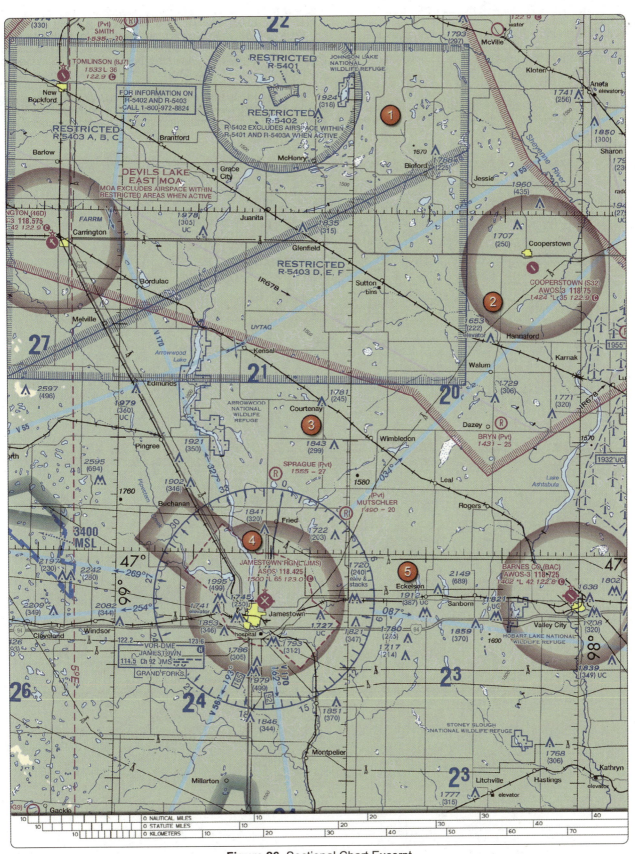

Figure 26. Sectional Chart Excerpt.
NOTE: Chart is not to scale and should not be used for navigation. Use associated scale.

13. (Refer to Figure 78 below, and Figure 79 on page 203.) At Sioux Gateway/Col Day (N42°24.16' W96°23.06'), which frequency should be used as a Common Traffic Advisory Frequency (CTAF) to self-announce position and intentions when the control tower is closed?

- A. 122.95 MHz.
- B. 119.45 MHz.
- C. 118.7 MHz.

Answer (C) is correct. (Chart Supplement)
DISCUSSION: Fig. 79 is the Chart Supplement excerpt for Sioux Gateway/Col Day Airport. Look for the section titled "Communications." On that same line, it states that the CTAF frequency is 118.7 MHz. It is also located on Fig. 78 in the Sioux Gateway Airport Data Description, indicated by a "C" surrounded by a shaded blue circle.

Answer (A) is incorrect. This is the UNICOM frequency, not the CTAF frequency. **Answer (B) is incorrect.** The ATIS (Automatic Terminal Information Service) frequency is 119.45 MHz and is not the CTAF frequency.

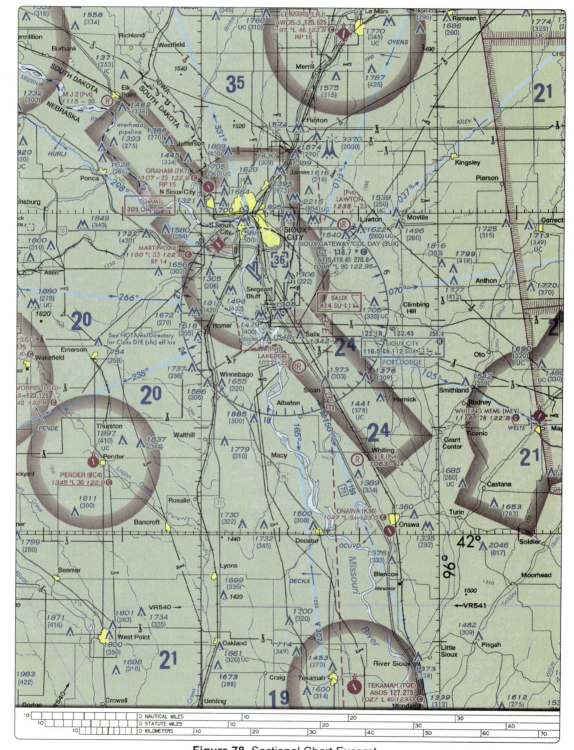

Figure 78. Sectional Chart Excerpt.
NOTE: Chart is not to scale and should not be used for navigation. Use associated scale.

SU 6: Radio Communications Procedures

64   **IOWA**

SIOUX CITY   N42°20.67′ W96°19.42′   NOTAM FILE SUX   OMAHA
     (L) VORTAC 116.5   SUX   Chan 112   313° 4.4 NM to Sioux Gateway/Col Bud Day Fld. 1087/9E.   HIWAS.   L-12I
     VOR unusable:
        280°-292° byd 25 NM   306°-350° byd 20 NM blo 3,000′
        293°-305° byd 20 NM blo 4,500′   350°-280° byd 30 NM blo 3,000′
        293°-305° byd 35 NM
     RCO 122.45 122.1R 116.5T (FORT DODGE RADIO)

SIOUX CITY

SIOUX GATEWAY/COL BUD DAY FLD   (SUX)   6 S   UTC −6(−5DT)   N42°24.16′ W96°23.06′   OMAHA
    1098   B   S4   **FUEL** 100LL, 115, JET A   OX 1, 2, 3, 4   Class I, ARFF Index—See Remarks   H-5C, L-12I
    NOTAM FILE SUX   IAP, AD
    RWY 13-31: H9002X150 (CONC-GRVD)   S-100, D-120, 2S-152,
      2D-220   HIRL
      RWY 13: MALS. VASI(V4L)—GA 3.0° TCH 49′. Tree.
      RWY 31: MALSR. VASI(V4L)—GA 3.0° TCH 50′.
    RWY 17-35: H6600X150 (ASPH-PFC)   S-65, D-80, 2S-102,
      2D-130   MIRL
      RWY 17: REIL. VASI(V4R)—GA 3.0° TCH 50′. Trees.
      RWY 35: PAPI(P4L)—GA 3.0° TCH 54′. Pole.
    LAND AND HOLD SHORT OPERATIONS
       LANDING   HOLD SHORT POINT   DIST AVBL
       RWY 13   17-35   5400
       RWY 17   13-31   5650
    ARRESTING GEAR/SYSTEM
       RWY 13 ←BAK-14 BAK-12B(B) (1392′)
                            BAK-14 BAK-12B(B) (1492′) →RWY 31

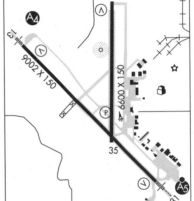

    AIRPORT REMARKS: Attended continuously. PAEW 0330-1200Z ‡ during
      inclement weather Nov-Apr. AER 31-BAK-12/14 located (1492′)
      from thld. Airfield surface conditions not monitored by arpt
      management between 0600-1000Z ‡ daily. Rwy 13-BAK-12/14
      located (1392′) from thld. All A-gear avbl only during ANG flying ops. Twr has limited visibility southeast of
      ramp near ARFF bldg and northeast of Rwy 31 touchdown zone. Rwy 31 is calm wind rwy. Class I, ARFF Index
      B. ARFF Index E fire fighting equipment avbl on request. Twy F unlit, retro-reflective markers in place. Portions
      of Twy A SE of Twy B not visible by twr and is designated a non-movement area. Rwy 13-31 touchdown and
      rollout rwy visual range avbl. When twr clsd, ACTIVATE HIRL Rwy 13-31; MIRL Rwy 17-35; MALS Rwy 13;
      MALSR Rwy 31; and REIL Rwy 17—CTAF.
    WEATHER DATA SOURCES: ASOS (712) 255-6474.   HIWAS 116.5 SUX. LAWRS.
    COMMUNICATIONS: CTAF 118.7   **ATIS** 119.45   **UNICOM** 122.95
      SIOUX CITY RCO 122.45 122.1R 116.5T (FORT DODGE RADIO)
   ® **SIOUX CITY APP/DEP CON** 124.6 (1200-0330Z ‡)
   ® **MINNEAPOLIS CENTER APP/DEP CON** 124.1 (0330-1200Z ‡)
      SIOUX CITY TOWER 118.7 (1200-0330Z ‡)   **GND CON** 121.9
    AIRSPACE: CLASS D svc 1200-0330Z ‡ other times **CLASS E**.
    RADIO AIDS TO NAVIGATION: NOTAM FILE SUX.
      SIOUX CITY (L) VORTAC 116.5   SUX   Chan 112   N42°20.67′ W96°19.42′   313° 4.4 NM to fld. 1087/9E.
       HIWAS.
      NDB (MHW) 233   GAK   N42°24.49′ W96°23.16′   at fld.
      SALIX NDB (MHW/LOM) 414   SU   N42°19.65′ W96°17.43′   311° 6.1 NM to fld. Unmonitored.
      TOMMI NDB (MHW/LOM) 305   OI   N42°27.61′ W96°27.73′   128° 4.9 NM to fld. Unmonitored.
      ILS 109.3   I-SUX   Rwy 31   Class IT.   LOM SALIX NDB. ILS Unmonitored when twr clsd. Glide path
        unusable coupled approach (CPD) blo 1805′.
      ILS 111.3   I-OIQ   Rwy 13   LOM TOMMI NDB. Localizer shutdown when twr clsd.
      ASR (1200-0330Z ‡)

SNORE   N43°13.96′ W95°19.66′   NOTAM FILE SPW.   OMAHA
    NDB (LOM) 394   SP   121° 6.8 NM to Spencer Muni.

SOUTHEAST IOWA RGNL   (See BURLINGTON)

Figure 79. Chart Supplement.

14. An ATC radar facility issues the following advisory to a pilot flying on a heading of 090°:

"TRAFFIC 3 O'CLOCK, 2 MILES, WESTBOUND..."

Where should the pilot look for this traffic?

A. East.
B. South.
C. West.

Answer (B) is correct. (AIM Para 4-1-14)
DISCUSSION: If you receive traffic information service from radar and are told you have traffic at the 3 o'clock position, traffic is in the direction of the right wingtip, or to the south.
Answer (A) is incorrect. East is the 12 o'clock position.
Answer (C) is incorrect. West is the 6 o'clock position.

15. An ATC radar facility issues the following advisory to a pilot flying on a heading of 360°:

"TRAFFIC 10 O'CLOCK, 2 MILES, SOUTHBOUND..."

Where should the pilot look for this traffic?

A. Northwest.
B. Northeast.
C. Southwest.

Answer (A) is correct. (AIM Para 4-1-14)
DISCUSSION: The controller is telling you that traffic is at 10 o'clock and 2 mi. 9 o'clock is the left wingtip, and 10 o'clock is 2/3 of the way from the nose of the airplane (12 o'clock) to the left wingtip. Thus, you are looking northwest.
Answer (B) is incorrect. Northeast would be in the 1 to 2 o'clock position. **Answer (C) is incorrect.** Southwest would be in the 7 to 8 o'clock position.

16. An ATC radar facility issues the following advisory to a pilot flying north in a calm wind:

"TRAFFIC 9 O'CLOCK, 2 MILES, SOUTHBOUND..."

Where should the pilot look for this traffic?

A. South.
B. North.
C. West.

Answer (C) is correct. (AIM Para 4-1-14)
DISCUSSION: Traffic at 9 o'clock is off the left wingtip. The nose of the airplane is 12 o'clock, the left wingtip is 9 o'clock, the tail is 6 o'clock, and the right wingtip is 3 o'clock. With a north heading, the aircraft at 9 o'clock would be west of you.
Answer (A) is incorrect. South would be the 6 o'clock position. **Answer (B) is incorrect.** North would be the 12 o'clock position.

17. (Refer to Figure 25 on page 205.) (Refer to Area 3.) If Dallas Executive Tower is not in operation, which frequency should be used as a Common Traffic Advisory Frequency (CTAF) to monitor airport traffic?

A. 127.25 MHz.
B. 122.95 MHz.
C. 126.35 MHz.

Answer (A) is correct. (ACUG)
DISCUSSION: In Fig. 25, find the Dallas Executive Airport just above area 3. When the Dallas Executive tower is not in operation, the CTAF is 127.25 MHz because that frequency is marked with a C, which indicates a CTAF.
Answer (B) is incorrect. The UNICOM frequency is 122.95 MHz. **Answer (C) is incorrect.** The ATIS frequency is 126.35 MHz.

18. (Refer to Figure 25 on page 205.) (Refer to Area 2.) The control tower frequency for Addison Airport is

A. 122.95 MHz.
B. 126.0 MHz.
C. 133.4 MHz.

Answer (B) is correct. (ACUG)
DISCUSSION: Addison Airport (Fig. 25, area 2) control tower frequency is given as the first item in the second line of the airport data to the right of the airport symbol. The control tower (CT) frequency is 126.0 MHz.
Answer (A) is incorrect. This is the UNICOM, not control tower, frequency for Addison Airport. **Answer (C) is incorrect.** This is the ATIS, not control tower, frequency for Addison Airport.

SU 6: Radio Communications Procedures

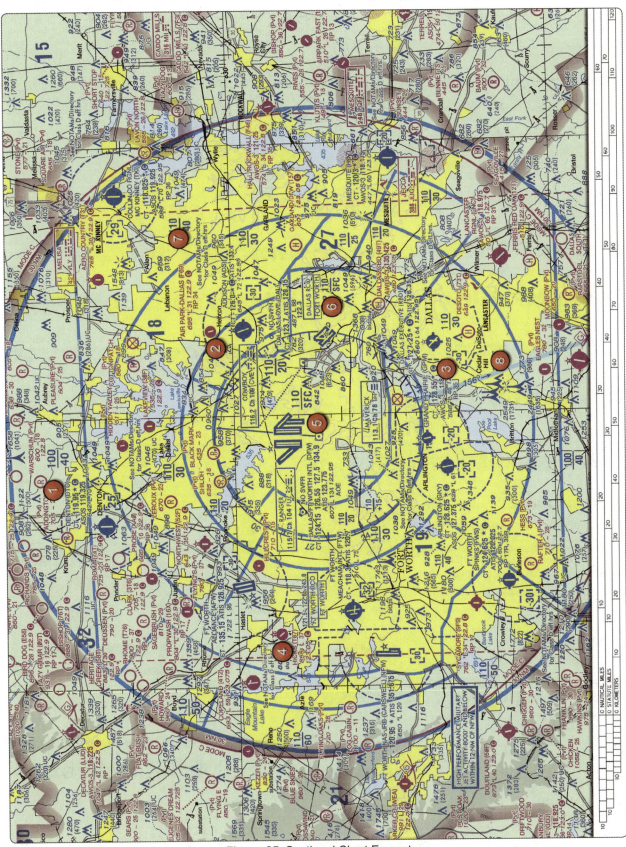

Figure 25. Sectional Chart Excerpt.
NOTE: Chart is not to scale and should not be used for navigation. Use associated scale.

GLEIM® FAA Test Prep Online

Study for and PASS your FAA knowledge test in a unique, easy-to-use program.
- Gain confidence by emulating tests as presented at the testing center.
- Customizable exams help you address and overcome weak areas.

Available for the following knowledge tests:

✈ **Sport Pilot**

✈ **Private Pilot**

✈ **Commercial Pilot**

✈ **Instrument Rating**

✈ **Remote Pilot**

✈ **Airline Transport Pilot**

✈ **Flight/Ground Instructor**

EXPAND YOUR REFERENCE LIBRARY

Pilot Handbook
- Comprehensive reference text to explain all aspects of flying
- Sections on flight reviews and instrument proficiency checks
- Color images and diagrams

Aviation Weather & Weather Services
- A simplified explanation of
  - AC 00-6, Aviation Weather
  - AC 00-45, Aviation Weather Services
- Color images and diagrams

Pilot Logbook
- Practical for all pilot skill levels, student through professional

www.GleimAviation.com/referencebooks

GleimAviation.com
800.874.5346 ext. 471

STUDY UNIT SEVEN
AIRPORT OPERATIONS

(16 pages of outline)

| 7.1 | Airport Operations | (37 questions) 207, 223 |

7.1 AIRPORT OPERATIONS

1. **Types of airports**, such as towered, non-towered, heliport, and seaplane bases, have specific operational requirements for each of the various types or classes of airspace. Situational awareness must be maintained at all times.

    a. Towered airport operations.

    1) Approaching aircraft: Tower control will provide instructions to either land straight-in or to enter the pattern on either the left or right downwind leg of the runway.

    2) Departing aircraft: Tower control will provide instructions to depart straight out or turn left or right after takeoff.

        a) Monitoring communications with ground control will help advise when aircraft are taxiing to a runway and which general direction they may be departing toward.

    b. Non-towered airport operations.

    1) Approaching aircraft: Pilots will self-announce their position when approaching airports and should state their intention to either land straight-in or enter the pattern on the downwind leg of the runway.

        a) Landing traffic should also announce their position on various legs of the traffic pattern, such as "base" or "final."

        b) Listen for the mentions of "left or right traffic" to determine which side of the runway the aircraft will be using in the pattern. Different aircraft may use different types of approaches.

    2) Departing aircraft: Similar to approaching aircraft, manned aircraft pilots will self-announce their intention to takeoff and make position reports in the vicinity of the airport after departure.

2. **Monitor and interpret ATC communications** to improve situational awareness and become familiar with typical ATC communications.

    a. The tower controller coordinates all aircraft activity on the active runway and in the vicinity of the airport.

    b. When an aircraft is ready to takeoff, the pilot addresses the tower, identifies their call sign and registration number, and states their intentions.

    c. The tower controller may then issue a clearance for takeoff if appropriate and provide an outbound departure heading.

    1) The tower may not clear the pilot due to traffic, e.g., "Bonanza six-six-four-two-one, hold short of Runway six, landing traffic."

        a) Pilots must read back all runway hold short instructions, e.g., "Hold short of Runway six, Bonanza six-six-four-two-one."

d. Tower control is also used for landing. Pilots generally contact tower control 10 to 15 NM out, so the controller has time to route them to the active runway and coordinate their approach with the other traffic.

   1) Pilots will address the tower, stating who they are, where they are, and what they want.

e. The Air Traffic Organization (ATO) does not have the authority to deny sUAS operations on the basis of equipage that exceeds the part 107 requirements.

   1) A remote pilot who wishes to operate in controlled airspace may do so by applying for a waiver.
   2) ATC may impose certain restrictions and require the remote pilot to maintain two-way communications with the tower, or at least be capable of monitoring ATC communications.

3. **Runway markings and signage** provide useful information for pilots during takeoff, landing, and taxiing that enhances safety and improve efficiency.

   a. A runway is marked in accordance with its present usage as a visual runway, nonprecision instrument runway, or precision instrument runway.

      1) **Visual runways** are used for visual flight rules (VFR) operations.

         a) **Designation markings** are numbers and letters determined by the approach direction. The runway number is the whole number nearest one-tenth the magnetic direction of the runway (e.g., a runway with a magnetic direction of 200° would be designated as runway 20). Letters differentiate between left (L), right (R), or center (C) parallel runways, if applicable.

            i) Two parallel runways -- "20L," "20R"
            ii) Three parallel runways -- "20L," "20C," "20R"

         b) **Centerline markings** are dashed white lines that identify the center of the runway, providing alignment guidance during takeoff and landing.

         c) **Optional markings**

            i) If the runway is used or intended to be used by international commercial transport, threshold markings are required.
            ii) If the runway is 4,000 ft. or longer and is used by jet aircraft, an aiming point marking is required.
            iii) Runway side stripes may be added if necessary.

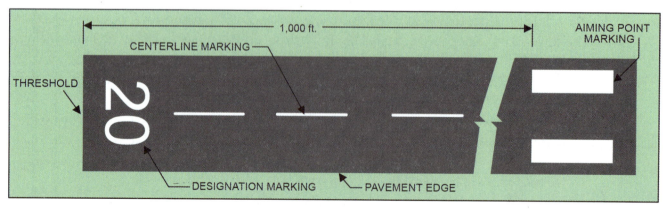

2) **Nonprecision instrument runways** are served by nonprecision instrument approaches, and their markings include

   a) Designation markings.
   b) Centerline markings.
   c) **Threshold markings.** These markings help you to identify the beginning of the runway that is available for landing. Threshold markings come in two configurations.

      i) A number of stripes designated according to the width of the runway or
      ii) A total of eight longitudinal stripes (four on each side of the centerline) equaling 100 ft. wide

   d) **Aiming point markers.** These markers serve as a visual aiming point during landing. They are two broad white stripes located on each side of the runway centerline approximately 1,000 ft. from the landing threshold.
   e) Runway side stripes. These may be added as necessary.

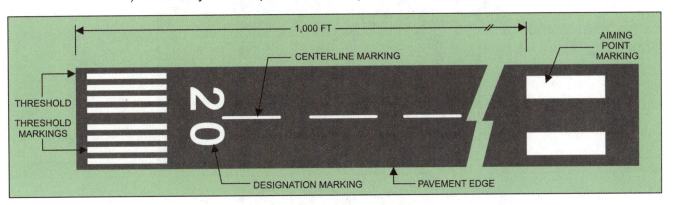

3) **Precision instrument runways** are served by precision instrument approaches.

   a) **Touchdown zone markings** identify the touchdown zone for landing operations and are coded to provide distance information in 500-ft. increments.

      i) These markings consist of groups of one, two, and three rectangular bars arranged on each side of the centerline, as shown below.

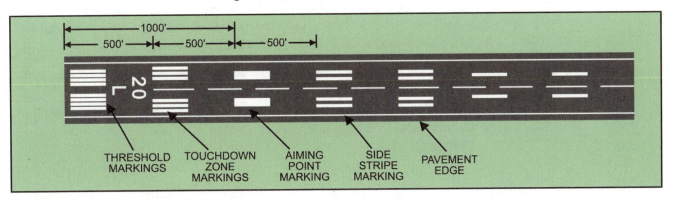

b. Additional Runway Markings

1) **Side stripe markings** are continuous white stripes located on each side of the runway to provide a visual contrast between the runway and the abutting terrain or shoulders.

2) **Runway shoulder markings** are yellow and may be used to supplement runway side stripes to identify the runway shoulder area as shown below. This area is not intended for use by aircraft.

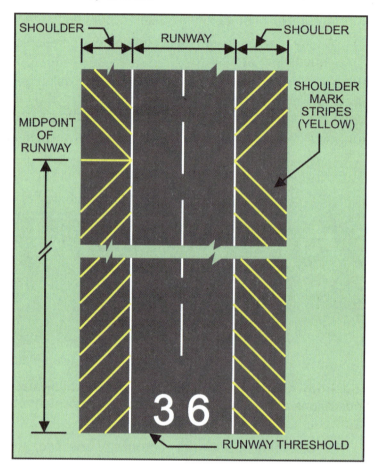

3) **Runway threshold bars** mark the beginning of the runway that is available for landing when the threshold has been relocated or displaced. The threshold bar is 10 ft. wide, white, and extends across the width of the runway.

a) **Relocated thresholds** are thresholds temporarily relocated (due to construction, maintenance, etc.) toward the departure end of the runway.

i) While methods for identifying the relocated threshold vary, the most common method is to use a threshold bar to mark the relocated threshold.

b) **Displaced thresholds** are thresholds not at the beginning of the paved runway.

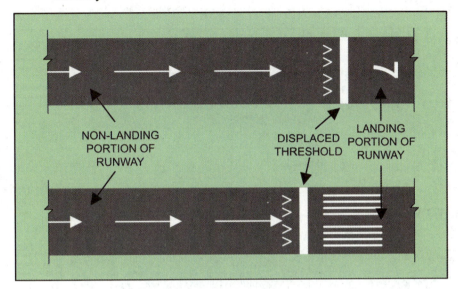

   i) The paved area before the displaced runway threshold (marked by arrows) is available for taxiing, the takeoff of aircraft, and a landing rollout from the opposite direction, but not for landing in the direction of the runway in question.

   ii) A threshold bar is located across the width of the runway at the displaced threshold.

   iii) White arrows are located along the centerline in the area between the beginning of the runway and the displaced threshold.

   iv) White arrowheads are located across the width of the runway just prior to the threshold bar.

4) **Chevrons** are yellow markings used to show pavement areas (e.g., blast pads, stopways, etc.) aligned with the runway that are unusable for landing, takeoff, and taxiing.

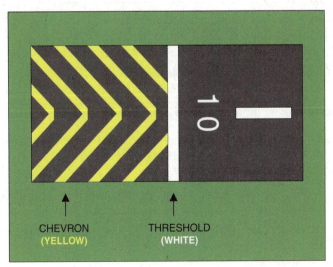

5) **Demarcation bars** separate runways with displaced thresholds from taxiways or areas marked by chevrons that precede the runway, as shown below. The demarcation bar is 3 ft. wide and is colored yellow since it is not on the runway.

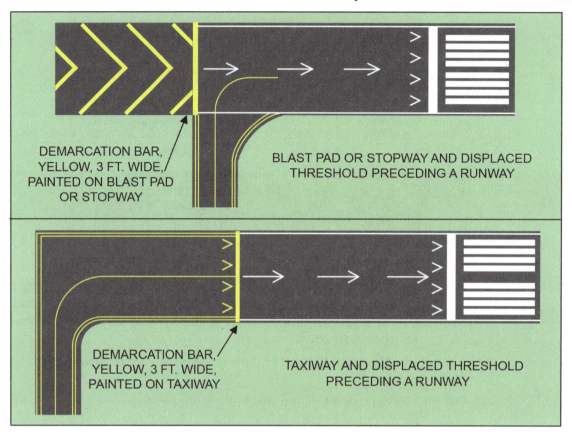

6) **Closed or temporarily closed runways** are visually managed differently.

a) A permanently closed runway has all runway lighting disconnected, all runway markings obliterated, and yellow crosses placed at each end of the runway and at 1,000-ft. intervals.

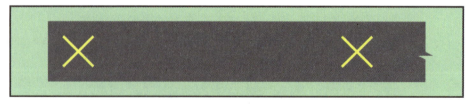

b) A temporarily closed runway is marked by yellow crosses placed only at each end of the runway.

i) An alternative is to place a raised lighted yellow cross at each end of the runway.

ii) A visual indication may not be present depending on the reason for the closure, the duration of the closure, airport configuration, and the existence (and operating hours) of a control tower.

SU 7: Airport Operations   213

c. **Taxiway and destination signs** guide manned aircraft on the airport surface.
   1) Destination signs have black characters on a yellow background with an arrow showing the direction of the taxiing route to the destination listed. Outbound destinations commonly show directions to the take-off runways.
      a) Signs I, J, and K are examples of destination signs as shown in Figure 65 on the next page.
         i) Sign K designates the direction of taxiway bravo.
   2) Taxiway location signs identify the taxiway on which an aircraft is currently located.
      a) Location signs feature a black background with yellow lettering and do not have directional arrows.
   3) Taxiway directional signs indicate the designation and direction of a taxiway.
      a) When turning from one taxiway to another, a taxiway directional sign indicates the designation and direction of a taxiway leading out of the intersection.
      b) Taxiway directional signs feature a yellow background with black lettering and directional arrows.
   4) When approaching taxiway holding lines from the side with continuous lines, the pilot should not cross the lines without an ATC clearance.
      a) Taxiway holding lines are painted across the width of the taxiway and are yellow.
   5) Many airports use an enhanced taxiway centerline marking consisting of a parallel line of yellow dashes on either side of the normal taxiway centerline.

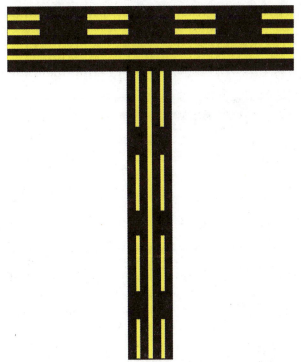

AIM Fig. 2-3-8. Enhanced Taxiway Centerline.

      a) These taxiway centerlines are enhanced for a maximum of 150 ft. prior to a runway holding position marking.
      b) They are used to warn the pilot of an approaching runway holding position marking. The pilot should prepare to stop unless the pilot has been cleared onto or across the runway by ATC.

6) A runway holding position sign is a mandatory instruction sign with white characters on a red background. It is located at the holding position on taxiways that intersect a runway or on runways that intersect other runways.

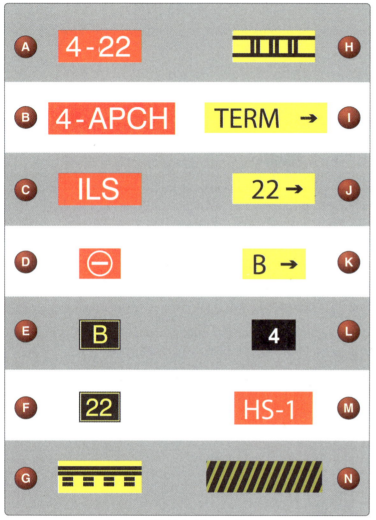

A. Runway Holding Position Sign
B. Holding Position Sign for a Runway Approach Area
C. Holding Position Sign for ILS Critical Area
D. Sign Prohibiting Aircraft Entry into an Area
E. Taxiway Location Sign
F. Runway Location Sign
G. Runway Boundary Sign
H. ILS Critical Area Boundary Sign
I. Direction Sign for Terminal
J. Direction Sign for Common Taxiing Route to Runway
K. Direction Sign for Runway Exit
L. Runway Distance Remaining Sign
M. Hold Short
N. Taxiway Ending Sign

Figure 65. U.S. Airport Signs.

d. **Vehicle roadway markings** define pathways for vehicles to cross areas of the airport used by aircraft.

1) Vehicle roadway markings are located at C in the airport planview (Figure 64) on the next page.

a) The edge of vehicle roadway markings may be defined by a solid white line or white zipper markings with a dashed white centerline separating opposite-direction vehicle traffic inside the roadway.

SU 7: Airport Operations

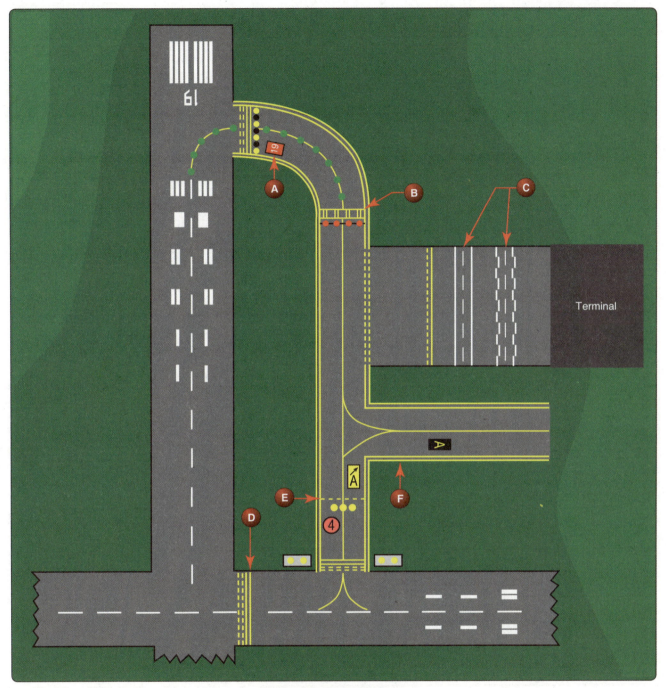

Figure 64. Airport Markings.

2) The letters below correspond to the airport markings in Figure 64.

    a) Holding Position Markings at Beginning of Takeoff Runway 19
    b) ILS Critical Area Boundary Marking
    c) Roadway Edge Stripes
    d) Runway Holding Position Marking
    e) Taxiway Holding Position Marker
    f) Taxiway Boundary

e. **Airport and heliport beacons** communicate in alternating colors: airport type or conditions present.

  1) Green alone or green and white identify a lighted land airport. Operation of the beacon at an airport located in Class B, C, D, or E surface areas during the day indicates that the weather is not VFR.

     a) Ground visibility less than 3 SM or
     b) Ceiling less than 1,000 ft.

  2) A lighted heliport may be identified by a green, yellow, and white rotating beacon.

  3) Military airports are indicated by beacons with two white flashes between each green flash.

4. **Established airport traffic patterns** ensure that air traffic flows into and out of an airport in an orderly manner.

  a. **Basic rectangular airport traffic patterns** are typically at an altitude of 1,000 ft. above the elevation of the airport, unless otherwise specified in the Chart Supplement. Using a common altitude is the key to minimizing collision risk.

    1) At all airports, the direction of traffic flow is to the left, unless right turns are indicated by

       a) Visual markings (i.e., traffic pattern indicators) on the airport
       b) Control tower instructions
       c) Depictions on charts

    2) The basic rectangular traffic pattern consists of five "legs" positioned in relation to the runway in use, as illustrated on the next page.

       a) The **departure leg** of the traffic pattern is a straight course aligned with and leading from the takeoff runway.
       b) The **crosswind leg** is horizontally perpendicular to the extended centerline of the takeoff runway. It is entered by making a 90° turn from the upwind leg.
       c) The **downwind leg** is flown parallel to the landing runway but in a direction opposite to the intended landing direction.
       d) The **base leg** is the transitional part of the traffic pattern between the downwind leg and the final approach leg.
       e) The **final approach leg** is a descending flight path starting at the completion of the base-to-final turn and extending to the point of touchdown.

    3) The **upwind leg** is commonly misunderstood to be another name for the departure leg.

       a) It is actually a separate leg of the pattern entirely.
       b) The upwind leg is used to side-step the departure leg. This may be done in the case of a go-around or aborted landing.

SU 7: Airport Operations

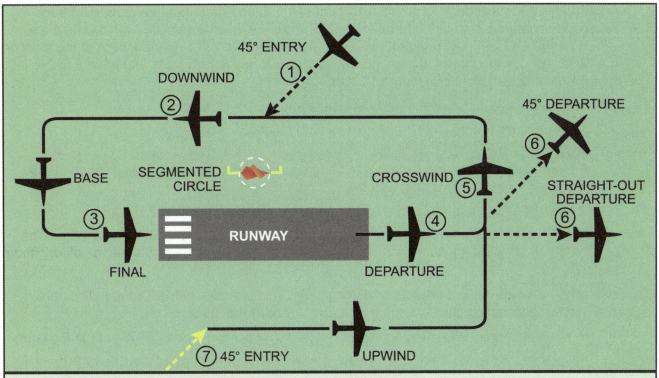

Key:
1. Enter pattern in level flight, abeam the midpoint of the runway, at pattern altitude.
2. Maintain pattern altitude until abeam approach end of the landing runway on the downwind leg.
3. Complete turn to final at least 1/4 mi. from the runway.
4. Continue straight ahead until beyond departure end of runway.
5. If remaining in the traffic pattern, commence turn to crosswind leg beyond the departure end of the runway, within 300 ft. of pattern altitude.
6. If departing the traffic pattern, continue straight out, or exit with a 45° left turn (right turn for right traffic pattern) beyond the departure end of the runway, after reaching pattern altitude.
7. There are a few airports in the U.S. that require a 45° entry to the upwind leg of the traffic pattern.

b. When **entering a traffic pattern** at an airport with an operating control tower, the controller will direct when and where pilots should enter the pattern.

1) Once the pilot is in the pattern, the controller may request that the pilot perform some maneuvers for better traffic spacing, including

a) Shortening or extending the downwind leg; increasing or decreasing the aircraft's speed; or performing a 360° turn or S-turns to provide spacing ahead of the aircraft.

2) To enter the traffic pattern at an airport without an operating control tower, inbound pilots are expected to observe other aircraft already in the pattern and wind indicators on the ground to conform to the traffic pattern in use.

a) Overfly the airport at least 500 to 1,000 ft. above the pattern before descending to the pattern altitude.

b) When approaching an airport for landing, the pilot should enter the traffic pattern at a 45° angle to the downwind leg at the midpoint of the runway at the proper traffic pattern altitude.

c. **Departing a traffic pattern** at airports with an operating control tower is guided by ATC.

1) At airports without an operating control tower, departures will be made straight out or with a 45° turn in the direction of the traffic pattern after reaching pattern altitude.

5. **Security identification display areas (SIDA)** are limited access areas that require a badge issued in accordance with procedures in 49 CFR Part 1542. Movement through or into these areas is prohibited without proper identification being displayed. If you are unsure of the location of a SIDA, contact the airport authority for additional information. Airports that have a SIDA must have the following information available:

    a. A description and map detailing boundaries and pertinent features;

    b. Measures used to perform the access control functions required under 49 CFR 1542.201(b)(1);

    c. Procedures to control movement within the secured area, including identification media required under 49 CFR 1542.201(b)(3); and

    d. A description of the notification signs required under 49 CFR 1542.201(b)(6).

6. **Longitude and latitude** lines provide a common grid system that is the key to navigation. The location of any point on the Earth can be determined by the intersection of the lines of longitude and latitude.

    a. **Lines of latitude**, or **parallels**, are imaginary circles parallel to the Equator. They are drawn as lines on charts running east and west around the world.

        1) They are used to measure degrees of latitude north (N) or south (S) of the Equator.

        2) Angular distance from the Equator to the pole is one-fourth of a circle, or 90°.

        3) The 48 conterminous states of the United States are located between 24° and 49°N latitude.

    b. **Lines of longitude**, or **meridians**, are drawn from the North Pole to the South Pole and are at right angles to the Equator and the parallels.

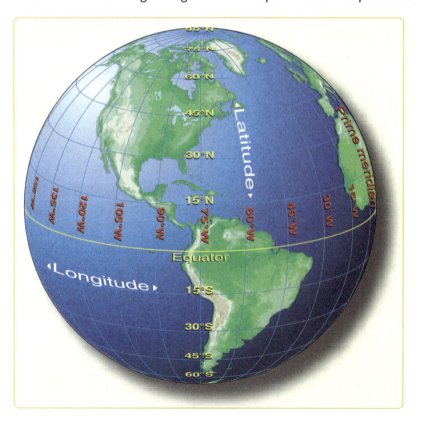

   1) The **Prime Meridian**, which passes through Greenwich, England, is used as the zero line from which measurements are made in degrees east (E) and west (W) to 180°.

   2) The 48 conterminous states of the United States are located between 67° and 125°W longitude.

   3) Because lines of longitude connect the poles, they mark the direction of true north and south.

SU 7: Airport Operations   219

c. Any specific geographical point on Earth can thus be located by reference to its latitude and longitude.

   1) EXAMPLES: Washington, D.C., is approximately 39°N latitude, 77°W longitude, and Chicago is approximately 42°N latitude, 88°W longitude.

   2) The lines of longitude and latitude are printed on aeronautical (e.g., sectional) charts with each degree subdivided into 60 equal segments called minutes; i.e., 1/2° is equal to 30' (the ' is the symbol for min.).

      a) Each minute shown on lines of longitude equals one nautical mile, and this scale may be used to measure distances on aeronautical charts.

d. The meridians are also useful for designating time zones. A day is defined as the time required for the Earth to make one complete revolution of 360°. Since the day is divided into 24 hr., the Earth revolves at the rate of 15° an hour.

   1) When the sun is directly above a meridian,

      a) It is noon at that meridian.
      b) To the west of that meridian, it is forenoon.
      c) To the east of that meridian, it is afternoon.

   2) The standard practice is to establish a time belt for each 15° of longitude. This makes a difference of exactly 1 hr. between each belt.

      a) The Continental United States has four time belts: Eastern (75°), Central (90°), Mountain (105°), and Pacific (120°).

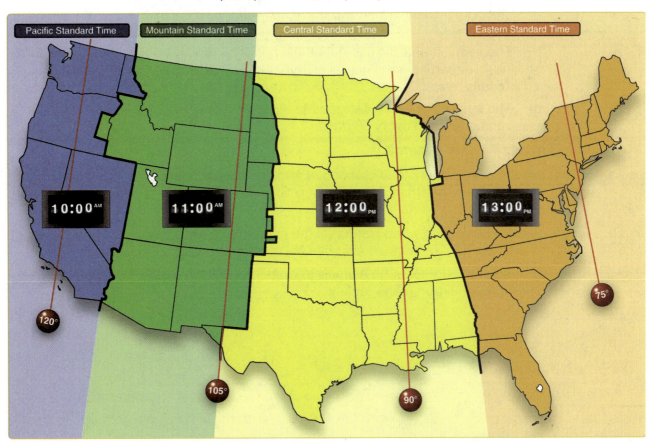

   3) The actual dividing lines are somewhat irregular because communities near the boundaries often find it more convenient to use the time designations of neighboring communities or trade centers.

7. **Aeronautical charts** are designed for visual navigation, with sectional charts being the most commonly used by pilots today.

   a. The charts have a scale of 1:500,000 [1 inch = 6.86 nautical miles (NM) or approximately 8 statute miles (SM)], which allows for more detailed information to be included on the chart.

      1) Sectional charts provide an abundance of information, including airport data, navigational aids, airspace, and topography.
      2) By referring to the chart legend, a pilot can interpret most of the information on the chart.
      3) A pilot should also check the chart for other legend information, which includes air traffic control (ATC) frequencies and information on airspace.
      4) These charts are revised every 56 days.

   b. The key to understanding each chart is the legend found at the front of every sectional chart. Use the legend sample on the following pages to locate every symbol on your current sectional chart or device, or review your local "VFR sectional" at www.faa.gov.

   c. **Chart Supplements**

      1) Chart Supplements include a listing of data on public and joint use airports, seaplane bases, and heliports; VFR airport sketches; NAVAIDs; communications data; weather data; airspace information; special notices; and operational procedures.

         a) Seven volumes cover the conterminous United States, Puerto Rico, and the Virgin Islands, with two additional volumes for Alaska and the Pacific territories.
         b) The supplements include data that cannot be readily depicted in graphic form; e.g., airport hours of operation, types of fuel available, runway data, lighting codes, etc.
         c) The supplements are designed to be used in conjunction with sectional charts and published every 56 days.

8. **Avoiding Bird and Wildlife Hazards**

   a. Many airports advise about the likelihood of wildlife hazards caused by large animals on the runway through the Chart Supplement U.S. and the Notice to Air Missions (NOTAM) system.

   b. Exercise extreme caution when warned of the presence of wildlife on and in the vicinity of airports or in areas of unmanned aircraft (UA) operation.

   c. If you observe deer or other large animals in close proximity to movement areas, advise the FSS, tower, or airport management.

SU 7: Airport Operations

Airports having control towers are shown in blue, all others in magenta. Consult Chart Supplement for details involving airport lighting, navigation aids, and services. Additional symbol information is in the Chart Users' Guide.

AIRPORTS

- Other than hard-surfaced runways
- Seaplane Base
- Hard-surfaced runways 1500 ft. to 8069 ft. in length
- Hard-surfaced runways greater than 8069 ft., or same multiple runways less than 8069 ft.
- Open dot within hard-surfaced runway configuration indicates approxmate VOR, VOR-DME, or VORTAC location.

All recognizable hard-surfaced runways, including those closed, are shown for visual identification. Airports may be public or private

ADDITIONAL AIRPORT INFORMATION

- ® Restricted or Private – (Soft surfaced runway, or hard surfaced runway less than 1500' in length.) Use only in emergency, or by specific authorization.
- Military – Other than hard-surfaced. All military airports are identified by abbreviations AFB, NAS, AAF, etc. For complete airport information consult, DOD FLIP.
- H Heliport Selected
- U Unverifield
- ⊗ Abandoned–paved, having landmark value, 3000 ft. or greater
- F Ultralight Flight Park Selected

Services—fuel available and field attended during normal working hours depicted by use of ticks around basic airport symbol. (Normal working hours are Mon thru Fri 10:00 A.M. to 4:00 P.M. local time. Consult Chart Supplement for service availability at airports with hard-surfaced runways greater than 8069 ft.

★ Rotating airport beacon in operation Sunset to Sunrise

AIRPORT DATA

Box indicators FAR 93 Special Air Traffic Rules & Airport Traffic Patterns

FSS NO SVFR

FAR 91 Location identifier

NAME (NAM)(PNAM)
CT – 118.3 * ⒸATIS 123.8
285 L 72 122.95
RP 23, 34
VFR Advsy 125.0
AOE

Runways with Right Traffic Patterns (public use)
RP Special conditions exist - see Chart Supplement

UNICOM

Airport of Entry

ICAO Location indicator shown outside contiguous U.S.

FSS – Flight Service Station
NO SVFR – Fixed wing special VFR flight is prohibited.
CT– 118.3 – Control Tower (CT) primary frequency
★ – Star indicates operation part-time (see tower frequencies tabulation for hours of operation).
Ⓒ – Indicates Common Traffic Advisory Frequencies (CTAF)
ATIS 123.8 – Automatic Terminal Information Service
ASOS/AWOS 135.42 – Automated Surface Weather Observing Systems (shown where full-time ATIS is not available).
Some ASOS/AWOS facilities may not be located at airports.
UNICOM – Aeronautical advisory station
VFR Advsy – VFR Advisory Service shown where full-time ATIS not available and frequency is other than primary CT frequency.
285 – Elevation in feet
  L – Lighting in operation sunset to sunrise
  ★L – Lighting limitations exist, refer to Airport/Facility Directory.
  72 – Length of longest runway in hundreds of feet; usable length may be less.

When information is lacking, the respective charactor is replaced by a dash. Lighting codes refer to runway edge lights and may not represent the longest runway or full length lighting.

RADIO AIDS TO NAVIGATION

- VHF OMNI RANGE (VOR)
- VORTAC
- VOR-DME
- Non-Directional Radiobeacon (NDB)
- NDB-DME
- Other facilities. i.e., FSS Outlet, RCO, etc.

COMMUNICATION BOXES

122.1R 122.6 123.6
OAKDALE Ⓐ
382 *116.8 OAK

Underline indicates no voice on this frequency.
Crosshatch indicates Shutdown Status
★ Operates less than continuous or On-Request.
Ⓐ ASOS/AWOS

122.1R
MIAMI

FSS radio providing voice communication

122.1R
CHICAGO CHI

Heavy line box indicates Flight Service Station (FSS). Frequencies 121.5, 122.2, 243.0 and 255.4 (Canada - 121.5, 126.7 and 243.0) are available at many FSSs and are not shown above boxes. All other frequencies are shown.

Certain FSSs provide Airport Advisory Service, see Chart Supplement.

R - Receive Only.

Frequencies above this line box are remoted to NAVAID site. Other FSS frequencies providing voice communication may be available as determined by altitude and terrain. Consult Chart Supplement for complete information.

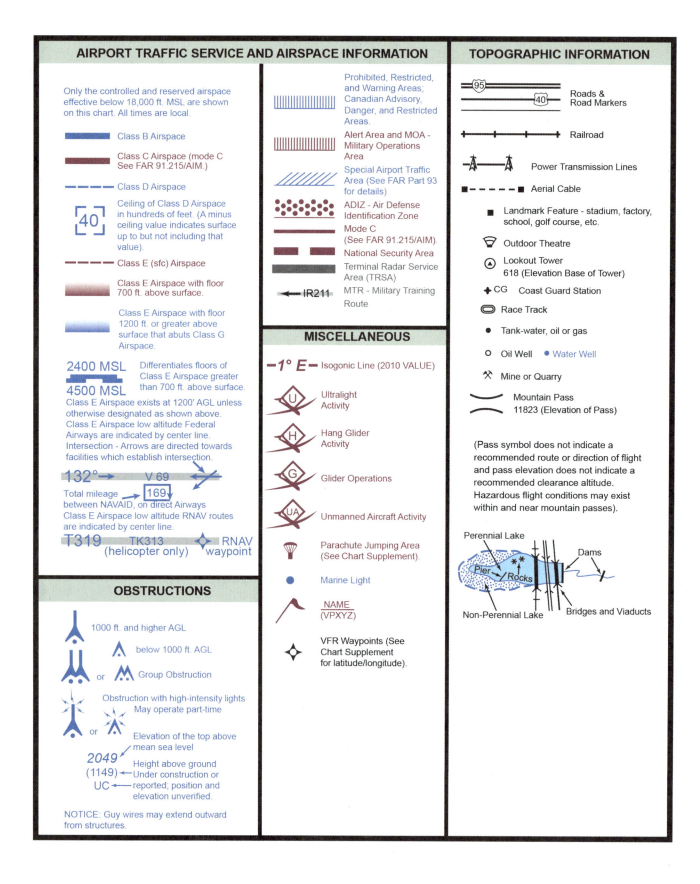

SU 7: Airport Operations

QUESTIONS

7.1 Airport Operations

1. (Refer to Figure 48 below.) Area C on the airport depicted is classified as a

    A. stabilized area.
    B. multiple heliport.
    C. closed taxiway.

Answer (C) is correct. (AIM Para 2-3-6)
    DISCUSSION: The taxiway marked by the arrow C in Fig. 48 has Xs on the taxiway, indicating it is closed.
    Answer (A) is incorrect. Stabilized areas are designed to be load bearing but may be limited to emergency use only. Area E on the airport indicates a stabilized area. **Answer (B) is incorrect.** Heliports are marked by Hs, not Xs.

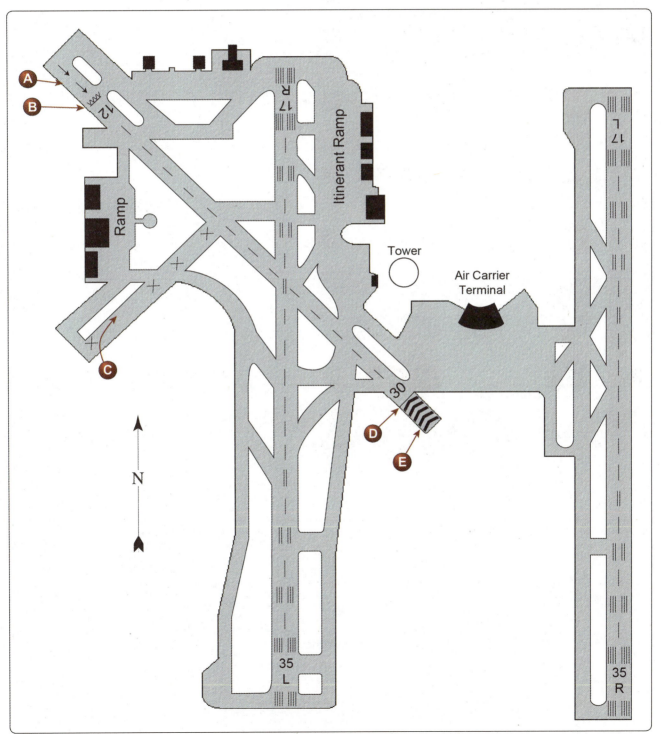

Figure 48. Airport Diagram.

224   SU 7: Airport Operations

2. (Refer to Figure 65 below.) (Refer to E.) This sign is a visual clue that

A. confirms the aircraft's location to be on taxiway "B."
B. warns the pilot of approaching taxiway "B."
C. indicates "B" holding area is ahead.

Answer (A) is correct. (AIM Para 2-3-9)
DISCUSSION: The taxiway location sign consists of a yellow letter on a black background with a yellow border. This sign confirms the pilot is on taxiway "B."
Answer (B) is incorrect. A direction sign with a yellow background, a black letter, and an arrow pointing to taxiway "B" would be required to warn a pilot that (s)he is approaching taxiway "B." **Answer (C) is incorrect.** A taxiway location sign defines a position on a taxiway, not a holding area.

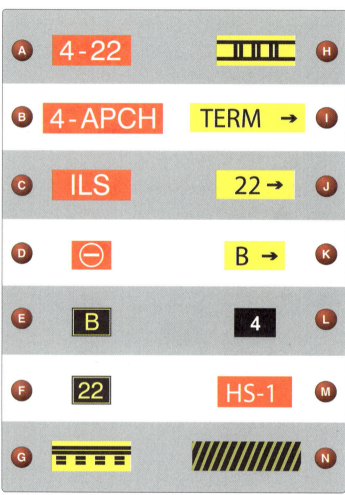

Figure 65. U.S. Airport Signs.

3. (Refer to Figure 65 above.) (Refer to F.) This sign confirms your position on

A. runway 22.
B. routing to runway 22.
C. taxiway 22.

Answer (A) is correct. (AIM Para 2-3-9)
DISCUSSION: A runway location sign has a black background with a yellow inscription and a yellow border. The inscription on the sign informs the pilot (s)he is located on Runway 22.
Answer (B) is incorrect. A direction sign with a yellow background and black inscription would be required to inform a pilot (s)he is routing to Runway 22. **Answer (C) is incorrect.** Only runways are numbered. Taxiways are always identified by a letter.

SU 7: Airport Operations

4. (Refer to Figure 65 on page 224.) Which sign identifies where aircraft are prohibited from entering?

A. D.
B. G.
C. B.

Answer (A) is correct. (AIM Para 2-3-8)
DISCUSSION: Mandatory instruction signs have a red background with a white inscription and are used to denote an entrance to a runway or critical area and areas where an aircraft is prohibited from entering.
Answer (B) is incorrect. "G" is a runway boundary sign.
Answer (C) is incorrect. "B" is a holding position sign for a runway approach area.

5. (Refer to Figure 65 on page 224.) Which sign is a designation and direction of an exit taxiway from a runway?

A. J.
B. F.
C. K.

Answer (C) is correct. (AIM Para 2-3-11)
DISCUSSION: Sign K designates the direction of taxiway B; while both J and K are destination signs, only K designates the route to a taxiway.
Answer (A) is incorrect. Though a destination sign, Sign J designates the direction of Runway 22, not the direction of a taxiway. **Answer (B) is incorrect.** Sign F is a location sign indicating that the aircraft is located on Runway 22.

6. The numbers 8 and 26 on the approach ends of the runway indicate that the runway is orientated approximately

A. 008° and 026° true.
B. 080° and 260° true.
C. 080° and 260° magnetic.

Answer (C) is correct. (AIM Para 2-3-3)
DISCUSSION: Runway numbers are determined from the approach direction. The runway number is the whole number nearest one-tenth the magnetic direction of the centerline. Thus, the numbers 8 and 26 on a runway indicate that the runway is oriented approximately 080° and 260° magnetic.
Answer (A) is incorrect. The ending digit, not a leading zero, is dropped. **Answer (B) is incorrect.** Runways are numbered based on magnetic, not true, direction.

7. What is the purpose of the runway/runway hold position sign?

A. Denotes entrance to runway from a taxiway.
B. Denotes area protected for an aircraft approaching or departing a runway.
C. Denotes intersecting runways.

Answer (C) is correct. (AIM Para 2-3-8)
DISCUSSION: Runway/runway hold position signs are a type of mandatory instruction sign used to denote intersecting runways. These are runways that intersect and are being used for "Land, Hold Short" operations or are normally used for taxiing. These signs have a red background with white lettering. Runway/runway hold position signs are identical to the signs used for taxiway/runway intersections.
Answer (A) is incorrect. A runway/runway hold position sign is located on a runway and denotes an intersecting runway, not the entrance to a runway from a taxiway. **Answer (B) is incorrect.** A runway approach area holding position sign protects an area from approaching or departing aircraft.

226   SU 7: Airport Operations

8. (Refer to Figure 64 below.) Which marking indicates a vehicle lane?

- A. A.
- B. C.
- C. E.

Answer (B) is correct. *(AIM Para 2-3-6)*
DISCUSSION: Vehicle roadway markings define a route of travel for vehicles to cross areas intended for use by aircraft. The roadway is defined by solid white lines, with a dashed line in the middle to separate traffic traveling in opposite directions. White zipper markings may be used instead of solid white lines to define the edge of the roadway at some airports.
Answer (A) is incorrect. This marking represents a surface painted holding position sign, not a vehicle lane. In this instance, the marking indicates the aircraft is holding short of Runway 19. **Answer (C) is incorrect.** This marking represents a standard taxiway holding position and is used by ATC to hold aircraft short of an intersecting taxiway.

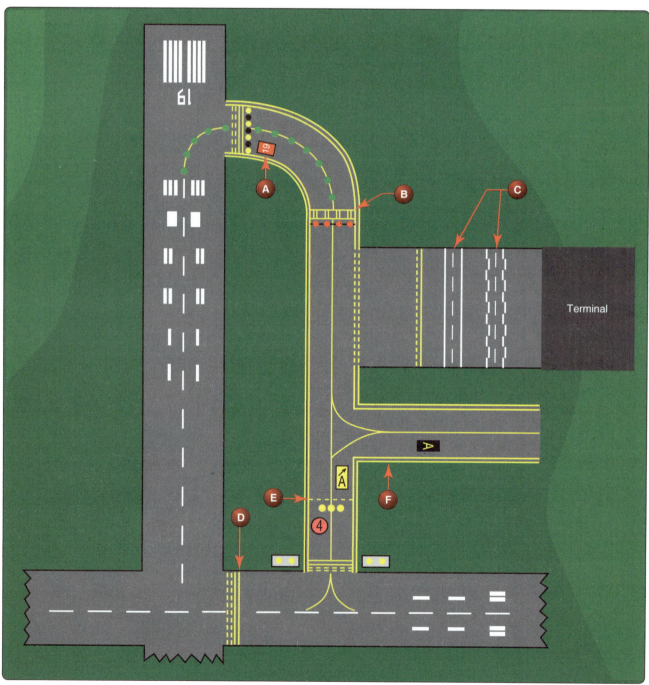

Figure 64. Airport Markings.

SU 7: Airport Operations

9. (Refer to Legend 15 below.) What depicts a Class E airspace that begins at 700 feet AGL?

- A. A dashed blue circle around an airport.
- B. A solid magenta circle around an airport.
- C. A magenta vignette around an airport.

Answer (C) is correct. (AIM Para 3-2-6)
DISCUSSION: Class E airspace floor begins at 700 ft. AGL. It is depicted by a magenta vignette circle or area around an airport.

Answer (A) is incorrect. A dashed blue circle around an airport depicts a Class D airspace. **Answer (B) is incorrect.** A solid magenta circle around an airport depicts Class C airspace.

DIRECTORY LEGEND 17

uncontrolled airports may contact ATC and FSS via VHF to a telephone connection to obtain an instrument clearance or close a VFR or IFR flight plan. They may also get an updated weather briefing prior to takeoff. Pilots will use four "key clicks" on the VHF radio to contact the appropriate ATC facility or six "key clicks" to contact the FSS. The GCO system is intended to be used only on the ground.

DEP CON—Departure Control. The symbol Ⓡ indicates radar departure control.
CLNC DEL—Clearance Delivery.
PRE TAXI CLNC—Pre taxi clearance.

VFR ADVSY SVC—VFR Advisory Service. Service provided by Non-Radar Approach Control.
  Advisory Service for VFR aircraft (upon a workload basis) ctc APP CON.
COMD POST—Command Post followed by the operator call sign in parenthesis.
PMSV—Pilot-to-Metro Service call sign, frequency and hours of operation, when full service is other than continuous. PMSV installations at which weather observation service is available shall be indicated, following the frequency and/or hours of operation as "Wx obsn svc 1900–0000Z‡" or "other times" may be used when no specific time is given. PMSV facilities manned by forecasters are considered "Full Service". PMSV facilities manned by weather observers are listed as "Limited Service".
OPS—Operations followed by the operator call sign in parenthesis.
CON
RANGE
FLT FLW—Flight Following
MEDIVAC
NOTE: Communication frequencies followed by the letter "X" indicate frequency available on request.

㉝ AIRSPACE

Information concerning Class B, C, and part-time D and E surface area airspace shall be published with effective times. Class D and E surface area airspace that is continuous as established by Rulemaking Docket will not be shown.
CLASS B—Radar Sequencing and Separation Service for all aircraft in CLASS B airspace.
CLASS C—Separation between IFR and VFR aircraft and sequencing of VFR arrivals to the primary airport.
TRSA—Radar Sequencing and Separation Service for participating VFR Aircraft within a Terminal Radar Service Area.
Class C, D, and E airspace described in this publication is that airspace usually consisting of a 5 NM radius core surface area that begins at the surface and extends upward to an altitude above the airport elevation (charted in MSL for Class C and Class D). Class E surface airspace normally extends from the surface up to but not including the overlying controlled airspace.
When part-time Class C or Class D airspace defaults to Class E, the core surface area becomes Class E. This will be formatted as:
AIRSPACE: CLASS C svc "times" ctc **APP CON** other times CLASS E:
or
AIRSPACE: CLASS D svc "times" other times CLASS E.
When a part-time Class C, Class D or Class E surface area defaults to Class G, the core surface area becomes Class G up to, but not including, the overlying controlled airspace. Normally, the overlying controlled airspace is Class E airspace beginning at either 700' or 1200' AGL and may be determined by consulting the relevant VFR Sectional or Terminal Area Charts. This will be formatted as:
AIRSPACE: CLASS C svc "times" ctc **APP CON** other times CLASS G, with CLASS E 700' (or 1200') AGL & abv:
or
AIRSPACE: CLASS D svc "times" other times CLASS G with CLASS E 700' (or 1200') AGL & abv:
or
AIRSPACE: CLASS E svc "times" other times CLASS G with CLASS E 700' (or 1200') AGL & abv.
NOTE: AIRSPACE SVC "TIMES" INCLUDE ALL ASSOCIATED ARRIVAL EXTENSIONS. Surface area arrival extensions for instrument approach procedures become part of the primary core surface area. These extensions may be either Class D or Class E airspace and are effective concurrent with the times of the primary core surface area. For example, when a part-time Class C, Class D or Class E surface area defaults to Class G, the associated arrival extensions will default to Class G at the same time. When a part-time Class C or Class D surface area defaults to Class E, the arrival extensions will remain in effect as Class E airspace.
NOTE: CLASS E AIRSPACE EXTENDING UPWARD FROM 700 FEET OR MORE ABOVE THE SURFACE, DESIGNATED IN CONJUNCTION WITH AN AIRPORT WITH AN APPROVED INSTRUMENT PROCEDURE.
Class E 700' AGL (shown as magenta vignette on sectional charts) and 1200' AGL (blue vignette) areas are designated when necessary to provide controlled airspace for transitioning to/from the terminal and enroute environments. Unless otherwise specified, these 700'/1200' AGL Class E airspace areas remain in effect continuously, regardless of airport operating hours or surface area status. These transition areas should not be confused with surface areas or arrival extensions.
(See Chapter 3, AIRSPACE, in the Aeronautical Information Manual for further details)

NE, 09 FEB 20XX to 05 APR 20XX

Legend 15. Chart Supplement.

10. (Refer to Figure 26 on page 229.) (Refer to Area 4.) You have been hired to inspect the tower under construction at 46.9N and 98.6W, near Jamestown Regional (JMS). What must you receive prior to flying your unmanned aircraft in this area?

A. Authorization from the military.
B. Authorization from ATC.
C. Authorization from the National Park Service.

Answer (B) is correct. (14 CFR 107.41)
DISCUSSION: There is a tower approximately 5 miles east of the Jamestown Regional airport with a height of 1,727 ft. MSL. The letters UC beneath the altitude indicate the tower is under construction. This tower is located within the boundary of a dashed magenta line, which indicated Class E controlled airspace starts at the surface. Operations in controlled airspace require prior authorization from ATC.
NOTE: Coordinates can be read as a decimal format or degrees-minutes-seconds. Similar to a clock, there are 60 seconds in a minute and 60 minutes in each degree. Therefore, 46.9N and 98.6W are the approximate decimal equivalents to 46 degrees 54 minutes and 98 degrees 36 minutes.
Answer (A) is incorrect. Operations in Class E controlled airspace require authorization from ATC, not the Military.
Answer (C) is incorrect. The tower under construction is located in Class E controlled airspace, not a national park.

11. (Refer to Figure 26 on page 229.) (Refer to Area 2.) What is the approximate latitude and longitude of Cooperstown Airport?

A. 47°25'N – 98°06'W.
B. 47°25'N – 99°54'W.
C. 47°55'N – 98°06'W.

Answer (A) is correct. (FAA-H-8083-25B Chap 16)
DISCUSSION: First locate the Cooperstown Airport on Fig. 26. It is just above 2, middle right of chart. Note that it is to the left (west) of the 98° line of longitude. The line of longitude on the left side of the chart is 99°. Thus, the longitude is a little bit more than 98°W, but not near 99°W.
With respect to latitude, note that Cooperstown Airport is just below a line of latitude that is not marked in terms of degrees. However, the next line of latitude below is 47° (see the left side of the chart, northwest of Jamestown Airport). As with longitude, there are two lines of latitude for every degree of latitude; i.e., each line is 30 min. Thus, latitude of the Cooperstown Airport is almost 47°30'N, but not quite. Accordingly, Cooperstown Airport's latitude is 47°25'N and longitude is 98°06'W.
Answer (B) is incorrect. Cooperstown is just west of the 98° line of longitude (not just east of 99°). **Answer (C) is incorrect.** Cooperstown is just south of the 47°30' line of latitude (not the 48°00' line).

SU 7: Airport Operations

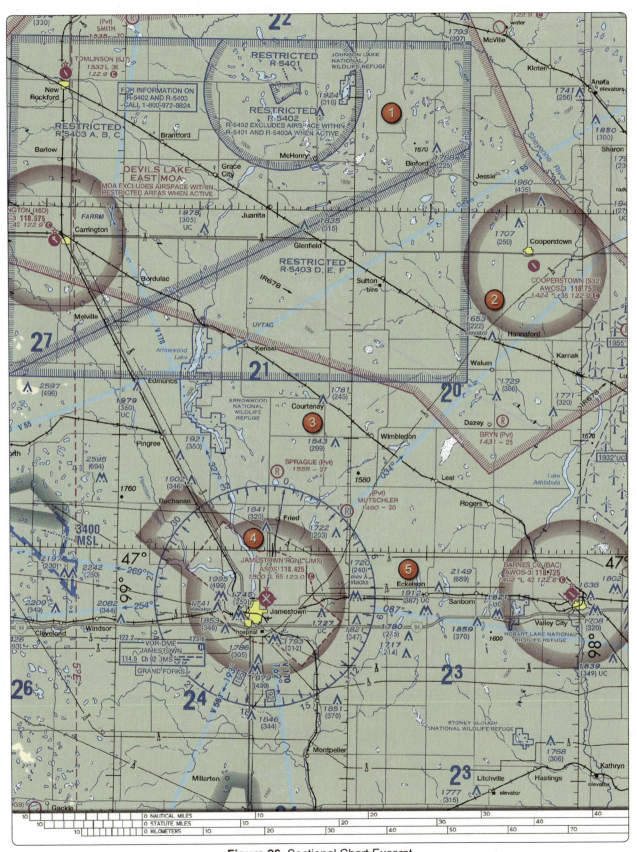

Figure 26. Sectional Chart Excerpt.
NOTE: Chart is not to scale and should not be used for navigation. Use associated scale.

230   SU 7: Airport Operations

12. (Refer to Figure 21 on page 231.) What airport is located approximately 47 (degrees) 40 (minutes) N latitude and 101 (degrees) 26 (minutes) W longitude?

A. Mercer County Regional Airport.
B. Semchenko Airport.
C. Garrison Airport.

Answer (C) is correct. (FAA-H-8083-25B Chap 16)
DISCUSSION: You are asked to locate an airport at 47°40'00"N latitude and 101°26'00"W longitude. Referring to the chart, find the longitude (vertical) 101° W line (increases to the west) and the latitude (horizontal) 48° line (decreases to the south). The longitude line to the west of 101° is 101° 30 min. (each additional crossline is 1 min.). Find 101° 26 min. by moving east four crosslines. The latitude line south of 48° is 47° 30 min. (each additional crossline is 1 min.). Find 47° 40 min. by moving north an additional 10 crosslines. These two coordinates (101°26'00"W and 47°40'00"N) intersect over Garrison Airfield.
Answer (A) is incorrect. The coordinates for Mercer County Regional are approximately 47° 17 min. 00 sec. N latitude and 101° 35 min. 00 sec. W longitude. **Answer (B) is incorrect.** The coordinates for Semchenko are approximately 47° 46 min. 00 sec. N latitude and 101° 16 min. 00 sec. W longitude.

13. (Refer to Figure 21 on page 231.) (Refer to Area 2.) Which airport is located at approximately 47°34'30"N latitude and 100°43'00"W longitude?

A. Linrud.
B. Makeeff.
C. Johnson.

Answer (B) is correct. (FAA-H-8083-25B Chap 16)
DISCUSSION: On Fig. 21, you are asked to locate an airport at 47°34'30"N latitude and 100°43'W longitude. Note that the 101°W longitude line runs down the middle of the figure. Accordingly, the airport you are seeking is 17 min. to the east of that line.
Each crossline is 1 min. on the latitude and longitude lines. The 48°N latitude line is approximately two-thirds of the way up the chart. The 47°30'N latitude line is about one-fourth of the way up. One-third up from 47°30'N to 48°N latitude would be 47°34'N. At this spot is Makeeff Airport.
Answer (A) is incorrect. Linrud is north of the 48°N latitude line. **Answer (C) is incorrect.** Johnson is south of the 47°30'N latitude line.

14. (Refer to Figure 21 on page 231.) (Refer to Area 3.) Which airport is located at approximately 47°21'N latitude and 101°01'W longitude?

A. Underwood.
B. Pietsch.
C. Washburn.

Answer (C) is correct. (FAA-H-8083-25B Chap 16)
DISCUSSION: On Fig. 21, find the 48° line of latitude (2/3 up the figure). Start at the 47°30' line of latitude (the line below the 48° line) and count down nine tick marks to the 47°21'N tick mark and draw a horizontal line on the chart. Next find the 101° line of longitude and go left one tick mark and draw a vertical line. The closest airport is Washburn.
Answer (A) is incorrect. Underwood is a city (not an airport) northwest of Washburn by about 1 in. **Answer (B) is incorrect.** Pietsch is north of the 48°00' latitude line.

15. (Refer to Figure 21 on page 231.) (Refer to Area 1.) After receiving authorization from ATC to operate a small UA near Minot International Airport (MOT) while the control tower is operational, which radio communication frequency could be used to monitor manned aircraft and ATC communications?

A. UNICOM 122.95.
B. ASOS 118.725.
C. CT-118.2.

Answer (C) is correct. (ACUG)
DISCUSSION: The Minot International Airport (Fig. 21, area 1) control tower frequency is given as the first item in the second line of the airport data to the right of the airport symbol. The control tower (CT) frequency is 118.2 MHz.
Answer (A) is incorrect. This is the UNICOM, not the control tower frequency, for Minot International Airport. **Answer (B) is incorrect.** This is the ASOS, not the control tower frequency, for Minot International Airport.

SU 7: Airport Operations

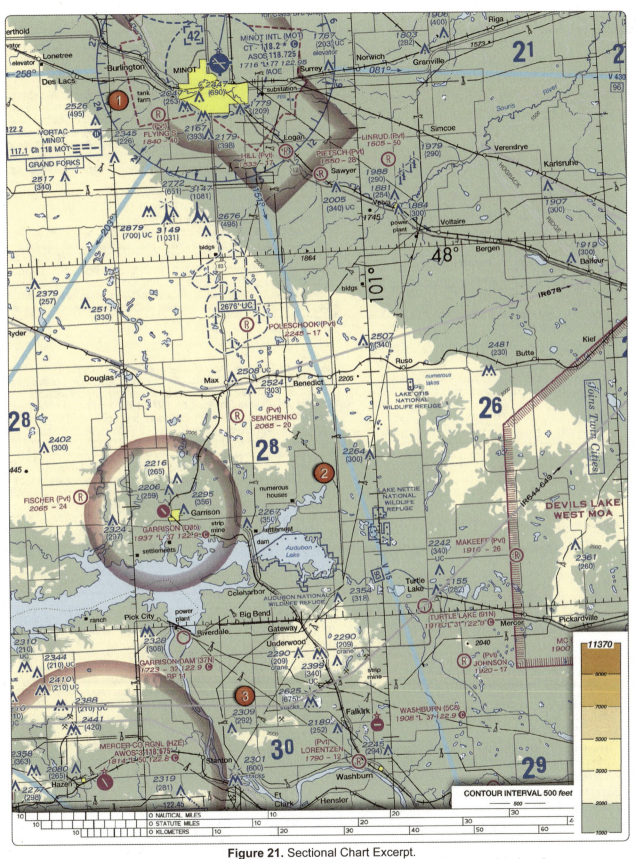

Figure 21. Sectional Chart Excerpt.
NOTE: Chart is not to scale and should not be used for navigation. Use associated scale.

16. Which is the correct traffic pattern departure procedure to use at a noncontrolled airport?

A. Depart in any direction consistent with safety, after crossing the airport boundary.
B. Make all turns to the left.
C. Comply with any FAA traffic pattern established for the airport.

Answer (C) is correct. (14 CFR 91.127)
DISCUSSION: Each person operating an aircraft to or from an airport without an operating control tower shall (1) make all turns of that aircraft to the left unless the airport displays approved light signals or visual markings indicating that turns should be made to the right, in which case the pilot shall make all turns to the right, and (2) in the case of an aircraft departing the airport, comply with any FAA traffic pattern for that airport.
Answer (A) is incorrect. The correct traffic pattern departure procedure at a noncontrolled airport is to comply with any FAA established traffic pattern, not to depart in any direction after crossing the airport boundary. **Answer (B) is incorrect.** The FAA may establish right- or left-hand traffic patterns, not only left-hand traffic.

17. Which statement about longitude and latitude is true?

A. Lines of longitude are parallel to the Equator.
B. Lines of longitude cross the Equator at right angles.
C. The 0° line of latitude passes through Greenwich, England.

Answer (B) is correct. (sUASSG Chap 11)
DISCUSSION: Lines of longitude are drawn from the north pole to the south pole and cross the equator at right angles. They indicate the number of degrees east and west of the 0° line of longitude, which passes through Greenwich, England.
Answer (A) is incorrect. Lines of latitude, not longitude, are parallel to the equator. **Answer (C) is incorrect.** The 0° line of longitude, not latitude, passes through Greenwich, England.

18. (Refer to Figure 20 on page 233.) (Refer to Area 3.) Determine the approximate latitude and longitude of Currituck County Airport.

A. 36°24'N – 76°01'W.
B. 36°48'N – 76°01'W.
C. 47°24'N – 75°58'W.

Answer (A) is correct. (FAA-H-8083-25B Chap 16)
DISCUSSION: On Fig. 20, find the Currituck County Airport, which is northeast of area 3. Note that the airport symbol is just to the west of 76° longitude (find 76° just north of Virginia Beach). There are 60 min. between the 76°W and 77°W lines of longitude, with each tick mark depicting 1 min. The airport is one tick mark to the west of the 76° line, or 76°01'W.
The latitude is below the 30-min. latitude line across the center of the chart. See the numbered latitude lines at the top (37°) of the chart. Since each tick mark represents 1 min. of latitude, and the airport is approximately six tick marks south of the 36°30'N latitude, the airport is at 36°24'N latitude. Thus, Currituck County Airport is at approximately 36°24'N – 76°01'W.
Answer (B) is incorrect. Currituck County Airport is south of the 36°30'N (not 37°00'N) line of latitude. **Answer (C) is incorrect.** Currituck County Airport is west (not east) of the 76°W line of longitude and 47°24'N is 11°N of the airport.

19. (Refer to Figure 20 on page 233.) Why would the small flag at Lake Drummond in area 2 of the sectional chart be important to a remote PIC?

A. The flag indicates a VFR check point for manned aircraft, and a higher volume of air traffic should be expected there.
B. The flag indicates a GPS check point that can be used by both manned and remote pilots for orientation.
C. The flag indicates that there will be a large obstruction depicted on the next printing of the chart.

Answer (A) is correct. (ACUG)
DISCUSSION: The small flag indicates a VFR checkpoint. A higher concentration of manned aircraft may be expected in the vicinity.
Answer (B) is incorrect. The flag indicates a VFR (not a GPS) checkpoint. **Answer (C) is incorrect.** A new obstruction may be depicted using the letters UC, meaning under construction, or will be reported via NOTAM.

SU 7: Airport Operations

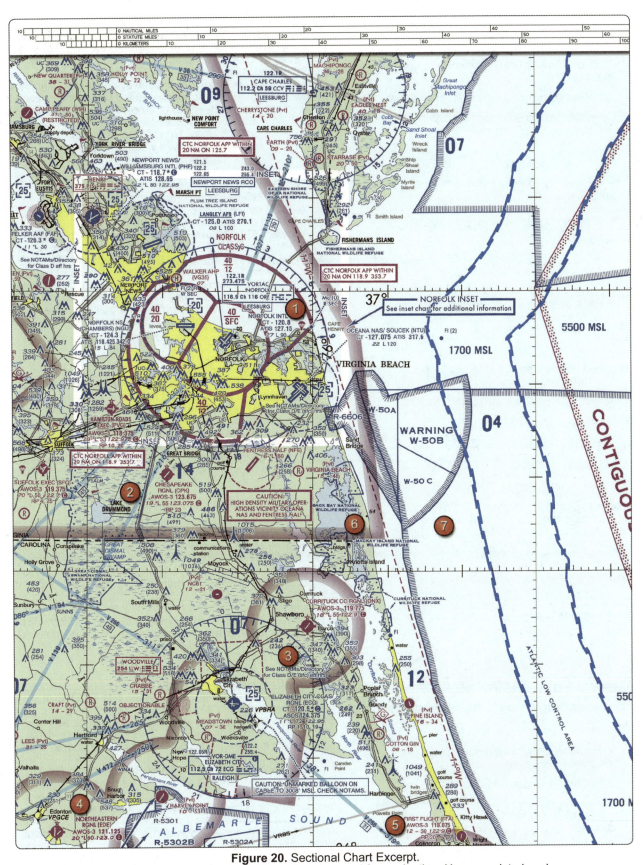

Figure 20. Sectional Chart Excerpt.
NOTE: Chart is not to scale and should not be used for navigation. Use associated scale.

20. What purpose does the taxiway location sign serve?

A. Provides general taxiing direction to named runway.

B. Denotes entrance to runway from a taxiway.

C. Identifies taxiway on which an aircraft is located.

Answer (C) is correct. (AIM Para 2-3-9)
   DISCUSSION: Taxiway location signs are used to identify a taxiway on which the aircraft is currently located. Taxiway location signs consist of a black background with a yellow inscription and yellow border.
   Answer (A) is incorrect. A runway destination sign, not a taxiway location sign, provides general taxiing information to a named runway. **Answer (B) is incorrect.** A runway holding position sign, not a taxiway location sign, identifies the entrance to a runway from a taxiway. Runway holding position signs consist of a red background with white inscription.

21. The recommended entry position to an airport traffic pattern is

A. 45° to the base leg just below traffic pattern altitude.

B. to enter 45° at the midpoint of the downwind leg at traffic pattern altitude.

C. to cross directly over the airport at traffic pattern altitude and join the downwind leg.

Answer (B) is correct. (AIM Para 4-3-3)
   DISCUSSION: The recommended entry position to an airport traffic pattern is to enter 45° at the midpoint of the downwind leg at traffic pattern altitude.
   Answer (A) is incorrect. The recommended entry to an airport traffic pattern is to enter 45° at the midpoint of the downwind, not base, leg and at traffic pattern altitude, not below. **Answer (C) is incorrect.** The recommended entry to an airport traffic pattern is to enter 45° at the midpoint of the downwind, not to cross directly over the airport and join the downwind leg. Also, flying at traffic pattern altitude directly over an airport is an example of poor judgment in collision avoidance precautions.

22. A lighted heliport may be identified by a

A. green, yellow, and white rotating beacon.

B. flashing yellow light.

C. blue lighted square landing area.

Answer (A) is correct. (AIM Para 2-1-9)
   DISCUSSION: A lighted heliport may be identified by a green, yellow, and white rotating beacon.
   Answer (B) is incorrect. A flashing yellow light is sometimes used to help a pilot locate a lighted water airport. It is used in conjunction with the lighted water airport's white and yellow rotating beacon. **Answer (C) is incorrect.** A lighted heliport may be identified by a green, yellow, and white rotating beacon, not a blue lighted square landing area.

23. (Refer to Figure 23 on page 235.) (Refer to Area 3.) What is the height of the lighted obstacle approximately 6 nautical miles southwest of Savannah International?

A. 1,498 feet MSL.

B. 1,531 feet AGL.

C. 1,548 feet MSL.

Answer (C) is correct. (ACUG)
   DISCUSSION: On Fig. 23, find the lighted obstacle noted by its proximity to Savannah International by being outside the surface area of the Class C airspace, which has a 5-NM radius. It is indicated by the obstacle symbol with arrows or lightning flashes extending from the tip. According to the numbers to the northeast of the symbol, the height of the obstacle is 1,548 ft. MSL or 1,534 ft. AGL.
   Answer (A) is incorrect. The unlighted tower 8 NM, not 6 NM, southwest of the airport has a height of 1,498 ft. MSL. **Answer (B) is incorrect.** An unlighted tower 9 NM, not 6 NM, southwest of the airport has a height of 1,531 ft. AGL.

24. (Refer to Figure 23 on page 235.) The flag symbols at Statesboro Bulloch County Airport, Claxton-Evans County Airport, and Ridgeland Airport are

A. outer boundaries of Savannah Class C airspace.

B. airports with special traffic patterns.

C. visual checkpoints to identify position for initial callup prior to entering Savannah Class C airspace.

Answer (C) is correct. (ACUG)
   DISCUSSION: On Fig. 23, note the flag symbols at Claxton-Evans County Airport (1 in. to the left of 2), at Statesboro Bulloch County Airport (2 in. above 2), and at Ridgeland Airport (2 in. above 3). These airports are visual checkpoints to identify position for initial callup prior to entering the Savannah Class C airspace.
   Answer (A) is incorrect. They do not indicate outer boundaries of the Class C airspace. The flags are outside the Class C airspace area, the boundaries of which are marked by solid magenta lines. **Answer (B) is incorrect.** Airports with special traffic patterns are noted in the Chart Supplement and also by markings at the airport around the wind sock or tetrahedron.

SU 7: Airport Operations

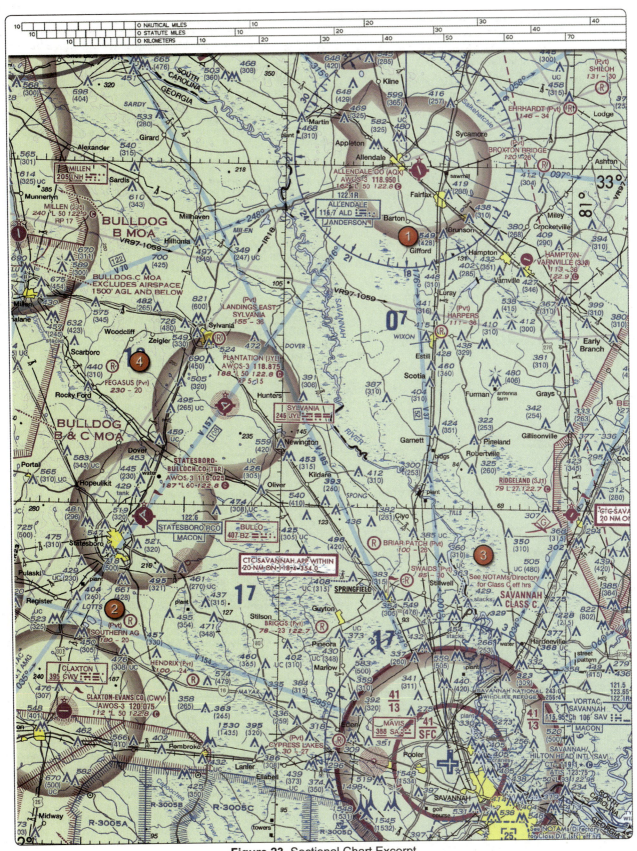

Figure 23. Sectional Chart Excerpt.
NOTE: Chart is not to scale and should not be used for navigation. Use associated scale.

25. An airport's rotating beacon operated during daylight hours indicates

A. there are obstructions on the airport.
B. that weather at the airport located in Class D airspace is below basic VFR weather minimums.
C. the Air Traffic Control tower is not in operation.

Answer (B) is correct. (AIM Para 2-1-9)
DISCUSSION: Operation of the airport beacon during daylight hours often indicates that weather at the airport located in controlled airspace (e.g., Class D airspace) is below basic VFR weather minimums, i.e., less than 1,000 ft. ceiling or 3 SM visibility. Note that there is no regulatory requirement for daylight operation of an airport's rotating beacon.
Answer (A) is incorrect. The obstructions near or on airports are usually listed in NOTAMs or the Chart Supplement as appropriate to their hazard. **Answer (C) is incorrect.** There is no visual signal of tower operation/non-operation.

26. A military air station can be identified by a rotating beacon that emits

A. white and green alternating flashes.
B. two quick, white flashes between green flashes.
C. green, yellow, and white flashes.

Answer (B) is correct. (AIM Para 2-1-9)
DISCUSSION: Lighted land airports are distinguished by white and green airport beacons. To further distinguish it as a military airport, there are two quick white flashes between each green.
Answer (A) is incorrect. White and green alternating flashes designate a lighted civilian land airport. **Answer (C) is incorrect.** Green, yellow, and white flashes designate a lighted heliport.

27. As standard operating practice, all inbound traffic to an airport without a control tower should continuously monitor the appropriate facility from a distance of

A. 25 miles.
B. 20 miles.
C. 10 miles.

Answer (C) is correct. (AIM Para 4-1-9)
DISCUSSION: As a standard operating practice, pilots of inbound traffic to an airport without a control tower should continuously monitor and communicate, as appropriate, on the designated Common Traffic Advisory Frequency (CTAF) from 10 mi. to landing.
Answer (A) is incorrect. All inbound traffic to an airport without a control tower should continuously monitor the CTAF from a distance of 10 mi., not 25 mi. **Answer (B) is incorrect.** All inbound traffic to an airport without a control tower should continuously monitor the CTAF from a distance of 10 mi., not 20 mi.

28. The most comprehensive information on a given airport is provided by

A. the Chart Supplements U.S.
B. Notices to Air Missions (NOTAMs).
C. Terminal Area Chart (TAC).

Answer (A) is correct. (FAA-H-8083-25B Chap 14)
DISCUSSION: Chart Supplements are a listing of data on record with the FAA on all open-to-the-public airports, seaplane bases, heliports, military facilities, and selected private use airports.
Answer (B) is incorrect. NOTAMs contain current notices to air missions that are considered essential to the safety of flight as well as supplemental data affecting other operational publications. **Answer (C) is incorrect.** A TAC is similar to a sectional chart, but the scale is larger. TACs provide an abundance of information in additional to airport data, such as navigational aids, airspace, and topography, but they are not the most comprehensive source for airport information.

29. (Refer to Figure 22 on page 237.) Weather information is available at the Coeur d'Alene (COE) Airport (area 2)

A. at the flight service station on the field.
B. from AWOS 3 135.075.
C. from UNICOM (CTAF) on 122.8.

Answer (B) is correct. (Sectional Chart, FAA-H-8083-25B Chap 13)
DISCUSSION: On the sectional chart excerpt, to the right of the airport, you will find in the information for the airport weather in the third line. It states the type of Automated Weather Observation System (AWOS) and the frequency of 135.075.
Answer (A) is incorrect. There is no flight service station on the field. This would be found in the Chart Supplement as FSS "on arpt" in the Communications section for this airport. **Answer (C) is incorrect.** The UNICOM (CTAF) is the Common Traffic Advisory Frequency.

SU 7: Airport Operations

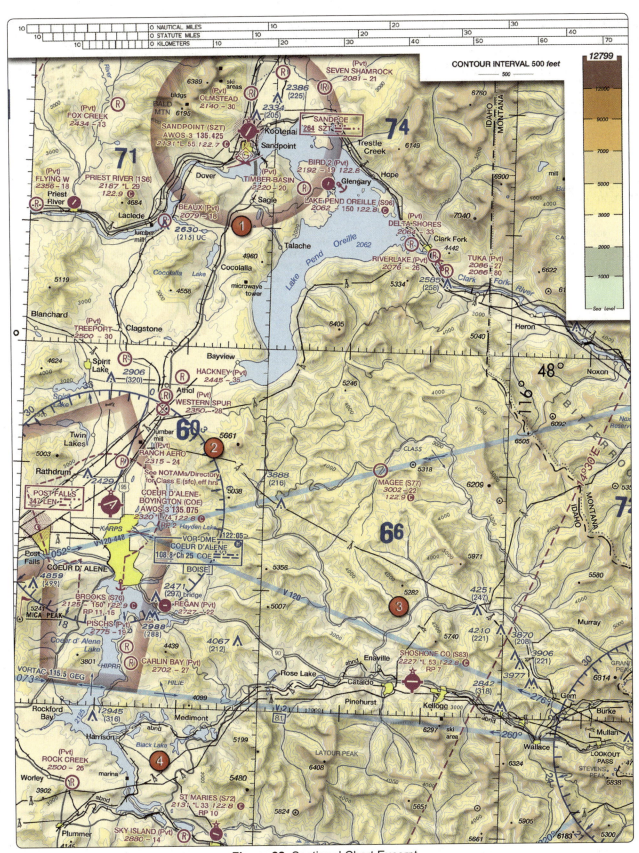

Figure 22. Sectional Chart Excerpt.
NOTE: Chart is not to scale and should not be used for navigation. Use associated scale.

30. (Refer to Figure 52 on page 239.) Traffic patterns in effect at Lincoln Municipal are

    A. to the right on Runway 14 and Runway 32; to the left on Runway 18 and Runway 35.

    B. to the left on Runway 14 and Runway 32; to the right on Runway 18 and Runway 35.

    C. to the right on Runways 14 - 32.

Answer (B) is correct. (Chart Supplement)
    DISCUSSION: Fig. 52 contains the Chart Supplement excerpt for Lincoln Municipal. For this question, you need to locate the runway end data elements, i.e., Rwy 18, Rwy 14, Rwy 32, Rwy 17, Rwy 35, and Rwy 36. Traffic patterns are to the left unless right traffic is noted by the contraction "Rgt tfc." The only runways with right traffic are Rwy 18 and Rwy 35.
    Answer (A) is incorrect. Traffic patterns are to the left, not right, for Rwy 14 and Rwy 32. Traffic patterns are to the right, not left, for Rwy 18 and Rwy 35. **Answer (C) is incorrect.** The traffic pattern for Rwy 14 and Rwy 32 is to the left, not right.

31. (Refer to Figure 52 on page 239.) Where is Loup City Municipal located with relation to the city?

    A. Northwest approximately 4 miles.

    B. Northwest approximately 1 mile.

    C. East approximately 7 miles.

Answer (B) is correct. (Chart Supplement)
    DISCUSSION: Fig. 52 contains the Chart Supplement excerpt for Loup City Municipal. On the first line, the third item listed, 1 NW, means that Loup City Municipal is located approximately 1 NM northwest of the associated city.
    Answer (A) is incorrect. 4 NW is the approximate location of LNK airport to the associated city, not Loup City Municipal airport. **Answer (C) is incorrect.** The airport is approximately 1 NM northwest, not 7 NM east, of the associated city.

NEBRASKA

LINCOLN (LNK) 4 NW UTC–6(–5DT) N40°51.05' W96°45.55'   **OMAHA**
  1219   B   S4   **FUEL** 100LL, JET A   TPA—See Remarks   ARFF Index—See Remarks   H–5C, L–10I
  NOTAM FILE LNK   IAP, AD 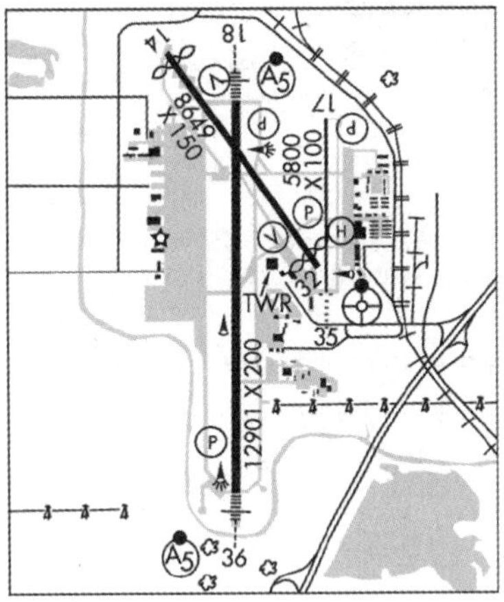
  RWY 18–36: H12901X200 (ASPH–CONC–GRVD)   S–100, D–200,
    2S–175, 2D–400   HIRL
    RWY 18: MALSR. PAPI(P4L)—GA 3.0° TCH 55'. Rgt tfc.   0.4%
    down.
    RWY 36: MALSR. PAPI(P4L)—GA 3.0° TCH 57'.
  RWY 14–32: H8649X150 (ASPH–CONC–GRVD)   S–80, D–170,
    2S–175, 2D–280   MIRL
    RWY 14: REIL. VASI(V4L)—GA 3.0° TCH 48'. Thld dsplcd 363'.
    RWY 32: VASI(V4L)—GA 3.0° TCH 50'. Thld dsplcd 470'.
    Pole.   0.3% up.
  RWY 17–35: H5800X100 (ASPH–CONC–AFSC)   S–49, D–60
    HIRL   0.8% up S
    RWY 17: REIL. PAPI(P4L)—GA 3.0° TCH 44'.
    RWY 35: ODALS. PAPI(P4L)—GA 3.0° TCH 30'. Rgt tfc.
  RUNWAY DECLARED DISTANCE INFORMATION
    RWY 14: TORA–8649   TODA–8649   ASDA–8649   LDA–8286
    RWY 17: TORA–5800   TODA–5800   ASDA–5400   LDA–5400
    RWY 18: TORA–12901   TODA–12901   ASDA–12901   LDA–12901
    RWY 32: TORA–8649   TODA–8649   ASDA–8286   LDA–7816
    RWY 35: TORA–5800   TODA–5800   ASDA–5800   LDA–5800
    RWY 36: TORA–12901   TODA–12901   ASDA–12901   LDA–12901
  AIRPORT REMARKS: Attended continuously. Birds invof arpt. Rwy 18 designated calm wind rwy. Rwy 32 apch holdline
    on South A twy. TPA–2219 (1000), heavy military jet 3000 (1781). Class I, ARFF Index B. ARFF Index C level
    equipment provided. Rwy 18–36 touchdown and rollout rwy visual range avbl. When twr clsd MIRL Rwy 14–32
    preset on low ints, HIRL Rwy 18–36 and Rwy 17–35 preset on med ints, ODALS Rwy 35 operate continuously on
    med ints, MALSR Rwy 18 and Rwy 36 operate continuously and REIL Rwy 14 and Rwy 17 operate continuously
    on low ints. VASI Rwy 14 and Rwy 32, PAPI Rwy 17, Rwy 35, Rwy 18 and Rwy 36 on continuously.
  WEATHER DATA SOURCES: ASOS (402) 474–9214. LLWAS
  COMMUNICATIONS: CTAF 118.5   **ATIS** 118.05   **UNICOM** 122.95
    RCO 122.65 (COLUMBUS RADIO)
  ® **APP/DEP CON** 124.0 (180°–359°) 124.8 (360°–179°)
    TOWER 118.5 125.7 (1130–0600Z‡)   **GND CON** 121.9   **CLNC DEL** 120.7
  AIRSPACE: CLASS C svc 1130–0600Z‡ ctc APP CON other times CLASS E.
  RADIO AIDS TO NAVIGATION: NOTAM FILE LNK.
    (H) **VORTACW** 116.1   LNK   Chan 108   N40°55.43' W96°44.52'   181° 4.4 NM to fld. 1370/9E
    POTTS NDB (MHW/LOM) 385   LN   N40°44.83' W96°45.75'   355° 6.2 NM to fld. Unmonitored when twr clsd.
    ILS 111.1   I–OCZ   Rwy 18.   Class IB   OM unmonitored.
    ILS 109.9   I–LNK   Rwy 36   Class IA   LOM POTTS NDB. MM unmonitored. LOM unmonitored when twr
    clsd.
  COMM/NAV/WEATHER REMARKS: Emerg frequency 121.5 not available at twr.

LOUP CITY MUNI (0F4)   1 NW   UTC–6(–5DT)   N41°17.20' W98°59.41'   **OMAHA**
  2071   B   **FUEL** 100LL   NOTAM FILE OLU   L–10H, 12H
  RWY 16–34: H3200X60 (CONC)   S–12.5   MIRL
    RWY 34: Trees.
  RWY 04–22: 2040X100 (TURF)
    RWY 04: Tree.   **RWY 22:** Road.
  AIRPORT REMARKS: Unattended. For svc call 308–745–1344/1244/0664.
  COMMUNICATIONS: CTAF 122.9
  RADIO AIDS TO NAVIGATION: NOTAM FILE OLU.
    WOLBACH (H) VORTAC 114.8   OBH   Chan 95   N41°22.54' W98°21.22'   253° 29.3 NM to fld. 2010/7E.

MARTIN FLD   (See SO SIOUX CITY)

Figure 52. Chart Supplement.

32. (Refer to Figure 71 on page 241.) (Refer to Area 1.) Dubey Airport is

A. a privately owned airport restricted to use.
B. a restricted military stage field within restricted airspace.
C. an airport restricted to use by sport pilots only.

Answer (A) is correct. (ACUG)
　DISCUSSION: Dubey Airport (south of 1) is a private, i.e., nonpublic-use, airport as indicated by the term "(Pvt)" after the airport name. Private airports that are shown on the sectional charts have an emergency or landmark value. The airport symbol with the letter "R" in the center means it is a nonpublic-use airport.
　Answer (B) is incorrect. Military airfields are labeled as AFB, NAS, AAF, NAAS, NAF, MCAS, or DND. **Answer (C) is incorrect.** Dubey is restricted by its use according to its owners and management.

33. (Refer to Figure 71 on page 241.) (Refer to Area 6.) Sky Way Airport is

A. an airport restricted to use by private and recreational pilots.
B. a restricted military stage field within restricted airspace.
C. a nonpublic-use airport.

Answer (C) is correct. (ACUG)
　DISCUSSION: Sky Way Airport (west of 6) is a private, i.e., nonpublic-use, airport as indicated by the term "(Pvt)" after the airport name or the letter "R" in the center of the airport symbol. Private airports that are shown on the sectional charts have an emergency or landmark value.
　Answer (A) is incorrect. Sky Way Airport (west of 6) is a private, i.e., nonpublic-use, airport as indicated by the term "(Pvt)" after the airport name or the letter "R" in the center of the airport symbol. This does not mean that only private and recreational pilots may use the airport. **Answer (B) is incorrect.** Military airfields are labeled as AFB, NAS, AAF, NAAS, NAF, MCAS, or DND.

SU 7: Airport Operations

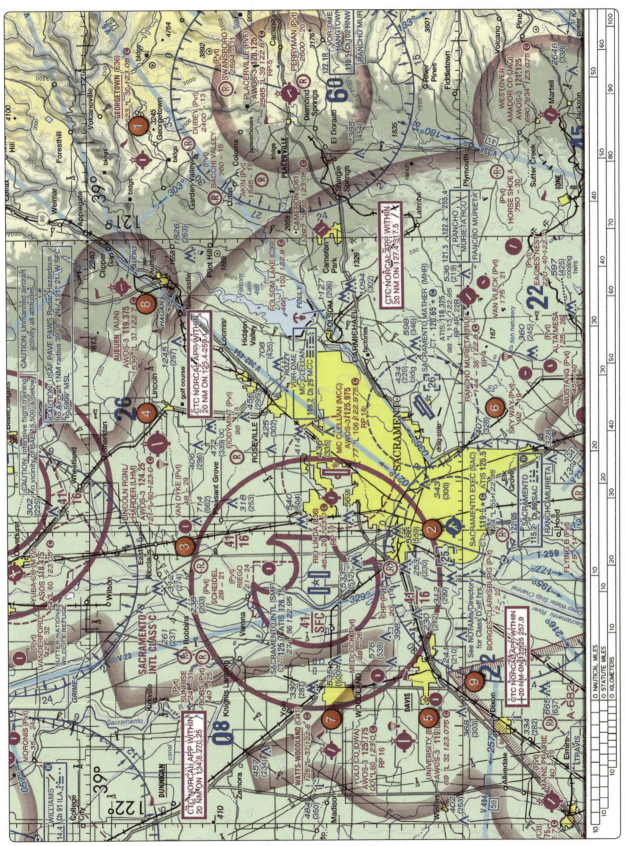

Figure 71. Sectional Chart Excerpt.
NOTE: Chart is not to scale and should not be used for navigation. Use associated scale.

34. Enhanced taxiway centerline markings are enhanced for a maximum of how many feet prior to the runway holding position markings?

A. 50
B. 100
C. 150

Answer (C) is correct. (AIM Para 2-3-4)
DISCUSSION: Enhanced taxiway centerlines will begin 150 ft. prior to the runway holding position markings to draw attention to the approaching runway entrance and holding position and to advise pilots to prepare to stop unless they have been cleared onto or across the runway by ATC.
Answer (A) is incorrect. Although the enhanced markings may be 50 ft., the maximum enhanced taxiway centerlines will begin 150 ft. from the runway holding position markings.
Answer (B) is incorrect. Although enhanced markings can often be 100 ft., the maximum enhanced taxiway centerlines will begin 150 ft. from the runway holding position markings.

35. The purpose of an enhanced taxiway centerline is to

A. identify the location of taxiing aircraft during low visibility operations.
B. highlight an approaching runway holding position marking.
C. supplement location signs in confirming the designation of the taxiway.

Answer (B) is correct. (AIM Para 2-3-4)
DISCUSSION: The enhanced taxiway centerline warns pilots that they are approaching a runway holding position marking and should prepare to stop unless they have been cleared onto or across the runway by ATC.
Answer (A) is incorrect. Geographic position markings provide location information at points along low visibility taxi routes to help identify locations and are found left of the taxiway centerline. **Answer (C) is incorrect.** Surface painted location signs are used to supplement location signs to assist pilots in confirming the designation of the taxiway on which the aircraft is located.

36. (Refer to Figure 59 on page 243.) (Refer to Area 2.) What kind of airport is Deshler (6D7)?

A. A private airport with a grass runway.
B. A public airport with a runway that is not a hard surface.
C. An abandoned paved airport having landmark value.

Answer (B) is correct. (ACUG)
DISCUSSION: According to the Sectional Chart Legend, a magenta circle with nothing indicated on the inside of the circle indicates that airport is not hard-surfaced.
Answer (A) is incorrect. There is not a letter "R" inside the magenta circle indicating it is a private airport. **Answer (C) is incorrect.** There is no "X" inside the magenta circle to indicate it is an abandoned paved airport having landmark value.

SU 7: Airport Operations 243

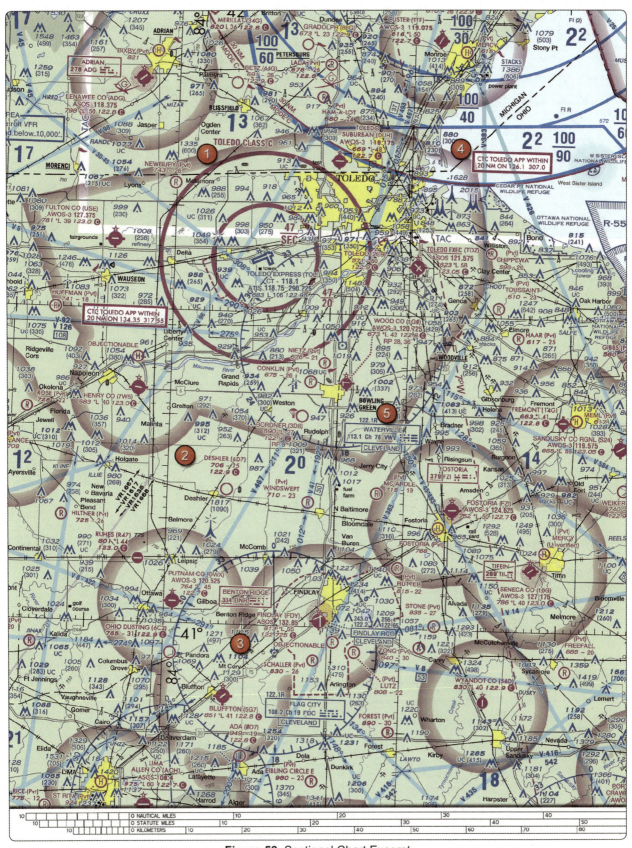

Figure 59. Sectional Chart Excerpt.
NOTE: Chart is not to scale and should not be used for navigation. Use associated scale.

37. (Refer to Figure 24 on page 245.) (Refer to Area 6.) What type of airport is Card Airport?

A. Public towered.
B. Public non-towered.
C. Private non-towered.

Answer (C) is correct. (ACUG)

DISCUSSION: Card Airport (southwest of area 6) is a private, i.e., nonpublic-use, airport as indicated by the term "(Pvt)" after the airport name and the magenta circle with the letter "R" in the center.

Answer (A) is incorrect. A public, towered airport is depicted with a blue airport symbol, not magenta. **Answer (B) is incorrect.** A public non-towered airport is depicted with a magenta symbol showing the runway complex, not the letter "R" in the center.

SU 7: Airport Operations

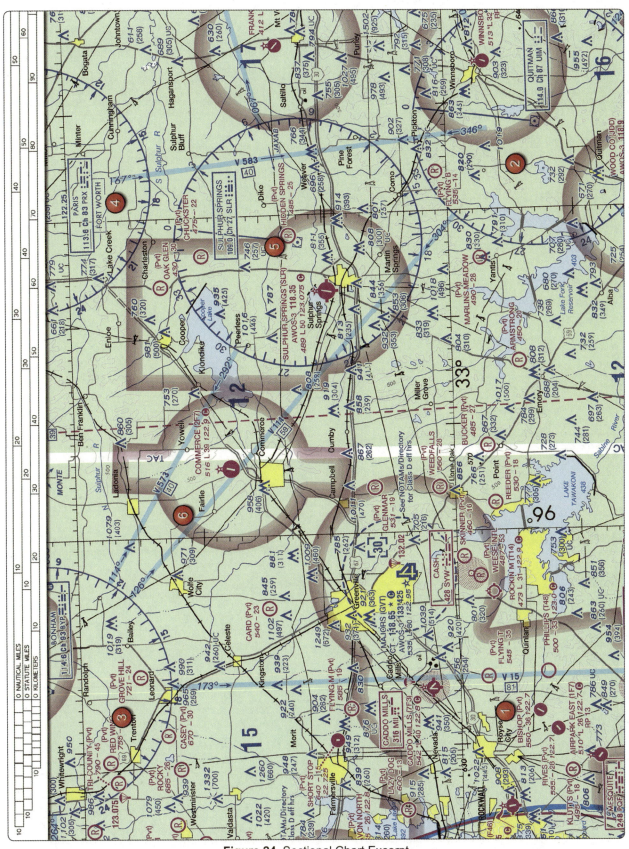

Figure 24. Sectional Chart Excerpt.
NOTE: Chart is not to scale and should not be used for navigation. Use associated scale.

STUDY UNIT EIGHT
AERONAUTICAL DECISION MAKING AND PHYSIOLOGY

(17 pages of outline)

8.1	Aeronautical Decision Making (ADM)	(19 questions) 247, 264
8.2	Physiology	(14 questions) 255, 268

8.1 AERONAUTICAL DECISION MAKING (ADM)

1. **ADM** is a systematic approach to the mental process used by unmanned aircraft (UA) pilots to determine consistently the best course of action in response to a given set of circumstances.

   a. **Effective team communication**

      1) The remote pilot in command (rPIC), person manipulating the controls, and visual observer (VO) must work out a method of communication, such as the use of a hand-held radio or other effective means, that would not create a distraction and allows them to understand each other. The rPIC should evaluate which method is most appropriate for the operation and should be determined prior to flight.

   b. **Task management**

      1) Tasks vary depending on the complexity of the operation. Depending on the area of the operations, additional crewmembers may be needed to safely operate. Enough crewmembers should be utilized to ensure no one on the team becomes overloaded. Once a member of the team becomes overworked, there is a greater possibility of an incident/accident.

2. **Crew resource management (CRM)** in single-pilot or multiperson crew configurations is the effective use of all personnel and material assets available to a pilot or a flight crew.

   a. CRM emphasizes good communication and other interpersonal relationship skills.

   b. CRM is a component of ADM, where the pilot of a small unmanned aircraft system (sUAS) makes effective use of all available resources: human resources, hardware, and information.

      1) Many remote pilots operating under Part 107 may use a VO, oversee other persons manipulating the controls of the UA, or any other person who the rPIC may interact with to ensure safe operations.

         a) Therefore, the rPIC must be able to function in a team environment and maximize team performance.

      2) This skill set includes situational awareness, proper allocation of tasks to individuals, avoidance of work overloads in self and in others, and effectively communicating with other members of the crew, such as VOs and persons manipulating the controls of an sUAS.

3. **Situational awareness** is pilot knowledge of where the UA is in regard to location, air traffic control, weather, regulations, operating status, and other factors that may affect flight.

    a. Situational awareness is the accurate perception of operational and environmental factors that affect the UA during a specific period of time.

        1) When situationally aware, the pilot has an overview of the total operation and is not fixed on one perceived significant factor.

        2) A pilot should maintain an awareness of the environmental conditions of the flight, such as spatial orientation of the UA and its proximity to terrain, traffic, weather, and airspace.

        3) To maintain situational awareness, all ADM skills should be used.

    b. **Obstacles to Maintaining Situational Awareness**

        1) Fatigue, stress, remote operation, and work overload can cause a pilot to lose overall awareness of the flight situation.

        2) Complacency can be an obstacle to situational awareness by reducing a pilot's effectiveness at the control station (CS).

4. **Hazardous attitudes** can contribute to poor pilot judgment and reduce situational awareness.

    a. **Antiauthority (*Don't tell me!*).** This attitude is found in people who do not like anyone telling them what to do. In a sense, they are saying, "No one can tell me what to do." They may be resentful of having someone tell them what to do or may regard rules, regulations, and procedures as silly or unnecessary. Of course, it is always your prerogative to question authority if you feel it is in error.

    b. **Impulsivity (*Do something quickly!*).** This is the attitude of people who frequently feel the need to do something -- anything -- immediately. They do not stop to think about what they are about to do, they do not determine the best alternative, and they do the first thing that comes to mind.

    c. **Invulnerability (*It won't happen to me.*).** Many people feel that accidents happen to others but never to them. They know accidents can happen, and they know that anyone can be affected. However, they never really feel or believe that they will be personally involved. Pilots who think this way are more likely to take chances and increase risk.

    d. **Macho (*I can do it.*).** Pilots who are always trying to prove that they are better than anyone else are thinking *I can do it -- I'll show them*. Pilots with this type of attitude will try to prove themselves by taking risks in order to impress others. While this pattern is thought to be a male characteristic, women are equally susceptible.

    e. **Resignation (*What's the use?*).** Pilots who think *What's the use?* do not see themselves as being able to make a great deal of difference in what happens to them. The pilot is apt to think that things go well due to good luck. When things go badly, the pilot may feel that someone is out to get him or her or may attribute the situation to bad luck. The pilot will leave the action to others, for better or worse. Sometimes, such pilots will even go along with unreasonable requests just to be nice.

SU 8: Aeronautical Decision Making and Physiology

5. **Hazard identification.** Hazards in the sUAS and its operating environment must be identified, documented, and controlled. The analysis process used to define hazards needs to consider all components of the system, based on the equipment being used and the environment in which it is being operated. The key question to ask during analysis of the sUAS and its operation is, "what if?" Small unmanned aircraft system rPICs are expected to exercise due diligence in identifying significant and reasonably foreseeable hazards related to their operations.

  a. **Risk analysis and assessment.** Risk is the future impact of a hazard that is not controlled or eliminated. It can be viewed as future uncertainty created by the hazard.

  b. **Risk management** is the part of the decision-making process that relies on situational awareness, problem recognition, and good judgment to reduce risks associated with each flight.

   1) The goal of risk management is to proactively identify safety-related hazards and mitigate the associated risks.

      a) Risk management is an important component of ADM. When a pilot follows good decision-making practices, the inherent risk in a flight is reduced or even eliminated.

      b) The ability to make good decisions is based on direct or indirect experience and education.

      c) A remote pilot must consider risk management to prevent the final link in the accident chain.

2) There are four risk elements involved in decisions made during a flight: the **P**ilot in command, the unmanned **A**ircraft, the en**V**ironment, and the **E**xternal pressures of the operation. You can remember these items using the PAVE checklist. In decision making, each risk element is evaluated to obtain an accurate perception of circumstances.

   a) **Pilot.** Consider such factors as competency, condition of health, mental and emotional state, level of fatigue, and many other variables.

   b) **Aircraft.** Assess performance, equipment, or airworthiness of the sUAS.

   c) **enVironment.** Consider a range of factors indirectly related to pilot or sUAS: weather, air traffic control, terrain, takeoff and landing areas, and surrounding obstacles.

   d) **External pressures.** Assessing factors relating to pilot, UA, and environment is largely influenced by the purpose of the operation. Decisions should be made in the context of why the flight is being made and how critical it is to maintain the schedule.

c. The risk assessment should use a conventional breakdown of risk by its two components: severity and likelihood of occurrence.

   1) Severity and likelihood criteria. Each level of severity and likelihood needs to be defined in terms that are realistic for the operational environment. This ensures each rPIC's decision tools are relevant to their operations and operational environment, recognizing the extensive diversity that exists.

      a) The definitions and construction of the matrix are left to the sUAS rPIC to design. An example of severity and likelihood definitions is shown in the following severity and likelihood criteria tables.

Severity of Consequences

Severity Level	Definition	Value
Catastrophic	Equipment destroyed, multiple deaths.	5
Hazardous	Large reduction in safety margins, physical distress, or a workload such that crewmembers cannot be relied upon to perform their tasks accurately or completely. Serious injury or death. Major equipment damage.	4
Major	Significant reduction in safety margins, reduction in the ability of crewmembers to cope with adverse operating conditions as a result of an increase in workload, or as a result of conditions impairing their efficiency. Serious incident. Injury to persons.	3
Minor	Nuisance. Operating limitations. Use of emergency procedures. Minor incident.	2
Negligible	Little consequence.	1

Likelihood of Occurrence

Likelihood Level	Definition	Value
Frequent	Likely to occur many times.	5
Occasional	Likely to occur sometimes.	4
Remote	Unlikely, but possible to occur.	3
Improbable	Very unlikely to occur.	2
Extremely Improbable	Almost inconceivable that the event will occur.	1

SU 8: Aeronautical Decision Making and Physiology

6. **Risk acceptance.** In the development of risk assessment criteria, sUAS rPICs are expected to develop risk acceptance procedures, including acceptance criteria and designation of authority and responsibility for risk management decision making.

   a. The acceptability of risk can be evaluated using a risk matrix. The matrix below shows three areas of acceptability. Risk matrices may be color coded: unacceptable (red), acceptable (green), and acceptable with mitigation (yellow).

   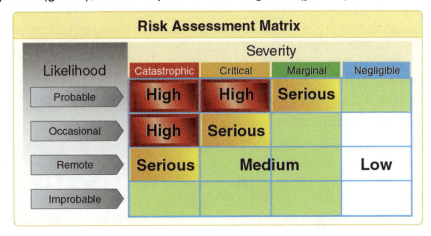

   1) **Unacceptable (Red).** Where combinations of severity and likelihood cause risk to fall into the red area, the risk would be assessed as unacceptable and further work would be required to design an intervention to eliminate that associated hazard or to control the factors that lead to higher risk likelihood or severity.

   2) **Acceptable (Green).** Where the assessed risk falls into the green area, it may be accepted without further action. The objective in risk management should always be to reduce risk to as low as practicable regardless of whether or not the assessment shows that it can be accepted as is.

   3) **Acceptable with Mitigation (Yellow).** Where the risk assessment falls into the yellow area, the risk may be accepted under defined conditions of mitigation.

      a) An example of this situation would be an assessment of the impact of an sUAS operation near a school yard. Scheduling the operation to take place when school is not in session could be one mitigation to prevent undue risk to the children that study and play there.

      b) Another mitigation could be restricting people from the area of operations by placing cones or security personnel to prevent unauthorized access during the sUAS flight operation.

   b. Other risk assessment tools for flight and operational risk management. Other tools can also be used for flight or operational risk assessments and can be developed by the rPICs themselves.

      1) The key is to ensure that all potential hazards and risks are identified and appropriate actions are taken to reduce the risk to persons and property not associated with the operations.

c. **Reducing risk.** Risk analyses should concentrate not only on assigning levels of severity and likelihood, but on determining why these particular levels were selected. This is referred to as root cause analysis and is the first step in developing effective controls to reduce risk to lower levels. In many cases, simple brainstorming sessions among crewmembers is the most effective and affordable method of finding ways to reduce risk. This also has the advantage of involving people who will ultimately be required to implement the controls developed.

1) It is also very easy to get quite bogged down in trying to identify all hazards and risks. That is not the purpose of a risk assessment. The focus should be upon those hazards that pose the greatest risks. As stated earlier, by documenting and compiling these processes, the rPIC can build an arsenal of safety practices that will add to the safety and success of future operations.

d. **Sample Hazard Identification and Risk Assessment**

1) EXAMPLE: I am the rPIC of an sUAS in the proximity of an accident scene shooting aerial footage. Much like pilots in manned aircraft must adhere to preflight action (14 CFR 91.103), I must adhere to preflight familiarization, inspection, and UA operations (14 CFR 107.49). Let's say that there is an obvious takeoff and landing site that I intend to use. What if, while I am operating a manned aircraft [emergency medical services (EMS) helicopter] requires use of the same area and I am not left with a suitable landing site? Furthermore, I am running low on power. If I consider this situation prior to flight, I can use the Basic Hazard Identification and Mitigation Process. Through this process, I might determine that an acceptable level of risk can be achieved by also having an alternate landing site and possibly additional sites at which I can sacrifice the UA to avoid imposing risk to people on the ground or to manned aircraft operations.

   a) It is really a simple process. I must consider the hazards presented during this particular operation, determine the risk severity, and then develop a plan to lessen (or mitigate) the risk to an acceptable level.

   b) By documenting and compiling these processes, I can build a catalog of safety practices that will add to the safety and success of future operations. Some proven methods that can help a new rPIC along the way are discussed further in this study unit.

2) Hazard identification. Using the Minimums (PAVE) Checklist for Risk Management, I will set personal minimums based upon my specific flight experience, health habits, and tolerance for stress, just to name a few.

   a) **P**ersonal: Am I healthy for flight and what are my personal minimums based upon my experience operating this sUAS? During this step, I will often use the IMSAFE checklist in order to perform a more in-depth evaluation:

      i) **I**llness – Am I suffering from any illness or symptom of an illness that might affect me in flight?

      ii) **M**edication – Am I currently taking any drugs (prescription or over-the-counter)?

      iii) **S**tress – Am I experiencing any psychological or emotional factors that might affect my performance?

      iv) **A**lcohol – Have I consumed alcohol within the last 8 to 24 hours?

      v) **F**atigue – Have I received sufficient sleep and rest in the recent past?

      vi) **E**motion – Am I emotional due to any factor? Bereavement, arguments, hostility, stress, etc.

   b) **A**ircraft: Have I conducted a preflight check of my sUAS (aircraft, CS, takeoff and landing equipment, etc.) and determined it to be in a condition for safe operation? Is the filming equipment properly secured to the UA prior to flight?

   c) En**V**ironment: What is the weather like? Am I comfortable and experienced enough to fly in the forecast weather conditions? Have I considered all of my options and left myself an "out?" Have I determined alternative landing spots in case of an emergency?

   d) **E**xternal Pressures: Am I stressed or anxious? Is this a flight that will cause me to be stressed or anxious? Is there pressure to complete the flight operation quickly? Am I dealing with an unhealthy safety culture? Am I being honest with myself and others about my personal operational abilities and limitations?

3) Risk assessment. After identifying hazards, I will again assess them with the Hazard Identification and Risk Assessment Process Chart.

4) Controlling risk. After I fully understand the hazards and risks by using the preceding steps, I must design and implement risk controls. These may be additional or changed procedures, additional or modified equipment, the addition of VOs, or any of a number of other changes.

   a) Residual and substitute risk. Residual risk is the risk remaining after mitigation has been completed. Often, this is a multistep process, continuing until risk has been mitigated down to an acceptable level necessary to begin or continue operation.

   b) After these controls are designed, but before the operation begins or continues, an assessment must be made of whether the controls are likely to be effective and/or if they introduce new hazards to the operation.

      i) The latter condition, introduction of new hazards, is referred to as substitute risk, a situation where the cure is worse than the disease.

      ii) The arrow in the figure above that returns back to the top of the diagram depicts the use of the preceding hazard identification, risk analysis, and risk assessment processes to determine if the modified operation is acceptable.

5) Starting the operation. Once appropriate risk controls are developed and implemented, I will begin the operation.

8.2 PHYSIOLOGY

1. **Dehydration** is the excessive loss of water from the body, as from illness or fluid deprivation.
    a. This fluid loss can occur in any environment. Causes include hot flight decks and flight lines, high humidity, diuretic drinks (i.e., coffee, tea, cola), as well as improper attire.
    b. Some common signs and symptoms of dehydration include headache, fatigue, cramps, sleepiness, dizziness, and with severe dehydration, lethargy and coma.
        1) Heat exhaustion often accompanies dehydration. Below are the first two stages of heat exhaustion, along with accompanying signs and symptoms.
            a) Heat stress (body temp., 99.5°-100° F) – reduces performance, decision-making ability, alertness, and visual capabilities.
            b) Heat exhaustion (body temp., 101°-105° F) – fatigue, nausea/vomiting, cramps, rapid breathing, and fainting.
    c. To help prevent dehydration and heat exhaustion, you should drink two to four quarts of water every 24 hours. Or, follow the generally prescribed eight-glasses-a-day rule.
        1) Because each individual is physiologically different, this is only to be used as a guide. Your daily fluid intake should be varied to meet your individual needs depending on work conditions, environment, and individual physiology.
        2) Other useful tips on avoiding heat exhaustion are limiting your daily intake of caffeine and alcohol (both are diuretics), properly acclimating to major weather and/or climate changes, and planning ahead by carrying sufficient fluids and choosing appropriate attire for the forecast conditions.

2. **Heat stroke** results from exposure to heat, leading to an excessive rise in body temperature and a failure of the body temperature regulating system.
    a. This acute medical emergency is characterized by body temperatures in excess of 105.8 °F.
        1) There may be a sudden and sustained loss of consciousness preceded by nausea, vertigo, headache, erratic behavior, and cerebral dysfunction.
    b. There will be a lack of sweating, and the skin will feel dry and hot.

3. **Alcohol** can be a significant self-inflicted stress factor.
    a. As little as 1 oz. of liquor, 1 bottle of beer, or 4 oz. of wine can impair flying skills.
        1) Even after your body has completely destroyed a moderate amount of alcohol, you can still be severely impaired for many hours by hangover.
        2) Alcohol also renders you much more susceptible to disorientation and hypoxia.
    b. The Federal Aviation Regulations prohibit remote pilots from operating an sUAS within 8 hr. after drinking any alcoholic beverage or while under the influence of alcohol.
        1) An excellent rule is to allow at least 12 to 24 hr. to pass before operating an sUAS, depending on how much you drank and the severity of the residual effects.

4. Pilot performance can be seriously impaired by both **prescription and over-the-counter** medications.

   a. Many medications, such as tranquilizers, sedatives, strong pain relievers, and cough-suppressant preparations, have primary effects that may impair judgment, memory, alertness, coordination, vision, and the ability to make calculations.

   1) Others, such as antihistamines, blood pressure drugs, muscle relaxants, and agents to control diarrhea and motion sickness, have side effects that may impair the same critical functions.

MOST COMMONLY EXPERIENCED SIDE EFFECTS AND INTERACTIONS OF OTC MEDICATIONS

	MEDICATIONS	SIDE EFFECTS	INTERACTIONS
PAIN RELIEF/ FEVER	ASPIRIN Alka-Seltzer Bayer Aspirin Bufferin	Ringing in ears, nausea, stomach ulceration, hyperventilation	Increase effect of blood thinners
	ACETAMINOPHEN Tylenol	Liver toxicity (in large doses)	
	IBUPROFEN Advil Motrin Nuprin	Upset stomach, dizziness, rash, itching	Increase effect of blood thinners
COLDS/FLU	ANTIHISTAMINES Actifed Dristan Benadryl Drixoral Cheracol-Plus Nyquil Chlortrimeton Sinarest Contac Sinutab Dimetapp	Sedation, dizziness, rash, impairment of coordination, upset stomach, thickening of bronchial secretions, blurring of vision	Increase sedative effects of other medications
	DECONGESTANTS Afrin Nasal Spray Sine-Aid Sudafed	Excessive stimulation, dizziness, difficulty with urination, palpitations	Aggravate high blood pressure, heart disease, and prostate problems
	COUGH SUPPRESSANTS Benylin Robitussin CF/DM Vicks Formula #44	Drowsiness, blurred vision, difficulty with urination, upset stomach	Increase sedative effects of other medications
BOWEL PREPARATIONS	LAXATIVES Correctol Ex-Lax	Unexpected bowel activity at altitude, rectal itching	
	ANTI-DIARRHEALS Imodium A-D Pepto-Bismol	Drowsiness, depression, blurred vision (see Aspirin)	
APPETITE SUPPRESSANTS	Acutrim Dexatrim	Excessive stimulation, dizziness, palpitations, headaches	Increase stimulatory effects of decongestants, interfere with high blood pressure medications
SLEEPING AIDS	Nytol Sominex	(Contain antihistamine) Prolonged drowsiness, blurred vision	Cause excessive drowsiness when used with alcohol
STIMULANTS	CAFFEINE Coffee, tea, cola, chocolate	Excessive stimulation, tremors, palpitations, headache	Interfere with high blood pressure medications

   b. The safest rule is to avoid sUAS operation while taking any medication, unless approved by the FAA.

   c. The table above lists the common over-the-counter medications and outlines some of their possible side effects that could affect your operating abilities. As with all drugs, side effects may vary with the individual.

d. FAA advice on over-the-counter medications:
   1) Read and follow label directions for use of medication.
   2) If the label warns of side effects, do not participate in sUAS operation until twice the recommended dosing interval has passed.
      a) EXAMPLE: If the label says "take every 4-6 hours," you should wait at least 12 hr. before operating an sUAS.
   3) Remember, the condition you are treating may be as disqualifying as the medication.
   4) As a pilot, you are responsible for your own personal preflight. Be wary of any illness that requires medicine to make you feel better.
   5) If an illness is serious enough to require medication, it is also serious enough to prevent you from operating an sUAS.
   6) Avoid mixing decongestants and caffeine (contained in coffee, tea, cola, chocolate).
   7) Beware of medications that use alcohol as a base for the ingredients.

5. **Hyperventilation**, an abnormal increase in the volume of air breathed in and out of the lungs, can occur subconsciously when you encounter a stressful situation in flight. This abnormal breathing flushes from your lungs and blood much of the carbon dioxide your system needs to maintain the proper degree of blood acidity.

   a. The resulting chemical imbalance in the body produces dizziness, tingling of the fingers and toes, hot and cold sensations, drowsiness, nausea, and a feeling of suffocation. Often you may react to these symptoms with even greater hyperventilation.
      1) Incapacitation can eventually result from incoordination, disorientation, and painful muscle spasms. Finally, unconsciousness can occur.
   b. The symptoms of hyperventilation subside within a few minutes after the rate and depth of breathing are consciously brought back under control.
      1) The buildup of the appropriate balance of carbon dioxide in your body can be hastened by controlled breathing in and out of a paper bag held over your nose and mouth. Also, talking, singing, or counting aloud often helps.

6. **Stress** from the pressures of everyday living can impair remote pilot performance, often in very subtle ways.

   a. When you are under more stress than usual, you should consider delaying operations until your difficulties have been resolved.
      1) Difficulties can occupy thought processes so as to decrease alertness.
      2) Distraction can so interfere with judgment that unwarranted risks are taken.
      3) Stress and fatigue can be a deadly combination.

7. **Fatigue** can be treacherous because it may not be apparent to you until serious errors are made.

    a. It is best described as either acute (short-term) or chronic (long-term).

        1) Acute fatigue is the everyday tiredness felt after long periods of physical or mental strain.

            a) Consequently, coordination and alertness can be reduced.
            b) Acute fatigue is prevented by adequate rest and sleep, as well as regular exercise and proper nutrition.

        2) Chronic fatigue occurs when there is not enough time for full recovery between episodes of acute fatigue.

            a) Performance continues to fall off, and judgment becomes impaired.
            b) Recovery from chronic fatigue requires a prolonged period of rest.

8. **Factors affecting vision.**

    a. Of the body senses, vision is the most important for safe flight. It is important for you to understand your eye's construction and the effect of darkness on the eye. Much of your operating will be conducted with a back-lit screen and your eyes continuously cycling through near and far vision.

        1) The **fovea** is a small, notched area that is located directly behind the lens on the retina. This area contains cones only.

            a) The fovea is where your vision is the sharpest. Thus, when you look directly at an object, the image is focused mainly on the fovea.
            b) The fovea field of vision is a conical field of only about 1°.

                i) To demonstrate how small a 1° field is, take a quarter and tape it to a flat piece of glass, such as a window. Now stand 4 1/2 ft. from the mounted quarter and close one eye. The area of your field of view covered by the quarter is a 1° field, similar to your fovea vision.

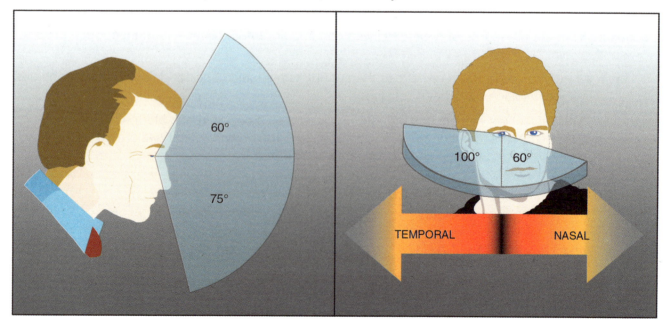

            c) The normal field of vision for each eye is about 135° vertically and about 160° horizontally, as shown above. The fovea field is the central 1° field.

- d) Your visual acuity (detail) drops off rapidly outside the fovea cone.
    - i) EXAMPLE: Outside of a 10° cone (centered on the fovea cone), you will see only about one-tenth of what you can see in the fovea cone.
- 2) Effective scanning is accomplished with a series of short, regularly spaced eye movements that bring successive areas of the sky into the central visual field.
    - a) Each eye movement should not exceed 10°.
    - b) Each area should be observed for at least 1 sec. to enable detection.
    - c) Most midair collisions occur during clear days when remote pilots may be less vigilant in scanning for traffic.
- b. The eyes are the first part of your body to suffer from low oxygen at altitude because the capillaries are very small and have a limited capacity to carry oxygen.
    - 1) Good vision depends on your physical condition. Fatigue, colds, vitamin deficiencies, alcohol, stimulants, smoking, or medication can seriously impair your vision.
        - a) EXAMPLE: Smoking lowers the sensitivity of the eyes and reduces night vision by approximately 20%.
- c. Various factors can affect the eye and cause things to be seen inaccurately.
    - 1) Haze, for example, can create the illusion of traffic or terrain being farther away than they actually are.

9. **Night flight** involves risks that are not present during daylight operations. To operate an sUAS safely at night, it is important for the rPIC to implement protocols to mitigate the risks identified for each operation.
    - a. **Circadian rhythm effects.** Avoid self-imposed stressors that can limit night vision (e.g., exhaustion, hypoglycemia/low blood sugar, and tobacco use).
    - b. **Obstacle Avoidance with Lack of Visual Cues**
        - 1) Survey the operational area before flight to identify possible obstacles.
        - 2) Check for sources of ground lighting and ensure the lights will not be turned on before and during the operation.
    - c. In the eyes, rods are distributed around the cones and do not lie directly behind the pupils, making **off-center viewing** (i.e., looking to one side of an object) important during night flight.
        - 1) During daylight, an object can be seen best by looking directly at it.
            - a) However, as the cones become less effective as the level of light decreases, you may not be able to see an object if you look directly at it.
            - b) Since the cones are at the center of vision, when they stop working in the dark, a night blind spot develops at your center of vision.
        - 2) After some practice, you will find that you can see things more clearly at night by looking to one side of them rather than directly at them.
            - a) Remember that rods do not detect objects while your eyes are moving, only during the pauses.

d. Adapting your eyes to darkness is an important aspect of night vision.

1) When entering a dark area, the pupils of the eyes enlarge to receive as much of the available light as possible.

2) It will take approximately 5 to 10 min. (with enough available light) for the cones to become moderately adjusted. After the adjustment, your eyes become 100 times more sensitive than they were before you entered the dark area.

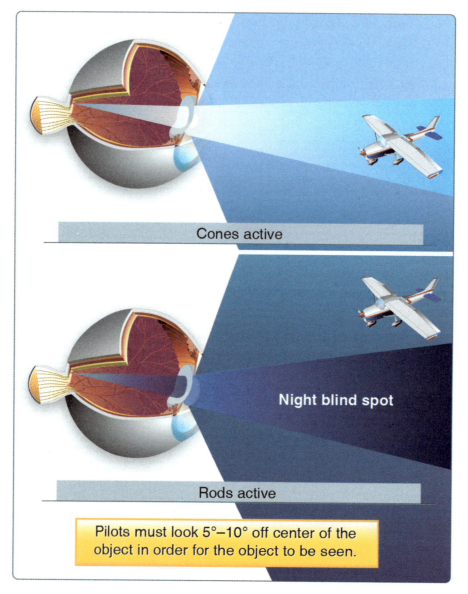

3) After about 30 min., the rods will be fully adjusted to darkness and become about 100,000 times more sensitive to light than they were in the lighted area.

   a) Since the rods can still function in light of 1/5,000 the intensity at which the cones cease to function, they are used for night vision.

4) The rods need more time to adjust to darkness than the cones do to bright light. Your eyes become adapted to sunlight in 10 sec., whereas they need 30 min. to adjust fully to a dark night.

SU 8: Aeronautical Decision Making and Physiology   261

   5) You must consider the adaptation process before and during night flight.

      a) First, your eyes should be allowed to adapt to the low level of light, and then they must be kept adapted.

      b) Next, you must avoid exposing your eyes to any bright light, which could cause temporary blindness, possibly resulting in serious consequences.

         i) Temporary blindness may result in illusions or "after images" during the time your eyes are recovering from the bright light.

10. **Night illusions.**

   a. In addition to night vision limitations, night illusions can cause confusion and distractions during night flying. The following discussion covers some of the common situations that cause illusions associated with night flying.

   b. **Motion parallax** refers to the apparent motion of stationary objects as viewed by an observer moving across the visual field. Near objects appear to move backward, past, or opposite the path of motion; far objects seem to move in the direction of motion or remain fixed. The rate of apparent movement depends on the distance the observer is from the object. The closer the object is to the observer, the faster it will appear to move.

   c. **Geometric perspective.** An object may appear to have a different shape when viewed at varying distances and from different angles. Geometric perspective cues include the following:

      1) Linear perspective -- parallel lines, such as roadway lights, power lines, and railroad tracks, tend to converge as distance from the observer increases.

      2) Apparent foreshortening -- the true shape of an object or a terrain feature appears elliptical when viewed from a distance.

      3) Vertical position in the field -- objects or terrain features farther away from the observer appear higher on the horizon than those closer to the observer.

d. A **false horizon** can occur when the natural horizon is obscured or not readily apparent. It can be generated by confusing bright stars and city lights. It can also occur while flying toward the shore of an ocean or a large lake. Because of the relative darkness of the water, the lights along the shoreline can be mistaken for stars in the sky.

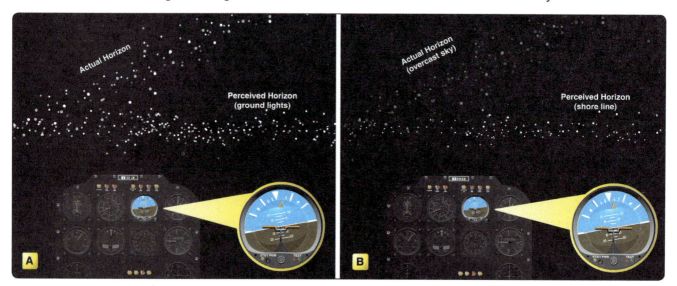

e. **Reversible perspective illusion** can occur when operating in proximity to other manned or unmanned aircraft on parallel courses. The UA operator may be unable to detect relative motion or determine whether the craft is moving away from or closer to the UA.

f. **Fascination (fixation)** is an illusion that occurs when a person becomes fixated on one task (e.g., looking at the sUAS control station) and forgets to look around (e.g., at the sUAS in flight).

g. Reduced lighting and contrast at night make visually discerning location, attitude, and direction of flight difficult. The rPIC cannot rely solely on anti-collision lighting or control station telemetry data displays (even in combination). As a result, night operations are subject to reduced operational ranges.

h. To safely operate in night conditions, the rPIC should do the following:

1) **Look 5° to 10° off-center** of the sUAS to help compensate for the night blind spot.
2) **Avoid looking at bright lights** after adapting to darkness (e.g., reduce the intensity of lighting on the control station).
3) **Designate one or more VOs**, if possible, to scan for other aircraft (strongly encouraged).
4) **Establish a night landing area** that is illuminated by lights (dimmed until needed, if able).
5) **Immediately land the sUAS** if unable to determine its location relative to another aircraft.

11. **Fitness for flight.**
    a. **Medical suitability**
        1) There are no certification requirements under Part 107, but regulations prohibit you from performing crewmember duties while you have a known medical condition or an aggravation of a known medical condition that would make you unable to fulfill your duties as rPIC.
    b. **Illness**
        1) Even a minor illness can seriously impair your performance as a pilot.
            a) Fever and other distracting symptoms can impair judgment, memory, alertness, and the ability to make calculations.
            b) Also, any medication you are taking to combat these symptoms may itself decrease your performance as a pilot.
        2) The safest rule is to avoid sUAS operation while suffering from any illness.
    c. **Medication**
        1) Pilot performance can be seriously impaired by both prescribed and over-the-counter medications.
            a) Many medications, such as tranquilizers, sedatives, strong pain relievers, and cough-suppressant preparations, have primary effects that may impair judgment, memory, alertness, coordination, vision, and the ability to make calculations.
            b) Others, such as antihistamines, blood pressure drugs, muscle relaxants, and agents to control diarrhea and motion sickness, have side effects that may impair the same critical functions.
        2) The safest rule is to avoid sUAS operation while taking any medication, unless approved by the FAA.

QUESTIONS

8.1 Aeronautical Decision Making (ADM)

1. The effective use of all available resources–human, hardware, and information–prior to and during flight to ensure the successful outcome of the operation is called

    A. Risk Management.
    B. Crew Resource Management.
    C. Safety Management System.

Answer (B) is correct. (sUASSG Chap 10)
    DISCUSSION: Crew resource management (CRM) in single-pilot or multi-person crew configurations is the effective use of all personnel and material assets available to a pilot or a flight crew.
    Answer (A) is incorrect. Risk management is the part of the decision-making process that relies on situational awareness, problem recognition, and good judgment to reduce risks associated with each flight. **Answer (C) is incorrect.** A safety management system is the formal, top-down, organization-wide approach to managing safety risk and assuring the effectiveness of safety-risk controls.

2. Safety is an important element for a remote pilot to consider prior to operating an unmanned aircraft system. To prevent the final "link" in the accident chain, a remote pilot must consider which methodology?

    A. Crew Resource Management.
    B. Safety Management System.
    C. Risk Management.

Answer (C) is correct. (sUASSG Chap 10)
    DISCUSSION: Risk management is the part of the decision-making process that relies on situational awareness, problem recognition, and good judgment to reduce risks associated with each flight.
    Answer (A) is incorrect. Crew resource management is the effective use of all personnel and material assets available to a pilot or a flight crew. **Answer (B) is incorrect.** A safety management system is the formal, top-down, organization-wide approach to managing safety risk and assuring the effectiveness of safety-risk controls.

3. Identify the hazardous attitude or characteristic a remote pilot displays while taking risks in order to impress others?

    A. Impulsivity.
    B. Invulnerability.
    C. Macho.

Answer (C) is correct. (sUASSG Chap 10)
    DISCUSSION: Pilots who are always trying to prove they are better than anyone else are thinking I can do it -- I'll show them. Pilots with this type of attitude will try to prove themselves by taking risks in order to impress others.
    Answer (A) is incorrect. Impulsivity is the attitude of people who frequently feel the need to do something -- anything -- immediately. **Answer (B) is incorrect.** Invulnerability is the attitude of people who feel that accidents happen to others but never to them.

4. You have been hired as a remote pilot by a local TV news station to film breaking news with a small UA. You expressed a safety concern and the station manager has instructed you to "fly first, ask questions later." What type of hazardous attitude does this attitude represent?

    A. Machismo.
    B. Invulnerability.
    C. Impulsivity.

Answer (C) is correct. (sUASSG Chap 10)
    DISCUSSION: Impulsivity (Do something quickly!) is the attitude of people who frequently feel the need to do something -- anything -- immediately. They do not stop to think about what they are about to do; they do not determine the best alternative; and they do the first thing that comes to mind.
    Answer (A) is incorrect. Pilots exhibiting the machismo attitude will try to prove themselves by taking risks in order to impress others. **Answer (B) is incorrect.** Pilots exhibiting the invulnerability attitude never believe that they will be personally involved in accidents.

5. When adapting crew resource management (CRM) concepts to the operation of a small UA, CRM must be integrated into

    A. the flight portion only.
    B. all phases of the operation.
    C. the communications only.

Answer (B) is correct. (sUASSG Chap 10)
    DISCUSSION: CRM is a component of ADM, where the pilot of sUAS makes effective use of all available resources: human resources, hardware, and information. CRM applies to all phases of the operation.
    Answer (A) is incorrect. CRM should be adapted to plan for all phases of the operation, not just the flight portion. **Answer (C) is incorrect.** CRM emphasizes good communication and other interpersonal relationship skills; however, it must be integrated into all phases of the operation.

SU 8: Aeronautical Decision Making and Physiology

6. A local TV station has hired a remote pilot to operate their small UA to cover news stories. The remote pilot has had multiple near misses with obstacles on the ground and two small UAS accidents. What would be a solution for the news station to improve their operating safety culture?

A. The news station should implement a policy of no more than five crashes/incidents within 6 months.

B. The news station does not need to make any changes; there are times that an accident is unavoidable.

C. The news station should recognize hazardous attitudes and situations and develop standard operating procedures that emphasize safety.

Answer (C) is correct. (sUASSG Chap 10)
   DISCUSSION: Hazards in the sUAS and its operating environment must be identified, documented, and controlled. The analysis process used to define hazards needs to consider all components of the system, based on the equipment being used and the environment it is being operated in.
   Answer (A) is incorrect. All operators should identify hazards and minimize risks. There is no quantifiable amount of accidents that is acceptable. **Answer (B) is incorrect.** Remote PICs are expected to exercise due diligence in identifying significant and reasonably foreseeable hazards related to their operations.

7. Risk management, as part of the aeronautical decision making (ADM) process, relies on which features to reduce the risks associated with each flight?

A. Application of stress management and risk element procedures.

B. The mental process of analyzing all information in a particular situation and making a timely decision on what action to take.

C. Situational awareness, problem recognition, and good judgment.

Answer (C) is correct. (sUASSG Chap 10)
   DISCUSSION: Risk management is that part of the ADM process that relies on situational awareness, problem recognition, and good judgment to reduce risks associated with each flight.
   Answer (A) is incorrect. Risk management relies on situational awareness, problem recognition, and good judgment, not the application of stress management and risk-element procedures, to reduce the risks associated with each flight. **Answer (B) is incorrect.** Judgment, not risk management, is the mental process of analyzing all information in a particular situation and making a timely decision on what action to take.

8. What is one of the neglected items when a pilot relies on short and long term memory for repetitive tasks?

A. Checklists.

B. Situational awareness.

C. Flying outside the envelope.

Answer (A) is correct. (AC 60-22)
   DISCUSSION: Neglect of checklists, flight planning, preflight inspections, etc., indicates a pilot's unjustified reliance on his or her short- and long-term memory for repetitive flying tasks.
   Answer (B) is incorrect. Situational awareness suffers when the operator falls behind the UA, which results in an inability to recognize deteriorating circumstances and/or misjudgment on the rate of deterioration. **Answer (C) is incorrect.** Flying outside the envelope occurs when the pilot believes (often in error) that the UA's high-performance capability meets the demands imposed by the pilot's (often overestimated) flying skills.

9. Hazardous attitudes occur to every pilot to some degree at some time. What are some of these hazardous attitudes?

A. Antiauthority, impulsivity, macho, resignation, and invulnerability.

B. Poor situational awareness, snap judgments, and lack of a decision making process.

C. Poor risk management and lack of stress management.

Answer (A) is correct. (sUASSG Chap 10)
   DISCUSSION: The five hazardous attitudes addressed in the ADM process are antiauthority, impulsivity, invulnerability, macho, and resignation.
   Answer (B) is incorrect. Poor situational awareness and snap judgments are indications of the lack of a decision-making process, not hazardous attitudes. **Answer (C) is incorrect.** Poor risk management and lack of stress management lead to poor ADM and are not considered hazardous attitudes.

10. In the aeronautical decision making (ADM) process, what is the first step in neutralizing a hazardous attitude?

A. Recognizing hazardous thoughts.
B. Recognizing the invulnerability of the situation.
C. Making a rational judgment.

Answer (A) is correct. (sUASSG Chap 10)
DISCUSSION: Hazardous attitudes, which contribute to poor pilot judgment, can be effectively counteracted by redirecting that hazardous attitude so that appropriate action can be taken. Recognition of hazardous thoughts is the first step in neutralizing them in the ADM process.
Answer (B) is incorrect. Invulnerability is a hazardous attitude. The first step in neutralizing a hazardous attitude is to recognize it. **Answer (C) is incorrect.** Before a rational judgment can be made, the hazardous attitude must be recognized then redirected so that appropriate action can be taken.

11. What is the antidote when a pilot has a hazardous attitude, such as "Antiauthority"?

A. Rules do not apply in this situation.
B. I know what I am doing.
C. Follow the rules.

Answer (C) is correct. (sUASSG Chap 10)
DISCUSSION: When you recognize a hazardous thought, you should correct it by stating the corresponding antidote. The antidote for the antiauthority ("Do not tell me!") hazardous attitude is "Follow the rules. They are usually right."
Answer (A) is incorrect. "Rules do not apply in this situation" is an example of the antiauthority hazardous attitude, not its antidote. **Answer (B) is incorrect.** "I know what I'm doing" is an example of the macho hazardous attitude, not an antidote to the antiauthority attitude.

12. What is the antidote when a pilot has a hazardous attitude, such as "Impulsivity"?

A. It could happen to me.
B. Do it quickly to get it over with.
C. Not so fast, think first.

Answer (C) is correct. (sUASSG Chap 10)
DISCUSSION: When you recognize a hazardous thought, you should correct it by stating the corresponding antidote. The antidote for the impulsivity ("Do something quickly!") hazardous attitude is "Not so fast. Think first."
Answer (A) is incorrect. "It could happen to me" is the antidote for the invulnerability, not impulsivity, hazardous attitude. **Answer (B) is incorrect.** "Do it quickly and get it over with" is an example of the impulsivity hazardous attitude, not its antidote.

13. What is the antidote when a pilot has the hazardous attitude of "Invulnerability"?

A. It cannot be that bad.
B. It could happen to me.
C. It will not happen to me.

Answer (B) is correct. (sUASSG Chap 10)
DISCUSSION: The antidote to counteract the attitude of invulnerability is thinking or saying, "It could happen to me."
Answer (A) is incorrect. "It cannot be that bad" describes the hazardous macho attitude, not invulnerability. **Answer (C) is incorrect.** "It will not happen to me" describes the hazardous attitude of invulnerability. It is not the antidote.

14. What is the antidote when a pilot has a hazardous attitude, such as "Macho"?

A. I can do it.
B. Taking chances is foolish.
C. Nothing will happen.

Answer (B) is correct. (sUASSG Chap 10)
DISCUSSION: When you recognize a hazardous thought, you should correct it by stating the corresponding antidote. The antidote for the macho ("I can do it") hazardous attitude is "Taking chances is foolish."
Answer (A) is incorrect. "I can do it" is an example of the macho hazardous attitude, not its antidote. **Answer (C) is incorrect.** "Nothing will happen" is an example of the invulnerability hazardous attitude, not an antidote to the macho attitude.

15. What is the antidote when a pilot has a hazardous attitude, such as "Resignation"?

A. What is the use?
B. Someone else is responsible.
C. I am not helpless.

Answer (C) is correct. (sUASSG Chap 10)
DISCUSSION: When you recognize a hazardous thought, you should correct it by stating the corresponding antidote. The antidote for the resignation ("What is the use?") hazardous attitude is "I am not helpless. I can make a difference."
Answer (A) is incorrect. "What is the use?" is an example of the resignation hazardous attitude, not its antidote. **Answer (B) is incorrect.** "Someone else is responsible" is an example of the resignation hazardous attitude, not its antidote.

SU 8: Aeronautical Decision Making and Physiology

16. Who is responsible for determining whether a pilot is fit to fly for a particular flight, even though he or she holds a current medical certificate?

A. The FAA.
B. The medical examiner.
C. The pilot.

Answer (C) is correct. (sUASSG Chap 10)
DISCUSSION: A number of factors, from lack of sleep to illness, can reduce a pilot's fitness to make a particular flight. It is the responsibility of the pilot to determine whether (s)he is fit to make a particular flight, even though (s)he holds a current medical certificate. Additionally, 14 CFR 61.53 prohibits a pilot who possesses a current medical certificate from acting as pilot in command, or in any other capacity as a required pilot flight crewmember, while the pilot has a known medical condition or an aggravation of a known medical condition that would make the pilot unable to meet the standards for a medical certificate.
Answer (A) is incorrect. The pilot, not the FAA, is responsible for determining whether (s)he is fit for a particular flight. **Answer (B) is incorrect.** The pilot, not the medical examiner, is responsible for determining whether (s)he is fit for a particular flight.

17. What is the one common factor which affects most preventable accidents?

A. Structural failure.
B. Mechanical malfunction.
C. Human error.

Answer (C) is correct. (sUASSG Chap 10)
DISCUSSION: Most preventable accidents, such as fuel starvation or exhaustion, VFR flight into IFR conditions leading to disorientation, and flight into known icing, have one common factor: human error. Pilots who are involved in accidents usually know what went wrong. In the interest of expediency, cost savings, or other often irrelevant factors, the wrong course of action (decision) was chosen.
Answer (A) is incorrect. Most preventable accidents have human error, not structural failure, as a common factor. **Answer (B) is incorrect.** Most preventable accidents have human error, not mechanical malfunction, as a common factor.

18. What antidotal phrase can help reverse the hazardous attitude of impulsivity?

A. Do it quickly to get it over with.
B. It could happen to me.
C. Not so fast, think first.

Answer (C) is correct. (sUASSG Chap 10)
DISCUSSION: Impulsivity is the attitude of people who frequently feel the need to do something, anything, immediately. They do not stop to think about what they are about to do. They do not select the best alternative but instead do the first thing that comes to mind. They should recognize this attitude and state the antidote, "Not so fast. Think first," before taking action.
Answer (A) is incorrect. "Do it quickly to get it over with" is the hazardous attitude of impulsivity, not the antidote. **Answer (B) is incorrect.** "It could happen to me" is the antidote for the hazardous attitude of invulnerability.

19. When a remote pilot-in-command and a visual observer define their roles and responsibilities prior to and during the operation of a small UA is a good use of

A. Crew Resource Management.
B. Authoritarian Resource Management.
C. Single Pilot Resource Management.

Answer (A) is correct. (AC 107-2A)
DISCUSSION: Crew resource management (CRM) is a component of aeronautical decision making through which the pilot of an sUAS makes effective use of all available resources: human resources, hardware, and information. CRM emphasizes good communication and other interpersonal relationship skills.
Answer (B) is incorrect. A remote PIC must be able to function in a team environment and maximize team performance using crew, not authoritarian, resource management. **Answer (C) is incorrect.** Crew resource management (CRM) in single-pilot or multiperson crew configurations is the effective use of all personnel and material assets available to a pilot or a flight crew.

8.2 Physiology

20. A pilot should be able to overcome the symptoms or avoid future occurrences of hyperventilation by

A. closely monitoring the flight instruments to control the airplane.
B. slowing the breathing rate, breathing into a bag, or talking aloud.
C. increasing the breathing rate in order to increase lung ventilation.

Answer (B) is correct. (AIM Para 8-1-3)
DISCUSSION: To recover from hyperventilation, the pilot should slow the breathing rate, breathe into a bag, or talk aloud.
Answer (A) is incorrect. Closely monitoring the flight instruments is used to overcome vertigo (spatial disorientation).
Answer (C) is incorrect. Increased breathing aggravates hyperventilation.

21. Rapid or extra deep breathing while using oxygen can cause a condition known as

A. hyperventilation.
B. aerosinusitis.
C. aerotitis.

Answer (A) is correct. (AIM Para 8-1-3)
DISCUSSION: Hyperventilation occurs when an excessive amount of carbon dioxide is passed out of the body and too much oxygen is retained. This occurs when breathing rapidly and especially when using oxygen.
Answer (B) is incorrect. Aerosinusitis is an inflammation of the sinuses caused by changes in atmospheric pressure.
Answer (C) is incorrect. Aerotitis is an inflammation of the inner ear caused by changes in atmospheric pressure.

22. When a stressful situation is encountered in flight, an abnormal increase in the volume of air breathed in and out can cause a condition known as

A. hyperventilation.
B. aerosinusitis.
C. aerotitis.

Answer (A) is correct. (AIM Para 8-1-3)
DISCUSSION: Hyperventilation occurs when an excessive amount of carbon dioxide is passed out of the body and too much oxygen is retained. This occurs when breathing rapidly and especially when using oxygen.
Answer (B) is incorrect. Aerosinusitis is an inflammation of the sinuses caused by changes in atmospheric pressure.
Answer (C) is incorrect. Aerotitis is an inflammation of the inner ear caused by changes in atmospheric pressure.

23. Which would most likely result in hyperventilation?

A. Emotional tension, anxiety, or fear.
B. The excessive consumption of alcohol.
C. An extremely slow rate of breathing and insufficient oxygen.

Answer (A) is correct. (AIM Para 8-1-3)
DISCUSSION: Hyperventilation usually occurs when one becomes excited or undergoes stress, which results in an increase in one's rate of breathing.
Answer (B) is incorrect. Hyperventilation is usually caused by some type of stress, not by alcohol. **Answer (C) is incorrect.** The opposite is true: Hyperventilation is an extremely fast rate of breathing that produces excessive oxygen.

24. A pilot experiencing the effects of hyperventilation should be able to restore the proper carbon dioxide level in the body by

A. slowing the breathing rate, breathing into a paper bag, or talking aloud.
B. breathing spontaneously and deeply or gaining mental control of the situation.
C. increasing the breathing rate in order to increase lung ventilation.

Answer (A) is correct. (sUASSG Chap 9, AIM Para 8-1-3)
DISCUSSION: A stressful situation can often lead to hyperventilation, which results from an increased rate and depth of respiration that leads to an abnormally low amount of carbon dioxide in the bloodstream. By slowing the breathing rate, breathing into a paper bag, or talking aloud, a pilot can overcome the effects of hyperventilation and return the carbon dioxide level in the bloodstream to normal.
Answer (B) is incorrect. Breathing deeply further aggravates the effects of hyperventilation. **Answer (C) is incorrect.** Increasing the rate of breathing will further aggravate the effects of hyperventilation.

SU 8: Aeronautical Decision Making and Physiology

25. Why is fatigue hazardous to flight safety?

A. The pilot hurries to get done in order to rest.
B. Fatigue may not be apparent to a pilot until serious errors are made (an impaired pilot is a dangerous pilot).
C. The pilot is lazy and rushes to get done quickly.

Answer (B) is correct. (sUASSG Chap 9, AIM Para 8-1-1)
DISCUSSION: Fatigue is one of the most treacherous hazards to flight safety because it may not become apparent to a pilot until serious errors are made.
Answer (A) is incorrect. The risk is not found in the pilot hurrying, but rather the risk is found in the diminished cognitive power that fatigue introduces to the situation, sometimes causing pilots to make serious errors before they realize how fatigued they are. **Answer (C) is incorrect.** The risk is not found in the pilot being lazy or rushing to complete a series of tasks, but rather the risk is found in the diminished cognitive power that fatigue introduces to the situation, sometimes causing pilots to make serious errors before they realize how fatigued they are.

26. What effect does haze have on the ability to see traffic or terrain features during flight?

A. Haze causes the eyes to focus at infinity.
B. The eyes tend to overwork in haze and do not detect relative movement easily.
C. All traffic or terrain features appear to be farther away than their actual distance.

Answer (C) is correct. (AIM Para 8-1-5)
DISCUSSION: Atmospheric haze can create the illusion of being at a greater distance and height from traffic or terrain than you actually are. The pilot who does not recognize this illusion will fly a lower approach.
Answer (A) is incorrect. In haze, the eyes focus at a comfortable distance, which may be only 10 to 30 ft. outside of the flight deck. **Answer (B) is incorrect.** In haze, the eyes relax and tend to stare outside without focusing or looking for common visual cues.

27. Which technique should a remote pilot use to scan for traffic? A remote pilot should

A. systematically focus on different segments of the sky for short intervals.
B. concentrate on relative movement detected in the peripheral vision area.
C. continuously scan the sky from right to left.

Answer (A) is correct. (AIM Para 4-4-14)
DISCUSSION: Due to the fact that eyes can focus only on a narrow viewing area, effective scanning is accomplished with a series of short, regularly-spaced eye movements that bring successive areas of the sky into the central vision field.
Answer (B) is incorrect. Detecting relative movement using peripheral vision concerns scanning for traffic at night. **Answer (C) is incorrect.** A pilot must continually scan successive, small portions of the sky. The eyes can focus only on a narrow viewing area and require at least 1 sec. to detect a faraway object.

28. The most effective method of scanning for other aircraft for collision avoidance during daylight hours is to use

A. regularly spaced concentration on the 3-, 9-, and 12-o'clock positions.
B. a series of short, regularly spaced eye movements to search each 10-degree sector.
C. peripheral vision by scanning small sectors and utilizing off-center viewing.

Answer (B) is correct. (AC 90-48D)
DISCUSSION: The most effective way to scan for other aircraft during daylight hours is to use a series of short, regularly spaced eye movements that bring successive areas of the sky into your central visual field. Each movement should not exceed 10°, and each area should be observed for at least one second to enable detection. Only a very small center area of the eye has the ability to send clear, sharply focused messages to the brain. All other areas provide less detail.
Answer (A) is incorrect. The spacing between the positions should be 10°, not 90°. **Answer (C) is incorrect.** This is the recommended nighttime scanning procedure.

29. Eye movements during daytime collision avoidance scanning should

A. not exceed 10 degrees and view each sector at least 1 second.
B. be 30 degrees and view each sector at least 3 seconds.
C. use peripheral vision by scanning small sectors and utilizing off-center viewing.

Answer (A) is correct. (AC 90-48D)
DISCUSSION: The most effective way to scan for other aircraft during daylight hours is to use a series of short, regularly spaced eye movements that bring successive areas of the sky into your central visual field. Each movement should not exceed 10°, and each area should be observed for at least 1 second to enable detection. Only a very small center area of the eye has the ability to send clear, sharply focused messages to the brain.
Answer (B) is incorrect. The spacing for the scan between positions should be 10°, not 30°. **Answer (C) is incorrect.** At night, collision avoidance scanning must use the off-center portions of the eyes. These portions are most effective at seeing objects at night. Accordingly, peripheral vision should be used, scanning small sectors and using off-screen viewing. This is in contrast to daytime searching for air traffic when center viewing should be used.

30. Most midair collision accidents occur during

A. hazy days.
B. clear days.
C. cloudy nights.

Answer (B) is correct. (AC 90-48D)
DISCUSSION: Most midair collision accidents and reported near midair collision incidents occur during good VFR weather conditions (i.e., clear days) and during the hours of daylight.
Answer (A) is incorrect. During hazy days, fewer pilots will be flying, and those who are will be more vigilant in their scanning for other traffic. **Answer (C) is incorrect.** During cloudy nights, fewer pilots will be flying, and those who are will be more vigilant in their scanning for other traffic.

31. Which is true regarding the presence of alcohol within the human body?

A. A small amount of alcohol increases vision acuity.
B. Consuming an equal amount of water will increase the destruction of alcohol and alleviate a hangover.
C. Judgment and decision-making abilities can be adversely affected by even small amounts of alcohol.

Answer (C) is correct. (sUASSG Chap 9)
DISCUSSION: As little as 1 oz. of liquor, 1 bottle of beer, or 4 oz. of wine can impair flying skills.
Answer (A) is incorrect. Alcohol decreases vision acuity. **Answer (B) is incorrect.** Time is the best method to ensure alcohol has metabolized in the body.

32. You are a remote pilot for a co-op energy service provider. You are to use your UA to inspect power lines in a remote area 15 hours away from your home office. After the drive, fatigue impacts your abilities to complete your assignment on time. Fatigue can be recognized

A. easily by an experienced pilot.
B. as being in an impaired state.
C. by an ability to overcome sleep deprivation.

Answer (B) is correct. (sUASSG Chap 9)
DISCUSSION: Fatigue, stress, and work overload can cause a pilot to become impaired by losing overall awareness of the flight situation.
Answer (A) is incorrect. Fatigue is not easily recognized. It can be treacherous because it may not be apparent until serious errors are made. **Answer (C) is incorrect.** Fatigue is not the ability to overcome sleep deprivation. Fatigue is overcome by periods of adequate rest and sleep as well as regular exercise and proper nutrition.

33. When preparing for a night flight, what should an sUAS pilot be aware of after assembling and conducting a preflight of an aircraft while using a bright flashlight or work light?

A. Once adapted to darkness, a persons eyes are relatively immune to bright lights.
B. It takes approximately 30 minutes for a persons eyes to fully adapt to darkness.
C. The person should use a flash light equipped with LED lights to facilitate their night vision.

Answer (B) is correct. (FAA-H-8083-3B Chap 10)
DISCUSSION: It takes approximately 30 min. for a person's eyes to fully adapt to darkness after being exposed to bright light.
Answer (A) is incorrect. A person's eyes will not be immune to bright lights after adapting to darkness. **Answer (C) is incorrect.** Being exposed to more bright light will prevent a person's eyes from adapting to darkness.

STUDY UNIT NINE
EMERGENCY PROCEDURES, MAINTENANCE, AND INSPECTIONS

(7 pages of outline)

9.1	Emergency Procedures	(4 questions) 271, 278
9.2	Maintenance and Inspection Procedures	(7 questions) 275, 279

9.1 EMERGENCY PROCEDURES

1. **Emergency planning and communication** are essential to offset any unexpected and unforeseen serious occurrence or situation that requires urgent, prompt action.

    a. In case of an in-flight emergency, the remote pilot in command (rPIC) is permitted to deviate from any rule of Part 107 to the extent necessary to respond to that emergency.

    1) Any rPIC who exercises this emergency power to deviate from the rules of Part 107 is required, upon FAA request, to send a written report to the Administrator explaining the deviation. Emergency action should be taken in such a way as to minimize injury or damage to property.

    b. Contingency planning should include an alternate landing/recovery site to be used in the event of an abnormal condition that requires a precautionary landing away from the original launch location.

    1) Incorporate the means of communication with air traffic control (ATC) (if required for the flight operation) as well as a plan for ground operations and securing the unmanned aircraft (UA) on the ground. This includes the availability of control stations capable of launch/recovery, communication equipment, and an adequate power source to operate all required equipment.

    2) Take into consideration all airspace constructs and minimize risk to other aircraft by avoiding congested areas to the maximum extent possible.

    c. When operating a UA in a commercial operation, the rPIC is responsible for briefing the participants about emergency procedures.

2. **Lithium-based batteries** can potentially pose hazards to UA operators as they are highly flammable and capable of ignition. A battery fire is an in-flight emergency that may cause loss of control (LOC) of the UA. Lithium battery fires can be caused when a battery short circuits, is improperly charged, is heated to extreme temperatures, is damaged as a result of a crash, is mishandled, or is simply defective. The most common type of lithium-based battery used in small unmanned aircraft systems (sUAS) is Lithium-Polymer (LiPo). The rPIC should consider following the manufacturer's recommendations, when available, to help ensure safe battery handling and usage.

   a. **Safe transportation, such as proper inspection and handling**
      1) Ensure careful storage of spare (uninstalled) lithium batteries.
      2) Prevent short circuits by placing each individual battery in the original retail packaging, a separate plastic bag, or a protective pouch or by insulating exposed terminals with tape.
      3) Do not allow spare batteries to come in contact with metal objects, such as coins, keys, or jewelry.
      4) Take steps to prevent objects from crushing, puncturing, or applying pressure on the battery.

   b. **Safe charging**
      1) Always use the proper charger/discharger for LiPo batteries.
      2) LiPo fires are rare but can occur quickly. Use a fireproof container whenever charging, discharging, or storing LiPo batteries.
      3) Store LiPo batteries in a safe fireproof container. Do not store them inside the aircraft or flight case.

   c. **Safe usage**
      1) LiPo batteries that are installed in an sUAS for power during the operation are not considered a hazardous material under Part 107.
      2) However, spare (uninstalled) LiPo batteries would meet the definition of hazardous material and may not be carried on the sUAS.
      3) LiPo batteries do not perform well in extremely cold temperatures.
         a) Some sUAS manufacturers place limitations on the acceptable temperature operating range.
         b) For cold weather operations, power on the sUAS and allow the battery to warm up to normal operating temperatures prior to starting your flight mission.

   d. **Risks of fires involving lithium batteries**
      1) When preparing to conduct sUAS operations, do not use any battery with signs of damage or defect.
         a) For example, check carefully for small nicks in the battery casing and be alert for signs of bubbling or warping during charging.
         b) Once the battery is installed and the sUAS takes flight, the rPIC or ground crew may not observe a battery fire until it is too late to land the aircraft safely.
         c) If a battery fire occurs, follow any manufacturer guidance for response procedures.

SU 9: Emergency Procedures, Maintenance, and Inspections

3. **Loss of aircraft control links** are critical to remote operation without an onboard pilot.
   a. UA operators rely on the command and control link to operate the aircraft. For example, an uplink transmits command instructions to the UA, and a downlink transmits the status of the aircraft and provides situational awareness to the rPIC or person manipulating the controls.
      1) **Lost link** is an interruption or loss of the control link between the control station and the UA, preventing control of the aircraft. As a result, the UA performs preset lost link procedures.
         a) Such procedures ensure that the UA
            i) Remains airborne in a predictable or planned maneuver, allowing time to re-establish the communication link, or
            ii) Autolands, if available, after a predetermined length of time or terminates the flight when the power source is depleted.
      2) A lost link is an abnormal situation but not an emergency. A lost link is not considered a flyaway.
      3) Follow the manufacturer's recommendations for programming lost link procedures prior to the flight.
         a) Examples of lost link procedures may include, when applicable,
            i) A route of flight that avoids flight over populated areas and
            ii) Communications procedures.
      4) Plan contingency measures if recovery of the UA is not feasible.
      5) **Flight termination** is the intentional and deliberate process of performing controlled flight to the ground. Flight termination may be part of lost link procedures, or it may be a contingency that you elect to use if further flight of the aircraft cannot be safely achieved or other potential hazards exist that require immediate discontinuation of flight.
         a) Execute flight termination procedures if you have exhausted all other contingencies.
         b) Flight termination points (FTPs), if used, or alternative contingency planning measures must
            i) Be located within power-off glide distance of the aircraft during all phases of flight
            ii) Be based on the assumption of an unrecoverable system failure
            iii) Take into consideration altitude, winds, and other factors

4. **Flyaways** are typically the product of a lost link.
   a. As a result, the UA is not operating in a predicable or planned manner. However in a flyaway, the preset lost link procedures are not established or are not being executed by the UA, creating an emergency situation.
      1) If a flyaway occurs while operating in airspace that requires authorization, notify ATC as outlined in the authorization.

5. **Global positioning system (GPS)** tools can be a valuable resource for flight planning and situational awareness during sUAS operation.

   a. However, as with manned aviation, rPICs in unmanned operations must avoid overreliance on automation and must be prepared to operate the unmanned aircraft manually if necessary.

      1) Prior to flight, check GPS NOTAMs for any known service disruptions in the planned location of the operation.

      2) Make a plan of action to prevent or minimize damage in the event of equipment malfunction or failure.

   b. Current NOTAM information, service outages, and status reports can be obtained from Flight Service as described in Study Unit 3, "Aviation Weather Services."

6. **Radio frequency (RF) spectrum** is divided into multiple bands defined by the wavelengths in distance and their frequency over time.

   a. The 2.4 GHz and 5.8 GHz systems are the unlicensed band RFs that most sUAS use for the connection between the control station (CS) and the UA.

      1) Note the frequencies are also used for computer wireless networks and the interference can cause problems when operating a UA in an area (e.g., dense housing and office buildings) that has many wireless signals.

      2) LOC and flyaways are some of the reported problems with sUAS frequency implications.

         a) To avoid frequency interference, many modern sUAS operate using a 5.8 GHz system to control the sUA and a 2.4 GHz system to transmit video and photos to the ground.

      3) Consult the sUAS operating manual and manufacturer's recommended procedures prior to operation.

         a) It should be noted that both RF bands (2.4 GHz and 5.8 GHz) are considered line of sight and the command and control link between the CS and the UA will not work properly when barriers are between the CS and the UA.

         b) Part 107 requires the rPIC or person manipulating the controls to be able to see the UA at all times, which should also help prevent obstructions from interfering with the line of sight frequency spectrum.

   b. Frequency spectrums used for UA operations are regulated by the Federal Communications Commission (FCC).

      1) Radio transmissions, such as those used to control a UA and to downlink real-time video, must use frequency bands that are approved for use by the operating agency.

      2) The FCC authorizes civil operations. Some operating frequencies are unlicensed and can be used freely (e.g., 900 MHz, 2.4 GHz, and 5.8 GHz) without FCC approval.

      3) All other frequencies require a user-specific license for all civil users, except federal agencies, to be obtained from the FCC. For further information, visit www.fcc.gov/licensing-databases/licensing.

9.2 MAINTENANCE AND INSPECTION PROCEDURES

1. **Maintenance of an sUAS** includes scheduled and unscheduled overhaul, repair, inspection, modification, replacement, and system software upgrades of the sUAS and its components necessary for flight. Whenever possible, the operator should maintain the sUAS and its components in accordance with manufacturer's instructions. The aircraft manufacturer may provide the maintenance program, or, if one is not provided, the applicant may choose to develop one.

    a. Scheduled maintenance. The sUAS manufacturer may provide documentation for scheduled maintenance of the entire UA and associated system equipment.

    　　1) There may be components of the sUAS that are identified by the manufacturer to undergo scheduled periodic maintenance or replacement based on time-in-service limits (such as flight hours, cycles, and/or the calendar days).

    　　2) All manufacturer-scheduled maintenance instructions should be followed in the interest of achieving the longest and safest service life of the sUAS.

    　　3) If there are no scheduled maintenance instructions provided by the sUAS manufacturer or component manufacturer, the operator should establish a scheduled maintenance protocol.

    　　　　a) This could be done by documenting any repair, modification, overhaul, or replacement of a system component resulting from normal flight operations, and recording the time-in-service for that component at the time of the maintenance procedure. Over time, the operator should then be able to establish a reliable maintenance schedule for the sUAS and its components.

    b. Unscheduled maintenance. During the course of a preflight inspection, the rPIC may discover that an sUAS component is in need of servicing (such as lubrication), repair, modification, overhaul, or replacement outside of the scheduled maintenance period as a result of normal flight operations or resulting from a mishap.

    　　1) In addition, the sUAS manufacturer or component manufacturer may require an unscheduled system software update to correct a problem. In the event such a condition is found, the rPIC should not conduct flight operations until the discrepancy is corrected.

2. **Preflight inspections** are required before each flight. The rPIC must inspect the sUAS to ensure that it is in a condition for safe operation, such as inspecting for equipment damage or malfunction(s). The preflight inspection should be conducted in accordance with the sUAS manufacturer's inspection procedures when available (usually found in the manufacturer's owner or maintenance manual) and/or an inspection procedure developed by the sUAS owner or operator.

    a. Creating an inspection program. As an option, the sUAS owner or operator may wish to create an inspection program for their UAS. The person creating an inspection program for a specific sUAS may find sufficient details to assist in the development of a suitable inspection program tailored to a specific sUAS in a variety of industry programs.

    b. Scalable preflight inspection. The preflight check as part of the inspection program should include an appropriate sUAS preflight inspection that is scalable to the UA program and operation to be performed prior to each flight. An appropriate preflight inspection should encompass the entire system in order to determine a continued condition for safe operation prior to flight.

c. 14 CFR Part 43, Appendix D – Scope and Detail of Items (as Applicable to the Particular Aircraft) To Be Included in Annual and 100-Hour Inspections. Another option and best practice may include the applicable portions of Part 43, Appendix D, as an inspection guideline correlating to the UA only.

  1) System-related equipment, such as, but not limited to, the CS, data link, payload, or support equipment, is not included in the list in Appendix D. Therefore, these items should be included in a comprehensive inspection program for the UA.

3. **Preflight inspection items** are often provided by the sUAS manufacturer through a written preflight inspection procedure. It is recommended that the rPIC ensure that the following inspection items are incorporated into the preflight inspection procedure required by Part 107 to help the rPIC determine that the sUAS is in a condition for safe operation.

   a. The preflight inspection should include a visual or functional check of the following items:

      1) Conditions of UAS components
      2) Airframe structure (including undercarriage), all flight control surfaces, and linkages
      3) Registration markings, for proper display and legibility
      4) Movable control surface(s), including airframe attachment point(s)
      5) Servo motor(s), including attachment point(s)
      6) Propulsion system, including powerplant(s), propeller(s), rotor(s), ducted fan(s), etc.
      7) Adequate energy supply for the intended operation and proper functionality of all systems (e.g., aircraft and control unit)
      8) Avionics, including control link transceiver, communication/navigation equipment, and antenna(s)
      9) Calibration of UAS compass prior to any flight
      10) Control link transceiver, communication/navigation data link transceiver, and antenna(s)
      11) Display panel, if used
      12) Ground support equipment, including takeoff and landing systems
      13) Control link correct connectivity established between the aircraft and the CS
      14) Correct movement of control surfaces using the CS
      15) Onboard navigation and communication data links
      16) Flight termination system, if installed
      17) Fuel for correct type and quantity
      18) Battery levels for the aircraft and CS
      19) Secure attachment of any equipment, such as a camera
      20) Communication with UA is verified and sUAS has acquired GPS location from the minimum number of satellites specified by the manufacturer
      21) UAS propellers for any imbalance or irregular operation
      22) All controller operation for heading and altitude
      23) Verify that the anti-collision light is operational (flight during civil twilight and night)
      24) At a controlled low altitude, fly within range of any interference and recheck all controls and stability

4. **Recordkeeping** for sUAS owners and operators is beneficial and easily achieved by documenting any repair, modification, overhaul, or replacement of a system component resulting from normal flight operations and recording the time-in-service for that component at the time of the maintenance procedure.

   a. Over time, the operator then should be able to establish a reliable maintenance schedule for the sUAS and its components. Recordkeeping that includes a record of all periodic inspections, maintenance, preventative maintenance, repairs, and alterations performed on the sUAS could be retrievable from either hardcopy and/or electronic logbook format for future reference.

      1) This includes all components of the sUAS: UA, CS, launch and recovery equipment, CS link equipment, payload, and any other components required to safely operate. Recordkeeping of documented maintenance and inspection events reinforces owner/operator responsibilities for airworthiness through systematic condition for safe flight determinations.

   b. Maintenance and inspection recordkeeping provides retrievable empirical evidence of vital safety assessment data defining the condition of safety-critical systems and components supporting the decision to launch.

   c. Recordkeeping of an sUAS may provide essential safety support for commercial operators that may experience rapidly accumulated flight operational hours/cycles.

   d. Methodical maintenance and inspection data collection can prove to be very helpful in the tracking of sUAS component service life, as well as systemic component, equipage, and structural failure events.

5. **Performing maintenance** is essential to safe operation, and the sUAS or component manufacturer may require certain maintenance tasks be performed by the manufacturer or by a person or facility (personnel) specified by the manufacturer.

   a. It is highly recommended that the maintenance be performed in accordance with the manufacturer's instructions.

      1) However, if the operator decides not to use the manufacturer or personnel recommended by the manufacturer and is unable to perform the required maintenance, the operator should consider the expertise of maintenance personnel familiar with the specific sUAS and its components.

         a) In addition, though not required, the use of certificated maintenance providers are encouraged, which may include repair stations, holders of mechanic and repairman certificates, and persons working under the supervision of these mechanics and repairmen.

   b. If the operator or other maintenance personnel are unable to repair, modify, or overhaul an sUAS or component back to its safe operational specification, then it is advisable to replace the sUAS or component with one that is in a condition for safe operation.

      1) It is important that all required maintenance be completed before each flight, preferably in accordance with the manufacturer's instructions or, in lieu of that, within known industry best practices.

QUESTIONS

9.1 Emergency Procedures

1. Damaged lithium batteries can cause

A. an inflight fire.
B. a change in aircraft center of gravity.
C. increased endurance.

Answer (A) is correct. (AC 107-2A App B)
DISCUSSION: Lithium-based batteries are highly flammable and capable of ignition. A battery fire could cause an in-flight emergency by causing loss of control (LOC).
Answer (B) is incorrect. Changes in center of gravity are caused by shifting weight. **Answer (C) is incorrect.** A damaged or short-circuited lithium battery could lose power and cause LOC, not increased endurance.

2. During your preflight inspection, you discover a small nick in the UA battery casing. What action should you take?

A. Throw it away with your household trash.
B. Use it as long as it will still hold a charge.
C. Follow the manufacturer's guidance.

Answer (C) is correct. (AC 107-2A Chap 7)
DISCUSSION: The remote pilot in command (rPIC) should consider following the manufacturer's recommendations, when available, to help ensure safe battery handling and usage.
Answer (A) is incorrect. Batteries should be properly disposed of according to the manufacturer's recommendations. **Answer (B) is incorrect.** Never use any battery with signs of damage or defect. You may not observe a battery fire until it is too late to land the aircraft safely.

3. What precautions should a remote pilot in command (rPIC) do to prevent possible in-flight emergencies when using lithium-based batteries?

A. Store the batteries in a freezer to allow proper recharging.
B. Follow the manufacturer's recommendations for safe battery handling.
C. Allow the battery to charge until it reaches a minimum temperature of 100°C.

Answer (B) is correct. (AC 107-2A App B)
DISCUSSION: Lithium-based batteries are highly flammable and capable of ignition. A battery fire could cause an in-flight emergency by causing a loss of control (LOC) of the sUA. Lithium battery fires can be caused when a battery short circuits, is improperly charged, is heated to extreme temperatures, is damaged as a result of a crash, is mishandled, or is simply defective. The rPIC should follow the manufacturer's recommendations, when available, to help ensure safe battery handling and usage.
Answer (A) is incorrect. The rPIC should follow the manufacturer's recommendations, not store the batteries in a freezer. **Answer (C) is incorrect.** The rPIC should follow the manufacturer's recommendations, not charge to an extreme temperature.

4. When using a small UA in a commercial operation, who is responsible for briefing the participants about emergency procedures?

A. The FAA inspector-in-charge.
B. The lead visual observer.
C. The remote pilot in command (rPIC).

Answer (C) is correct. (AC 107-2A)
DISCUSSION: The remote pilot is responsible for briefing the participants about emergency procedures when operating a small UA in a commercial operation.
Answer (A) is incorrect. The FAA inspector-in-charge is not responsible for briefing the participants. **Answer (B) is incorrect.** The lead visual observer is not responsible for briefing the participants.

9.2 Maintenance and Inspection Procedures

5. Under what condition should the operator of a small UA establish scheduled maintenance protocol?

A. When the manufacturer does not provide a maintenance schedule.
B. UAS does not need a required maintenance schedule.
C. When the FAA requires you to, following an accident.

Answer (A) is correct. (AC 107-2A Chap 7)
DISCUSSION: If there are no scheduled maintenance instructions provided by the sUAS manufacturer or component manufacturer, the operator should establish a scheduled maintenance protocol.
Answer (B) is incorrect. The operator should maintain the sUAS and its components in accordance with manufacturer's instructions, or if one is not provided, the applicant may choose to develop one. **Answer (C) is incorrect.** The FAA requires a report within 10 calendar days of an accident resulting from an operation that caused injury or damage, not a scheduled maintenance protocol.

6. According to 14 CFR Part 107, the responsibility to inspect the small unmanned aircraft system (sUAS) to ensure it is in a safe operating condition rests with the

A. visual observer.
B. remote Pilot in Command.
C. owner of the sUAS.

Answer (B) is correct. (14 CFR 107.49)
DISCUSSION: Before each flight, the remote pilot in command (rPIC) must inspect the sUAS to ensure that it is in a condition for safe operation, such as inspecting for equipment damage or malfunction(s).
Answer (A) is incorrect. The rPIC, not the visual observer, is responsible for ensuring that the sUAS is in a condition for safe operation. **Answer (C) is incorrect.** The rPIC, not the owner of the sUAS, is responsible for ensuring that the sUAS is in a condition for safe operation.

7. Scheduled maintenance should be performed in accordance with the

A. Contractor requirements.
B. Manufacturer's suggested procedures.
C. Stipulations in 14 CFR Part 43.

Answer (B) is correct. (AC 107-2A Chap 7)
DISCUSSION: Whenever possible, the operator should maintain the sUAS and its components in accordance with manufacturer's instructions. The aircraft manufacturer may provide the maintenance program, or if one is not provided, the applicant may choose to develop one.
Answer (A) is incorrect. If there are no scheduled maintenance instructions provided by the sUAS manufacturer or component manufacturer, the operator should establish a scheduled maintenance protocol. There is no requirement to follow contractor requirements. **Answer (C) is incorrect.** 14 CFR Part 43 is applicable to aircraft having a U.S. airworthiness certificate; foreign-registered civil aircraft used in common carriage or carriage of mail under the provisions of 14 CFR Part 121 or 135; and airframe, aircraft engines, propellers, appliances, and component parts of such aircraft.

8. Which of the following source of information should you consult **first** when determining what maintenance should be performed on an sUAS or its components?

A. Local pilot best practices.
B. 14 CFR Part 107.
C. Manufacturer guidance.

Answer (C) is correct. (AC 107-2A Chap 7)
DISCUSSION: There may be components of the sUAS that are identified by the manufacturer to undergo scheduled periodic maintenance or replacement based on time-in-service limits. All manufacturer scheduled maintenance instructions should be followed in the interest of achieving the longest and safest service life of the sUAS.
Answer (A) is incorrect. Manufacturer guidance, not local pilot best practices, should be consulted first when determining what maintenance should be performed. **Answer (B) is incorrect.** 14 CFR Part 107 provides guidance and best practices on how to inspect and maintain an sUAS, which includes first consulting with the manufacturer.

9. How often is the remote pilot in command (rPIC) required to inspect the sUAS to ensure that it is in a condition for safe operation?

A. Annually.
B. Monthly.
C. Before each flight.

Answer (C) is correct. (14 CFR 107.49)
DISCUSSION: Before each flight, the rPIC must inspect the sUAS to ensure that it is in a condition for safe operation, such as inspecting for equipment damage or malfunction(s).
Answer (A) is incorrect. A preflight inspection should be completed prior to each flight, not annually. **Answer (B) is incorrect.** A preflight inspection should be completed prior to each flight, not monthly.

10. During the preflight inspection, who is responsible for determining the unmanned aircraft (UA) is safe for flight?

A. The pilot in command.
B. The visual observer.
C. The UA manufacturer.

Answer (A) is correct. (14 CFR 107.49)
DISCUSSION: During the preflight inspection, the pilot in command is responsible for determining whether the UA is in condition for safe flight.
Answer (B) is incorrect. The remote pilot is the final authority for an operation and responsible for the preflight inspection. **Answer (C) is incorrect.** Maintenance should always occur in accordance with the manufacturer's instructions. Occasionally, certain tasks may only be completed by the manufacturer or specified party. However, the preflight inspection is the responsibility of the remote PIC.

11. What actions should the operator of an sUAS do if the manufacturer does not provide information about scheduled maintenance?

A. The operator should contact the FAA for a minimum equipment list.
B. The operator should establish a scheduled maintenance protocol.
C. The operator should contact the NTSB for component failure rates for their specific sUAS.

Answer (B) is correct. (AC 107-2A Chap 7)
DISCUSSION: If there are no scheduled maintenance instructions provided by the sUAS manufacturer or component manufacturer, the operator should establish a scheduled maintenance protocol.
Answer (A) is incorrect. The operator should establish a scheduled maintenance protocol. The FAA does not provide minimum equipment lists. **Answer (C) is incorrect.** The operator should establish a scheduled maintenance protocol. The NTSB does not provide component failure rates for specific sUAS.

APPENDIX A
REMOTE PILOT PRACTICE TEST

The following 60 questions have been randomly selected from the questions in our remote pilot test bank. You will be referred to figures (charts, tables, etc.) throughout this book. Be careful not to consult the answers or answer explanations when you look for and at the figures. Topical coverage in this practice test is similar to that of the FAA pilot knowledge test. Use the correct answer listing on page 286 to grade your practice test.

NOTE: Our **FAA Test Prep Online** provides unlimited Study and Test Sessions for your personal use. See the discussion on page 5 in the introduction of this book.

1. When may a remote pilot reduce the intensity of an aircraft's lights during a night flight?

A — At no time may the lights of an sUAS be reduced in intensity at night.
B — When a manned aircraft is in the vicinity of the sUAS.
C — When it is in the interest of safety to dim the aircraft's lights.

2. A remote PIC is operating an sUAS at night. A nearby homeowner complains about the ultra-bright LED strobe anti-collision lights. The remote pilot in command (rPIC) reduces the intensity of the light to avoid a confrontation. Is this sUAS operation in compliance with 14 CFR Part 107?

A — Compliant with Part 107.
B — Not compliant with Part 107.
C — Part 107 does not apply in this scenario.

3. Which Category of small UA must have an airworthiness certificate issued by the FAA?

A — 4
B — 3
C — 2

4. Which Category of operations over people is limited to sUAS that weigh 0.55 pounds or less, including everything that is on board or attached?

A — Category 1.
B — Category 2.
C — Category 3.

5. Which of the following UA may only operate in "FAA-recognized identification areas"?

A — A new UA produced after the compliance date with standard Remote ID capabilities.
B — An existing or home-built UA that is later equipped with a Remote ID broadcast module.
C — Any UA that does not have Remote ID capabilities.

6. If the UA or Remote ID broadcast module indicates that the equipment is not functioning properly while the UA is in flight, the Remote PIC must

A — Land the UA as soon as practicable.
B — Transfer control of the UA to a visual observer.
C — Immediately report the malfunction to the FAA.

7. When preparing for a night flight, what should an sUAS pilot be aware of after assembling and conducting a preflight of an aircraft while using a bright flashlight or work light?

A — Once adapted to darkness, a persons eyes are relatively immune to bright lights.
B — It takes approximately 30 minutes for a persons eyes to fully adapt to darkness.
C — The person should use a flash light equipped with LED lights to facilitate their night vision.

8. For aviation purposes, ceiling is defined as the height above the Earth's surface of the

A — lowest reported obscuration and the highest layer of clouds reported as overcast.
B — lowest broken or overcast layer or vertical visibility into an obscuration.
C — lowest layer of clouds reported as scattered, broken, or thin.

9. A blue segmented circle on a Sectional Chart depicts which class airspace?

A — Class B.
B — Class C.
C — Class D.

10. (Refer to Figure 75 on page 101.) The airspace surrounding the Gila Bend AF AUX Airport (GXF) (area 6) is classified as Class

A — B.
B — C.
C — D.

11. (Refer to Figure 26 on page 99.) (Refer to Area 2.) What hazards to aircraft may exist in areas such as Devils Lake East MOA?

A — Unusual, often invisible, hazards to aircraft such as artillery firing, aerial gunnery, or guided missiles.
B — Military training activities that necessitate acrobatic or abrupt flight maneuvers.
C — High volume of pilot training or an unusual type of aerial activity.

12. (Refer to Figure 25 on page 205.) (Refer to Area 3.) If Dallas Executive Tower is not in operation, which frequency should be used as a Common Traffic Advisory Frequency (CTAF) to monitor airport traffic?

A — 127.25 MHz.
B — 122.95 MHz.
C — 126.35 MHz.

13. (Refer to Figure 26 on page 229.) (Refer to Area 2.) What is the approximate latitude and longitude of Cooperstown Airport?

A — 47°25'N – 98°06'W.
B — 47°25'N – 99°54'W.
C — 47°55'N – 98°06'W.

14. (Refer to Figure 23 on page 235.) The flag symbols at Statesboro Bulloch County Airport, Claxton-Evans County Airport, and Ridgeland Airport are

A — outer boundaries of Savannah Class C airspace.
B — airports with special traffic patterns.
C — visual checkpoints to identify position for initial callup prior to entering Savannah Class C airspace.

15. (Refer to Figure 19 on page 139.) You are planning a flight in southern Georgia at 1300Z. What condition should you expect?

A — Ceiling 1,000 to 3,000 ft. and/or visibility 3 to 5 mi. with moderate turbulence.
B — Ceiling 1,000 to 3,000 ft. and/or visibility 3 to 5 mi. and temperatures below freezing.
C — Ceiling less than 1,000 ft. and/or visibility less than 3 mi. and temperatures above freezing.

16. (Refer to Figure 15 on page 137.) During the time period from 0600Z to 0800Z, what visibility is forecast for KOKC?

A — Greater than 6 statute miles.
B — Possibly 6 statute miles.
C — Not forecasted.

17. (Refer to Figure 15 on page 137.) In the TAF from KOKC, the "FM (FROM) Group" is forecast for the hours from 1600Z to 2200Z with the wind from

A — 160° at 10 knots.
B — 180° at 10 knots.
C — 180° at 10 knots, becoming 200° at 13 knots.

18. (Refer to Figure 48 on page 223.) Area C on the airport depicted is classified as a

A — stabilized area.
B — multiple heliport.
C — closed taxiway.

19. Who is responsible for determining whether a pilot is fit to fly for a particular flight, even though he or she holds a current medical certificate?

A — The FAA.
B — The medical examiner.
C — The pilot.

20. (Refer to Figure 26 on page 229.) (Refer to Area 4.) You have been hired to inspect the tower under construction at 46.9N and 98.6W, near Jamestown Regional (JMS). What must you receive prior to flying your unmanned aircraft in this area?

A — Authorization from the military.
B — Authorization from ATC.
C — Authorization from the National Park Service.

21. You have been hired as a remote pilot by a local TV news station to film breaking news with a small UA. You expressed a safety concern and the station manager has instructed you to "fly first, ask questions later." What type of hazardous attitude does this attitude represent?

A — Machismo.
B — Invulnerability.
C — Impulsivity.

22. What is one of the neglected items when a pilot relies on short and long term memory for repetitive tasks?

A — Checklists.
B — Situational awareness.
C — Flying outside the envelope.

23. What is the antidote when a pilot has the hazardous attitude of "Invulnerability"?

A — It cannot be that bad.
B — It could happen to me.
C — It will not happen to me.

24. What effect, if any, does high humidity have on aircraft performance?

A — It increases performance.
B — It decreases performance.
C — It has no effect on performance.

25. (Refer to Figure 65 on page 224) (Refer to F.) This sign confirms your position on

A — runway 22.
B — routing to runway 22.
C — taxiway 22.

26. A military air station can be identified by a rotating beacon that emits

A — white and green alternating flashes.
B — two quick, white flashes between green flashes.
C — green, yellow, and white flashes.

27. (Refer to Figure 26 on page 201.) (Refer to Area 2.) While monitoring the Cooperstown CTAF you hear an aircraft announce that they are midfield left downwind to RWY 13. Where would the aircraft be relative to the runway?

A — The aircraft is East.
B — The aircraft is South.
C — The aircraft is West.

28. Which is the correct traffic pattern departure procedure to use at a noncontrolled airport?

A — Depart in any direction consistent with safety, after crossing the airport boundary.
B — Make all turns to the left.
C — Comply with any FAA traffic pattern established for the airport.

29. (Refer to Figure 52 on page 239.) Traffic patterns in effect at Lincoln Municipal are

A — to the right on Runway 14 and Runway 32; to the left on Runway 18 and Runway 35.
B — to the left on Runway 14 and Runway 32; to the right on Runway 18 and Runway 35.
C — to the right on Runways 14 - 32.

30. In accordance with 14 CFR Part 107, except when within a 400' radius of a structure, at what maximum altitude can you operate small UA?

A — 500 feet AGL.
B — 400 feet AGL.
C — 600 feet AGL.

31. When a control tower located on an airport within Class D airspace ceases operation for the day, what happens to the airspace designation?

A — The airspace designation normally will not change.
B — The airspace remains Class D airspace as long as a weather observer or automated weather system is available.
C — The airspace reverts to Class E or a combination of Class E and G airspace during the hours the tower is not in operation.

32. The term "angle of attack" is defined as the angle between the

A — chord line of the wing and the relative wind.
B — airplane's longitudinal axis and that of the air striking the airfoil.
C — airplane's center line and the relative wind.

33. An ATC radar facility issues the following advisory to a pilot flying on a heading of 360°:

"TRAFFIC 10 O'CLOCK, 2 MILES, SOUTHBOUND..."

Where should the pilot look for this traffic?

A — Northwest.
B — Northeast.
C — Southwest.

34. Which factor would tend to increase the density altitude at a given airport?

A — An increase in barometric pressure.
B — An increase in ambient temperature.
C — A decrease in relative humidity.

35. During your preflight inspection, you discover a small nick in the UA battery casing. What action should you take?

A — Throw it away with your household trash.
B — Use it as long as it will still hold a charge.
C — Follow the manufacturer's guidance.

36. An air mass moving inland from the coast in winter is likely to result in

A — rain.
B — fog.
C — frost.

37. A local TV station has hired a remote pilot to operate their small UA to cover news stories. The remote pilot has had multiple near misses with obstacles on the ground and two small UAS accidents. What would be a solution for the news station to improve their operating safety culture?

A — The news station should implement a policy of no more than five crashes/incidents within 6 months.
B — The news station does not need to make any changes; there are times that an accident is unavoidable.
C — The news station should recognize hazardous attitudes and situations and develop standard operating procedures that emphasize safety.

38. Why is fatigue hazardous to flight safety?

A — The pilot hurries to get done in order to rest.
B — Fatigue may not be apparent to a pilot until serious errors are made (an impaired pilot is a dangerous pilot).
C — The pilot is lazy and rushes to get done quickly.

39. In which environment is aircraft structural ice most likely to have the highest accumulation rate?

A — Cumulus clouds with below freezing temperatures.
B — Freezing drizzle.
C — Freezing rain.

40. (Refer to Figure 23 on page 94 and Legend 1 on page 95.) (Refer to Area 3.) For information about glider operations at Ridgeland Airport, refer to

A — notes on the border of the chart.
B — the Chart Supplement.
C — the FNS NOTAM search portal online.

41. (Refer to Figure 2 on page 187.) If an unmanned airplane weighs 33 pounds, what approximate weight would the airplane structure be required to support during a 30° banked turn while maintaining altitude?

A — 34 pounds.
B — 47 pounds.
C — 38 pounds.

42. What could be a consequence of operating a small unmanned aircraft above its maximum allowable weight?

A — Faster speed.
B — Shorter endurance.
C — Increased maneuverability.

43. Before each flight, the rPIC must ensure that

A — Objects carried on the sUAS are secure.
B — The site supervisor has approved the flight.
C — ATC has granted clearance.

44. To ensure that the unmanned aircraft center of gravity (CG) limits are not exceeded, follow the aircraft loading instructions specified in the

A — *Pilot's Operating Handbook or UAS Flight Manual.*
B — *Aeronautical Information Manual (AIM).*
C — *Aircraft Weight and Balance Handbook.*

45. You are operating a 1280 g (2.8 lb.) quadcopter for your own enjoyment. Is this operation subject to 14 CFR Part 107?

A — Yes, this operation is subject to Part 107.
B — No, this operation is not subject to Part 107.
C — Yes, all aircraft weighing over .55 lb. are subject to Part 107.

46. Which of the following source of information should you consult **first** when determining what maintenance should be performed on an sUAS or its components?

A — Local pilot best practices.
B — 14 CFR Part 107.
C — Manufacturer guidance.

47. According to 14 CFR Part 107, the responsibility to inspect the small unmanned aircraft system (sUAS) to ensure it is in a safe operating condition rests with the

A — visual observer.
B — remote Pilot in Command.
C — owner of the sUAS.

48. A person may not act as a crewmember of a small UA if alcoholic beverages have been consumed by that person within the preceding

A — 8 hours.
B — 12 hours.
C — 24 hours.

49. If there is thunderstorm activity in the vicinity of an airport at which you plan to land, which hazardous atmospheric phenomenon might be expected on the landing approach?

A — Precipitation static.
B — Wind-shear turbulence.
C — Steady rain.

50. What conditions are necessary for the formation of thunderstorms?

A — High humidity, lifting force, and unstable conditions.
B — High humidity, high temperature, and cumulus clouds.
C — Lifting force, moist air, and extensive cloud cover.

51. Which weather phenomenon signals the beginning of the mature stage of a thunderstorm?

A — The appearance of an anvil top.
B — Precipitation beginning to fall.
C — Maximum growth rate of the clouds.

52. One weather phenomenon which will always occur when flying across a front is a change in the

A — wind direction.
B — type of precipitation.
C — stability of the air mass.

53. One of the most easily recognized discontinuities across a front is

A — a change in temperature.
B — an increase in cloud coverage.
C — an increase in relative humidity.

54. What are characteristics of unstable air?

A — Turbulence and good surface visibility.
B — Turbulence and poor surface visibility.
C — Nimbostratus clouds and good surface visibility.

55. A stable air mass is most likely to have which characteristic?

A — Showery precipitation.
B — Turbulent air.
C — Poor surface visibility.

56. The amount of water vapor which air can hold depends on the

A — dewpoint.
B — air temperature.
C — stability of the air.

57. The wind at 5,000 feet AGL is southwesterly while the surface wind is southerly. This difference in direction is primarily due to

A — stronger pressure gradient at higher altitudes.
B — friction between the wind and the surface.
C — stronger Coriolis force at the surface.

58. Where does wind shear occur?

A — Only at higher altitudes.
B — Only at lower altitudes.
C — At all altitudes, in all directions.

59. Under what condition would a small UA not have to be registered before it is operated in the United States?

A — When the aircraft weighs less than .55 pounds on takeoff, including everything that is on-board or attached to the aircraft.
B — When the aircraft has a takeoff weight that is more than .55 pounds, but less than 55 pounds, not including fuel and necessary attachments.
C — All small UA need to be registered regardless of the weight of the aircraft before, during, or after the flight.

60. According to 14 CFR Part 48, when must a person register a small UA with the Federal Aviation Administration?

A — All civilian small UAs weighing greater than .55 pounds must be registered regardless of its intended use.
B — When the small UA is used for any purpose other than as a model aircraft.
C — Only when the operator will be paid for commercial services.

PRACTICE TEST LIST OF ANSWERS

Listed below are the answers to the practice test. To the immediate right of each answer is the page number on which the question, as well as correct and incorrect answer explanations, can be found.

Q. #	Answer	Page	Q. #	Answer	Page	Q. #	Answer	Page	Q. #	Answer	Page
1.	C	68	16.	A	136	31.	C	90	46.	C	279
2.	B	68	17.	B	137	32.	A	185	47.	B	279
3.	A	70	18.	C	223	33.	A	204	48.	A	64
4.	A	71	19.	C	267	34.	B	163	49.	B	164
5.	C	71	20.	B	228	35.	C	278	50.	A	165
6.	A	72	21.	C	264	36.	B	162	51.	B	165
7.	B	270	22.	A	265	37.	C	265	52.	A	164
8.	B	135	23.	B	266	38.	B	269	53.	A	164
9.	C	92	24.	B	163	39.	C	166	54.	A	169
10.	C	100	25.	A	224	40.	B	94	55.	C	169
11.	B	98	26.	B	236	41.	C	187	56.	B	167
12.	A	204	27.	A	200	42.	B	186	57.	B	163
13.	A	228	28.	C	232	43.	A	63	58.	C	166
14.	C	234	29.	B	238	44.	A	186	59.	A	58
15.	C	138	30.	B	58	45.	B	60	60.	A	62

APPENDIX B
INTERPOLATION

The following is a tutorial based on information that has appeared in the FAA's *Pilot's Handbook of Aeronautical Knowledge*. Interpolation is required in questions found in the following subunit: Study Unit 4, Subunit 1, "Effects of Weather on Performance" (pages 141, 162)

1. To interpolate means to compute intermediate values between a series of given values.
   a. In many instances when performance is critical, an accurate determination of the performance values is the only acceptable means to enhance safe flight.
   b. Guessing to determine these values should be avoided.
2. Interpolation is simple to perform if the method is understood. The following are examples of how to interpolate, or accurately determine the intermediate values, between a series of given values.
3. The numbers in column A range from 10 to 30, and the numbers in column B range from 50 to 100. Determine the intermediate numerical value in column B that would correspond with an intermediate value of 20 placed in column A.

A	B
10	50
20	X = Unknown
30	100

   a. It can be visualized that 20 is halfway between 10 and 30; therefore, the corresponding value of the unknown number in column B would be halfway between 50 and 100, or 75.
4. Many interpolation problems are more difficult to visualize than the preceding example; therefore, a systematic method must be used to determine the required intermediate value. The following describes one method that can be used.
   a. The numbers in column A range from 10 to 30 with intermediate values of 15, 20, and 25. Determine the intermediate numerical value in column B that would correspond with 15 in column A.

A	B
10	50
15	
20	
25	
30	100

   b. First, in column A, determine the relationship of 15 to the range between 10 and 30 as follows:

$$\frac{15 - 10}{30 - 10} = \frac{5}{20} \text{ or } 1/4$$

   1) It should be noted that 15 is 1/4 of the range between 10 and 30.

288   Appendix B: Interpolation

    c.   Now determine 1/4 of the range of column B between 50 and 100 as follows:

$$100 - 50 = 50$$
$$1/4 \text{ of } 50 = 12.5$$

       1)   The answer 12.5 represents the number of units, but to arrive at the correct value, 12.5 must be added to the lower number in column B as follows:

$$50 + 12.5 = 62.5$$

    d.   The interpolation has been completed and 62.5 is the actual value which is 1/4 of the range of column B.

5.   Another method of interpolation is shown below:

    a.   Using the same numbers as in the previous example, a proportion problem based on the relationship of the number can be set up.

Proportion: $\dfrac{5}{20} = \dfrac{X}{50}$

$$20X = 250$$
$$X = 12.5$$

       1)   The answer, 12.5, must be added to 50 to arrive at the actual value of 62.5.

6.   The following example illustrates the use of interpolation applied to a problem dealing with one aspect of airplane performance:

Temperature (°F)	Takeoff Distance (ft.)
70	1,173
80	1,356

    a.   If a distance of 1,173 feet is required for takeoff when the temperature is 70°F and 1,356 feet is required at 80°F, what distance is required when the temperature is 75°F? The solution to the problem can be determined as follows:

$$\dfrac{5}{10} = \dfrac{X}{183}$$
$$10X = 915$$
$$X = 91.5$$

       1)   The answer, 91.5, must be added to 1,173 to arrive at the actual value of 1,264.5 ft.

CROSS-REFERENCES TO THE FAA ACS CODES

Knowledge Test Reports list the Airman Certification Standards (ACS) code of each question answered incorrectly. The total number of questions missed may differ from the number of ACS codes shown on the report if more than one question is missed for a certain code. We have created an online cross-reference of all the questions from our remote pilot knowledge test bank to their ACS codes to help you determine which Gleim subunits to focus on.

> To view the online listing of questions and ACS codes, visit www.GleimAviation.com/ACSXRefs.
>
> To determine what topic each code pertains to, the ACS may be viewed at www.faa.gov/training_testing/testing/acs.

The codes are derived from the Remote Pilot ACS, which consists of Areas of Operation arranged in a logical sequence, beginning with Regulations and ending with Operations. Each Area of Operation includes appropriate tasks, and each task begins with an objective that states what the applicant should know, consider, and/or do. The ACS then lists the aeronautical knowledge elements relevant to each task. Each task element is assigned a unique code, such as UA.I.A.K1, which can be broken down as follows:

- UA = Applicable ACS (Unmanned Aircraft Systems)
- I = Area of Operation (Regulations)
- A = Task (General)
- K1 = Task element Knowledge 1 (Applicability of 14 CFR Part 107 to small unmanned aircraft operations)

In the online cross-reference, we present our study unit/question number and our answer to the right of each code. For example, a cross-reference to 4-1 represents our Study Unit 4, question 1. Multiple questions may be associated with a single ACS code. Applicants should study the entire task elements of any identified weaknesses instead of merely studying specific questions.

The FAA will periodically revise the existing codes and add new ones. As Gleim learns about any changes, we will update our materials.

ABBREVIATIONS AND ACRONYMS IN *REMOTE PILOT FAA KNOWLEDGE TEST PREP*

14 CFR	Federal Aviation Regulations	ILS	Instrument landing system
AAAM	Association for Advancement of Automotive Medicine	IR	instrument route
AC	Advisory Circular	KTC	knowledge testing center
ACR	Airman Certification Representative	LIDAR	Light detection and ranging
ACS	Airman Certification Standards	LiPO	lithium-polymer
ACUG	Aeronautical Chart Users' Guide	LOC	loss of control
ADM	aeronautical decision making	mb	millibar
ADS-B	Automatic Dependent Surveillance-Broadcast	METAR	aviation routine weather report
AGL	above ground level	MOA	Military Operations Area
AIM	*Aeronautical Information Manual*	MOC	means of compliance
AIRMET	Airmen's Meteorological Information	mph	miles per hour
AIS	abbreviated injury scale	MSL	mean sea level
AKTR	Airman Knowledge Test Report	MTR	Military Training Route
ASOS	automated surface observing system	MVFR	marginal VFR
ATC	Air Traffic Control	NAS	National Airspace System
ATIS	Automatic Terminal Information Service	NEXRAD	next generation radar
ATO	Air traffic organization	NM	nautical mile
AWOS	automated weather observing system	NOTAM	notice to air missions
AWS	*Aviation Weather Services*	NSA	national security area
AWSS	automated weather sensor system	NTSB	National Transportation Safety Board
CFI	Certificated Flight Instructor	NWS	National Weather Service
CFR	Code of Federal Regulations	PAVE	Pilot, Aircraft, enVironment, External pressures
CG	center of gravity	PIC	pilot in command
CoA	Certificate of Authorization	PROG	short-range surface prognostic charts
CONUS	continental United States	RF	radio frequency
CoW	Certificate of Waiver	RID	remote identification
CRM	crew resource management	ROC	Regional Operations Center
CS	control station	rPIC	remote PIC
CT	control tower	RVR	runway visible range
CTAF	Common Traffic Advisory Frequency	SAA	Special Activity Airspace
DOC	declaration of compliance	SFC	surface
DOD	Department of Defense	SIDA	security identification display area
DOT	Department of Transportation	SIGMET	Significant Meteorological Information
DPE	Designated Pilot Examiner	SIGWX	significant weather charts
FAA	Federal Aviation Administration	SM	statute mile
FAA-H-8083-1B	*Weight and Balance Handbook*	sUA	small unmanned aircraft
FAA-H-8083-3B	*Airplane Flying Handbook*	sUAS	small unmanned aircraft system
FAA-H-8083-25B	*Pilot's Handbook of Aeronautical Knowledge*	*sUASSG*	*Small Unmanned Aircraft Systems Study Guide*
FBO	Fixed-Base Operator	TAF	terminal aerodrome forecast
FCC	Federal Communications Commission	TFR	temporary flight restriction
FL	flight level	TRSA	terminal radar service area
FPV	first-person view	TSA	Transportation Security Administration
FRIA	FAA-recognized identification area	UA	unmanned aircraft
FSS	Flight Service Station	UAS	unmanned aircraft system
FTN	Flight Tracking Number	UNICOM	Aeronautical advisory communications station
FTP	Flight termination point	UTC	Coordinated Universal Time
GCS	ground control station	VFR	visual flight rules
GMT	Greenwich mean time	VHF	very high frequency
GPS	Global Positioning System	VLOS	visual line of sight
Hg	mercury	VO	visual observer
IACRA	Integrated Airmen Certification and/or Rating Application	VOR	Victor airways or Federal airways
		VR	visual route
ICAO	International Civil Aviation Organization	WINGS	pilot proficiency program
IFR	instrument flight rules	Z	Zulu or UTC time

INDEX OF LEGENDS AND FIGURES

<u>Legend</u>
1	Sectional Aeronautical Chart	95
15	Chart Supplement	227

<u>Figure</u>
1	Lift Vector	185
2	Load Factor Chart	178, 187
12	Aviation Routine Weather Reports (METAR)	134
15	Terminal Aerodrome Forecasts (TAF)	137
19	Low-Level Significant Weather (SIGWX) Prognostic Charts	139
20	Sectional Chart Excerpt	91, 107, 233
21	Sectional Chart Excerpt	109, 199, 231
22	Sectional Chart Excerpt	197, 237
23	Sectional Chart Excerpt	94, 111, 235
24	Sectional Chart Excerpt	93, 245
25	Sectional Chart Excerpt	97, 205
26	Sectional Chart Excerpt	99, 201, 229
31	Chart Supplement	198
48	Airport Diagram	223
52	Chart Supplement	239
59	Sectional Chart Excerpt	105, 243
64	Airport Markings	215, 226
65	U.S. Airport Signs	214, 224
71	Sectional Chart Excerpt	241
75	Sectional Chart Excerpt	101
78	Sectional Chart Excerpt	67, 103, 202
79	Chart Supplement	203

INDEX

Abbreviated Injury Scale (AIS). 13
Abbreviations in book. 291
Accident reporting. 13
    Information. 14
    Submitting the report. 13
ADS-B Out. 29, 54
Aerodynamic forces. 172
Aeronautical
    Charts. 220
    Decision making (ADM). 247
    Knowledge recency. 33
Ailerons. 171
Aiming point markers. 209
Air masses. 152
Aircraft
    Call signs. 193
    Stability. 175
    Turn. 174
Airman Certification Standards (ACS). 289
Airport
    Advisory areas. 80
    Operations. 207
    Traffic patterns. 23, 216
Airspace
    Authorizations. 35
    Classification. 73
    Controlled. 22, 35, 82
    Waivers. 35
ALC-451. 32
Alcohol and drugs. 19, 30, 255
Alert areas. 79
Angle of attack. 172
Applicant. 12
    Produced sUAS. 44
Application
    Instructions. 16
    Process. 30
ATC
    Authorizations. 84
    Communications. 207
Atmospheric pressure. 148
Automated
    Operations. 28
    Surface Observing System (ASOS). 132
    Weather Observing System (AWOS). 132
Automatic terminal information service (ATIS). . . . 192
Aviation Routine Weather Report. 116

Balloons, flight beneath. 84
Basic weather minimums. 83
Batteries, lithium. 272
Beacons. 216
Bernoulli's principle. 172
Briefing, weather. 113

Canard. 171
Careless or reckless operation. 18
Category
    1 operation. 37
    2 operation. 37
    3 operation. 38
    4 operation. 38
Ceiling. 119, 161
Centerline marking. 208
Certificate of Waiver (CoW). 34
Chart supplements. 220
Chevrons. 211
Civil twilight operations. 28
Class
    B airspace. 74
        VFR transition route. 81
    C airspace. 74
    D airspace. 75
    E airspace. 76
    G airspace. 77
Clouds. 155
Common Traffic Advisory Frequency (CTAF). . . . 190
Communication
    Effective team. 247
    Radio procedures. 189
Condition for safe operation. 14, 17
Confirmation of Identification. 55
Control
    Links. 273
    Station (CS). 12
Controlled
    Airspace. 22, 35, 82
    Firing areas. 79
Coriolis force. 143
Corrective lenses. 12
Crew resource management (CRM). 247
Crosswind leg, traffic pattern. 216

Damage, property. 13
Daylight operations. 19
Declaration of compliance (DOC). 12, 45
Dehydration. 255
Demarcation bars. 212
Demonstration of compliance. 14
Density altitude. 141
Departure leg, traffic pattern. 216
Descriptors, weather. 118
Designation marking. 208
Destination signs. 213
Displaced threshold. 211
Downwind leg, traffic pattern. 216
Drones. 11
DroneZone. 34
Dropping objects. 18

Elevator. 171
Emergency action. 18, 271
Endurance. 180
Exposed rotating parts. 50

False records. 12
Fatigue. 258
FDC NOTAMs. 88
Federal Communications Commission (FCC). 274
Final approach leg, traffic pattern. 216
Flaps. 172
Flight
    Controls. 171
    Fitness. 263
    Hazards. 84
    Service. 88, 113
    Termination. 273
Flyaways. 273
Fog. 160
Foreign civil aircraft. 16
Frequency spectrum. 274
Fronts. 153

Global positioning system (GPS). 274
Ground effect. 174

Hail. 159
Hazardous
    Attitudes. 248
    Material. 22
    Operations. 18
Hazards
    Bird and wildlife. 220
    Flight. 84
    Identification. 249
Heat stroke. 255
High pressure system. 151
Hyperventilation. 257

ICAO station identifier. 116, 122
Icing. 158
Impact kinetic energy. 49
In-flight emergency. 18, 271
    Regulatory deviation. 18
    Reporting requirements. 18
Inspection. 24
    Emergency airborne. 85
    Preflight. 275
    Procedures. 275
Integrated Airmen Certificate and/or Rating
    Application (IACRA). 31
Intensity or proximity, weather. 118
Interpolation. 287

Knowledge test. 2
    Report. 8, 289

LAANC. 35, 89
Laser operations. 86
Latitude and longitude. 218
Lightning. 161
LiPo. 272
Load factor. 178
Loading and performance. 175
Longitude and latitude. 218
Lost link. 273
Low
    Altitude authorization and notification
        capability (LAANC). 35, 89
    -Level significant weather chart. 129
    Pressure system. 151

Maintenance
    Of sUAS. 47
    Persons who perform. 277
    Procedures. 275
    Scheduled. 275
    Unscheduled. 275
Means of compliance (MOC). 12, 48
Medical conditions. 17, 19
Meridians. 218
METAR. 116
Military
    NOTAMs. 88
    Operations areas (MOAs). 79
    Training routes (MTRs). 80
Modification of an sUAS. 39
MULTICOM. 190
Multiple
    Category sUAS. 15
    sUAS operation prohibition. 22

National
    Airspace System (NAS). 82
    Security areas (NSAs). 79
    Transportation Safety Board (NTSB) reporting. . . 14
NEXRAD. 131
Night
    Flight. 259
    Illusions. 261
    Operations. 21, 28
Nonprecision instrument runways. 209
NOTAM (D). 88
Notice of identification. 54
Notices to Air Missions (NOTAMs). 23, 88

Index

Obscurations to visibility, weather. 119
Obstructions. 143
Operating
    In the vicinity of an airport. 23
    Instructions. 41
    Limitations. 26
Operational area selection. 38
Operations
    Careless or reckless. 18
    From moving vehicles. 19
    Over people. 36, 39
    While impaired. 19

Parachute jump areas. 81
Parallels. 218
Part 107. 11
Performance data. 176
Person manipulating the controls. 12
Phonetic alphabet. 193
Physical or mental incapacitations. 17
Pointer NOTAMs. 88
Precipitation. 118, 155
    Static (P-static). 85
Precision instrument runways. 209
Preflight inspection. 14, 24, 275
Pressure. 151
    Gradient force. 142
    Variation. 149
Prevailing visibility. 117
Previously manufactured sUAS. 15
Prime Meridian. 218
Product labeling. 56
Prohibited areas. 78
Published VFR routes. 81

Radar observations. 131
Radio
    Frequency (RF) spectrum. 274
    Phraseology. 194
    Procedures. 189
Recordkeeping. 15, 277
Recurrent training. 33
Relocated threshold. 210
Remote
    Identification (RID). 51
        Alternatives. 53
        Message elements. 55
    Pilot in command (rPIC). 12, 27
        Responsibility and authority. 18
Required components. 43
Requirements
    Eligibility. 2, 30
    Registration. 16

Reserve power. 181
Restricted
    Access sites. 40
    Areas. 78
Reviewers and contributors. iv
Right-of-way rules. 22
Risk
    Acceptance. 251
    Assessment. 25, 249
Rotating parts, exposed. 50
Rudder. 171
Runway
    Closed, temporarily closed. 212
    Markings. 208, 210
    Precision and nonprecision instrument. 209
    Visual range (RVR). 117

SAA NOTAMs. 88
Sectional chart symbology. 220
Security
    Disqualification. 33
    Identification display areas (SIDA). 218
See and avoid. 17, 22
Sensor status indicators. 121
Serious injury. 13
Short-Range Surface Prognostic (PROG) Chart. . . 125
Shoulder markings. 210
Side stripe markings. 210
Situational awareness. 248
Sky condition, weather. 119, 123
Small unmanned aircraft (sUA). 11, 12
    System (sUAS). 11, 12
        Foreign-owned and operated. 16
Special-use airspace. 78
Spoilers. 172
Squall. 119
Stabilator. 171
Stable air. 146
Stalls. 172
Standard remote identification. 51
Stress. 257
Sufficient power. 14, 25

Task management. 247
Taxiway
    Lights. 216
    Signs. 213
Temperature
    Conversion formulas. 147
    Inversions. 146
    Variations. 147
Temporary flight restrictions (TFRs). 80
Terminal
    Aerodrome forecast (TAF). 122
    Radar service area (TRSA). 81
Testing. 14
Thermal plumes. 86
Threshold
    Bars. 210
    Displaced. 211
    Markings. 209
    Relocated. 210
Thunderstorms. 156
Tornadoes. 157
Touchdown zone markers. 209
Traffic
    Advisory procedures. 190
    Patterns. 23, 216
        Departing. 217
        Entering. 217
Transportation of property. 22, 29
Trim systems. 172

UAS
    Data Exchange. 89
    Marking. 16
    Registration. 16
UNICOM. 191
Unmanned aircraft (UA). 12
Unstable air. 146
Upwind leg, traffic pattern. 216

Valid period date and time. 122
Vehicle roadway markings. 214
VFR corridor. 81
Visibility, weather chart. 117, 122
Vision. 258
    Aids. 20
    Unaided. 20
Visual
    Line of sight (VLOS). 19
    Observer (VO). 12, 21
    Runway. 208
Voluntary consensus standards bodies. 12

Waivers. 34
Waiving the sparsely-populated area provision. . . . 19
Warning areas. 79
Water vapor. 154
Weather. 123
    Briefing. 113
    Effects on performance. 141
    Minimums. 83
    Services. 113
Weight. 176
Wind. 142
    METAR. 117
    Shear. 123
    TAF. 122
Wire environment. 86

AUTHORS' RECOMMENDATIONS

AIRCRAFT OWNERS AND PILOTS ASSOCIATION (AOPA)

AOPA is the largest, most influential aviation association in the world, with two thirds of all pilots in the United States as members. AOPA's most important contribution to the world's most accessible, safest, least expensive, friendliest, easiest-to-use general aviation environment is its lobbying on our behalf at the federal, state, and local levels. AOPA also provides legal services, advice, and other assistance to the aviation community.

We recommend that you become an AOPA member to get the most out of AOPA's resources. To join, call 1-800-USA-AOPA or visit the AOPA website at www.aopa.org.

ASSOCIATION FOR UNMANNED VEHICLE SYSTEMS INTERNATIONAL (AUVSI)

The AUVSI is the world's largest organization devoted exclusively to advancing the unmanned systems and robotics industries. AUVSI provides its members with a unified voice in advocacy for policies and regulations that encourage growth and innovation. It educates the public and media on the safe and beneficial uses of unmanned systems and enables market growth by offering its members custom resources that can help them realize their full industry potential. AUVSI's Remote Pilots Council also provides local networking for certificated remote pilots and a forum for feedback to the FAA.

Learn more about AUVSI at www.auvsi.org.

ACADEMY OF MODEL AERONAUTICS (AMA)

The AMA is the world's largest model aviation association, representing a membership of more than 195,000 people from every walk of life, income level, and age group. The purpose of this self-supporting, non-profit organization is to promote the development of model aviation as a recognized sport and recreation activity. They are the official national body for model aviation in the United States.

The AMA sanctions more than 2,000 model competitions throughout the country each year, and certifies official model flying records on a national and international level. It organizes the annual National Aeromodeling Championships, the world's largest model airplane competition. The AMA is the chartering organization for more than 2,500 model airplane clubs across the country, offering its chartered clubs official contest sanction, insurance, and assistance in acquiring and maintaining flying sites.

Membership is open to anyone interested in model aviation. Consider joining the AMA today at www.modelaircraft.org.

GLEIM® Reference Books

Pilot Handbook

- Comprehensive ground school text in outline format
- Expanded weather coverage
- Sections on flight reviews and instrument proficiency checks
- Color images and diagrams

FAR/AIM

- Expanded indexes
- Full-color graphics

Aviation Weather & Weather Services

- A detailed explanation of weather
- A reorganization of
  - AC 00-6, *Aviation Weather*
  - AC 00-45, *Aviation Weather Services*
- Color graphics of weather depictions

Pilot Logbook

- Versatile and durable
- Ideal for pilots of all skill levels
- Professional quality at an affordable price
- The new standard in logbooks

800.874.5346 ext. 471
GleimAviation.com/referencebooks